MW00448667

GOVERNMENT BY
INVESTIGATION

THE BROOKINGS INSTITUTION

The Brookings Institution is a private nonprofit organization devoted to research, education, and publication on important issues of domestic and foreign policy. Its principal purpose is to bring the highest quality independent research and analysis to bear on current and emerging policy problems. Interpretations or conclusions in Brookings publications should be understood to be solely those of the authors.

THE GOVERNANCE INSTITUTE

The Governance Institute (http://thegovernanceinstitute.org/) is a small nonprofit, nonpartisan organization that since 1986 has, on its own or in cooperation with other entities, explored the functioning and interaction of governmental institutions to help them address specific problems, such as encouraging law firm pro bono programs; evaluating mechanisms to ease contentiousness in federal judicial selection; developing and monitoring the operation of a protocol by which federal appellate judges alert Congress to technical drafting problems in enacted legislation; and enhancing the fairness and effectiveness of the Justice Department's immigration courts. The Institute has enjoyed a long and mutually productive relationship with the Brookings Institution—particularly its Governance Studies program—but it is not a part of Brookings.

GOVERNMENT BY INVESTIGATION

CONGRESS, PRESIDENTS, AND THE
SEARCH FOR ANSWERS 1945–2012

PAUL C. LIGHT

THE GOVERNANCE INSTITUTE

BROOKINGS INSTITUTION PRESS

Washington, D.C.

Copyright © 2014

THE BROOKINGS INSTITUTION

1775 Massachusetts Avenue, N.W., Washington, DC 20036.

www.brookings.edu

All rights reserved. No part of this publication may be reproduced or transmitted in any form or by any means without permission in writing from the Brookings Institution Press.

Library of Congress Cataloging-in-Publication data

Light, Paul Charles.
  Government by investigation : Congress, presidents, and the search for answers, 1945–2012 / Paul C. Light, Governance Institute.
      pages   cm
  Includes bibliographical references and index.
  ISBN 978-0-8157-2268-7 (pbk. : alk. paper)
  1. Governmental investigations—United States.   I. Title.
  JF1525.C58L54 2013
  353.4'630973—dc23   2013016767

10 9 8 7 6 5 4 3 2 1

Printed on acid-free paper

Typeset in Minion and Univers Condensed

Composition by R. Lynn Rivenbark
Macon, Georgia

Contents

Acknowledgments   vii

1 Introducing the Search for Answers   1

2 Counting Investigations   11

3 Creating Footprints   56

4 Making Investigations Count   126

5 Creating High-Impact Investigations   191

Appendixes

A Interview Respondents   217

B Sources   221

C Investigation Résumés, 1945–2012   225

D Supporting Statistical Analysis   249

Notes   269

Index   303

Acknowledgments

I have always viewed acknowledgments as the beginning of a denouement. This book is now done, but there are still questions to be answered, and answers to be questioned. If I have done my work well, the book will provoke healthy debate about when and how to use investigations to address breakdowns in government performance.

This denouement has been six years in coming. I started designing my research plan in September 2006 after conversations with my friends and colleagues at the Governance Institute in Washington, D.C., and originally expected to finish three years later. The research took three years longer, because the investigatory histories were so dense, the questions increasingly complicated, the coding more difficult, and the data analysis more intricate. By the time I completed the initial draft of the book and began revisions in late 2011, it only seemed logical to expand the time frame to cover the first term of the Obama administration, which added more investigatory histories to my reading list.

Now that the book is finished, I have the honor of thanking the many people who helped along the way. This book could not have been completed without my research assistant, Todd L. Ely, who worked on the project for two years as a doctoral student at the Wagner School of Public Service and is now an assistant professor at the University of Colorado, Denver. Todd was tireless in compiling the early lists of investigations that competed for space in my final list of the 100 most significant investigations between

1945 and 2012. He was also central to initial coding decisions on many of the footprint and impact measures presented later in the book. He was indispensable to the work.

Once Todd left for Denver, I relied on a small corps of research assistants to track down information, check my coding, transcribe interviews, and build files, and will be forever grateful. I also relied on steady support from my dean, Ellen Schall, and the associate deans, Rogan Kersh and Tyra Liebmann, as they built Wagner's reputation for excellence, and from my always-available executive assistant, Iveliz Vazquez. I fully expect Dean Shall's successor, Sherry Glied, and her team to continue the school's remarkable rise.

I also relied on generous financial support from the Smith Richardson Foundation to keep the project moving through the five years of data collection and initial analysis and consider the foundation's senior program officer for domestic public policy, Mark Steinmeyer, both a friend and leader. He was always gracious as the grant was extended year after year, and he never wavered in his encouragement.

Alongside this dedicated help and encouragement, I owe my greatest thanks to my friends and colleagues associated with the Governance Institute. The Institute's founder, Robert A. Katzmann, convinced me to take on the project, gave me constant feedback and support, and provided essential reassurance on early drafts. In turn, the Governance Institute's president, Russell Wheeler, was a tireless ally, confidant, and adviser throughout the entire project. I can guarantee that there is not a single sentence in this book that he did not read at least twice, and many that he read thrice and more. He checked every draft, coached me on revision plans, counseled patience when I needed it, and questioned analytic conclusions when they warranted it. He made this book better at every turn.

The book was also supported by a long list of friends, colleagues, anonymous peer reviewers, respondents, and the four readers who wrote endorsements on the back cover. I also benefited greatly from my small team of personal supporters, including Cesar Alfonso, Clara Janis, Katherine Rappaport, Bryna Sanger, and Robyn Stein. My children remain at the center of the list—ever patient, loving, and a source of constant joy. My students also made a difference, too, by asking questions, catching typos and grammatical errors along the way, and providing so much curiosity in my classes.

Finally, the Brookings Institution put enormous energy and patience into bringing this book to publication, including financial support for publication, a welcoming embrace, ample editing energy, and a dedication to quality. Darrell West provided both financial and intellectual resources to the effort, while Christopher Kelaher pushed the manuscript through the arduous review process. Janet Walker—and Elizabeth Forsyth, who worked with her—was absolutely essential in bringing this book to fruition, and I thank her for the work and dedication in taking the book across the finish line.

I am responsible for the errors in this book, however. Having worked on it from 2006 to 2013, there are no doubt many. I trust readers will take them in stride and add new ideas to the search for answers about improving government performance.

ONE

Introducing the Search for Answers

This book is about the 100 most significant investigations of government between 1945 and 2012. All of the investigations were designed to fix a breakdown in a government performance.

In an ideal investigatory world, all 100 investigations would have asked every possible question, assessed every possible answer, and fixed the breakdown once and for all. But in the real world covered by this book, one group of investigations asked most of the questions, assessed the available answers, and mostly fixed the breakdown, while a second group muddled through to minimal effect. This book is designed to explain the differences.

Every decade provided legendary investigations to the 100: Pearl Harbor and communists in government during the 1940s, and continuing with quiz shows and Sputnik in the 1950s, crime rates and the Vietnam War in the 1960s, Watergate and domestic spying in the 1970s, Social Security and the shuttle *Challenger* in the 1980s, Clinton misconduct and early warning about terrorism in the 1990s, and the Iraq War and financial meltdown in the 2000s.

Every decade also contributed forgotten or less visible investigations: commodity speculation and government reorganization in the 1940s, airport safety and drug prices in the 1950s, White House news management and defense stockpiling in the 1960s, welfare fraud and the General Services Administration in the 1970s, Indian affairs and government mismanagement in the 1980s, Ruby Ridge and Y2K in the 1990s, and mine safety and the Solyndra loan in the 2000s.

But whether legendary or forgotten, all 100 investigations were historically significant. Their ultimate success in fixing the breakdown had varied, but their historical significance at the top of the investigatory record between 1945 and 2012 did not. Significance was never a measure of investigatory weight or impact, but how history was served—and that is what placed them at the very top of the investigatory pile.

Just because all 100 were historically significant does not mean they operated in the same way. They addressed different breakdowns, reacted to separate triggers, took diverse institutional homes, moved forward from different venues such as committees, subcommittees, or commissions, targeted different issues, adopted different purposes, and used various methodologies. They also searched for answers about problems created by past decisions to act, as well as past decisions not to act.

As such, the post–World War II investigatory agenda reflects the two faces of power described by Peter Bachrach and Morton S. Baratz in 1962. There are times when the "mobilization of bias" supports decisions to act, some of which set the stage for future government breakdowns. There are also times when this mobilization of bias leads to "nondecisions" that reinforce the status quo by preventing action on pressing issues. As Bachrach and Baratz show, "Power is exercised when A participates in the making of decisions that affect B. But power is also exercised when A devotes his energies to creating or reinforcing social and political values and institutional practices that limit the scope of the political process to public consideration of only those issues which are comparatively innocuous to A."[1]

This second face of power results in nondecisions that can eventually lead to a large-scale investigation. This was clearly the case with the 1965 traffic safety investigation, where the automobile industry and its allies in Congress and the presidency had successfully suppressed action for decades, just as the tobacco industry would suppress action until the 1993 tobacco investigation began reversing the course of policy. Both investigations were clearly designed to change nondecisions to decisions.

A DISTINCTION WITH A DIFFERENCE

At first glance, the 100 investigations examined here resemble the more traditional inquiries launched every day by congressional committees, obscure presidential task forces, public interest groups, the media, and a host of quasi-independent monitoring agencies such as the federal Offices of Inspectors General and Government Accountability Office.

After all, these investigations used many of the same tools in the same search for answers about the same kinds of breakdowns. They held hearings, presented opening statements and calls to order, questioned witnesses, collected documents, searched for patterns of fact, assigned blame, and almost always produced lengthy reports. Although some of my investigations also produced draft legislation, issued subpoenas, filed contempt citations, and even issued articles of impeachment, they can still be easily confused with standard oversight.

Despite the differences, investigations generally produce a much heavier imprint on history than ordinary oversight. Oversight obviously involves investigating, and investigations often begin with routine oversight, but the former usually occurs in now-and-again hearings, while the latter was described by one of my respondents as "oversight on steroids."[2] Oversight is clearly important for monitoring ongoing government performance, uncovering failures, and sending warning shots, but it is usually brief and all-too-easily ignored and quickly forgotten.

In turn, investigations are also a form of monitoring and prevention, but they are usually longer, more visible, and controversial. Investigations give Congress and the president a particularly significant platform for finding the answers to what one of my respondents called the "big-ticket" failures that undermine the faithful execution of the laws. Simply stated, oversight and investigation are best viewed as separate species within the same genus.

This is not to argue that all of my investigations produced great impact by fixing underlying problems, however. To the contrary, despite their initial promises to repair past mistakes and prevent future failures, just forty investigations achieved a great deal or fair amount of impact in their search for answers, compared with sixty that produced some, little, or no impact at all.[3]

The sixty less successful investigations were often long, broad, free to investigate, visible, serious, and thorough as they pursued the facts about a breakdown. Many left heavy footprints on investigatory practice, and met the test of the good investigation discussed in the next chapter. But even the heaviest investigations sometimes failed to improve government performance. Again, simply stated, they were historically significant, but had little impact.

Given this mixed track record of impact, the key question for this book is why some of the investigations succeeded, while so many others failed. This book addresses the question using more than thirty "demographic" measures that answer the who, what, where, when, how, and why of each investigation.

An investigation's location in history is measured at its starting date by
(1) historical period, (2) presidential administration (Truman through Obama),
(3) Watergate (before or after), (4) the president's term of office (first or second),
and (5) whether it began in an election year. There are four historical periods
covered by this book: the post–World War II period (1945 to 1960), the Great
Society (1961–Nixon's resignation in mid-1974), the congressional resurgence
(mid-1974 to 1994), and divided government (1995 to 2012).

An investigation's structure and modus operandi are measured by (1) institutional home (Congress or the presidency, and the House or the Senate),
(2) venue (full committees, special congressional bodies, subcommittees, or
commissions), (3) trigger (police patrol or fire alarm), (4) issue (domestic or
foreign), (5) breakdown (process, policy, or personal misconduct), (6) purpose
(repair or prevention), and (7) investigatory method (fact finding or blame setting). As used in this book, the term "special congressional bodies" refers to
joint, select, or special committees or subcommittees.

The party control surrounding an investigation is measured by (1) party
control of Congress and the presidency (unified or divided), (2) party control
of Congress (unified or divided), (3) Democratic or Republican control of
Congress and the presidency, (4) Democratic or Republican control of the
presidency, (5) Democratic or Republican control of Congress, (6) Democratic or Republican control of the House, and (7) Democratic or Republican
control of the Senate.

The footprint of each investigation is measured by its (1) length, (2) breadth,
(3) complexity of the breakdown, (4) leadership, (5) freedom to investigate,
(6) public visibility, (7) seriousness, (8) thoroughness, (9) leverage, (10) durability, and (11) bipartisanship.

Matched against each other as potential predictors of impact, the statistical analysis and fifty case studies presented in this book yield a relatively
short list of findings that should help future investigators to achieve maximum impact.

The overall analysis suggests that investigations have a greater impact
when they (1) seek to repair the breakdown at hand and (2) use fact finding
as their primary investigatory methodology. Many other choices lead to heavier investigatory footprints, including the use of blue-ribbon commissions,
for example, but these two basic decisions appear to be the ultimate predictors of investigatory impact. Investigators may not be able to travel through
time to less quarrelsome eras, but they can shape the odds of success. This
book provides several options for doing so, especially in pursuing answers
about why a breakdown occurred and how it might be fixed.[4]

INTRODUCING THE LIST

Building my list of the 100 most significant investigations conducted by Congress and the president during the seventy years following World War II was a challenging task. For one reason, many investigations have already been listed by scholars such as David C. W. Parker and Matthew Dull (1,015 congressional hearings on government waste and malfeasance), Amy B. Zegart (668 presidential commissions), Thomas R. Wolanin (99 blue-ribbon presidential commissions), Jordan Tama (51 major national security commissions), and David R. Mayhew (35 high-publicity congressional investigations), not to mention the long lists compiled by Congressional Quarterly, the Congressional Research Service, the House and Senate historians, and the several dozen investigations described as exemplars by my ninety-six respondents.[5]

Building on this research, my list of highly significant inquiries involved six years of careful reading, multiple rounds of additions and subtractions, and a long list of difficult decisions as investigations were added one-by-one to the final 100. Acknowledging that my decision to cap the list at 100 investigations involved many subjective judgments about significance, or the lack thereof, the final list contains more than enough variation to answer tough quantitative and qualitative questions about the sources of eventual impact.

I am not the first to attach terms such as "major," "significant," or "high publicity" to congressional and presidentially initiated investigations. Congressional Quarterly has long done so in building the annual list of major investigations in its *Congressional Quarterly Almanac* and in assigning stories for its *CQ Weekly* reports, as have many others, such as the nonpartisan Project on Government Oversight and the many scholars who have featured specific big-ticket investigations in their work.

Most of these lists contain investigations of single breakdowns by a single committee, subcommittee, or blue-ribbon commission during a single moment in time. The unit of analysis is almost always the hearing set or single commission, not the investigatory topic. Thirty-six of these single-venue investigations made my list, but so did sixty-four multi-venue investigations by multiple committees, special congressional bodies, subcommittees, and even commissions. My sum-greater-than-the-whole rule for creating these packages asked whether these multiple investigations focused on the same broad government breakdown, not on a specific event within the breakdown such as the Alger Hiss case, My Lai massacre, or Vincent Foster's 1993 suicide. Whether these subsequent multi-venue reviews occurred simultaneously, because investigators joined the fray from both branches and both chambers of Congress, or were separated over time, all were packaged together within an encompassing breakdown.

Thus did the Alger Hiss case end up within the communists-in-government investigation, My Lai within the Vietnam War investigation, and Foster within the White House misconduct investigation. As appendix C shows, the number of packaged investigations rose steadily between 1945 and 2012: just seven of the twenty-three investigations in the post–World War II period, ten out of nineteen in the Great Society period, twenty-two of twenty-seven during the congressional resurgence, and twenty-five of thirty-one during the divided government era as Congress and the president piled on when big breakdowns occurred, then moved onto other business after the headlines were gone.[6]

Once I completed this process, I designated the primary investigator in each package. This decision was not based on a first-enter/first-primary basis, or on the simple number of hearings produced within a single venue. Rather, the decision was based on a careful reading of the investigatory record that covered the entire package. Despite multiple possibilities, for example, I designated the House Un-American Activities Committee (HUAC) as the primary investigator on communists in government, the Senate Foreign Affairs Committee as the primary investigator on the Vietnam War, and the House Committee on Government Reform and Oversight (and its successor, the Committee on Government Reform) on White House conduct. Despite other hearing sets within the package, these were the primaries that I coded for my analysis of cause and effect.[7]

MAKING JUDGMENTS

As noted, creating my list of 100 investigations involved a mix of subjective and objective questions. Was the investigation long or short, complex or narrow, and led by a visible investigator or a little-known chairman? Was it free to follow every lead or tightly controlled by the congressional leadership or president, visible or largely ignored, and serious or frivolous? And was it thorough or superficial, too prominent to be ignored in its time or quickly buried, bipartisan or partisan, and durable in standing over the long term or rarely remembered? In short, why did each investigation exist, whom did it serve, and how did it reach a conclusion, if a conclusion was reached at all?

The investigations of the 1974 Nixon pardon and 2001 Enron collapse show the wide variation among the inquiries on my list.

The exceedingly brief 1975 investigation of President Gerald Ford's pardon of Richard Nixon made my list entirely because of Ford's forty-five-minute appearance before the House Judiciary Subcommittee on Criminal

Justice on October 17, 1975. Ford made every effort to downplay his testimony, cautioning the subcommittee's chairman, Rep. William L. Hungate (D-Mo.), that his testimony was offered entirely "in a spirit of cooperation," but without any intention "to detract on this occasion or in any other instance, from the generally recognized rights of the President to preserve the confidentiality of internal discussions of communications whenever it is properly within his constitutional responsibility to do so."[8]

Yet Ford appeared nonetheless. As the first president in history to testify before Congress, Ford decided that it was time to put the rapidly spreading pardon rumors to rest:

> My appearance at this hearing of your distinguished subcommittee of the House Committee on the Judiciary has been looked upon as an unusual historic event—one that has no firm precedent in the whole history of Presidential relations with the Congress. Yet, I am here not to make history, but to report on history.
>
> The history you are interested in covers so recent a period that it is not well understood. If, with your assistance, I can make for better understanding of the pardon of former President Nixon, then we can help to achieve the purpose I had for granting the pardon when I did.
>
> That purpose was to change our national focus. I wanted to do all I could to shift our attention from the pursuit of a fallen President to the pursuit of the urgent needs of a rising nation. Our Nation is under the severest of challenges now to employ its full energy and efforts in the pursuit of a sound and growing economy at home and a stable and peaceful world around us.
>
> We would needlessly be diverted from meeting those challenges if we as a people were to remain sharply divided over whether to indict, bring to trial and punish a former President, who is already condemned to suffer long and deeply in the shame and disgrace brought upon the office that he held.[9]

After providing an explanation of the president's power to grant pardons and a detailed history of his decision, Ford concluded with a simple sentence: "I assure you that there never was at any time any agreement whatsoever concerning a pardon to Mr. Nixon if he were to resign and I were to become President."[10]

Ford's testimony was carefully crafted, but dramatic and precedent setting nonetheless. Although the pardon investigation is easily judged as short, narrow, not particularly serious or thorough, and certainly not bipartisan in its general thrust even though a Republican president appeared before a Democratic House, it earned its place on my list in part because of the attendant visibility and the hoped-for resolution of persistent public doubts about the alleged quid pro quo. Whether the investigation will lead to future presidential appearances is still in doubt, but its significance is not.

In contrast, the Enron investigation left a much heavier footprint and was more easily included on the list. Media coverage was intense, as was congressional scrutiny. The Congressional Research Service issued 22 separate reports on the collapse in 2001–02, while the Government Accountability Office issued 130 reports, including one in April 2002 titled "Protecting the Public's Interest: Considerations for Addressing Selected Regulatory Oversight, Auditing, Corporate Governance, and Financial Reporting Issues."[11] The report provided not only a history of events, but also strongly worded recommendations for action.

The investigation was hardly a model of coherence, however. Congress launched at least four separate investigations, three by full committees (the Senate Commerce, Senate Governmental Affairs, and House Energy and Commerce committees) and one by a subcommittee (the House Financial Services Committee's Subcommittee on Capital Markets, Insurance, and Government-Sponsored Enterprises). Rep. Henry Waxman (D-Calif.) also launched a separate review as the ranking member of the House Oversight and Government Reform Committee. Each investigation covered a key event in the collapse, but the House Financial Services Committee and its chairman Mike Oxley (R-Ohio) eventually claimed the lead.

More important for measuring its eventual impact on government performance, the investigation produced sweeping reforms to prevent future accounting deception and failed regulation through the Sarbanes-Oxley Act, so named for its co-sponsors, Sen. Paul Sarbanes (D-Md.) and Oxley. The investigation itself also created a heavy investigatory footprint based on its length, breadth, complexity, well-known leadership, freedom to investigate, visibility, seriousness, thoroughness, leverage, durability, and bipartisanship. The investigation would have earned the heaviest possible footprint score but for the persistent partisanship of the hearings, which is easily identifiable in Waxman's breakaway investigation and plausibly linked to its use of blame setting.

PLAN OF THE BOOK

This book examines the history and patterns among the 100 investigations using legislative histories, contemporary media coverage, research articles, and ninety-six "not for attribution" interviews with former members of Congress, executive branch officers, congressional staffers, scholars, journalists, and other investigatory experts listed in appendix A.[12]

Chapter 2 begins with a more detailed definition of terms and a discussion of the methods and sources I used in compiling my list. The chapter continues with a demographic description of the list as a whole, giving specific examples of what I label "forgotten investigations" that made the final tally. It ends with an analysis of the investigatory climate before and after Watergate and during unified and divided party control of government.

Chapter 3 reviews the prevailing definition of what constitutes the "good investigation" and introduces a set of both quantitative and qualitative measures for estimating the relative significance, or footprint, of each investigation. Using my eleven weights to create a summary score, the chapter ranks the footprints created by each of my 100 investigations, followed by another demographic profile using the measures discussed above. The chapter moves forward with examples of light-, middle-, and heavyweight investigations, discusses blue-ribbon commissions in more detail, proceeds with an effort to predict the final footprint scores, and ends with specific advice to investigators on increasing the footprint of their efforts.

Chapter 4 examines each investigation's impact in repairing or preventing future government breakdowns. Acknowledging the subjective nature of impact and the limits of judging long-term investigatory impacts, the chapter assigns a simple four-point impact score to each investigation and offers a demographic profile of the results. It then discusses six specific types of impact: (1) reforming broken bureaucracies, (2) repairing failed policies, (3) reversing course on national strategies, (4) enhancing accountability, (5) setting the agenda for future action, and (6) resolving doubts about a particular event.[13] The chapter continues with further analysis of the sources of impact, another examination of blue-ribbon commissions, and advice to investigators on increasing the impact of their work.

Chapter 5 starts with a history of the one investigation I admired most and the one I admired least. It continues with a short review of the book's findings, and concludes with a set of broad principles that underpin high-impact investigations. If a good investigation involves both quality and impact, investigators must make hard choices. But these choices must be made in the context of a broader set of core foundations that they must maintain as they start their journey to answers.

AUTHOR'S NOTE

This book is written for two very different audiences: current and would-be investigators and those who study investigations. My hope is to resolve some of the long-standing debates about what constitutes the good investigation, while helping investigators to make thoughtful choices in pursuing impact. These are not mutually exclusive goals, but they do create a more readable book for investigators. For example, all of the percentages that underpin my key findings are presented in the demographic overviews in chapters 2–4, while the supporting statistical analyses are reserved for appendix D.

However, this book involves more than another inventory of investigations. It also introduces new measures of the characteristics, weight, and impact of investigations, many of which are based on my reading of the available record, including my own involvement in the 1983 National Commission on Social Security Reform on behalf of Rep. Barber B. Conable Jr. (R-N.Y.), implementation of the President's Commission on the Shuttle *Challenger* Accident on behalf of the National Academy of Public Administration, and involvement in the 1989 government mismanagement investigation as a senior consultant to Sen. John Glenn's (D-Ohio) Senate Governmental Affairs Committee. I believe that my judgments about each investigation are fair, although others might reach different judgments about the contours of any given investigation. I also recognize that some of my judgments will provoke disagreement. Therefore, this book is best read as a search for answers about investigations, not as a final conclusion about any given inquiry.

TWO

Counting Investigations

Each of the 100 investigations covered in this book left its own mark on history and followed its own path to impact or irrelevance. If not absolutely unique, each investigation nevertheless created its own story, including some that became the grist of Academy Award and Pulitzer Prize winners, not to mention ongoing speculation on what really went wrong.

Each investigation had its own timeline, for example. Some lasted for years, as investigators scoured the country looking for plots against the nation such as communist infiltration of government, illegal lobbying, or China's theft of U.S. nuclear secrets, while others moved quickly to address urgent breakdowns such as the Gulf oil spill, limit the contagion from rapidly spreading disasters such as the 1987 savings and loan collapse, or resolve doubts about lingering controversies such as allegations that the Reagan campaign had contacted Iran in an effort to delay the release of the fifty-two U.S. hostages being held in Tehran and thereby prevent an "October surprise" that might assure President Jimmy Carter's reelection.[1]

Each investigation was also sparked by some kind of government breakdown, whether the result of a decision or a nondecision. Some were presaged by a tragic word or two such as the "uh oh" uttered by the shuttle *Challenger* pilot, Navy Captain Michael J. Smith, just nanoseconds before he and his crew were killed in a preventable explosion. Others were launched after yet another news story about government waste or another "Golden Fleece" award that Sen.

William Proxmire (D-Wis.) pioneered as a way to highlight "the biggest, most ridiculous, or most ironic example of wasteful spending for the month."[2] Others still were ignited by a surprise such as quiz show rigging revealed by the media, a whistle-blower, or the release of a best seller. Finally, still others began with a seemingly innocuous "my-eyes-glaze-over" hearing on the Defense Department's bloated stockpiles of spare engine parts, clothing, dental floss, nose spray, and even bubonic plague vaccine.[3]

Each investigation had a somewhat different purpose as well. Some trivialized national disgraces such as the Ku Klux Klan's brutal tactics during the civil rights movement, minimized systemic problems surrounding technical failures such as the Three Mile Island nuclear power plant meltdown, or glossed over the broader causes of front-page events such as the May 4, 1970, killing of four Kent State University students during a Vietnam War protest. Others pursued the facts about hidden abuses such as the federal government's domestic spying operation during the same war and the Reagan administration's Iran-Contra program, which raised money for Nicaraguan anticommunist rebels from secret arms sales to Iran.[4]

Finally, each investigation had its own structure and modus operandi. Some of the investigations were designed for partisan advantage by focusing on personal misconduct, such as the Clinton administration's alleged misuse of the White House Christmas card list to raise campaign cash and the transformation of the Lincoln bedroom into the "Fat Cat Hotel" for "Friends of Bill," or by firing a warning shot about the potential regulation of a beloved game such as professional baseball. Others, such as the 9/11 investigation, embraced bipartisanship as they sought the facts about what went wrong in the past and what must go right in the future.

Yet even as each investigation created its own résumé, all 100 stand together as significant efforts to address a government failure, be it to fix the problem or to exploit it for political and institutional advantage. All 100 can also be compared against each other using measures such as their length, call to action, seriousness, and bipartisanship. In turn, these and other measures can be used to explain the footprints that the investigations left behind and to predict their eventual impact on government performance.

This chapter begins with short vignettes about three iconic investigations that illustrate the concept of historical significance. It then explains how investigations differ from traditional oversight, discusses my methodology for selecting the 100 investigations on my list, and provides a brief introduction to the list itself, along with a demographic profile of the 100 investigations and an analysis of basic investigatory patterns over the past seven decades.

THREE ICONIC INVESTIGATIONS

The 9/11 terrorist attacks, Watergate cover-up, and alleged communist infiltration of government all offer initial glimpses of what gave an investigation the historical significance to reach my list of the 100 most significant government investigations during the seventy years following World War II.

Start with the 9/11 investigation, which will likely remain at or near the top of every list of significant investigations in U.S. history, in no small part because of its leverage as the nation launched its war on terrorism. Led by former New Jersey governor Tom Kean (R-N.J.) as chair and former Rep. Lee Hamilton (D-Ind.) as vice chair, but with both acting as co-chairs and always appearing side by side, the National Commission on Terrorist Attacks upon the United States not only produced a best-selling final report that remains an essential resource on intelligence and coordination challenges inside the executive branch, but also stands as an exemplar of nonpartisan cooperation toward impact.[5]

This result was hardly preordained by the mere appointment of another blue-ribbon commission, however. Under enormous pressure to help the United States to avoid another attack, perhaps even a biological, chemical, or nuclear attack, Kean and Hamilton drafted the final report with what *New York Times* reporter Philip Shenon calls "trepidation." "There were several potential land mines," Shenon writes, "maybe the wording of the passages about al-Qaeda and its purported links to Iraq, maybe some[thing] about the way Bush and Clinton were described, maybe something about the report's treatment of American relations with Saudi Arabia or Israel."[6]

In the end, Kean and Hamilton decided to steer the commission away from naming names in a flurry of blame setting. As Shenon reports, they wanted to prove that "it was still possible for loyal Republicans and loyal Democrats to agree on what was best for national security."[7] Although there had been conflict over the course of the highly charged investigation, Kean and Hamilton had forged an esprit de corps that served the commission well.

Continue this historical tour with Watergate, which also resides at or near the top of every list of the most significant investigations and remains an oft-cited historical marker of declining public trust in government. Along with the investigations of the Vietnam War, Watergate is still cited as an accelerant for the resurgence of Congress as an investigatory institution.[8] Moreover, Watergate seems to produce a new history every year, memories of Pulitzer Prizes and the once-robust press, and lasting concerns about presidential abuse of power.

The investigation was led by a seven-member Senate select committee chaired by a folksy southern chairman named Sam Ervin (D-N.C.). The Senate did not act alone, however. Archibald Cox uncovered key evidence as

Watergate special prosecutor, while the *Washington Post* and *New York Times* produced one breakthrough story after another as the scandal expanded from what Nixon's press secretary initially called a "third-rate" burglary of the Democratic National Committee's offices in June 1972 to a full-blown conspiracy to cover up the incident.[9]

The investigation obviously had great impact, starting with Nixon's resignation and continuing with the passage of a long list of laws designed to protect privacy, promote transparency in government, regulate campaign finance, and expand freedom of information. The investigation also provoked a series of additional investigations, such as Sen. Frank Church's (D-Idaho) inquiry into intelligence agency abuses, and sparked a renaissance in congressional oversight.

Conclude with the bitter post–World War II investigation of communists in government so frequently associated with the rise and fall of Sen. Joseph McCarthy (R-Wisc.). Although he had only been in the Senate three years when he broke into the public consciousness, he launched a secondary investigation in this package with his 1950 "Enemies Within" speech in Wheeling, West Virginia. His charges were both inflammatory and deceptively specific:

> While I cannot take the time to name all the men in the State Department who have been named as members of the Communist party and members of a spy ring, I have here in my hand a list of 205 that were known to the Secretary of State as being members of the Communist party and who, nevertheless, are still working and shaping policy in the State Department.[10]

McCarthy waffled on the exact number of State Department communists in the following weeks, but his charges raised the "Red Scare" to new prominence.[11] Almost immediately after his five-hour floor speech detailing each of his cases, the Senate passed Senate Resolution 23 ordering the Foreign Relations Committee "to investigate whether there are employees in the State Department disloyal to the United States." Chaired by Sen. Millard E. Tydings (D-Md.), the investigation held thirty-one hearings during its six-month inquiry, but reached an entirely equivocal conclusion. In a very real sense, its conclusion marked the beginning of the end for McCarthy. Noting McCarthy's cries of "whitewash," the subcommittee launched a scathing attack against a fellow senator rarely spoken in the chamber, let alone written in a public report:

From the very outset of our inquiry, Senator McCarthy has sought to leave the impression that the subcommittee has been investigating him and "disloyalty in the State Department." The reason for the Senator's concern is now apparent. He had no facts to support his wild and baseless charges, and lived in mortal fear that this situation would be exposed.

Few people, cognizant of the truth in even an elementary way have, in the absence of political partisanship, placed any credence in the hit-and-run tactics of Senator McCarthy. He has stooped to a new low in his cavalier disregard of the facts . . . Starting with nothing, Senator McCarthy plunged headlong forward, desperately seeking to develop some information, which colored with distortion and fanned by a blaze of bias would forestall his day of reckoning.[12]

The Senate was hardly the only investigator involved in the war against shadows. The House Un-American Activities Committee (HUAC) launched its salvo first, moving early and hard on the issue in its long trail of hearings, while establishing itself as the prime investigator in the overall package. Established as a special investigatory committee in 1938 and converted to a full committee in 1945, HUAC was unrelenting in its pursuit of infiltration and treason.

The HUAC 1948 hearings on communist infiltration of the executive branch ignited a fire of other investigations, launched Nixon's rise to the national ticket in 1952, and produced reams of front-page newspaper coverage. The committee's investigation also produced the first televised hearings in history, which pitted former *Time* magazine senior editor and admitted former communist Whittaker Chambers against the State Department's former director of special political affairs, Alger Hiss. In turn, the investigation led to Hiss's eventual perjury conviction.

The HUAC hearings were augmented by a host of parallel, often competing hearings led by at least a half dozen other congressional committees and subcommittees, each with a slightly different variation on the communists-in-government theme. The result was a massive investigation that is still enshrined in the national security forms that every presidential nominee must complete as a necessary (but not dispositive) condition for confirmation. It appears on my list of the heaviest investigations between 1945 and 2012.

Despite its long-lasting effects on everything from national security clearances to persistent fears of censorship and blacklists, the investigation began to flag with McCarthy's own downfall after he launched yet another investigation as the new chairman of the Senate Government Affairs Committee in 1953. Having earned his reputation by attacking the long-maligned State Department, McCarthy decided to take on a much bigger target, the Army and World War II hero Major General Ralph W. Zwicker.

McCarthy's unsubstantiated attacks provoked a wave of criticism from the Army, President Dwight D. Eisenhower, his own Republican colleagues, and most famously Edward R. Murrow, host of the popular CBS news program *See It Now*. On March 9, 1954, Murrow devoted his entire half-hour broadcast to "A Report on Senator Joseph R. McCarthy." Murrow's scathing commentary marked a turning point in the investigation: "His primary achievement has been in confusing the public mind, as between the internal and the external threats of Communism . . . The actions of the junior Senator from Wisconsin have caused alarm and dismay amongst our allies abroad, and given considerable comfort to our enemies. And whose fault is that? Not really his. He didn't create this situation of fear; he merely exploited it—and rather successfully."[13]

The Senate censured McCarthy nine months later, and he died in 1957 before the end of his second term in office.

A DISTINCTION WITH A DIFFERENCE REVISITED

There is no shortage of candidates for a list of significant investigations, in large measure because the term "investigation" is defined so broadly that it has no operational meaning. As Roger Davidson argued in 1977, "It is no simple task to discern just what is and what is not a congressional investigation."[14] The House and Senate Joint Committee on the Organization of Congress echoed the comment in 1993:

> There are no authoritative, comprehensive statistics on the amount of oversight or even the number of specialized investigations throughout the history of the Congress. This absence is, in part, because scholars have disagreed as to what constitutes oversight and, therefore, how it should be measured as well as the difficulty and high research costs of quantifying congressional activities.[15]

Despite this confusion, investigations have certain characteristics that generate more historical significance than the day-to-day inquiries that Congress and presidents so often pursue. Compared to these inquiries, most investigations have a discrete beginning and end, last longer, often involve more complex issues, and generally produce visible products such as final reports, admonishments, recommendations, and legislative proposals. Although simple oversight hearings sometimes cascade to full-blown investigations, most have a set beginning and expected end. And many generate intense competition within and across the branches, as multiple investigators fight for leverage in the search for answers—thus sixty-one of the investigations involved more than one congressional venue and the occasional blue-ribbon commission.

Beyond their sheer historical weight, investigations can be distinguished from routine oversight by their focus, stature, identity, intensity, linkages, slack, and coverage. Together, these seven characteristics provide a general template for distinguishing investigations from other forms of government monitoring. This framework undergirds the choices made in building the list of the most significant investigations used in this book.

Focus

First, investigations are driven by a government breakdown, be it an urgent event such as the shuttle *Challenger* accident, a persistent problem such as illegal lobbying and corruption, or a failed policy such as federal banking regulation, the Vietnam War, or the Enron collapse. Some of these breakdowns are uncovered through routine "police patrol" oversight, while others involve "fire alarms" created by urgent events, and still others by one followed by another.

The 1963 investigation of alleged news management during the Cuban missile crisis seems like a perfect example of a police patrol hidden behind a fire alarm. Led by the House Government Operations Subcommittee on Foreign Operations and Information, the inquiry centered on federal "secrecy directives" issued during the thirteen-day nuclear stand-off. As the Defense Department's assistant secretary for public affairs told the subcommittee at one point in a December 1962 hearing, government has an "inherent right to lie to save itself when it's going up into a nuclear war."[16]

Yet, much as the investigation might have looked like a pop-up storm, it was actually the culmination of an eleven-year review. By wrapping the Cuban missile investigation in a fire alarm, the subcommittee was able to draw national attention to its work and attract leading journalists and newspaper publishers to the witness table. By then, the subcommittee was almost finished with its report on what the public needs to know, and when it needs to know it. As noted later in this chapter, the long-running investigation laid the foundation for the Freedom of Information Act of 1966 and was mentioned as one of several sparks for the act's further expansion following the Vietnam War. Congressional Research Service scholar Harold C. Relyea gave John E. Moss (D-Calif.) full credit for the act and his persistence in conducting hearing after hearing on the seemingly minor and certainly mundane facets of government information management.[17]

Stature

Second, investigations have a discernible stature, or standing, that towers above most appropriations and authorization oversight hearings. Congress and the president often use "investigation" to signal their commitment to resolve a particular problem such as the shuttle *Challenger* and *Columbia* disasters or, at the very least, to show their concern for issues such as campus unrest during the Vietnam War, intelligence agency abuses, or prevention of terrorism.

The Obama administration sent just such a signal in announcing the 2010 National Commission on Fiscal Responsibility and Reform, which was cochaired by former Wyoming senator Alan Simpson (R) and former Clinton White House chief of staff Erskine Bowles. Although Obama later distanced himself from the commission and its findings, his announcement was filled with promise:

> For far too long, Washington has avoided the tough choices necessary to solve our fiscal problems—and they won't be solved overnight. But under the leadership of Erskine and Alan, I'm confident that the Commission I'm establishing today will build a bipartisan consensus to put America on the path toward fiscal reform and responsibility. I know they'll take up their work with the sense of integrity and strength of commitment that America's people deserve and America's future demands.[18]

Congress is hardly immune to similar grandeur, especially when it creates a select or special investigatory committee. For example, it sent its own grand signal in May 1995 when it created the Senate Special Committee to Investigate Whitewater Development Corporation and Related Matters under Senate Resolution 120. The Senate could have given the committee authority to review everything from Vince Foster's suicide to the seemingly unjustified White House travel office firings (often called "Travelgate"), and the allegedly improper 1993 White House scrutiny of secret FBI security clearance files (often called "Filegate"). Although these incidents eventually made their way into the House Clinton conduct investigation, the Senate clearly believed that Whitewater was unrelated, in part because it occurred long before Clinton became president. Nevertheless, as Sen. Alfonse D'Amato (R-N.Y.) told his colleagues the day he took the helm of the case, Whitewater had created a national crisis of confidence:

Mr. President. Whitewater is a very serious matter. Some questions raised by Whitewater go to the very heart of our democratic system of government. We must determine whether the public trust has been abused. We must ascertain whether purely private interests have been placed above the public trust. The American people have a right to know the full facts about Whitewater and related matters . . . Congress has the responsibility to serve as the public's watchdog. We would be derelict in our duties if we did not pursue these Whitewater questions. The Senate must proceed in an evenhanded, impartial, and thorough manner. We have a constitutional responsibility to resolve these issues . . . The American people expect and deserve a thorough inquiry committed to the pursuit of truth. That is the American way.[19]

Like so many of the Clinton conduct investigations, the sixty days of public hearings produced little by way of significant findings, but nonetheless marked the inquiry as one of the most significant of the post–World War II period.[20]

Identity

Third, investigations tend to develop a brand identity as the go-to source for answers and fixes. This identity shapes media coverage and is often advertised as a way to show comprehensive concern. The public comes to know the investigation, if they know it at all, more by its leader than by its subject—for example, the Warren (Kennedy assassination), Kerner (urban riots), Scowcroft (strategic missile forces), Packard (defense procurement fraud), Hart and Rudman (preventing terrorism), and 9/11 commissions and the McCarthy (communists in government), Kefauver (organized crime and drug price fixing), and Waxman (tobacco) investigations.

A case in point is the 1975 investigation of intelligence agency abuses led by Sen. Frank Church (D-Idaho), which is discussed in chapter 5 as the top investigation on my list. The investigation covered a host of topics from assassination plots to domestic spying, some that were first announced in front-page exposés in the *New York Times* and others that were uncovered as Church's Senate Select Committee on Intelligence Activities continued its fifteen-month review. Although the House launched a parallel investigation chaired by Rep. Otis Pike (D-N.Y.), the Church Committee was widely recognized as the lead inquiry, produced a deeper list of findings, and issued a stunning indictment of Congress itself:

While the evidence in the Committee's Report emphasizes the misguided or improper activities of a few individuals in the executive branch, it is clear that the growth of intelligence abuses reflects a more general failure of our basic institutions.

Throughout its investigation, the Committee has carefully inquired into the role of presidents and their advisors with respect to particular intelligence programs. On occasion, intelligence agencies concealed their programs from those in higher authority, more frequently it was the senior officials themselves who, through pressure for results, created the climate within which the abuses occurred. It is clear that greater executive control and accountability is necessary.

The legislative branch has been remiss in exercising its control over the intelligence agencies. For twenty-five years Congress has appropriated funds for intelligence activities. The closeted and fragmentary accounting which the intelligence community has given to a designated small group of legislators was accepted by the Congress as adequate and in the best interest of national security. There were occasions when the executive intentionally withheld information relating to intelligence programs from the Congress, but there were also occasions when the principal role of the Congress was to call for more intelligence activity, including activity which infringed the rights of citizens. In general, as with the executive, it is clear that Congress did not carry out effective oversight.[21]

Intensity

Fourth, investigations often help Congress and the president to focus on a particular breakdown, which often generates intense pressure for action. Although presidents have certainly used blue-ribbon investigations to make problems disappear, they have also created commissions to issue fast, fact-based recommendations through an intense study process.[22] Similarly, Congress often has used investigations to assert its institutional prerogatives in the Constitution's separation of powers, confirm its bipartisan commitment to fact finding, leverage its capacity for blame setting during divided government, and resolve doubts about long-standing controversies.

Consider the 1991–92 investigation of Vietnam prisoners of war (POWs) and soldiers missing in action (MIAs) as an example. Led by the Senate Select Committee on POW/MIA Affairs, and chaired by decorated Vietnam War veteran, and future presidential candidate, Sen. John Kerry (D-Mass.), the investigation was designed to resolve twenty years of doubts about the fate of U.S. military personnel captured or lost in Southeast Asia. Kerry's committee took its job seriously, holding twenty-two hearings, calling 144 witnesses, examining thousands of documents and photos, and finally issuing a 1,000-page, heavily footnoted report. Despite its overall weight, however, the investigation did little either to put the issue to rest or spark demands for relief, in part because it was based far more on rumor than hard facts. As such, it followed the pattern of half a dozen previous inquiries dating back to hearings of the House Foreign Affairs Committee from 1969 to 1973, the House Select Committee from 1975 to 1976, and the House International Relations Committee from 1978 to 1991, as well as parallel hearings of the Senate Armed Services, Foreign Relations, and Veterans' Affairs committees over the same long march.

Linkages

Fifth, new investigations are often tied to their predecessors, as familiar breakdowns emerge anew or old ones remain unresolved. Although appropriations and authorizing committees also tie their work to prior hearings, investigations tend to involve punctuations, or moments of intense activity, often linked in an almost predictable sequence based on continued problems fixing a specific problem such as Social Security, banking regulation, space exploration, and government fraud, waste, and abuse. And although wars and military interventions may not be breakdowns in and of themselves, they often produce grist for the investigatory mill dating back to the Board of War appointed by the Continental Congress to investigate the calamity at Valley Forge during the winter of 1778.[23]

The Defense Department's penchant for poor procurement judgments is almost always in the news, including reports in 2012 about the $17,000 Blackhawk helicopter oil drip pans.[24] At least five procurement investigations made the list of top investigations presented later in this chapter, including two deep investigations of procurement fraud, the first during and after World War II and the second during and after the Reagan administration's rapid defense buildup.

The 1985 Blue-Ribbon Commission on Defense Management is arguably the most visible in this set of separate investigations, the most controversial of which involved alleged profiteering in the purchase of defense material. The profiteering investigation was launched in 1962 after President Kennedy described the Defense Department's $8 billion stockpile as a "questionable burden on public funds" and a "potential source of unconscionable profits" and was led by Sen. Stuart Symington (D-Mo.) and his Armed Services Committee's National Stockpile and Naval Petroleum Reserves Subcommittee. Symington orchestrated sixty hearings between March 28, 1961, and January 30, 1962, en route to a null finding about Kennedy's complaint.

Placing the blame for the growth in profiteering squarely on the Eisenhower administration, Symington's investigation examined every commodity from rubber to steel, but eventually took aim at Eisenhower's former treasury secretary, George Humphrey. Humphrey became secretary only months after leaving the M. A. Hanna Mining Company, which had signed a contract to deliver 125 million pounds of steel-strengthening nickel just four days before Eisenhower became president.

Humphrey was a nearly perfect investigatory target. He had been president of Hanna's mining subsidiary when the company set what one Defense Department witness called an "objectionable" price for the desperately needed nickel, retained his stock even after his confirmation as treasury secretary, and described the Symington investigation as "pure baloney." "They don't dare attack Ike directly, so they are attacking me," he told the *Christian Science Monitor* in August 1962. "This is a stab in the back." Despite the circumstantial evidence, the subcommittee never reached a firm conclusion about either Humphrey or the more general profiteering. It simply faded away after the subcommittee rejected Symington's draft report, although the document was cited in the legislative history of the 1978 Ethics in Government Act. The final report was released as a draft and never formally approved.[25]

Slack

Sixth, investigations generally have excess capacity or "slack" as part of their mission, especially when established through law or executive order. Blue-ribbon commissions are almost always given independent budgets and separate office space, as are select and special congressional committees and subcommittees, especially when they are established as temporary investigatory venues.

This slack is not necessarily automatic, however. The 1976 House Select Committee on Assassinations won its budget and staffing in part through an apples-and-oranges comparison of three past investigations, one by the President's Commission on the Assassination of John F. Kennedy (the Warren Commission), a second by the Federal Bureau of Investigation involving the Patty Hearst kidnapping, and a third by the New York State government of fraud in its Medicaid long-term programs. According to the select committee, the Warren Commission had its own full-time staff of 83, with another 150 FBI and 60 Secret Service agents on detail, the Federal Bureau of Investigation spent

$2.6 million in the first three months of the Hearst investigation, and New York State's Medicaid review had a staff of 421 and a yearly budget of $6 million, while building on the work of forty grand juries.[26] The about-to-be-created House select committee argued its case for budget and staff as follows:

> The committee feels strongly that the integrity of this investigation is contingent upon the independence of our investigative efforts. The executive branch agencies, which were utilized in the past, are the very agencies whose previous performance may be the subject of a part of this investigation. The committee, therefore, cannot employ the services of the executive branch agencies. Both the size of the staff and the budget requirements are predicated on the necessity of conducting a comprehensive, impartial investigation.[27]

Despite its flawed comparisons of three completely unrelated inquiries, the select committee won a $6.5 million budget and a full-time staff of 170, giving it the independence for its wide-ranging and ultimately unsatisfying result.

Coverage

Seventh, investigations tend to be designed for maximum media coverage featuring well-rehearsed scripts and supported by long lists of protagonists such as the 9/11 victims and antagonists such as investment bankers, baseball players, and discredited lobbyists. Whereas many oversight hearings are conducted at the subcommittee level with minimal coverage and third-tier witnesses called forward from within the executive branch, many of my 100 investigations were launched with a parade of first-tier witnesses from both inside and outside government.

The 1950 investigation of organized crime involved just such a parade. Launched in 1950 by the Senate Special Committee to Investigate Organized Crime in Interstate Commerce, the investigation was led by up-and-coming political star Estes Kefauver (D-Tenn.). Drawing upon its own history of holding televised hearings, including ones that featured notorious figures such as the alleged "godfather" of organized crime, Frank Costello,[28] the Kefauver Committee eventually felt well qualified to provide its own advice on handling television coverage in the future:

> 1. No television network or station shall use for the hearings a commercial sponsor not specifically approved in writing by the committee or its designated representative, and no sponsor shall be charged

by a network or station more than such reasonable amount as may be consistent with the usual charges for other programs emanating from a public source.

2. No commercial announcement shall be broadcast from the hearing room.

3. Breaks for station identification during the hearings shall be limited to 10 seconds.

4. No network or station shall make any comment or commercial announcement during the testimony of a witness, or interrupt the broadcasting of the testimony of a witness for the purpose of making any such comment or announcement.

5. During each pause or intermission in the hearings, the network may make a commercial announcement lasting not more than 1 minute and, except in the case of a newspaper, magazine, or other publication of general circulation referring to reports of the hearings to appear in its columns, such commercial shall be institutional in character and shall make no reference to the hearings.

6. No local station shall interrupt any portion of the broadcasting of the hearings as received from a network for the purpose of making any spot or other commercial announcement.

7. A network or station may, at any time, make a complete break from the broadcasting of the hearings for the purpose of broadcasting other programs.

8. At the beginning and end of the broadcasting of the hearings for any day, the network carrying the hearings shall make the following announcement or its equivalent: These hearings are brought to you as a public service by the X Company in cooperation with the Y Television Network.[29]

THE INVENTORY OF INVESTIGATIONS

Just as experts disagree on when oversight stops and investigation begins, they also disagree on the most significant in any given historical period. Indeed, the problem in creating a final list of the most significant investigations from World War II to the end of Obama's first term was not having too few candidates and associated inventories, but having too many. Some of the available lists are comprehensive, while others are selective; some are based on explicit criteria such as media coverage, while others are based on participant observation and memory; some are based on hard criteria and careful vetting, while others are presented as examples to prove a point; and some are clearly advertised as significant examples, while others can be found in asides at workshops and conferences. But together, the many lists can be used to build a population of possibilities that can be winnowed down to 100.

Building a List

The search for the 100 most significant investigations between 1945 and 2012 began with a thorough review of potential candidates identified by a long list of sources summarized in appendix B. Some of these sources merely provided examples of significant investigations, while others offered lists of every important investigation from a certain period, but all of the candidates were reviewed unless they involved a Senate confirmation investigation such as the nominations of Robert Bork and Clarence Thomas for the Supreme Court or a House or Senate internal investigation of their members or staff such as Bobby Baker's alleged influence peddling as secretary to the Senate majority leader.

My search continued by developing detailed introductory résumés of roughly 125 candidates culled from contemporary investigatory history. Each of these two- to three-page forms contained extensive background information on the investigation's history, characteristics, leadership, and general outcome. These reports helped me to compare historical signatures among competing investigations and included background reports and key Congressional Quarterly documents for further analysis.

Finally, my search for candidates ended with a series of subjective decisions regarding the boundaries of each investigation. Simply asked, at what point does a single investigation become part of a much larger whole? Although thirty-nine investigations involved a single congressional committee, special congressional body, subcommittee, or a single blue-ribbon commission, the other sixty-one involved multiple, often nearly simultaneous hearings by other committees, subcommittees, and even an occasional blue-ribbon commission that were packaged into one inquiry. Consider three examples of these "packaged" investigations:

—The investigation of communists in government during the late 1940s and early 1950s involved seven hearing sets that ran from 1948 all the way through Sen. Joseph McCarthy's censure in 1954. It involved dozens of hearings by HUAC, the Senate Committee on Foreign Relations, the Senate Committee on Government Operations and its Special Subcommittee on Investigations (which now operates as the Permanent Subcommittee on Investigations), and a Senate Select Committee to Study Censure Charges (that is, against McCarthy). Five of these hearing sets showed up on David R. May-hew's list of high-publicity investigations in chapter 2 of his seminal book *Divided We Govern.*[30]

—The long-running investigation of the Vietnam War, which ran from hearings on deception in the evidence underpinning the 1964 Gulf of Tonkin Resolution all the way through the My Lai massacre and the secret war in Cambodia, involved parallel and often conflicting hearing sets by liberal Sen. J. William Fulbright (D-Ark.) and his Committee on Foreign Relations[31] and by conservative John C. Stennis (D-Miss.) and his Preparedness Subcommittee of the Armed Services Committee. Three of the ongoing hearing sets made Mayhew's list.

—The 1985 investigation of Defense Department procurement fraud involved separate hearing sets by the President's Blue-Ribbon Commission on Defense Management (Packard Commission), the House Armed Services Committee, the Senate Armed Services Committee, the Senate Governmental Affairs Committee and its Subcommittee on Oversight of Government Management, the House Committee on Energy and Commerce, and the Joint Economic Committee and its Subcommittee on International Trade, Finance, and Security Economics. None of these hearing sets made Mayhew's list.

The World War II Procurement Package

Packaging multiple hearing sets into single investigations carries certain risks, not the least of which are the potentially heavier footprints that might come from such couplings. Packaged investigations may be more likely to produce greater investigatory impact as well, in part because the level of surrounding activity may increase the leverage so closely associated with fixing or preventing a breakdown.

Nevertheless, it is difficult, if not impossible, to separate many of the competing investigations that surrounded some of the breakdowns covered in this book, such as the four on civil unrest in the mid-1960s, six on the savings and loan crisis in the late 1980s, seven on communist infiltration of government starting in the 1940s, eight on the 2008 financial collapse, nine on the 1981 Social Security financing crisis, ten on the 2001 Enron debacle, fifteen on the Iraq War, and seventeen on technology transfers to China in the late 1990s. Some of these packages obviously involved sharp-elbowed competition in real time, while others involved multiple investigations over long periods. Regardless of the duration, packaging is the best available option for defining the total investigation as the unit of analysis for this book, not the single set of hearings.

Consider the long-running investigation of World War II procurement fraud as a particularly difficult packaging decision. Launched by then-senator Harry S. Truman (D-Mo.) on March 1, 1941, the Senate Special Committee to Investigate the National Defense Program worked through one fraud case after another until 1948, when it was terminated by Senate resolution. The seven-year investigation is listed by the Senate historian as one of the most important investigations ever conducted by the body and is the first inquiry on my list.

Launched with Franklin D. Roosevelt's blessing, Truman's investigation produced a thorough inventory of scandal and demands for reform, but also gave the novice senator the political visibility to join the national ticket in 1944. The Senate historian makes the connection between the investigation and Truman's future as follows:

> No senator ever gained greater political benefits from chairing a special investigating committee than did Missouri's Harry S. Truman . . . During the three years of Truman's chairmanship, the committee held hundreds of hearings, traveled thousands of miles to conduct field inspections, and saved millions of dollars in cost overruns. Earning nearly universal respect for his thoroughness and determination, Truman erased his earlier public image as an errand-runner for Kansas City politicos. Along the way, he developed working experience with business, labor, agriculture, and executive branch agencies that would serve him well in later years. In 1944, when Democratic Party leaders sought a replacement for controversial Vice President Henry Wallace, they settled on Truman, thereby setting his course directly to the White House.[32]

The investigation did not end with Truman's move to 1600 Pennsylvania Avenue, however. Although still known as the Truman Committee, the committee's investigation of wartime fraud continued under two different chairmen and reached its most visible moment in a series of highly visible hearings on the nation's sizable investment in Howard Hughes's "flying boat," better known as the Spruce Goose for its ungainly shape.[33] Initially authorized during World War II, the amphibious craft (formally the H-4 Hercules) became a sensational example of government waste, in part because it was so large and in part because it could barely rise from the water in its one flight test. The Republican majority concluded that the plane was "an unwise and unnecessary expense as a wartime project" and a waste of desperately needed resources.

With a new Republican majority in power, the investigation was driven forward with even greater intensity, prompting the Democratic minority to demand rules for investigatory conduct and procedural limits on "fishing expeditions."[34] The hearings are still cited in the coverage of contemporary issues such as the financial crisis.

The investigation shows the potential value of combining highly visible inquiries into single investigatory packages. Although the Spruce Goose investigation was undeniably substantial, obviously well covered, and created at least some deterrence against cost overruns, it can be easily described as merely one, albeit highly visible, of dozens of postwar hearings on defense fraud, waste, and abuse. Operating under yearly reauthorizations from 1941 to 1948, the committee issued fifty-one reports, held 432 public and 300 private hearings, called 1,798 witnesses (who made 2,284 appearances), and issued forty-three volumes of testimony.[35] The flying boat controversy was just one on the list.

Moreover, the committee continues to exist in its distinguished offspring. Its primary responsibilities moved to the Senate Committee on Executive Expenditures in 1948, which became the Committee on Government Operations in 1952, which became the Committee on Governmental Affairs in 1977, which became the Committee on Homeland Security and Governmental Affairs in 2005. Although the committee has conducted extensive procurement investigations over the years, its Permanent Subcommittee on Investigations is often cited as the Truman Committee's resting place. It is a case well made on the subcommittee's own website:

> The Permanent Subcommittee on Investigations was originally authorized by Senate Resolution 189 on January 28, 1948. At its creation in 1948, the Subcommittee was part of the Committee on Expenditures in the Executive Departments. The Subcommittee's records and broad investigative jurisdiction over government operations and national security issues, however, actually antedate its creation, since it was given custody of the jurisdiction of the former Special Committee to Investigate the National Defense Program (the so-called "War Investigating Committee," or "Truman Committee"), chaired by Senator Harry S. Truman during the Second World War and charged with exposing waste, fraud, and abuse in the war effort and war profiteering.[36]

The historical record suggests that the World War II procurement investigation had little lasting impact on government performance, positive or negative, but its historical shadow can be easily seen in the permanent subcommittee's subsequent role in dozens of other significant investigations.

The List of Investigations

Box 2-1 presents the final list of the 100 most significant investigations between 1945 and 2012. Some of the investigations had a great deal of impact on government performance, while others had little or none; and some involved serious domestic and foreign crises, while others addressed seemingly trivial offenses.[37] However, the decision to include one investigation in box 2-1 and exclude another was not based on either impact or importance, but rather on historical significance. As noted in the introduction to this book, some of the twenty-five investigations that missed the final list created heavy footprints and impact, but not the significance needed to reach the final 100.[38]

The Forgotten

The most familiar investigations on my list tend to remain part of investigatory lore (the Warren Commission, 9/11), come down from dusty bookshelves when similar breakdowns occur (Internal Revenue Service [IRS] misconduct, lobbying abuse, defense fraud), return to the fore as exemplars of the good investigation (Vietnam, intelligence community abuses), or provide the plotlines for films such as *All the President's Men, Good Night and Good Luck, JFK, Quiz Show, The Aviator, The China Syndrome,* and *The Godfather.*

So noted, a handful of "forgotten" investigations also made my list. Often conducted with little media coverage and sometimes led by obscure committees and little-known chairmen, these investigations often laid the groundwork for major legislation such as the Freedom of Information Act or solved problems before they became catastrophes.

Recall the 1963 investigation of Kennedy's alleged news manipulation as one of several examples of forgotten investigations. Launched by the Subcommittee on Foreign Operations and Government Information on March 19 under the broad title of "Government Information Plans and Policies," the investigation only involved eight hearings between March and June, but raised significant questions about government transparency and freedom of information. As chairman of the subcommittee, John E. Moss argued in his opening statement, the investigation reflected a long-standing interest "in breaking down barriers to a freer flow of information to the Congress and to the public." Moss also noted the ongoing tension about what the public should know when, how, and why:

> There is management of the news. It always has existed in Government at all levels just as it exists in every private business. Everybody wants to put out information in a way to show his actions in the best

BOX 2-1. The Federal Government's Most Significant Investigations,
1945–2012

1940s

Pearl Harbor (1945)
World War II procurement fraud (1945)
Agriculture commodity speculation (1947)
Communists in Hollywood (1947)
Government reorganization (1947)
Communists in government (1948)
Atomic Energy Commission operations
    (1949)

1950s

Organized crime in America (1950)
Reconstruction Finance Corporation
    mismanagement (1950)
Bureau of Internal Revenue corruption
    (1951)
Conduct of the Korean War (1951)
Airport safety (1952)
Justice Department operations (1952)
Dixon-Yates power contract (1954)
Federal Housing Administration
    mismanagement (1954)
Air Force preparedness for the cold war
    (1956)
Campaign finance corruption (1956)
Labor racketeering (1957)
Sherman Adams misconduct (1957)
Sputnik launch (1957)
Drug industry practices (1959)
Munitions lobby (1959)
Quiz show rigging (1959)

1960s

Agriculture commodity leasing (1962)
Defense Department stockpiling (1962)
Lobbying by foreign governments (1962)

Military "muzzling" (1962)
Government information management
    (1963)
Kennedy assassination (1963)
State Department security procedures
    (1963)
TFX fighter aircraft contract (1963)
Traffic safety (1965)
Crime in America (1965)
Ku Klux Klan activities (1965)
Conduct of the Vietnam War (1966)
Central Intelligence Agency financing of
    private organizations (1967)
Urban riots (1967)
Executive branch reorganization (1969)

1970s

Kent State campus unrest (1970)
Justice Department antitrust settlement
    (1972)
Energy shortages (1973)
Watergate (1973)
Nixon pardon (1974)
Intelligence agency abuses (1975)
Welfare fraud (1975)
South Korean lobbying (1977)
General Services Administration
    corruption (1978)
Three Mile Island nuclear accident (1979)

1980s

Educational quality (1981)
Social Security financing crisis (1981)
Superfund implementation (1981)
Abscam congressional sting (1982)
Bombing of Beirut Marine barracks (1983)
Central America policy (1983)

BOX 2-1. The Federal Government's Most Significant Investigations, 1945–2012 (continued)

1980s (cont.)

Strategic missile forces (1983)

Defense Department fraud, waste, and abuse (1985)

Space shuttle *Challenger* accident (1986)

Wedtech defense procurement decision (1986)

Government response to the human immunodeficiency virus (HIV) epidemic (1987)

Savings and loan crisis (1987)

White House Iran-Contra program (1987)

Base closing and realignment (1988)

Indian Affairs corruption (1988)

Government mismanagement (1989)

Housing and Urban Development scandal (1989)

1990s

Vietnam prisoners of war (POWs) and missing in action (MIAs) (1991)

1980 "October surprise" (1992)

Tobacco industry practices (1993)

U.S. intelligence agencies in the post–cold war era (1994)

Clinton conduct (1995)

Gulf War syndrome (1995)

Ruby Ridge siege (1995)

Waco Branch Davidian siege (1995)

Whitewater allegations (1995)

Secret arms shipments to Bosnia (1996)

Aviation security and safety in an age of terrorism (1996)

Internal Revenue Service taxpayer abuse (1996)

Technology transfers to China (1997)

1996 campaign finance abuses (1997)

Clinton impeachment (1998)

Preventing terrorist attacks (1998)

Year 2000 technology problem (1998)

2000s

Enron collapse (2001)

White House energy task force (2001)

9/11 terrorist attacks (2002)

Conduct of the Iraq War (2003)

Department of Homeland Security implementation and operations (2003)

Space shuttle *Columbia* accident (2003)

Abramoff lobbying tactics (2004)

Government response to Hurricane Katrina (2005)

Steroid abuse in baseball (2005)

Mine safety (2007)

Quality of care for wounded warriors (2007)

U.S. attorney firings (2007)

2008 financial collapse (2008)

Stimulus oversight (2009)

Deficit reduction (2010)

Gulf oil spill (2010)

Fast and Furious gun-walking operation (2011)

Solyndra Corporation (2011)

possible light. Recognizing this, the subcommittee, from its incep-
tion, has addressed itself to a central and overriding problem of making available the facts on the activities of Government and the
activities of those who are charged with the responsibility of running
the Government.[39]

The Moss hearings began with a "who's who" of newspaper editors, all
arguing that the Kennedy administration had used information as "weaponry"
in shaping public opinion about the missile crisis. The investigation was short,
relatively narrow, not particularly complex, barely visible, and led by a little-
known investigator. However, it was also serious, thorough, and free to pursue
every lead. Although the investigation produced plenty of partisan disagreement as the Republican minority took the Kennedy administration to task, it
created lasting effects nonetheless. It may have left a relatively light footprint
on the investigatory landscape, but scored at the very top of the impact scale
in chapter 4.

The investigation seems eerily relevant in light of the October 2012
attacks in Benghazi, Libya, that claimed the lives of the U.S. ambassador J.
Christopher Stevens and three other Americans. The resulting "spin" of the
event, whether accidental or intended, suggests that news management
remains an issue worthy of investigation, which the House and Senate
promptly demonstrated in their own hearings on the events of the day. The
investigations began with a House Oversight and Government Reform Committee hearing on October 10, 2012, which featured contradictory testimony
about the Obama administration's initial version of events as well as allegations that the United States had reduced security at the mission in the days
before the attack. The hearings contributed to the December withdrawal of
the United Nations ambassador Susan Rice from consideration for appointment as secretary of state.[40]

The investigation of State Department security procedures during the
same year is a second example of a forgotten investigation. Few historians
know the story well, and even fewer recall the allegations regarding an obscure
State Department official named Otto Otepka either. Otepka became a central witness in a three-year probe of the Kennedy administration's alleged
evasion of the State Department's security procedures created during the
communists-in-government probe.

Led by the Senate Judiciary Committee's Special Subcommittee to Investigate the Administration of the Internal Security Act and Other Internal
Security Laws, the investigation lasted until 1966, involved forty-two hearings,
and produced a four-volume report with twenty separate sections. Although

it made the *New York Times* front page only once, the investigation centered on the Senate's constitutional right to examine State Department operations.

The hearings had an obvious "hook": the summary firing of Otepka for the alleged release of classified documents in his congressional testimony. Asked for documents on the security clearance of several Kennedy administration aides, Otepka complied with a list, but not the full documents. According to the *New York Times*, the subcommittee vice chairman, Sen. Thomas J. Dodd (D-Conn.), viewed the firing as "a serious challenge to responsible government and an affront to the Senate."[41] The full committee's final report explored the firing in excruciating detail, offering a history of Otepka's career, an inventory of positive performance ratings, and a full review of his decision to provide the documents. The subcommittee's own summation was the single most important statement for moving the investigation onto my list:

> The impact this case had had upon personnel security in the executive branch of our Government has been far greater than is generally recognized. This impact has been both positive and negative.
>
> On the plus side, a number of improvements in security policies and procedures have been put into effect administratively to cure lapses or supply deficiencies to which Mr. Otepka and other witnesses called attention. Another plus is the inspiring example Otto Otepka has set in remaining steadfast to the uncompromising principles and high standards which should and do motivate a majority of the professional security officers who serve our Government.
>
> The most outstanding negative aspect of the Otepka case has been its chilling effect upon all those Government employees, both in and out of the security field, who may quite reasonably see it as an object lesson teaching that honor and virtue involves stepping on the toes of entrenched authority, or calls for disclosing matter embarrassing to officials in high places.[42]

Viewed as a whole, the investigation had modest impact at best on the State Department, which never reinstated Otepka. Otepka was hardly a glamorous figure, and the rules he enforced were already becoming passé, but the investigation was a harbinger of congressional resurgence nonetheless.[43] As such, it can rightly be seen as one of several sparks for more aggressive congressional monitoring.

Moreover, the investigation occurred during a period of unified government and under a popular president, which is itself a sign of congressional assertiveness, and deserves a place on the most significant investigations on my list. However, it did not have the grand visibility of the organized crime,

Watergate, lobbying, 9/11, or banking investigations and did not produce a particularly large media or public reaction. It was "inside baseball" to a large extent, but important baseball nonetheless.

The Y2K, or Year 2000, investigation is a third and final example of a forgotten investigation. With the turn of the calendar to 2000 looming only three years in the future, an obscure House subcommittee led by a little-known chairman launched a multiyear investigation of U.S. preparedness for potential computer problems in "mission-critical" agencies such as the Social Security Administration.

The Y2K problem was created by the federal government's long use of two-digit codes such as "98" or "99" to demarcate years. Adopted as a cost-saving practice in the 1950s and 1960s and enshrined in antiquated computer language, investigators in both chambers argued that the federal government's information systems would collapse when confronted by two zeros on January 1, 2000. "The lagging response to this problem," Sen. Daniel Patrick Moynihan (D-N.Y.) told his colleagues in November 1997, "is without excuse."[44]

A brief review of the historical record might lead one to assign lead responsibility for the investigation to the Senate's Special Committee on the Year 2000 Technology Problem, which began its work in 1998 under Senate Resolution 7. However, the driver of actual implementation of the Y2K "fix" is more appropriately assigned to Rep. Stephen Horn (R-Calif.), a former public administration professor and university president who took control of the issue as chairman of the House Government Reform Committee's Subcommittee on Government Management, Information, and Technology. Horn proved a tireless, albeit unheralded, advocate of immediate action to reprogram federal computers and held hearing after hearing as part of his broad monitoring effort. The Senate claimed much of the credit for "the bug that didn't bite," as the *Washington Post* called it, but Horn and his subcommittee did the heavy lifting in preventing a federal disaster.[45] Even then, the U.S. Naval Observatory's Internet website listed January 1, 2000, as January 1, 19100.[46]

Other forgotten investigations appear on my list, including the investigation of what was then called the Bureau of Internal Revenue (1951), drug industry pricing (1959), General Services Administration (GSA) corruption (1978),[47] government mismanagement (1989), and the Solyndra Corporation's $535 million loan default (2011), which 2012 Republican presidential candidate Mitt Romney featured the day after he reached the magic number of delegates needed for his party's presidential nomination.[48] (Romney also mentioned the GSA's briefly infamous, outrageously expensive Las Vegas employee conference featuring a clown and a psychic, but the resulting investigation was brief and inconsequential.)

A DEMOGRAPHIC OVERVIEW

Each of the 100 investigations has a separate demographic profile that describes its place in history, investigatory characteristics, and the party in power at the start of its inquiry. This is not to claim that each investigation is unique, but rather that important patterns help to explain the eventual impact of each search for answers. These demographic markers are summarized in the three categories described below: history, investigatory characteristics, and party context.

Readers should note again that the demographic profiles in this book focus on the primary investigator in each of the 100 inquiries. At some point in every packaged investigation, one committee, subcommittee, or commission emerged as the lead investigator, and the others fell to the wayside. Although the competition sometimes came from within the same chamber or between the key standing committees in the House and Senate, the investigatory history is often quite clear regarding the eventual source of the main investigatory engagement. Merely being the first venue to launch an investigation set was rarely enough to win control of a given inquiry. Rather, the lead tended to belong to the venue with the strongest historical claim to the issue at hand.

History

An investigation's location in history is marked by five measures: (1) historical period, (2) presidential administration (Truman through Obama), (3) Watergate (before or after), (4) the president's term of office (first or second), and (5) whether it began in an election year. As noted earlier, the four historical periods covered by this book start with the post–World War II period (1945 to 1960), and continue with the Great Society (1961 to Nixon's resignation in mid-1974), the congressional resurgence (mid-1974 to 1994), and divided government (1995 to 2012).

Many scholars have argued, for example, that Congress has abandoned its constitutional obligation to monitor the executive branch. According to Thomas E. Mann and Norman J. Ornstein, authors of *The Broken Branch*, oversight may be essential for keeping mistakes from happening, but has declined since the early 1990s.[49] Acknowledging "exceptions that prove the rule," Mann and Ornstein argue that oversight of foreign and national security "virtually collapsed" during the George W. Bush administration. Writing in 2006, these two seasoned congressional overseers do not mince words: "With little or no midcourse corrections in decision-making and implementation, policy has been largely adrift. Occasionally—as during the aftermath of Hurricane Katrina last year—the results have been disastrous."[50]

However, the history of my 100 investigations suggests that Mann and Ornstein may have overstated the recent trends in the overall number of inquiries, but perhaps not the quality. At least measured by the number of big-ticket investigations, Congress did not back away from investigating breakdowns in government performance over the past two decades. All told, Congress launched and led twenty-five investigations during divided government, compared with twenty during the congressional resurgence, thirteen during the Great Society era, and twenty-two during the post–World War II period.

Nevertheless, Mann and Ornstein are quite right to note that Congress throttled back on foreign policy investigations beginning with the new Republican majority in 1995. Congress launched and led just five foreign-issue investigations during the Clinton, George W. Bush, and Obama administrations, compared with eight during the Ford, Carter, Reagan, and George H. W. Bush administrations, six during the Kennedy, Johnson, and Nixon administrations, and nine during the Truman and Eisenhower administrations. At least according to my list, foreign policy is fading as grist for congressional review.

Viewed through these measures of historical time, my 100 investigations showed the following trends:

—Measured by historical eras, twenty-three of the investigations were launched from 1945 to 1961 (the post–World War II period), another nineteen were launched from 1961 through the first half of 1974 (the Great Society period), twenty-seven from late 1974 to 1994 (the congressional resurgence period), and thirty-one from 1995 to 2012 (the divided government period).

—Ranked by administration, fifteen were launched during the Clinton administration, fourteen during the Reagan administration, thirteen each during the Truman and George W. Bush administrations, ten during the Eisenhower administration, seven each during the Kennedy and Johnson administrations, five each during the Nixon, George H. W. Bush, and Obama administrations, and three each during the Ford and Carter administrations.

—Measured in political time, sixty-one were launched in the first term of a presidential administration, compared with thirty-nine in the second term; in turn, forty were launched in a presidential or midterm election year, while sixty began in a nonelection year.

—Finally, using Watergate as the historical dividing line, forty-two investigations were launched before Nixon's 1974 resignation, while fifty-eight were initiated after. Watergate is just a date, of course, but one that is widely viewed as a defining moment in the nascent congressional resurgence of power.[51]

At least using simple numbers, these patterns generally support David C. W. Parker and Matthew Dull's argument that congressional investigations of the executive branch became more frequent after Nixon's resignation.[52]

However, much of the increase reflects the growing use of presidential blue-ribbon commissions in the post-Watergate era. Congress created just one commission before Watergate and seven after, while presidents created seven before Watergate and thirteen after. As one of my respondents put it, Congress began "outsourcing" investigations just like presidents did, albeit at a much lower rate. Subtract these commissions from the post-Watergate count, and the total number of investigations increased ever-so-slightly from thirty-four to thirty-eight, hardly a notable surge.

Investigatory Characteristics

An investigation's structure and modus operandi are measured using seven investigatory characteristics: (1) institutional home (Congress or the presidency, the House or the Senate), (2) venue (full committees, special congressional bodies, subcommittees, or commissions), (3) trigger (police patrol or fire alarm), (4) issue (domestic or foreign), (5) breakdown (process, policy, or personal misconduct), (6) purpose (repair or prevention), and (7) investigatory method (fact finding or blame setting).

There are two ways to compare the seven characteristics and their nineteen separate components against each other. The first uses statistical correlations to search for yes-no relationships that show the size and statistical significance of every potential relationship. A quarter of the correlations among these measures were significant.[53]

The second uses simple percentages to suggest underlying patterns among the correlations. Because correlations merely show the presence or absence of a relationship, not the if-then direction, percentages are the most accessible tool for indicating a possible cause for each significant result by asking whether one measure, such as the institutional home, seems to be a possible driver of methodology. At this point in the book, however, it is up to the reader to make the judgment.

INSTITUTIONAL HOME

An investigation's primary institutional home is located either in Congress or the presidency. Further, if an investigation is located in Congress, it has a secondary home in either House or the Senate. As the investigatory résumés at the end of this book show, the two branches and two chambers often compete against each other to claim the primary role in the search for answers about highly visible breakdowns such as *Challenger*, 9/11, Hurricane Katrina, or the 2008 financial collapse.

Even less visible breakdowns can spark intense competition. The 1997 investigation of technology transfers to China actually involved competing reviews by the two branches and both chambers of Congress. The Senate Intelligence Committee finally wrested primary investigatory control after battling nine full committees, three special congressional bodies, two presidential commissions, and two subcommittees.

Given the long time period covered by this book, and the relatively modest rise of presidential commissions, it is no surprise that eighty of the 100 investigations in box 2-1 were housed in Congress, while just twenty were housed in the presidency. Within Congress, the Senate led forty-nine investigations, while the House led just thirty-one. As noted later, the presidency became more involved in investigations over time, but Congress kept up with the gains.

Viewed by branch of government, institutional home produced the following significant correlations with other investigatory characteristics:

—Congressional investigations were much less likely than presidential investigations to take place in commissions (10 percent of congressional investigations versus 100 percent of presidential investigations).

—Congressional investigations were more likely than presidential investigations to aim for repair, not prevention (65 percent versus 35 percent).

—Congressional investigations were more likely than presidential investigations to use blame setting in their search for answers rather than fact finding (61 percent versus 30 percent).

—Congressional investigations were more likely to be triggered by fire alarms than presidential investigations (58 percent versus 40 percent).

Measured across the four investigatory eras, Congress conducted twenty-two investigations during the World War II period, thirteen during the Great Society era, twenty during the congressional resurgence, and twenty-five during the divided government period. Looking back across the periods, congressional activity shows a dip during the 1960s, followed by steady upward growth from 1961 to 2012.

Viewed next by chamber of Congress, a secondary institutional home in the House or Senate produced the following significant correlations with other investigatory characteristics:

—House investigations were more likely than Senate investigations to be conducted by subcommittees (52 percent of House investigations versus 35 percent of Senate investigations).

—House investigations were more likely than Senate investigations to be triggered by fire alarms (71 percent of House investigations versus 51 percent of Senate investigations).

—House investigations were more likely than Senate investigations to target personal misconduct (26 percent of House investigations versus 8 percent of Senate)

—In turn, Senate investigations were more likely to target breakdowns in process (57 percent of Senate investigations versus 36 percent of House).

Among the eighty investigations conducted by Congress, the House and Senate reversed positions as the most active investigatory chamber after Watergate. Whereas the Senate launched twenty-eight of its total investigations before Watergate and another twenty-one after, the House launched just seven of its total investigations before Watergate but twenty-four after. House activity obviously increased dramatically, while the Senate began to fade

The House gained ground with the Senate in two steps. First, the ninety-one House Democrats elected in 1974 helped turn once moribund committees and subcommittees into more aggressive investigatory venues in matchups against presidents of the other party. Second, the fifty-four House Republicans elected in 1994 not only led their party back into the majority, but helped turn the same now-activated committees and subcommittees into more partisan instruments in the matchup against a Democratic president. These new members were ready to pick away at Clinton whenever possible, and they moved up the investigatory hierarchy quickly as older chairmen were removed because they were judged too soft on the president. The changes produced an almost immediate increase in the number of congressional investigations during both unified and divided government.

Within the presidency, the number of investigations began to rise in 1961 and held steady all the way through 2012. Whereas the presidency housed just one investigation during the post–World War II period, it housed six in the Great Society era, seven during the congressional resurgence, and six again during the divided government era. Converted into percentages, the number of presidential investigations increased from just 4 percent of all investigations in the first historical period to 32 percent in the second and 30 percent in the third before dropping back to 19 percent in the fourth. The number of presidential investigations remained steady over the three final periods, but were overwhelmed as congressional activity hit its seventy-year high as it rose from thirteen during the Great Society era to twenty during the congressional resurgence and twenty-five during the divided government period.

VENUE

An investigation's venue is defined as the primary institutional entity that conducts the primary inquiry: full committee, special congressional body, subcommittee, or commission. Among the eighty investigations conducted by Congress, subcommittees conducted thirty-three, full committees conducted twenty-three, special congressional bodies conducted sixteen, and commissions conducted the final eight. Commissions were the exclusive venue for all twenty presidential investigations.

However, whereas presidential investigations always took place in blue-ribbon commissions either created by the president through executive order or capture, the House and Senate varied greatly in their chosen investigatory venue. Within the House, subcommittees led 52 percent of the investigations, full committees led 29 percent, special congressional bodies led 16 percent, and commissions led 3 percent. Within the Senate, subcommittees led 35 percent of investigations, while full committees also led 29 percent, special congressional bodies led 22 percent, and blue-ribbon commissions led 14 percent.

Investigatory venue produced the following significant correlations with other investigatory characteristics:

—Investigations conducted by commissions were more likely to be sparked by police patrols than investigations conducted by the other three venues (64 percent of commissions versus 39 percent for full committees, 38 percent for special congressional bodies, and 36 percent for subcommittees).

—Investigations conducted by special congressional bodies were more likely to focus on foreign issues than investigations conducted by any of the other three venues (56 percent for special congressional bodies versus 32 percent for full committees, 24 percent for subcommittees, and 32 percent for commissions.)

—Investigations conducted by commissions were less likely to target personal misconduct than investigations conducted by any of the other three venues (0 percent of commissions focused on misconduct versus 22 percent of full committees, 13 percent of special congressional bodies, and 15 percent of subcommittees), while investigations of process and process breakdowns were more evenly spread out across all four venues.

—Investigations conducted by commissions were more likely to engage in fact finding than investigations conducted by any of the other three venues (75 percent of commissions versus 30 percent for full committees, 38 percent for special bodies, and 33 percent for subcommittees).

According to historical trends, full committees became more active in the divided government period, accounting for just three investigations during the post–World War II period, seven during the Great Society period, three during the congressional resurgence, and ten during the divided government period. In addition, the largest concentration of full committee investigations (seven) came during the George W. Bush administration, while the rest were evenly spread out in ones or twos over the other presidential administrations.

TRIGGER

An investigation can be triggered by a fire alarm or police patrol. As the terms suggest, fire alarms are generated by urgent events, while police patrols involve regular "beats" that occasionally reveal the presence of a major breakdown. Applied to traditional congressional oversight, Matthew D. McCubbins and Thomas Schwartz define the terms as follows:

> *Police Patrol Oversight:* Analogous to the use of real police patrols, police-patrol oversight is comparatively centralized, active, and direct: at its own initiative, Congress examines a sample of executive-agency activities, with the aim of detecting and remedying any violations of legislative goals. . . . An agency's activities might be surveyed by any of a number of means such as reading documents, commissioning scientific studies, conducting field observations, and holding hearings to question officials and affected citizens.[54]
> *Fire Alarm Oversight:* Analogous to the use of real fire alarms, fire-alarm oversight is less centralized and involves less active and direct intervention than police-patrol oversight: instead of examining a sample of administrative decisions, looking for violations of legislative goals, Congress establishes a system of rules, procedures, and informal practices that enable individual citizens and organized interest groups to examine administrative decisions (sometimes in prospect), to charge executive agencies with violating congressional goals, and to seek remedies from agencies, courts, and Congress itself.

Fifty-five of the 100 investigations listed in box 2-1 were sparked by fire alarms, while forty-five were triggered by police patrols. Separated by branch, fire alarms accounted for 60 percent of all congressional investigations and 41 percent of all presidential investigations. Separated by chamber, fire alarms triggered 71 percent of House investigations, compared with 49 percent of Senate investigations.

Investigatory trigger produced the following significant correlations with other investigatory characteristics:

—Police patrols were more likely to spark investigations of process and policy breakdowns than investigations of personal misconduct (40 percent of process investigations and 58 percent of policy investigations versus just 2 percent of personal misconduct investigations)

—Fire alarms were more likely than police patrols to be linked to investigations that used blame setting than fact finding (67 percent of investigations sparked by fire alarms adopted a blame setting methodology versus 33 percent of police patrols).

Tracked over time, fire alarms triggered 47 percent of all investigations conducted during the post–World War II period and continued to rise period by period until hitting their high at 65 percent of the investigations conducted during the divided government period, while police patrols dropped from 52 percent during the post–World War II period to just 36 percent during divided government.

Among the eighty congressional investigations, 63 percent of the House investigations conducted before Watergate were sparked by fire alarms, compared with 77 percent of the investigations conducted after. In turn, 44 percent of the Senate investigations conducted before Watergate were triggered by fire alarms, compared with 56 percent of the investigations conducted after. Among the twenty presidential investigations, 42 percent of the investigations conducted before Watergate were sparked by fire alarms, compared with 38 percent of the investigations conducted after.

ISSUE

An investigation's primary issue falls into two very broad categories: domestic or foreign. Domestic investigations include social and economic breakdowns such as welfare fraud, crime, taxpayer abuse, campaign finance abuses, and ethical misconduct, while the latter includes foreign issue breakdowns such as terrorist attacks, intelligence failures, national security breaches, failed wars, illegal spying, and defense waste.

Despite compelling targets on each list, sixty-seven of the 100 investigations focused on domestic issues, leaving thirty-three on foreign issues. Domestic issues appear to raise greater electoral stakes for both branches and may provide easier access to core information and conclusions, while foreign issues have tended to be reserved for special congressional bodies and the presidency.

Investigatory issue produced the following significant correlations with other investigatory characteristics:

—Investigations of foreign issues were more likely than investigations of domestic issues to focus on policy and process breakdowns than misconduct breakdowns (55 percent of policy breakdowns and 42 percent of process breakdowns involved foreign issues, respectively, versus just 3 percent of misconduct). The two issues did not generate significant correlations with other investigatory characteristics with the other two breakdowns.

—Investigations of foreign issues were more likely than investigations of domestic issues to use fact finding in their search for answers (61 percent versus 37 percent).

From a historical perspective, changes in the list of investigatory issues and breakdowns may reflect historical "punctuations" in the number of new programs and policies created during periods of great activity, such as the New Deal or Great Society. If there are punctuations in the new programs and agencies, there may also be punctuations in government investigations.[55] According to Frank R. Baumgartner, Christopher Green-Pedersen, and Bryan D. Jones, these breakthroughs reflect a "disjoint and episodic trace" of policy activities that build up over history. "As new participants with fresh ideas break into the inner circle of policy-making, the system is jolted; there is nothing smooth about the process of adjustment in democratic societies."[56]

If policies rise in punctuations, perhaps investigations also rise as new agencies, policies, and codes of conduct are created, and old agencies, policies, and codes age past impact. In this theory of punctuated policy equilibrium, the number of domestic-issue investigations during and after the Great Society era should have soared. In reality, the percentages actually fell from 68 percent during the Great Society era to 59 percent during the congressional resurgence. Although there may be an investigatory punctuation in the numbers somewhere, my list is not large enough to show it.

Moreover, despite the Johnson administration's punctuation in domestic programs, the House became steadily more interested in foreign issues over time, even as the Senate moved toward domestic concerns and the presidency held steady. Only 13 percent of the House investigations conducted before Watergate focused on foreign policy, compared with 29 percent of the investigations conducted after. In contrast, 48 percent of the Senate investigations conducted before Watergate focused on foreign policy, compared with 22 percent conducted after.

Presidential investigations of foreign issues also increased after Watergate, albeit from none to a few. None of the seven presidential commissions conducted before Watergate focused on foreign issues, compared with four of the investigations conducted after.

BREAKDOWN

An investigation's raison d'être involves a breakdown in government process, policy, or conduct. Big-ticket breakdowns are rarely in short supply, but even when they are, some investigators will create an imaginary breakdown by transforming a small mistake into a massive crisis.

Indeed, some political scientists argue that government bureaucracies are designed to fail. Terry M. Moe made just such an argument in explaining his theory of public bureaucracy: "Just as policy can get watered down through compromise, so can structure—and it almost always does. In the economic system, organizations are generally designed to succeed. In the political system, public bureaucracies are designed in no small measure by participants who explicitly want them to fail."[57]

Participants may want bureaucracies to fail, but they cannot always design the specific failure. In fact, the 100 investigations suggest that government process, policy, and conduct break down for many reasons—surprise attacks, rank incompetence, public resistance, congressional meddling, inadequate resources, a changing world, and political sabotage. Grouped into the three broad categories described above, forty-eight of the 100 investigations dealt with process failures, another forty addressed policy failures, and just twelve targeted personal misconduct.

Investigatory breakdowns produced the following significant correlations with other investigatory characteristics:

—Investigations of process and misconduct breakdowns were more likely to focus on repair than investigations of policy breakdowns (77 percent for process and 67 percent for misconduct, respectively, versus 33 percent for policy breakdowns).

—Investigations of personal misconduct were more likely to adopt a blame-setting methodology than investigations of process or policy breakdowns (92 percent of misconduct breakdowns adopted blame setting versus 52 percent of process breakdowns and 48 percent of policy breakdowns, respectively).

As with the analysis of investigatory issues, history showed little evidence of punctuations among investigatory breakdowns. The largest number of process investigations occurred during the Truman (eight), Reagan (eight), Clinton (nine), and George W. Bush (eight) administrations, for example, while the largest number of policy investigations occurred during the Eisenhower (seven) and Johnson (six) administrations, and the largest number of misconduct investigations occurred during the Clinton administration (three). This variation could be the product of partisan conflict for sure, but could also reflect the lack of major policy or process breakdowns during a given period of time, minimal public interest, committee competition, or "investigation fatigue" from a flood of prior process or policy inquiries.

However, investigatory targets did change before and after Watergate. Policy breakdowns were central in 52 percent of the investigations conducted before Watergate, compared with 31 percent of the investigations conducted after, while process breakdowns were central in 38 percent of the investigations conducted before Watergate, compared with 55 percent of the investigations conducted after.

It could be that the rise of process breakdowns as an investigatory topic is the true measure of a post–Great Society punctuation as government strained to meet a growing agenda with an antiquated bureaucracy, public concerns about "big government" increased, and trust in government fell. Each of the investigations of personal misconduct barely changed its relative standing after Watergate, rising ever so slightly from 10 percent before to 14 percent after.

Each of the three investigatory bodies, the House, Senate, and presidency, followed this general trend toward a greater focus on process. Thus, 25 percent of the House investigations conducted before Watergate focused on process, compared with 41 percent of the investigations conducted after; 44 percent of the Senate investigations conducted before Watergate also focused on process compared with 67 percent conducted after; and 29 percent of the presidential investigations conducted before Watergate focused on process, compared with 48 percent of the investigations conducted after. These post-Watergate increases in process investigations were almost entirely offset by declining interest in policy, leaving personal misconduct investigations roughly unchanged in percentage terms over the two periods.

Nevertheless, Democrats have at least some cause for complaint about the wide-ranging Clinton conduct investigations launched by the Republican majority that took office in 1995. Although only two of the five House investigations over the rest of the Clinton administration involved personal misconduct, the first was long and brutal, while the second led directly to a Senate impeachment trial.

Moreover, my decision to package all of the Clinton conduct hearings into a single investigation clearly understates the Republican majority's appetite for investigating personal misconduct. According to a committee-by-committee inventory of misconduct allegations written and released in 2001 by Rep. Henry Waxman's (D-Calif.) staff, the president and first lady faced more than fifty separate inquiries during the first four years of the new Republican House majority alone (1995–99). According to the staff report titled "Unsubstantiated Allegations of Wrongdoing Involving the Clinton Administration," the Clinton investigation involved an unprecedented abuse of investigatory authority:

> Over the past six years, Chairman Dan Burton of the House Government Reform Committee and other Republican leaders have repeatedly made sensational allegations of wrongdoing by the Clinton Administration. In pursuing such allegations, Chairman Burton alone has issued over 900 subpoenas; obtained over 2 million pages of documents; and interviewed, deposed, or called to testify over 350 witnesses. . . . Chairman Burton or other Republicans have charged that Deputy White House Counsel Vince Foster was murdered as part of a cover-up of the Whitewater land deal; that the White House intentionally maintained an "enemies list" of sensitive FBI files; that the IRS targeted the President's enemies for tax audits; that the White House may have been involved in "selling or giving information to the Chinese in exchange for political contributions"; that the White House "altered" videotapes of White House coffees to conceal wrongdoing; that the Clinton Administration sold burial plots in Arlington National Cemetery; that prison tape recordings showed that former Associate Attorney General Webster Hubbell was paid off for his silence; that the Attorney General intentionally misled Congress about Waco; and that problems with the White House e-mail archiving system are "the most significant obstruction of Congressional investigations in U.S. history" and "reach much further" than Watergate.[58]

PURPOSE

An investigation's purpose can be divided into two broad goals: (1) repair of a past or current breakdown, or (2) prevention of a future breakdown. Both purposes can be viewed as methods for solving what political scientists and legal scholars have long labeled the delegation dilemma.

The dilemma is simple to explain, but difficult to solve. Facing a growing workload on the one hand, and increased polarization on the other, Congress and the president have been unable to reach agreement on urgent issues without delegating increased responsibility to the bureaucracy. Ambiguity begets agreement. Much as Congress and the president may want to believe that their policy decisions are clear and final, their bureaucratic agents have substantial power to alter implementation to satisfy their own incentives, and often have little choice given the statutory ambiguity embedded in most legislation. As Mathew D. McCubbins argues, this broad congressional delegation of administrative discretion has weakened the faithful execution of the laws:

> To many critics of legislative delegation, the growth of the federal bureaucracy has been irresponsible, as delegations to agencies have become ever more general. In the critics' view, those sweeping delegations of authority represent a colossal failure of institutional nerve. Facing public clamor to do something about such pressing problems as the safety of food or drug products, but unable to agree on precisely how to solve the problems, Congress repeatedly has passed the buck by establishing more federal agencies. Many of these critics argue for a dismantling of the administrative state and for a revival of the nondelegation doctrine. But the delegation of authority is a fact of modern life.[59]

Investigations help address the delegation dilemma in two ways: (1) they can repair past breakdowns using ex post controls such as reorganization, reversal, expansion, or termination, or (2) they can prevent future breakdowns using ex ante controls such as new or expanded accountability mechanisms, policy and procedures, or the resolution of public doubts regarding a particular event or controversy.[60] In concept, resolving doubts obviates the need for repair or policy change and thereby becomes part of an ex ante control by default.

Divided into these two purposes, fifty-nine of my investigations focused on repair, while forty-one focused on prevention. Viewed across institutional home, repair dominated 65 percent of investigations conducted by Congress, compared with just 38 percent of the investigations conducted by the presidency. Congress may have greater electoral and institutional incentives to protect past legislation by focusing on repair, while presidents may have equally powerful incentives either to maintain their reputations as "managers in chief" or to avoid blame by focusing on prevention.

Investigations conducted by the House and Senate did not vary on investigatory purpose. Repair was the driver in 68 percent of investigations conducted by the House, compared with 62 percent of the investigations conducted by the Senate.

Investigatory purpose produced just one significant correlation that has not already been discussed: investigations designed to repair a past or current breakdown were more likely to involve fact finding than investigations designed to prevent a future breakdown (62 percent to 38 percent).

According to the historical trend lines, it is still important to note the role of time on repair and prevention. Repair reached its high point during divided government, while remaining steady during the three earlier periods. Two-thirds of the investigations during divided government focused on repair, compared with just over half during the three preceding eras. Contrasting the first two periods against the second two smooths these differences slightly, leaving repair at the helm in 55 percent of the investigations conducted before Watergate, compared with 62 percent of the investigations conducted after.

Viewed by institutional home, the Watergate dividing line had a small effect on investigatory purposes in all three institutional homes, the House, Senate, and presidency. Of the congressional investigations, 57 percent conducted before Watergate focused on repair, compared with 70 percent of the investigations conducted after. In turn and not surprising, the House and Senate also showed more interest in repair after Watergate, while the presidency's interest remained about the same (43 percent of the investigations conducted before and 36 percent after).

METHOD

An investigation's primary methodology for conducting an inquiry can involve fact finding or blame setting. The former involves a bottom-up, first-the-facts approach, while the latter involves a top-down, find-the-culprit path. Sorted into these two categories, forty-five of the investigations in box 2-1 involved fact finding, while fifty-five used blame setting.

The two methods are not mutually exclusive, however. Fact finding can lead to blame setting, while blame setting often starts with at least some fact finding. Even when investigations blend methods, however, they tend to adopt an underlying norm favoring one over another.

For example, some conspiracy theorists, congressional investigators, and at least one filmmaker have long argued that the President's Commission on the Assassination of President Kennedy (the Warren Commission) was driven to place the blame solely on Lee Harvey Oswald and assembled the facts accordingly. Others maintain that the commission considered alternative theories, but found no facts to support allegations that the Soviet Union, Cuba, or organized crime aided and abetted the assassination.

Although all of the correlations between method and other investigatory characteristics have already been discussed, time did leave a mark within the post-Watergate period. Comparing the two periods that followed Nixon's resignation, the percentage of fact finding dropped from 52 percent in the congressional resurgence to 39 percent during divided government. This slight drop between the two most recent eras provides a small hint of the growth in investigatory partisanship during the Clinton and George W. Bush presidencies. The hint will be addressed in the next section.

Party Control

The party control surrounding an investigation is marked by seven measures: (1) party control of Congress and the presidency (unified or divided), which is often referred to as party control of government (unified or divided), (2) party control of the two chambers of Congress (unified or divided), (3) Democratic or Republican control of Congress and the presidency, (4) Democratic or Republican control of the presidency, (5) Democratic or Republican control of the two chambers of Congress, (6) Democratic or Republican control of the House, and (7) Democratic or Republican control of the Senate. These measures can be combined to examine matchups between House or Senate majorities of one party and presidents of the other party.

BY THE NUMBERS

Here and throughout the book, unified government is defined as single-party control of the presidency and both chambers of Congress, while divided government is defined as split-party control between the presidency and at least one of the two chambers of Congress. A divided Congress automatically produces divided government between one chamber and the president.

Based on the sheer number of investigations during unified and divided party control, Congress and the president appear quite capable of conducting significant investigations under either divided or unified government:

—Thirty-seven of the investigations occurred during unified party control of government, while sixty-three occurred during divided party control.

—Thirty-one occurred during Democratic control of government, while just six occurred during Republican control.

—Fifty occurred during Democratic control of the presidency, while fifty occurred during Republican control.

—Eighty-three occurred during unified party control of the House and Senate, while seventeen occurred during divided party control.

—Sixty occurred during Democratic control of the House and Senate, while twenty-three occurred during Republican control.

—Seventy-two occurred during Democratic control of the House, while twenty-eight occurred during Republican control.

—Sixty-five occurred during Democratic control of the Senate, while thirty-five occurred during Republican control.

There is one more number hidden in the interstices of party control presented above: forty-five of the eighty congressional investigations involved a matchup between a House or Senate majority of one party and a president of the other party. House Democratic majorities launched fourteen, House Republican majorities launched seven, Senate Democratic majorities launched fourteen, and House Republican majorities launched ten. Although it has mixed effects on investigatory footprints and impact, divided government is not a barrier to launching an investigation in the first place.

Although this inventory echoes Mayhew's conclusion that high-publicity investigations can occur during either unified or divided government, it is too early in this analysis to encourage Mayhew to retitle his book *Divided We Govern and Investigate.* Investigations can spring up during divided government, but the as-yet-to-be-answered question is whether they produce heavy footprints and high impact. Alas, there are very few cases available to produce a definitive answer.

PARTY CONTROL AND INVESTIGATORY CHARACTERISTICS

The simple number of divided government investigations at any point in history addresses only the "when" of investigatory activity, not the where, what, how, and why. If Parker and Dull are right that divided government creates "more and more intensive investigations," the trend should show up among the divided government inquiries on my list. But the differences between unified and divided government investigations are more occasional than consistent.

"Not so fast," Parker and Dull might say. "Your time period is too long. The quarrels worsened after Watergate":

> After 1975, party leaders were invigorated by post-Watergate reforms. The discretion of committee chairs waned, and the chairs became answerable to congressional parties. Many of the behavioral norms and expectations of the earlier era, such as apprenticeship and consensus seeking, also began to erode. The majority party increasingly dominated the flow of business by putting the post-1975 reforms to work: restricting minority rights on the floor, frequently adopting closed rules for legislation, and ignoring seniority when assigning committee chairs, relying instead on a member's willingness to support the party's legislative priorities.[61]

Watergate marks the start of a long list of changes in American politics, not the least of which was a renewed interest in investigations. But if divided government generated more quarrelsome investigations after Watergate, as Parker and Dull argue, it is not immediately apparent in the distribution of investigatory triggers, issues, purposes, and methodologies. Rather, divided government after Watergate had its major effects on investigatory homes, venues, and breakdowns:

—The percentage of all divided government investigations launched by the presidency increased from 11 percent before Watergate to 23 percent after, while the percentage launched by Congress fell.

—The percentage of all divided government investigations launched by the House increased from 16 percent before Watergate to 50 percent after, while the Senate's percentage share plunged from 74 percent before to just 27 percent after.

—The percentage of all divided government investigations conducted by commissions doubled from 16 percent before Watergate to 32 percent after, while the percentage conducted by subcommittees dropped from 47 percent before to 25 percent after.

—The percentage of all divided government investigations that targeted policy breakdowns fell from 53 percent before Watergate to 30 percent after, while the share of process breakdowns rose from 32 to 57 percent, and the share of personal misconduct investigations remained steady.

EXPLORING PARTY MATCHUPS

These patterns of where, who, and what do not confirm or deny the persistent claims that Republican congressional majorities have used the investigatory process to undermine, embarrass, and frustrate Democratic presidents. However, the list does provide an opportunity to explore the evidence when the House or Senate was matched up against presidents of the other party in an investigation. Despite the relatively small numbers of matchups available for comparison, there are wisps of Republican angst among several of the investigatory characteristics discussed above:

—Matched against a president of the other party, House Democratic majorities and Senate Republican majorities were the most likely to answer fire alarms (86 percent and 70 percent of their investigations, respectively), followed by House Republicans and Senate Democrats only slightly behind (57 percent).

—Matched against a president of the other party, House and Senate Republicans were the most likely to examine domestic issues (71 percent and 70 percent of their investigations, respectively), followed by House and Senate Democrats only slightly behind (57 percent each).

—Matched against a president of the other party, Senate Republicans were the most likely to target process breakdowns (80 percent of their investigations), while House and Senate Democrats were the most likely to target policy breakdowns (50 percent each), and House Republicans were the most likely to focus on personal misconduct (43 percent).

—Matched against a president of the other party, House Democrats and House Republicans were equally likely to set course for repair (71 percent of each of their investigations), while Senate Democrats showed a slight preference for repair (57 percent), and Senate Republicans split evenly between repair and prevention.

—Matched against a president of the other party, Senate Republicans were the most likely to use blame setting (80 percent of their investigations), followed by House Republicans (71 percent), House Democrats (57 percent), and Senate Democrats (50 percent).

Wisps though they are, the general Republican preference for blame setting, and the specific House Republican interest in personal misconduct, lends at least some credence to Democratic complaints about Republican "extremism" and the rise of what Thomas E. Mann and Norman J. Ornstein call "asymmetric polarization."[62] If Mann and Ornstein are correct in blaming Republicans for planting the seeds of dysfunction in the legislative process, they would no doubt see the same trends in at least some of the comparisons above. After all, of the seventeen investigations that involved House or Senate Republican matchups with a Democratic president, thirteen occurred after 1995.

CONCLUSION

Congressional and presidential investigations have clearly changed over the past seventy years. Divided government may not be to blame, but the political, economic, and social climate appears to be pushing investigations in certain directions that may undermine their value for impact on government performance. Before they turn to footprints and impacts in the next two chapters, investigators can already draw a handful of lessons from my analysis of the 100 investigations:

—Congress has bounced back as an institutional home. Despite a drop in activity during the Great Society period, Congress surged back to a record-setting pace after 1994 and is likely to maintain its four-to-one numerical edge far into the future. Although presidents have used blue-ribbon commissions to become a genuine force in the investigatory process, Congress has learned how to use commissions, too. Moreover, commissions are the only investigatory venue at the president's disposal and cannot be used too often without creating charges of "dodge ball" and "kick-the-can."

The House surged as an investigatory destination, while the Senate faded. The House did not surpass the Senate during a single presidency or the last few years. Instead, its investigatory agenda grew slowly and steadily from just three investigations under Ford and one under Carter, to four under Reagan, three under George H. W. Bush, five each under Clinton and George W. Bush, and three under Obama. The House gained momentum in part by recruiting more aggressive investigators as committee and subcommittee chairs, and in part by launching larger numbers of policy and misconduct investigations than the Senate. Although the Republicans launched dozens of investigations against Clinton between 1995 and 2000, most of the inquiries were insignificant and only made my list as part of the Clinton conduct inquiry discussed earlier in this chapter.

Full committees have also bounced back as an investigatory venue, while subcommittees have faded. This fall and rise suggests several potential trends that bear further examination. First, full committees may be creaming the oversight agenda for maximum visibility. Second, the declining freedom to investigate discussed in chapter 3 may be best managed at the full committee level. Finally, investigatory resources may be pooling at the full committee levels, as the House, in particular, has cut its staff.[63]

—Blue-ribbon commissions, whether congressionally or presidentially created, may have reached their peak as an investigatory venue, perhaps because of commission fatigue. Although the number of commissions rose dramatically after Watergate, there may be little room for more in the future. So noted, there may still be at least some extra room for new commissions on foreign issues, especially if Congress continues to back away from the subject area. Even as the number of congressionally sponsored foreign issue investigations plummeted from nine in the post–World War II period to just two during the 1995–2012 divided government period, the number of foreign issue commissions rose from zero to five. Congress created much of the vacuum that commissions now fill.

—Fire alarms have become the dominant investigatory trigger. It is not clear whether this focus is because of recent crises, such as the *Challenger*

accident, the Waco siege, 9/11, Hurricane Katrina, a series of mine disasters, the Gulf oil spill, the Solyndra Corporation default, or the Fast and Furious gun-walking operation, or because of electoral and time pressures that have caused the number of police patrol investigations to decline. What is clear is that fire alarms produce more visible and high-pressure investigations, discussed in the next chapter.

—*Domestic issues have become the dominant topic for investigations, pushing foreign issues to a modern low as an investigatory concern over the past two decades.* Focusing on domestic issues has become good politics, whether because the domestic budget has become the target for deep budget cuts in an age of austerity or because voters still want more of virtually everything the federal government delivers, but worry that the bureaucracy cannot or will not deliver.

—*Process and personal misconduct breakdowns may be driving out policy breakdowns as investigatory concerns.* The number of investigations that addressed process and personal misconduct breakdowns hit its peak during the last two decades covered by this analysis, while the number of policy investigations hit its nadir. This reversal of investigatory fortune appears to reflect contemporary realities as the federal bureaucracy continues to age and atrophy and a scandal-hungry, 24/7 press intensifies its search for personal misbehavior.

—*Many of today's investigations have become salvage operations.* There are many potential explanations for the steady rise in repair investigations during divided government, most notably the rising number of visible government breakdowns. Investigators simply have no choice when shuttles explode, attacks occur, and government agencies fail to execute the laws because of persistent cutbacks or bureaucratic sclerosis.[64]

—*Finally, investigators may be losing their fact-finding skills.* Fact finding requires curiosity, questions, and an open mind, while blame setting often involves little more than targets, subpoenas, and a foregone conclusion. Given today's tight legislative calendar, 24/7 campaigns, and a public appetite for scandal, investigators have ample reason to pursue what one of my respondents called "Jeopardy" investigations where the culprit is known before the first question is asked. In contrast, "Joe Friday" investigations that focus on "just the facts" can end up just about anywhere and are much more expensive. In fact, one of the reasons POGO wrote its 60-page, glossy, fast-paced, example-filled *Art of Congressional Oversight* is that members and staff had stopped reading the 160-page, single-spaced, densely packed *Congressional Oversight Manual*, which is written by Congress itself.

This summary not only describes the changing nature of investigations over time, but also lays the foundation for assessing investigatory footprints in chapter 3. Designed as a measure of the good investigation, an inquiry's weight is based on simple indicators of its length, breadth, complexity, leadership, freedom to investigate, visibility, seriousness, thoroughness, pressure, and durability.

As the next chapter shows, each investigation leaves a footprint on history. Some investigations are largely invisible, while others are rarely off camera. Some are serious and thorough, while others are mostly for show. And some create the pressure for action, while others exert little influence at all.

The challenge is to measure the elements of this implied good investigation with enough precision to show how footprints vary and why they matter. Doing so involves a heavy dose of judgment, which must be based on further readings of legislative history, scholarly research, and story after story about who did what, when, where, and how. Alas, these sources are not always clear, and the final judgments are difficult. Thus the next two chapters on footprints and impacts can be read as speculative to an extent, but are grounded in careful readings of history and analysis nonetheless.

THREE

Creating Footprints

The mere announcement of an investigation can create the promise of significance, including a measure of deterrence based on fear and foreboding. This spark often follows a highly visible government breakdown and the engagement of a well-known investigator such as Jack Brooks, Barney Frank, Frank Church, Tom Davis, Robert Dole, Sam Ervin, John Glenn, Lee Hamilton, Charles Grassley, J. William Fulbright, Tom Kean, Herbert Hoover, Estes Kefauver, Carl Levin, George Mitchell, Warren Rudman, Brent Scowcroft, Donna Shalala, John Stennis, Harry Truman, or Henry Waxman.

The early moments of an investigation also begin creating the "footprint" of the effort based on eleven attributes of the "good investigation." Is the investigation long, broad, complex, led by a well-known investigator, given the freedom to investigate, visible, serious, thorough, a force for action, durable, and bipartisan? Based on the answers, some investigations emerge as heavyweights, while others are best described as middleweights or lightweights.

Before describing the eleven weights and the eleven-point summary score, it is important to note that footprints are not necessarily a predictor of impact. An investigation can be a perfect example of the good investigation but have little or no impact, while another can be a perfect disaster yet have significant impact. Similarly, some of the eleven weights are very strong predictors of eventual impact, while others have either a negative effect or no effect at all. But this distinction is not an issue here. Rather, this chapter deals with the footprint of an investigation and asks a simple question: How do the 100 investigations measure up against the conventional image of an inquiry done right?

Consider Rep. Waxman's (D-Calif.) 1993–94 tobacco investigation as a heavyweight that also had significant impact. Fifteen years after he called tobacco industry executives to account before his Energy and Commerce Subcommittee on Health, Congress finally gave the Food and Drug Administration (FDA) authority to regulate the industry's products. Waxman did not claim outright credit for the Family Smoking Prevention and Tobacco Control Act of 2009, but his leading role in setting the agenda was undeniable. As he remembered the initial investigation a few years before Congress finally acted, he noted the need for patience as the essence of eventual impact:

> Congress didn't pass any tobacco legislation that year. But by calling the tobacco executives before Congress and releasing thousands of pages of internal tobacco industry documents, Congress had an enormous impact on the public attitudes toward the tobacco industry and on national policy.
>
> After the hearings, state attorneys general across the nation brought lawsuits against the tobacco industry that restricted tobacco advertising and produced a settlement worth over $200 billion. FDA tried to regulate tobacco. And state and local governments enacted laws to eliminate exposure to toxic secondhand smoke.
>
> It would be wrong to ascribe these accomplishments to the congressional hearings. It took the hard work of thousands of dedicated activists to build public support for these important tobacco control initiatives. But without question, those congressional hearings 12 years ago had a galvanizing effect.[1]

The historical record confirms Waxman's belief. The investigation was long, broad, complex, serious, thorough, and visible, generating effects well into the future. Waxman's investigation was obviously not the only force at work in shaping the tobacco agenda, but it was certainly an exemplary investigation, which is why it ranks so high on the list of heavy-footprint investigations presented later in this chapter.

Before presenting these rankings, the chapter discusses what constitutes the good investigation, the recent debate about the alleged decline in investigatory activity, and my method for weighing the footprint created by each of the 100 investigations. The chapter then turns to my ratings of each investigation's footprint and rankings of the full list, followed by a demographic analysis of the rankings, short vignettes on some of the heavyweights, middleweights, and lightweights on the list, and an analysis of what creates a heavyweight footprint.

As noted below, investigatory footprints offer an opportunity to assess the modus operandi of a given inquiry and involve eleven measures of investigatory weight: (1) length, (2) breadth, (3) complexity, (4) leadership, (5) freedom to investigate, (6) visibility, (7) seriousness, (8) thoroughness, (9) leverage, (10) durability, and (11) bipartisanship. Although these measures do not cover every attribute of the good investigation, they do capture the core elements of what the nonpartisan Project on Government Oversight (POGO) calls "doing it right."

THE "GOOD INVESTIGATION"

Congressional oversight and investigations are generally viewed as a pure constitutional good. Done well, they give both Congress and the president a check on administrative action, enact desperately needed process and policy repairs, and prevent future breakdowns through enhanced accountability and deterrence. Done poorly, they undermine faithful execution of the laws and give the president ample reason to believe that Congress is not watching.

The basic foundation of a good investigation is built upon a specific process for conducting the inquiry. Simply put, investigators cannot fail if they pick the right targets, ask the right questions, use the right tools, generate the right coverage, and make the right choices. It hardly matters whether Democrats or Republicans are in charge, or so the argument goes; a good investigation produces a good result. Defined almost entirely by conduct and process, the good investigation is not so much a work of art as artful work and is, therefore, more about understanding breakdowns than solving them.[2]

The following pages use the past research on oversight to help to describe the good investigation. Thus, as Joel Aberbach writes in his seminal 1990 study, *Keeping a Watchful Eye: The Politics of Congressional Oversight*, expectations of oversight often run far beyond reality:

> Because of the high standards set for oversight (a high level of activity carried out in a systematic and comprehensive way and contributing to a "rational" process of congressional priority setting), those who advocate oversight as a mechanism for enhancing congressional control of administration and policy have rarely been content with what is done. The incentives of the elected members, it

seems, do not mesh well with behaviors expected by many advocates of an enhanced congressional oversight role.[3]

Doing It Right

No organization has done more to promote the good investigation than the nonpartisan Project on Government Oversight. POGO is the go-to organization for congressional oversight training and the author of the primary congressional oversight manual, *The Art of Congressional Oversight: A User's Guide to Doing It Right*. POGO is not the only good-government organization that monitors congressional monitoring, but it is also the lead advocate for the good investigation.

POGO makes this case in its introductory message to congressional staffers on the art of their work:

> The bottom line is that Congress is equal in power to the executive branch, just as it is to the judiciary branch. Congress has the right to information and should demand it. The oversight functions of Congress are essential to creating an accountable federal government and upholding our democracy's checks and balances system. We are writing this guide because we have discovered that Congress has lost sight of these essential points and has forgotten its strength.[4]

This view is echoed in many of the histories and commentary on both small- and large-scale oversight. David H. Rosenbloom argues that oversight is one of many tools for monitoring the growth of the federal administrative state. Simply put, oversight gives Congress the freedom to delegate authority to the executive. "In the 1930s and early 1940s, the concept of delegation had not yet received the broad legitimacy it would later achieve," he writes. Even as delegation increased, "The fear that delegation would lead to totalitarianism was frequently voiced and apparently real."[5]

Summarizing a long list of legislation enacted immediately after World War II, Rosenbloom concludes that this new congressional role is primarily about delegation, regulation of administrative procedures, supervision of agencies, and detailed, systematic attention to public works projects and spending."[6]

Frederick A. O. Schwarz converts this argument into a more practical list of congressional obligations. Testifying in 2007 as the former chief counsel to the Senate Select Committee to Study Governmental Operations with Respect to Intelligence Activities (the Church Committee), Schwarz offers the following inventory of oversight responsibilities and characteristics:

—Congressional oversight is essential to ensuring the fair and effective deployment of law enforcement and national security powers. On matters as diverse as political corruption and counterterrorism, Congress serves the nation best when it vigorously ensures that federal law is applied in a fair, just, and effective manner.

—Oversight, therefore, need not be a partisan matter. Neither Republicans nor Democrats want a system where prosecutors are fired on partisan grounds. No one wants the "national security" or the "executive privilege" label to be applied to obscure partisan goals or to hide abusive exercises of power. Oversight is a shared responsibility. And before facts are fully aired, nobody should prejudge the matter.

—Far too much information about governmental conduct is kept secret. There are, of course, legitimate secrets. They should be protected. But, as the Church Committee concluded thirty years ago, many secrecy stamps serve no national interest. Rather, they shield governmental mistakes and misdeeds from public sight. This is no less true of assertions of "executive privilege," which should not be treated as having the talismanic effect of shutting down all inquiry. It is Congress's duty to sift responsibly claims of secrecy or privilege to determine the credible from the flawed.

—The Church Committee showed that Congress has several procedural means to handle secrecy claims. Even in the case where a presidential advisor can make a colorable claim that some of their [sic] testimony is covered by a privilege, Congress should proceed to secure testimony and use the means deployed by the Church Committee to ensure a full airing of the matter under investigation.[7]

As the perceived quantity of oversight and investigations has declined, the good-government community has developed a detailed definition of the good investigation and recommendations for producing it. The definition is rooted less in the actual outcome of a given inquiry or the faithful execution of the laws and more in the exercise of checks and balances.

The good investigation generally follows a particular modus operandi of inquiry. Although POGO's manual is about "doing it right," it is also about "doing it for the right reasons." Oversight and investigations remedy the travail created by ambiguous legislation, presidential signing statements,[8] and the overall weakening of executive accountability.

POGO's oversight guide also provides a step-by-step examination of just how to "do it right" and is unabashed about its view of the good investigation, a term it uses side-by-side with oversight throughout its sixty-page, double-space, easily accessible, and thoughtfully tabbed text. The guide is also unabashed in its strong recommendations about what investigators should and should not do in creating good investigations:

> Congressional investigators should work together. This means you should be building relationships with other staffers doing meaningful oversight across the aisle or in the other Chamber. They may be your best sources of advice, documents, and contacts.
>
> Investigators should not get intimidated. Meaningful congressional oversight is hard work. It is time- and resource-consuming. Given that you are trying to address fraud, waste, and abuse, people will become defensive and may even go on the offensive against you. You will need to develop a thick skin.
>
> Congressional oversight should not be a partisan issue. While it is a given that certain issues will, by their nature, lead to partisan disagreements, there are some issues that should transcend politics.[9]

POGO hardly expects investigations to be perfect in every way, but the guide sets a very high bar indeed. Looking back to the basic demographic profile presented in chapter 2, there is at least some evidence that Congress is no longer doing it POGO's way, if it ever did it right at all.

Doing It Well

Doing it right through heavy footprints is quite different from doing it well through eventual impact, however. Unfortunately, the overall impact of an investigation depends on the broader environment surrounding each inquiry. As noted, an investigation can do it right, but still fall short of eventual impact in repairing a government breakdown or preventing one in the future.

Aberbach warned in a 2002 update to his book that ideology and politics are unavoidable in shaping ultimate consequences. "Oversight is difficult to divorce from political context, and when there is divided government, intense partisanship, and skepticism about the role of government as well as doubts about the way that programs are being implemented, conditions are ripe for conflict and contentious hearings."[10]

As such, the quality of an investigation is based more on opinion than on absolute proof. Some see intense partisanship as a precursor for destructive (itself a judgment) oversight, while others see it is as a perfectly reasonable expression of majority control. In turn, some see the freedom to investigate as an essential ingredient of high-impact investigations, while others see tight majority control of the investigatory and oversight agenda as a tool for holding executive agencies accountable to changing public expectations. Nevertheless, the political science literature is laden with hints, even longings for research, about how each tool of control works under which conditions. Simply asked, when do certain kinds of efforts to control actually produce control? It is a question well worth asking and one that I address in chapter 4.

The More, the Better

The contemporary call for good investigations is built in part on the notion that there has been a general decline in investigatory activity and quality over the past seventy years. One reason investigators need to do it right is because they need to do more.

However, the total number of investigations on my list grew from forty-two before Watergate (1945 to mid-1974) to fifty-eight after Nixon's resignation (mid-1974 to 2012). Moreover, focusing solely on the congressional investigations that underpin so much concern about declining oversight, there were thirty-five investigations before Nixon's resignation and forty-five after, a nearly 30 percent increase that suggests more engagement, not less. Calculated on a per-year basis, however, the number of investigations held steady at 1.2 per year before and after Watergate, even though removing blue-ribbon commissions from the totals actually shows a decline from 1.2 investigations per year before Watergate to 0.7 investigation per year.

Given this mash-up of findings, perhaps POGO and others should stop using raw numbers to make the case for more oversight. As Aberbach clearly shows, some types of congressional oversight declined between 1961 and 1997, others remained constant, and "primary-purpose" oversight increased dramatically.

On the one hand, Aberbach shows that Congress actually conducted more oversight from 1993 to 1997 than during any comparable period dating back to 1961: "In many ways, these figures are not surprising. With divided government, increased partisanship, and continued intense debate about how to deploy resources, one would expect Congress to be quite vigilant in overseeing the executive."[11]

On the other hand, Aberbach also shows that Congress conducted fewer hearings and meetings on authorizations, reauthorizations, and amendments to ongoing programs, all of which offer important opportunities for oversight. "Some of the decline in hearings is due to a lack of interest in starting new programs," he writes, "but it is clear that there are other political factors at work as well, such as the difficulty of building a consensus behind many reauthorization bills in an ideologically divided Congress where party margins are relatively slim, problems with controversial amendments tacked onto bills (for example, abortion), and the increasing use of appropriations bills to fund unauthorized programs and omnibus vehicles to legislate with little committee input."[12]

Having titled his article "What's Happened to the Watchful Eye?," Aberbach provides a simple answer:

> Based on the data and related materials utilized in this analysis—though ideally one would want information from more sources and some comparative over-time data on different kinds of oversight (personal investigations, programmatic oversight, etc.)—the answer, if I can take liberties with the watchful eye metaphor, is that one congressional eye is wide open and, presumably, seeing what the majorities on congressional committees want it to see, and the other eye is almost shut.[13]

This opinion was echoed in some of my interviews. "It's premature to declare oversight dead," one think-tank scholar told me. "There are other points in history when Congress has been counted out—the question is whether members have the motivation and skill to seize [the] opportunity and whether Congress can supply the resources. I hesitate to leap to the conclusion that Congress is permanently disabled—I'd argue that opportunity times motivation equals rebound. Based on the current situation, however, oversight is on life support."

CREATING WEIGHT

Every investigation leaves its own footprint on investigatory history. This footprint is not a surrogate for historical significance, though it is tempting to argue that "heavier" investigations are more significant than their lighter peers on my list. Nor is footprint a measure of impact, although many of the measures discussed below do affect eventual impact, albeit through a chain of cause and effect that begins with investigatory characteristics such as trigger, breakdown, purpose, and investigatory method.

Rather, footprint indicates an investigation's overall weight in claiming and consuming resources such as time, expertise, and staff; setting course on a broad, serious, thorough, and bipartisan search for answers about what it defines as a complex issue; operating with full freedom to follow every lead in a serious, thorough inquiry; creating intense leverage for action; and establishing durable influence into the future. Broken into each of its eleven weights, a footprint reveals the basic context and modus operandi of an investigation; summed into a single eleven-point score, it reveals the basic character of the effort.

Again, just because an investigation creates a heavy footprint does not mean that it will produce a great deal of impact. Although chapter 4 shows a very strong relationship with impact, the relationship is not perfect. Even though 75 percent of the heavyweight investigations discussed below produced a great deal or fair amount of impact, the other 25 percent created some, or little or none.

Impact is not the issue for this chapter, however. The issue is footprint and the measures that sum to an eleven-point score. Before turning to the rating of each investigation and the ranking of my full list, it is important to understand the basic components of the measure.

The Eleven Weights

By definition, all of the investigations on my list were historically significant. However, all did not create particularly heavy footprints.

When it mostly came to an end in mid-2012, for example, the House Energy and Commerce Committee's investigation of the Solyndra Corporation had established itself as a long, visible, serious, and high-leverage investigation, but had failed to achieve much weight as a particularly broad, complex, thorough, influential, or bipartisan effort. Lacking a well-known investigator at the helm and given little freedom to act by the House Republican leadership, the investigation generated a relatively light footprint on the investigatory landscape. Was it a significant investigation? Yes. Did it create a heavy historical footprint? No. And did it create discernible impact? Also no.

The following discussion is based on similar assessments of the 100 investigations chronicled in this book. As readers already know, however, many of the investigations involved multiple committees, subcommittees, and even the occasional blue-ribbon commission. As already noted, congressional investigators often pile onto a breakdown, but usually move back to their core interests once the news clippings are collected and the prime investigator takes control.

Regardless of the competition involved in these investigations, a primary investigator always emerged from the pack and determined both the footprint and ultimate impact of the effort. Some competitors simply dropped out as a dominant committee or commission took charge; others were merely piling on to gain a measure of credit for whatever might come of the review;

and still others were designated as the lead by Congress itself through formal resolutions or the creation of select committees and subcommittees.

Once I identified the primary investigator and built a demographic profile around its history, characteristics, and political setting, I moved forward with objective and subjective judgments regarding each of the eleven footprint weights discussed below.[14]

LENGTH

The good investigation takes enough time to complete its inquiry, but comes to closure without dissipating the urgency associated with its launch. The clock starts ticking with the investigation's launch, often revealed through legislative authorization, a presidential order, a first press release, or, most frequently, a first hearing; the clock stops ticking with the last hearing, a final report, a bang at a press event, or a whimper as the investigation fades from the agenda without notice. Length is weighted in two categories: less than one year (zero) or one year or more (one). The one-hearing investigation of the Nixon pardon is the shortest investigation on my list, while the twenty-four-year investigation of obsolete military bases is by far the longest and will last until at least 2015 and the completion of its final round of recommended closings. The near-simultaneous House investigations of the Solyndra Corporation and the Justice Department's Fast and Furious "gun-walking" operation both had lasted more than a year by the time this book went to press and will probably continue in the wake of the 2012 elections, which left the status quo in place, albeit with slightly lower Republican margins in the House and Senate. Forty-three of my investigations lasted less than a year, while fifty-seven lasted a year or longer.

BREADTH

The good investigation examines the widest range of potential causes and consequences of the crisis at hand. Simply asked, did the investigation move quickly to a limited destination or prepare for a more complicated, even unpredictable search for answers? Breadth is weighted in two categories: narrow (zero) or broad (one). Here, one can assume that every breakdown contains both situational causes, such as technical errors or a simple lack of character, and systemic angles, such as organizational structure or the absence of lobbying controls. Looking back to the post–World War II period, for example, the Hoover Commission's investigation of government organizations in the late 1940s and early 1950s examined a long list of systemic failures that included duplication and overlap, antiquated management practices, and personnel failures, while the 1947 investigation of communist infiltration of the motion picture industry and the 1959 investigation of deceptive broadcasting practices in quiz shows such as *The $64,000 Question* were unquestionably visible, but showed little interest in the broader systemic issues that may have caused the breakdowns at hand. Sixty-one of my investigations were narrowly pursued, while thirty-nine were designed for a broader inquiry.[15]

COMPLEXITY

The good investigation embraces the complexity of the issue at hand, thereby avoiding the reductionist temptation to reduce a crisis to a simple event or technical flaw. Simply asked again, did the investigation define the breakdown at hand in relatively simple terms or view it as a more complicated, even tangled, set of potential cause and effect? This initial definition can be sorted into two categories: simple (zero) or complex (one). The investigations of the shuttle *Columbia* disaster and Three-Mile Island nuclear power plant accident began with the search for human error and technical failures and mostly stopped there. In contrast, the investigations of the eerily similar shuttle *Challenger* tragedy and Gulf oil spill started at the same place, but moved toward a more complex definition of the underlying economic, political, and organizational causes of each breakdown. Sixty-one of my investigations worked with a simple definition of the breakdown, while thirty-nine worked with a complex definition.

LEADERSHIP

The good investigation attracts well-known leadership as a source of ideas, credibility, and leverage in promoting its findings. Although being known is not enough to produce a high-impact result, it rarely hurts. Leadership is weighted in two categories: little known (zero) or well known (one). Some of the nation's most talented investigators, such as Rep. Tom Lantos (D-Calif.), were generally little known both before and after their investigations,[16] while others, such as Alan Greenspan, were well known when they took the chairmanship of their inquiries and continued in the news for decades after. Little-known leaders were at the helm of sixty-five of my investigations, while well-known leaders took on thirty-five.

FREEDOM TO INVESTIGATE

The good investigation is free to investigate every lead and examine any angle without interference from party leaders, lobbyists, or government itself. It is one thing to charter a broad commission about a complex issue, but quite another to give it the resources and encouragement to ask any question. Simply asked, was an investigation given significant leeway to operate without interference from either inside actors such as the party leadership or outside actors such as the White House? The investigations of Clinton White House conduct were tightly controlled by House speaker Newt Gingrich (R-Ga.) in 1995, but not the investigation of the year 2000 computer problem later in 1999. The former was obviously laden with political significance, while the latter was generally viewed as a "good government" issue that warranted little leadership control. Freedom to investigate is weighted in two categories: little or no freedom (zero) or moderate to high freedom (one). Forty-six of my investigations operated with little or no freedom to investigate beyond the boundaries of their institutional leadership, while fifty-four were generally free to set and pursue their investigatory agenda as they deemed appropriate.

VISIBILITY

The good investigation generates enough visibility to create public interest in its issue and advance pressure for its recommendations. Some investigations of highly controversial issues such as communists in government, Central Intelligence Agency abuses, the shuttle *Challenger* accident, and steroid abuse in professional baseball were highly visible, in part because of the allegations involved, while others such as the inquiries about airport safety, government information management, strategic missile basing, and Gulf War syndrome were barely noticed. Visibility is weighted in two categories: lower (zero) or higher (one). Thirty-seven of my investigations were almost invisible even inside Washington, while sixty-three were visible both inside the capital city and in the country writ large.

SERIOUSNESS

The good investigation is serious about honoring its commitment to a broad and complex investigation, assuming, of course, that it has enough resources and freedom to act. Just as members of Congress can be described as workhorses or show horses, so, too, can investigations. Seriousness is weighted in two categories: lower (zero) or higher (one). Even though the 1965 investigation of the Ku Klux Klan was the beginning of the end of the House Un-American Activities Committee (HUAC), it nonetheless had an air of insincerity from the start. In contrast, the 1975 investigation of intelligence agency misconduct was anything but frivolous in exposing the government's inventory of domestic spying, assassination plots, eavesdropping, and abridgments of civil rights. Although all of my investigations began with grand commitments to serious review, forty-one of them did not follow through, while fifty-nine did.

THOROUGHNESS

The good investigation is not just serious about its work, but is also ready to dive below the available, but often superficial, answers into the contested issues that might explain the crisis at hand. After all, it is one thing to set a broad agenda and define a breakdown in complex terms and quite another to follow through on these early commitments. Based on a reading of legislative histories, hearing transcripts, witness lists, final reports, staff memos, and even the inventory of investigatory documents, thoroughness is weighted in two categories: lower (zero) or higher (one). Whereas the 9/11 investigation was based on a thorough review of what it called "failures in imagination, policy, capabilities, and management," the Iraq War investigation was highly fragmented and often cursory at best regarding the administration's rosy scenarios about a quick end to the conflict. Forty-four of my investigations were generally superficial, while fifty-six were thorough.

LEVERAGE

The good investigation builds leverage for implementation by creating strong linkages with advocates, promoting early commitments to action, targeting its recommendations to specific actors, and even drafting possible legislation and regulations. Based again on a reading of the historical record, leverage is weighted in two categories: lower (zero) or higher (one). Some investigations begin to exert leverage by gaining legislative commitments before they are launched, others generate leverage by exploiting real and artificial deadlines for action, and still others amplify their leverage by focusing on what will happen if the nation does not act, thereby "looking backward in order to look forward," as the 9/11 Commission's final report put it.[17] Thirty-two of my investigations generated little leverage for action, while sixty-eight had the connections to create legislative and executive attention.

DURABILITY

The good investigation produces a body of work that can withstand the test of time, not to mention the metaphorical dusty shelves in forgotten libraries or the oddly titled "cyber cemeteries" of more recent vintage. Some investigations set precedents for future investigatory conduct or aggressive partisan action, others become models for subsequent inquiries on the same or other breakdowns, still others produce ongoing statutory breakthroughs and program expansion that become central to government performance, and the findings of others continue to produce repairs and prevent breakdowns decades after they conclude. Durability is weighted in two categories:

lower (zero) or higher (one). Although durability is a subjective measure, it is often easy to identify. Reagan's 1981 National Commission on Excellence in Education is a case in point. The investigation was not particularly visible during its two-year review, but gained prominence as its *Nation at Risk* report became an anchor for a thirty-year educational reform effort.[18] Sixty-three of my investigations did not have enduring influence, while thirty-seven created effects, references, and readership well into the future.

BIPARTISANSHIP

The good investigation makes every effort to maintain a bipartisan position as it pursues its inquiry. However, investigations can be intensely partisan in a bipartisan period, just as they can be astutely bipartisan in a partisan era. The measure is weighted in two categories: lower (zero) or higher (one). Bipartisanship, or the lack thereof, can be identified through a variety of historical markers found in hearing records, press releases, split votes, and final dissents. It is also discernible in media reports. Some investigations, such as the Clinton impeachment inquiry, were undeniably partisan, while others, such as the 1951 and 1996 reviews of Internal Revenue Service operations, were astutely bipartisan. Similarly, some investigations, such as Herbert Hoover's 1949 government reorganization review, were created as partisan instruments, but eventually moved toward bipartisanship. Forty-six of my investigations were partisan, and fifty-four were bipartisan.

Ranking Footprints

Summed into a final score from zero to eleven, these weights produce an individual footprint for each investigation. The final scores are presented in box 3-1.

A Note on Bipartisanship

Bipartisanship is often described as the sine qua non of the good investigation. POGO's admonition, quoted above and repeated here, is its very first recommendation to investigators: "Congressional investigators should work together," POGO says early in its oversight manual. "This means you should be building relationships with other staffers doing meaningful oversight across the aisle or in the other Chamber. They may be your best sources of advice, documents, and contacts. They may even drop a completed investigation into your lap—as it's been known to happen that a Member halts their [sic] staff's investigation because it's too hot, and that colleague may need someone else to take over."[19]

BOX 3-1. Federal Investigatory Footprints of 100 Investigations,
Ranked from Heaviest to Lightest, 1945–2012

Heavyweight *(footprints 8–11)*

Score	Investigation
11	Intelligence agency abuses (1975)
11	Social Security financing crisis (1981)
11	9/11 terrorist attacks (2002)
11	2008 financial collapse (2008)
10	Government reorganization (1947)
10	Bureau of Internal Revenue corruption (1951)
10	Sputnik launch (1957)
10	Conduct of the Vietnam War (1966)
10	Watergate (1973)
10	Space shuttle *Challenger* accident (1986)
10	Savings and loan crisis (1987)
10	Base closing and realignment (1988)
10	Tobacco industry practices (1993)
10	Preventing terrorist attacks (1998)
10	Enron collapse (2001)
10	Quality of care for wounded warriors (2007)
9	Organized crime in America (1950)
9	Urban riots (1967)
9	Defense Department fraud, waste, and abuse (1985)
9	Conduct of Iraq War (2003)
9	Deficit reduction (2010)
8	World War II procurement fraud (1945)

Score	Investigation
8	Air force preparedness for the cold war (1956)
8	Drug industry practices (1959)
8	Kennedy assassination (1963)
8	Traffic safety (1965)
8	Indian Affairs corruption (1988)
8	Government mismanagement (1989)
8	U.S. intelligence agencies in the post–cold war era (1994)
8	Internal Revenue Service taxpayer abuse (1996)
8	Year 2000 technology problem (1998)
8	Gulf oil spill (2010)

Middleweight *(footprints 4–7)*

Score	Investigation
7	Communists in government (1948)
7	Airport safety (1952)
7	Labor racketeering (1957)
7	Crime in America (1965)
7	Executive branch reorganization (1969)
7	White House Iran-Contra program (1987)
7	Vietnam prisoners of war (POWs) and missing in action (MIAs) (1991)
7	Aviation security and safety (1996)
7	Stimulus oversight (2009)
6	Munitions lobby (1959)

BOX 3-1. Federal Investigatory Footprints of 100 Investigations,
Ranked from Heaviest to Lightest, 1945–2012 (continued)

Middleweight (cont.)

Score	Investigation
6	Educational quality (1981)
6	Strategic missile forces (1983)
6	Department of Homeland Security implementation and operations (2003)
6	Mine safety (2007)
5	Pearl Harbor (1945)
5	Quiz show rigging (1959)
5	State Department security procedures (1963)
5	Energy shortages (1973)
5	Ruby Ridge siege (1995)
5	Government response to the human immunodeficiency virus (HIV) epidemic (1987)
5	Gulf War syndrome (1995)
5	Technology transfers to China (1996)
5	1996 campaign finance abuses (1997)
5	Steroid abuse in baseball (2005)
5	Government response to Hurricane Katrina (2005)
4	Reconstruction Finance Corporation mismanagement (1950)
4	Campaign finance corruption (1956)
4	Defense Department stockpiling (1962)
4	Government information management (1963)
4	Welfare fraud (1975)

Score	Investigation
4	General Services Administration corruption (1978)
4	Three Mile Island nuclear accident (1979)
4	Central America policy (1983)
4	Housing and Urban Development scandal (1989)
4	Clinton impeachment (1998)
4	Solyndra Corporation (2011)
4	Fast and Furious gun-walking operation (2011)

Lightweight *(footprints 1–3)*

Score	Investigation
3	Communists in Hollywood (1947)
3	Agriculture commodity speculation (1947)
3	Dixon-Yates power contract (1954)
3	Sherman Adams misconduct (1957)
3	Lobbying by foreign governments (1962)
3	Agriculture commodity leasing (1962)
3	Ku Klux Klan activities (1965)
3	South Korean lobbying (1977)
3	Abscam congressional sting (1982)
3	Whitewater allegations (1995)
3	Waco Branch Davidian siege (1995)
3	Space shuttle *Columbia* accident (2003)
2	Atomic Energy Commission operations (1949)
2	Conduct of Korean War (1951)

(continued)

BOX 3-1. Federal Investigatory Footprints of 100 Investigations,
Ranked from Heaviest to Lightest, 1945–2012 (continued)

Score	Lightweight (cont.) Investigation	Score	Investigation
		1	Federal Housing Administration mismanagement (1954)
2	Justice Department operations (1952)		
		1	Central Intelligence Agency financing of private organizations (1967)
2	Military "muzzling" (1962)		
2	TFX fighter aircraft contract (1963)	1	Justice Department antitrust settlement (1972)
2	Kent State campus unrest (1970)	1	Nixon pardon (1974)
2	Superfund implementation (1981)	1	Wedtech defense procurement decision (1986)
2	Bombing of Beirut Marine barracks (1983)	1	1980 "October surprise"(1992)
2	Clinton conduct (1995)	1	Secret arms shipments to Bosnia (1996)
2	Abramoff lobbying tactics (2004)		
2	U.S. attorney firings (2007)	1	White House energy task force (2001)

Whether it is the product of unified government, national interest, institutional norms, or personal relationships between chairs and ranking members or between commission co-chairs, bipartisanship is often celebrated as the driver of all good things that follow. How can investigators fulfill their role as "the public's only hope for truth," as POGO implies, if they allow partisanship to shape their work?[20]

Moreover, even if bipartisanship is not essential for truth, it is the right thing to do for the party in power. "Remember," POGO argues in its very last "doing it right" directive, "although it may sound counter-intuitive, one of the best things you can do for your party if it is in the White House is conduct rigorous and regular oversight of the executive branch. This can prevent the growth of problems that may generate media attention and can negatively impact your party in the next election."[21] Given POGO's frequent use of the word "investigation" in its text, the advice also applies to the general description of the good investigation discussed in this chapter.

PARTISANSHIP IN PLAY

Partisanship is featured in both *Divided We Govern* and "Divided We Quarrel," but for very different reasons.[22] In essence, Mayhew argues that

Congress produces visible investigations in spite of the partisanship associated with divided government, while Parker and Dull argue that Congress produces longer investigations because of it.

Partisanship is also featured in the contemporary conversation about dysfunctional government and nowhere more visibly than in Thomas E. Mann and Norman J. Ornstein's *It's Even Worse Than It Looks: How the American Constitutional System Collided with the New Politics of Extremism.* Although they argue that the polarization is "asymmetric," meaning that Republicans are more divisive, even nastier than Democrats, the result is the same: a parliamentary system that grinds to a halt. It hardly matters who started the brawl. What matters is its effect:

> Partisan polarization is undeniably the central and most problematic feature of contemporary American politics. Political parties today are more internally unified and ideologically distinct than they have been in over a century. This pattern is most evident in the Congress, state legislatures, and other bastions of elite politics, where the ideological divide is wide and where deep and abiding partisan conflict is the norm. But it also reaches the activist stratum of the parties and into the arena of mass politics, as voters increasingly sort themselves by ideology into either the Democratic or Republican Party and view politicians, public issues, and even facts and objective conditions through distinctly partisan lenses.[23]

Today's bitter partisanship is nothing new per se. It has driven many of the party realignments in history and was central to the grand debates that preceded the Civil War, the New Deal, and the Reagan revolution. But today's partisanship does seem much more intense and has changed the parties into what Jonathan Rauch calls "ideological clubs" that have a strict political dress code:

> Northeastern Republicans were once much more liberal than Southern Democrats. Today more or less all conservatives are Republicans and more or less all liberals are Democrats. To some extent the sorting of parties into blue and red happened naturally as voters migrated along the terrain of their convictions, but the partisans of the political class have been only too happy to prod the voters along . . . Perhaps more significant, both parties also got busy using their computer programs and demographic maps to draw wildly complicated new district boundaries that furnished their incumbents with safe congressional seats. Today House members choose their voters

rather than the other way around, with the result that only a few dozen districts are competitive.[24]

And if this partisanship affects everything from presidential appointments to legislative productivity, it must surely affect investigation, too. Yet it is not necessarily clear that bipartisanship is essential for eventual impact. Bipartisanship can certainly create the gloss of consensus, but there are always times when investigatory findings provoke intense disagreement when recommendations hit the House and Senate floor. The question, therefore, is not whether bipartisanship is the antidote to stalemate, but whether it matters to investigatory impact. As chapter 4 suggests, the answer is not so much.

PARTISANSHIP BY DESIGN

More to the point of investigatory designs, investigations are often designed to generate the partisanship that may frustrate impact. The potential for partisanship was certainly built into the 2010 National Commission on Fiscal Responsibility and Reform, for example. Despite the commission's mandate to produce bipartisan consensus, it was almost perfectly designed to fail.

The seeds of failure were planted in the appointments process. Six of the commission members were to be appointed by the president, including two from "private life" and the co-chairs, three each by the two parties in the Senate, and three each by the two parties in the House. Once all the heads were counted, Democrats had a ten-commissioner majority led by the Senate's second-in-command Dick Durbin (D-Ill.), while Republicans had a seven-vote minority led by avowed budget hawk and rising star Rep. Paul Ryan (R-Wisc.). Although Simpson and Bowles eventually managed to win an eleven-vote majority in favor of their $4 trillion deficit-busting package, they needed three more votes to reach the fourteen-vote supermajority required for formal approval.[25] "I think they just had a unique opportunity with extraordinary powers and the chance to solve the problem rather than just kick it down the road," commission member Alice Rivlin said. "Unfortunately they didn't do it. It's the basic polarization over entitlements and taxes. They had to do both, and they couldn't get to agreement unless they did both."[26]

A DEMOGRAPHIC OVERVIEW

There are many ways to analyze the relationships between the eleven footprints, but none offers a faster introduction than correlations. According to this simple yes-no test in which higher correlations signal higher significance, thirty-four of the fifty-five relationships among the eleven weights are statistically significant and positive, while one is statistically significant and negative.[27] Thus, for example, the freedom to investigate is positively correlated with breadth, complexity, well-known leadership, seriousness, thoroughness, durability, and bipartisanship.

The only strong negative correlation in the mix is between visibility and length—as visibility increased, length decreased, and vice versa. The negative, but significant correlation confirms what Anthony Downs describes as the issue-attention cycle. Policymakers also clearly understand that public interest ebbs and flows over time. According to Downs, "American public attention rarely remains sharply focused upon any one domestic issue for very long—even if it involves a continuing problem of crucial importance to society." Instead, an issue "suddenly leaps into prominence, remains there for a short time, and then—although still largely unresolved—gradually fades from the center of public attention."[28] Perhaps the issue-attention cycle holds for investigations, too.

Setting aside these and other correlations for the if-then predictive analysis until later in this chapter, the rest of this demographic profile is based on simple percentage comparisons that show the potential effects of history, investigatory characteristics, and party control on the combined measure of the total eleven-point footprint for each investigation. Because historical dividing lines such as Watergate, investigatory characteristics such as institutional home, and party control are set before investigations begin, they must be viewed as predictors of footprints, not vice versa.

History

Tracked across the four historical periods (post–World War II, the Great Society, the congressional resurgence, and the most recent period, divided government) or compared before and after Watergate, history left its mark on some of the eleven footprint weights and not on others:

—The percentage of long investigations held steady across the four periods at an average of 57 percent.

—The percentage of broad investigations also held steady at an average of 39 percent.

—The percentage of complex investigations rose steadily from 26 percent during the post–World War II period to 49 percent during divided government.

—The percentage of investigations with well-known leadership seesawed over the four periods, dropping from 39 percent during the post–World War

II period to 16 percent during the Great Society era, rising back up to 48 percent during the congressional resurgence, and then falling back to 32 percent during divided government.

—The percentage of investigations with the freedom to investigate fell dramatically from 74 percent and 68 percent in the post–World War II and Great Society periods, respectively, to just 44 percent and 39 percent during the congressional resurgence and divided government, respectively.

—The percentage of visible investigations held steady at an average of 62 percent over the four periods.

—The percentage of serious investigations rose steadily over the four periods, from 48 percent during the post–World War II period to 65 percent during divided government.

—The percentage of thorough investigations held steady over the four periods at an average of 57 percent.

—The percentage of high-leverage investigations held steady at an average of 75 percent during the first (post–World War II), third (congressional resurgence), and fourth (divided government) historical periods, but stood at just 37 percent during the second (Great Society).

—The percentage of durable investigations held steady at an average of 37 percent during the four periods.

—The percentage of bipartisan investigations also seesawed slightly over the four periods, hitting 60 percent and 59 percent, respectively, during the post–World War II and congressional resurgence periods, while dropping to 47 percent and 48 percent during the Great Society and divided government, respectively.

Even though historical periods and Watergate produced little variation in these weights, presidential terms and election years left their own marks on each footprint weight. The president's term of office did not produce any significant differences in the percentages of longer, visible, high-leverage, and bipartisan investigations, but first terms were more likely to produce narrower investigations (70 percent for first terms versus 46 percent for second), simpler investigations (71 percent versus 46 percent), fewer familiar leaders at the helm (69 percent versus 59 percent), and less serious (46 percent versus 33 percent), thorough (52 percent versus 31 percent), and durable (71 percent versus 51 percent) investigations. Investigations launched during election years produced similar patterns when compared with investigations launched in nonelection years. The heightened electoral concerns of first terms and election years did not change the general modus operandi of investigatory history, but they did produce tighter and less durable footprints, suggesting that many were designed to make a more focused imprint on the political calendar.

Investigatory Characteristics

The eleven-point footprint score is much easier to analyze in three separate weight classes: lightweight (footprint scores of one to three), middleweight (four to seven), and heavyweight (eight to eleven). Within these three categories, thirty-one of my investigations were lightweights, another thirty-seven were middleweights, and thirty-two were heavyweights.

INSTITUTIONAL HOME

Institutional branch and chamber produced minimal effects on weight class. Indeed, Congress and the presidency produced almost exactly the same percentage of heavyweights (33 percent versus 30 percent, respectively). However, separating Congress into chambers, the Senate was twice as likely to produce heavyweights as the House (40 percent for the Senate versus 26 percent for the House), even though the House smoothed out the difference with a higher percentage of middleweights than the Senate (40 percent for the House versus 26 percent for the House).

These patterns held steady in the pre- and post-Watergate comparisons.

VENUE

Investigatory venue produced significant effects on weight class. Commissions produced the highest percentage of heavyweights (50 percent), followed by joint, select, or special congressional bodies (31 percent), subcommittees (28 percent), and full committees (17 percent). As the correlations show, commissions were the most likely source of heavyweight investigations, while full committees and subcommittees were the destination most likely to produce lightweights.

All but one of these differences remained unchanged in the pre- and post-Watergate comparisons. However, the percentage of heavyweights led by commissions increased from 38 percent before Nixon's resignation to 55 percent after.

TRIGGER

Investigatory trigger produced significant effects on weight class. Fire alarms produced a higher percentage of lightweights (42 percent versus 28 percent), while police patrols produced more heavyweights (38 percent versus 28 percent). Police patrols also produced more middleweights (44 percent versus 33 percent).

Watergate amplified these associations. Whereas 30 percent of police patrols produced heavyweights before Watergate, 48 percent produced heavyweights after. Most of these gains came from a sharp reduction in the percentage of police patrol lightweights, which fell from 45 percent before Watergate to just 4 percent after. Although fire alarms became the dominant trigger after Watergate, they were equally unlikely to be linked with heavyweights after Nixon's departure (30 percent before versus 26 percent after), perhaps because they involved less breadth, complexity, seriousness, and thoroughness and perhaps because investigators simply do not know how to produce the good investigation under the tight deadlines created by urgent events.

ISSUE

Investigatory issue did not produce any significant impact on weight class either directly or over history.

BREAKDOWN

Breakdown produced significant effects on weight class. Process and policy breakdowns produced more heavyweights than personal misconduct investigations (35 percent for process and 33 percent for policy versus 17 percent for personal misconduct), while misconduct breakdowns produced more lightweights than process or policy (67 percent for misconduct versus 27 percent for process and 25 percent for policy). Investigations of personal misconduct clearly produce highly visible investigations, but not necessarily the breadth, complexity, well-known leadership, seriousness, thoroughness, and durability associated with heavier footprints.

The pre- and post-Watergate comparisons produced mixed lines across these patterns. Process breakdowns produced more heavyweights after Watergate than before (25 percent before versus 38 percent after), but process breakdowns produced roughly the same effects (32 percent versus 39 percent). In turn, personal misconduct breakdowns produced more heavyweights before Watergate than after (25 percent versus 13 percent).

PURPOSE

Investigatory purpose produced significant effects on weight class. Investigations that focused on repair produced twice as many heavyweights as investigations that focused on prevention (41 percent versus 20 percent), but repair and prevention produced roughly equal percentages of lightweights (31 percent versus 32 percent), meaning that prevention had its greatest effects in producing middleweights (49 percent for prevention versus 29 percent for repair).

These differences were even more striking when compared before and after Watergate. Investigations that focused on repair were almost twice as likely to produce heavyweights after Watergate as before (26 percent before versus 50 percent after), but investigations that focused on prevention were more than three times as likely to produce heavyweights before Watergate as after (32 percent before versus just 9 percent after). Although most of the weight was lost to the middleweight category, investigators arguably became much better at repair, but prevention became more difficult.

METHOD

Investigatory method produced significant effects on weight class. Fact-finding investigations produced more than twice as many heavyweights as blame-setting investigations (47 percent versus 20 percent), while blame setting produced almost three times as many lightweights as fact finding (44 percent versus 16 percent).

Watergate amplified these differences. Fact finding was more tightly linked with heavyweights after Watergate (32 percent before versus 58 percent after), while blame setting produced fewer heavyweights after Watergate (26 percent before versus 16 percent after). The gains for fact finding came from a sharp decline in the percentage of lightweights, which fell from 32 percent before Watergate to just 4 percent after. Blame setting clearly produces visibility, but few of the other markers of the good investigation.

Party Control

Party control has a long and distinguished history in the study of congressional and presidential investigations. Much as bipartisanship is honored, even deified, as essential for the good investigation, it would not receive so much attention if it were always present. For many observers, and most certainly for Parker and Dull, divided government is at the root of the bitterness that seems to pervade the investigatory process. It is also viewed as the strike plate for failure and the rationale for using blue-ribbon commissions to reduce partisanship.

At least according to the following review, however, divided government does not threaten the good investigation. Congress and the president are still quite capable of good investigations under divided control of government or Congress. And neither party has a particular advantage in producing good investigations when they control government as a whole, the White House, Congress, the House, or the Senate.

PARTY CONTROL AND THE ELEVEN FOOTPRINTS

Party control also played a mixed role in shaping each of the eleven investigatory weights, with divided government the most favorable for some weights and unified government the most favorable for others, but Democrats were more likely than Republicans to generate more of the attributes of the good investigation:

—Unified and divided party control of government produced generally equal levels of investigatory length, breadth, freedom to investigate, and bipartisanship. However, unified government produced greater complexity (43 percent for divided government versus 30 percent for unified), visibility (67 percent versus 54 percent), leverage (71 percent versus 60 percent), and durability (41 percent versus 30 percent), but also lower levels of seriousness (54 percent versus 62 percent), thoroughness (49 percent versus 70 percent), and bipartisanship (51 percent versus 60 percent).

—Democratic and Republican control of government produced generally equal levels of investigatory complexity, well-known leadership, seriousness, thoroughness, leverage, and bipartisanship. However, Democratic control of both branches was associated with shorter (56 percent for Democratic control versus 67 percent for Republican control) and less visible (26 percent versus 83 percent) investigations, but more breadth (40 percent versus 17 percent), freedom to investigate (55 percent versus 33 percent), and thoroughness (71 percent versus 48 percent).

—Democratic and Republican control of the presidency produced generally equal levels of investigatory length, breadth, complexity, leverage, seriousness, thoroughness, durability, and bipartisanship. However, Democratic control of the presidency was associated with less familiar leadership (30 percent versus 44 percent), less freedom to investigate (29 percent versus 59 percent), and less visibility (58 percent versus 68 percent).

—Unified and divided party control of Congress produced generally equal levels of investigatory length, breadth, complexity, well-known leadership, visibility, seriousness, thoroughness, and durability. However, divided control of Congress produced less freedom to investigate (29 percent versus 59 percent), less thoroughness (35 percent versus 61 percent), and less leverage (66 percent versus 77 percent).

—Democratic and Republican control of Congress produced generally equal levels of investigatory length, complexity, visibility, leverage, and durability. However, Democratic control produced more breadth (42 percent versus 30 percent), more familiar leadership (38 percent versus 26 percent), more freedom to investigate (57 percent versus 44 percent), more seriousness (62 percent versus 48 percent), more thoroughness (58 percent versus 48 percent), and more bipartisanship (55 percent versus 40 percent).

—Democratic and Republican control of the House produced generally equal levels of investigatory breadth, complexity, familiar leadership, visibility, seriousness, and durability. However, Democratic control produced less visibility (60 percent versus 71 percent) and less leverage (65 percent versus 75 percent), but more length (64 percent versus 54 percent), more freedom to investigate (58 percent versus 43 percent), more thoroughness (60 percent versus 46 percent), and more bipartisanship (58 percent versus 43 percent).

—Democratic and Republican control of the Senate produced generally equal levels of investigatory length, complexity, familiar leadership, visibility, leverage, durability, and bipartisanship. However, Democratic control was associated with greater breadth (43 percent versus 31 percent), greater freedom to investigate (63 percent versus 37 percent), greater seriousness (66 percent versus 46 percent), and greater thoroughness (63 percent versus 43 percent), but also lower levels of visibility (59 percent versus 69 percent).

As these comparisons suggest, Democratic control generally produced more of the attributes of the good investigation, including freedom to investigate, well-known leadership, seriousness, thoroughness, and bipartisanship, while Republican control generally produced more of the visibility, leverage, and durability also associated with good investigations.

Not surprising given the earlier analysis, Watergate created few dividing lines in comparisons among the eleven separate weights. Democratic investigations were given greater freedom to investigate than Republican investigations before and after Watergate, while Republican investigations were more visible, high leverage, and influential than Democratic investigations also before and after Watergate. However, party control of government moved toward parity on investigatory complexity, visibility, thoroughness, and leverage after Watergate, but left unified government as the condition of choice for seriousness and bipartisanship and divided government as the condition of choice for durability.

PARTY CONTROL AND WEIGHT CLASS

Party control of government produced negligible effects in determining investigatory footprints when separated into the three weight classes. Looking down the range of potential associations, only four measures of party control showed significant effects on weight:

—Unified and divided government split the lightweights, middleweights, and heavyweights into thirds by almost exactly the same percentages.

—Democratic control of government produced more heavyweights than Republican control (33 percent versus 17 percent).

—Democratic and Republican control of the presidency divided the weight classes into thirds again by almost exactly the same percentages.

—Unified and divided congresses produced almost equal percentages of heavyweights (33 percent for unified versus 29 percent for divided).

—Democratic control of Congress produced more heavyweights than Republican control (37 percent versus 22 percent).

—Democratic control of the House produced more heavyweights than Republican control (35 percent versus 25 percent).

—Democratic control of the Senate produced more heavyweights than Republican control (37 percent versus 23 percent).

Additionally, House Democratic majorities produced more heavyweights when matched against Republican presidents than House Republican majorities when matched against Republican presidents (28 percent versus 14 percent), while Senate Democratic majorities produced more heavyweights when matched against Republican presidents than Senate Republican majorities when matched against Democratic presidents (64 percent versus 20 percent). The Watergate dividing line did not produce significant changes in these patterns, which seem to suggest that House and Senate Democratic majorities and Senate Republicans majorities produce more of the good investigations so admired among good government groups.

Moreover, if the post-Watergate quarrels cited by Parker and Dull had an impact on footprints, it is not apparent in the before-and-after patterns compared across the three weight classes. To the contrary, the relationship between party control and weight class moved ever so slightly toward parity over time.

—Divided control of government produced almost equal percentages of heavyweights before and after Watergate (26 percent versus 34 percent), as did unified government (30 percent versus 36 percent). The pattern suggests movement toward parity.

—Democratic control of government produced fewer heavyweights before and after Watergate (30 percent versus 50 percent). Although I cannot provide a before-and-after comparison during Republican control because the party never controlled government between 1945 and mid-1974, I can report that Republican control after Watergate produced fewer heavyweights than Democratic control (17 percent versus 50 percent).

—Democratic control of the presidency produced equal percentages of heavyweights before and after Watergate (30 percent each), while Republican control of the presidency produced fewer heavyweights before Watergate (27 percent) than after (37 percent). The pattern shows movement toward parity.

—Unified party control of both chambers of Congress produced fewer heavyweights before Watergate (30 percent) than after (35 percent), while divided control produced fewer heavyweights before Watergate (0 percent) than after (33 percent). The pattern suggests movement toward parity.

—Democratic control of both chambers of Congress produced fewer heavyweights before Watergate (31 percent) than after (46 percent), while Republican control produced roughly equal percentages of heavyweights before (25 percent) and after (21 percent). The pattern shows more drift toward parity.

—Democratic control of the House produced fewer heavyweights before Watergate (29 percent) than after (41 percent), while Republican control produced exactly the same percentage of heavyweights both before and after (25 percent). The pattern shows strong movement toward parity as Democrats lost most of their edge after Watergate.

—Democratic control of the Senate produced fewer heavyweights before Watergate (31 percent) than after (45 percent), while Republican control produced the same result (17 percent before and 24 percent after). The pattern shows a drift toward parity as Democratic control of the Senate produced fewer heavyweights after Watergate.

Despite the general absence of strong differences between these variations of party control, these findings suggest that unified government is not always what it appears to be. Unified government under Democrats produced somewhat more heavyweights than unified government under Republicans, as did Democratic control of both chambers, and Democratic control of the House or the Senate. It is not clear, however, whether Democrats gained their edge because they had more investigatory practice over the decades, or because Republicans were willing to trade weight for visibility. What is clear is that Democratic control is no guarantor of a good investigation or divided government a barrier.

THE INDIRECT EFFECTS OF PARTY CONTROL ON FOOTPRINTS

Party control did not produce any direct effects on the eleven footprints or the overall score. However, it did have significant indirect effects by shaping the direct associations between other measures such as investigatory characteristics and the eleven footprints. Commissions and fact finding may produce significant percentages of heavyweights, for example, but they produce much heavier investigations during divided government than during unified.

The following review shows these and other indirect effects of divided government by comparing the relationships between all of my investigatory characteristics and each of the eleven footprint weights. Using only the differences between divided and unified government that exceeded 10 percent, the review can be expressed as a simple chain running from party control → investigatory characteristics → each of the eleven footprints.

—Divided government produced larger percentages of long investigations that were conducted by commissions (47 percent versus 36 percent) and used fact finding (52 percent versus 38 percent). However, unified government produced larger percentages of long investigations that were conducted by Congress (71 percent versus 61 percent), the House (78 percent versus 63 percent), full committees (67 percent versus 56 percent), and subcommittees (77 percent versus 60 percent), examined foreign issues (73 percent versus 45 percent), targeted personal misconduct (67 percent versus 56 percent), and used blame setting (76 percent versus 59 percent).

—Divided government produced larger percentages of broad investigations that were conducted by the presidency (55 percent versus 44 percent), the Senate (50 percent versus 37 percent), and commissions (71 percent versus 46 percent), were triggered by police patrols (52 percent versus 32 percent), targeted process breakdowns (48 percent versus 33 percent), set course for repair (50 percent versus 38 percent), and used fact finding (59 percent versus 38 percent). However, unified government produced larger percentages of broad investigations that were conducted by full committees (31 percent versus 21 percent), targeted personal misconduct (33 percent versus 11 percent), and used blame setting (38 percent versus 27 percent).

—Divided government produced larger percentages of complex investigations that were led by the presidency (82 percent versus 44 percent), joint, select, and special congressional bodies (42 percent versus 25 percent), and commissions (88 percent versus 55 percent), were triggered by police patrols (65 percent versus 32 percent), examined foreign issues (50 percent versus 27 percent), targeted a process (42 percent versus 24 percent) or policy (57 percent versus 41 percent) breakdown, set course for repair (47 percent versus 33 percent), and used fact finding (69 percent versus 25 percent). However, unified government produced larger percentages of complex investigations that targeted personal misconduct (33 percent versus 11 percent) and used blame setting (38 percent versus 21 percent).

—Divided government produced larger percentages of investigations with well-known leadership that were conducted by the presidency (55 percent versus 33 percent), the House (25 percent versus 11 percent), subcommittees (42 percent versus 15 percent), and commissions (59 percent versus 46 percent), were triggered by fire alarms (33 percent versus 13 percent), examined foreign issues (50 percent versus 36 percent), targeted process breakdowns (42 percent versus 30 percent), and set course for repair (42 percent versus 29 percent). However, unified government produced larger percentages of investigations with well-known leadership when they targeted personal misconduct (33 percent versus 11 percent).

—Although divided government did not produce any indirect effects on the freedom to investigate, unified government more than compensated, with larger percentages of investigations that had the freedom to investigate when they were conducted by the House (56 percent versus 42 percent) or full committees (56 percent versus 21 percent), were triggered by fire alarms (60 percent versus 45 percent), examined foreign issues (64 percent versus 50 percent), targeted personal misconduct (33 percent versus 22 percent), set course for prevention (57 percent versus 40 percent), and used blame setting (57 percent versus 41 percent).

—Divided government produced larger percentages of visible investigations that were conducted by Congress (69 percent versus 50 percent), the House (67 percent versus 44 percent), the Senate (69 percent versus 53 percent), full committees (79 percent versus 67 percent), and subcommittees (65 percent versus 31 percent), were triggered by fire alarms (83 percent versus 60 percent), examined foreign issues (68 percent versus 36 percent), targeted process breakdowns (65 percent versus 47 percent) and personal misconduct (89 percent versus 67 percent), set course for prevention (76 percent versus 63 percent), and used blame setting (74 percent versus 48 percent). However, unified government produced larger percentages of visible investigations that were conducted by special congressional bodies (75 percent versus 64 percent) and commissions (73 percent versus 59 percent), were triggered by police patrols (55 percent versus 39 percent), and used fact finding (69 percent versus 58 percent).

—Divided government produced larger percentages of serious investigations that were conducted by commissions (50 percent versus 39 percent) and triggered by police patrols (83 percent versus 64 percent). However, unified government produced larger percentages of serious investigations that were conducted by the presidency (100 percent versus 81 percent) and full committees (56 percent versus 29 percent), were triggered by fire alarms (67 percent versus 40 percent), examined domestic issues (73 percent versus 56 percent), examined foreign issues (73 percent versus 55 percent), targeted personal misconduct (33 percent versus 22 percent), set course for prevention (75 percent versus 44 percent), and used blame setting (57 percent versus 35 percent).

—Divided government produced no indirect effects toward a greater percentage of thorough investigations. However, unified government produced larger percentages of thorough investigations that were conducted by the House (79 percent versus 42 percent), full committees (56 percent versus 29 percent), special congressional bodies (75 percent versus 50 percent), and subcommittees (69 percent versus 45 percent), were triggered by fire alarms (60 percent versus 40 percent), examined domestic issues (69 percent versus 44 percent), targeted process (77 percent versus 55 percent), policy (65 percent versus 52 percent), and personal misconduct (33 percent versus 22 percent) breakdowns, set course for repair (56 percent versus 40 percent), and used blame setting (57 percent versus 29 percent).

—Divided government produced larger percentages of high-leverage investigations that were conducted by Congress (79 percent versus 57 percent), the House (79 percent versus 56 percent), the Senate (77 percent versus 58 percent), full committees (71 percent versus 56 percent), and subcommittees (75 percent versus 46 percent), examined foreign issues (73 percent versus 46 percent), targeted process breakdowns (94 percent versus 47 percent), and used either fact finding (76 percent versus 63 percent) or blame setting (71 percent versus 57 percent). However, unified government produced larger percentages of high-leverage investigations that were conducted by the presidency (67 percent versus 46 percent) and targeted policy breakdowns (71 percent versus 52 percent) and personal misconduct (67 percent versus 56 percent).

—Divided government produced larger percentages of durable investigations that were conducted by Congress (40 percent versus 25 percent), the House (33 percent versus 22 percent), the Senate (42 percent versus 26 percent), and commissions (65 percent versus 46 percent), were triggered by fire alarms (43 percent versus 20 percent), examined foreign issues (55 percent versus 18 percent), targeted process breakdowns (45 percent versus 12 percent) and personal misconduct (22 percent versus 0 percent), set course for repair (50 percent versus 19 percent), and used fact finding (59 percent versus 31 percent). However, unified government produced larger percentages of durable investigations when they set course for prevention (44 percent versus 28 percent).

—Divided government produced the largest percentages of bipartisan investigations that were conducted by the presidency (91 percent versus 78 percent), special congressional bodies (50 percent versus 39 percent), and subcommittees (94 percent versus 73 percent), were triggered by police patrols (87 percent versus 50 percent), targeted policy breakdowns (65 percent versus 47 percent), and used fact finding (79 percent versus 56 percent). However, unified government produced larger percentages of bipartisan investigations that were conducted by the House (44 percent versus 29 percent) and full committees (56 percent versus 14 percent), were triggered by fire alarms (67 percent versus 33 percent), targeted process breakdowns (71 percent versus 58 percent) and personal misconduct (33 percent versus 0 percent), and set course for prevention (69 percent versus 56 percent).

All told, divided government produced more than sixty indirect effects on the eleven footprints, compared with fifty-two for unified government. Investigators might note that unified government had particularly significant indirect effects on seriousness and thoroughness, while divided government had particularly significant effects on visibility and durability.

It is not clear that investigators have any choice at all regarding investigatory characteristics, although there have been plenty of contests between the institutions on who owns an investigation, what kinds of triggers matter, which issues carry the greatest weight, and why some breakdowns should be avoided and when. What is clear is that some investigatory characteristics produce more of the favored weights during divided government, while others produce more during unified government. If durability is the key footprint for impact, and the next chapter shows that it absolutely is, investigators have ten ways to generate more during divided government, compared to just one during unified government.

As for the twenty-eight blue-ribbon commissions discussed above, divided and unified government both had indirect effects on commissions with well-known leadership, freedom to investigate, seriousness, thoroughness, and leverage. Divided government produced larger percentages of commissions than unified government when they were triggered by fire alarms (80 percent versus 40 percent), examined domestic issues (50 percent versus 33 percent), targeted a process breakdown (70 percent versus 20 percent), and moved toward repair (80 percent versus 40 percent). However, unified government produced larger percentages of heavy commitment investigations when commissions targeted policy breakdowns (50 percent versus 14 percent), set course for prevention (33 percent versus 0 percent), and used blame setting (20 percent versus 0 percent). All in all, it is not a stunning inventory of the salutary effects of unified government nor an endorsement of divided government.

A QUESTION STILL UNANSWERED

These patterns suggest that party control affects at least some choices that produce heavier footprints and eventual impact, while further analysis of the party matchups between House and Senate majorities of one party and presidents of the other offers another chance to ask whether divided government is the bane of the good investigation.

Recall from chapter 2 that the number of matchups is limited at best—just fourteen cases when House Democrats faced a Republican president, seven when House Republicans faced a Democrat, fourteen when Senate Democrats faced a Republican, and ten when Senate Republicans faced a Democrat. The comparisons suggest that Republican majorities were the culprits in rising investigatory conflict:

—Senate Democratic majorities had the highest average footprint score at 7.3 and the highest percentage of heavyweights (64 percent). Matched against a president of the other party, Senate Democrats scored nine firsts among the eleven footprints, one second, and one third. Senate Democrats were the most likely to produce long (tied with House Republican majorities at 71 percent each), broad (64 percent), complex (57 percent), serious (71 percent), thorough (64 percent), durable (tied with Senate Republican majorities at 50 percent), and bipartisan (64 percent) investigations, with well-known leadership (57 percent) and freedom to investigate (79 percent); the second most likely to produce visible (79 percent) investigations; and the third most likely to produce high-leverage (79 percent) investigations, although all four matchups produced relatively high levels of leverage.

—Senate Republican majorities had the second highest average footprint score at 5.2, but the third highest percentage of heavyweights (20 percent). Matched against a president of the other party, Senate Republican majorities scored two firsts, seven seconds, and two fourths. They were the most likely to produce visible (80 percent) and durable investigations (50 percent); the second most likely to produce long (tied with House Democratic majorities at 50 percent), broad (40 percent), complex (30 percent), high-leverage (80 percent), and bipartisan (40 percent) investigations with well-known leadership (30 percent) and freedom to investigate (60 percent); and the least likely to produce serious (30 percent) and thorough (30 percent) investigations.

—House Democratic majorities had the third highest average footprint score at 4.9 and the lowest percentage of heavyweights (14 percent). Matched against a president from the other party, House Democratic majorities scored two seconds, seven thirds, and two fourths. They were the second most likely to produce long (50 percent) and serious (50 percent) investigations; the third most likely to produce investigations with well-known leadership (29 percent) and freedom to investigate (50 percent) as well as visible (71 percent), serious (60 percent), high-leverage (79 percent), durable (36 percent), and bipartisan (36 percent) investigations; and the least likely to produce broad (21 percent) and complex (21 percent) investigations.

—House Republican majorities had the lowest average footprint score at 4.7 and the third highest percentage of heavyweights (27 percent). Matched against a president from the other party, House Republican majorities had two firsts, one second, three thirds, and five fourths. On the one hand, House Republican majorities were the most likely to produce high-leverage investigations (86 percent), second most likely to produce serious investigations (86 percent), and tied with Senate Democrats as most likely to produce long investigations (71 percent each). On the other hand, House Republican majorities were the third most likely to produce broad (29 percent) and complex (29 percent) investigations, and the least likely to produce visible (57 percent), durable (29 percent), bipartisan (29 percent) investigations with the freedom to investigate (29 percent) and well-known leadership (14 percent).

So is this evidence that House Republicans are more quarrelsome facing a Democratic president? Perhaps so, especially given the restrictions on freedom to investigate and low levels of bipartisanship. And is this also evidence that Senate Democrats are the most likely to generate the good investigation? Perhaps so, too, especially given the high marks for seriousness, thoroughness, and bipartisanship.

Yet the more interesting finding here may be the general tendency of the House and Senate to create distinctive investigatory habits regardless of the party in power. The House produced the lowest percentages on all eleven measures, while the Senate produced the highest. At least for big-ticket investigations, the House appears quite willing to boil the investigatory tea, as George Washington might have put it in his famous conversation with Thomas Jefferson, while the Senate seems quite willing to cool it. These are just wisps from a question still unanswered, of course, but well worth watching if polarization continues upward.

AN INVENTORY OF EXAMPLES

Each of these investigations tended to earn its footprint score through somewhat different paths—some as a function of length, others based on the freedom to investigate, and still others based on the early leverage created through appointment of a special congressional body. Thus, even though a group of investigations may share the same footprint, they have histories well worth exploring through vignettes from the three weight classes, a discussion of works in progress, and a final note on the salutary effects of blue-ribbon commissions on investigatory weight.

Heavyweights

The list of heavyweights in box 3-1 is generously populated by well-known investigations of visible national breakdowns such as the Vietnam War (1966), Watergate (1973), Social Security (1981), the *Challenger* accident (1986), the 9/11 terrorist attacks (2003), and the 2008 financial collapse. All have their own stories to tell, as do the two heavyweights discussed below.

SPUTNIK (1957)

The successful Soviet launch of a 184-pound satellite called Sputnik on October 4, 1957, was arguably the most important event in 1950s cold war history. Soon followed by the failed launch of a U.S. satellite, Sputnik prompted a wave of newspaper headlines highlighting the specter of nuclear war and Soviet supremacy, even as members of Congress worked through reams of data leaking from the Defense Department's secret 1957 report *Deterrence and Survival in the Nuclear Age.*[29]

The Senate's investigation was almost invisible in the flood of fear that followed, however. Aggressively chaired by future president Lyndon B. Johnson (D-Tex.), the inquiry moved quickly to assess the need to accelerate the U.S. space program. Although the investigation lasted just eight months, the Senate Armed Services Committee's Preparedness Subcommittee held thirty hearings and released its seventeen recommendations when Johnson rose to speak to his colleagues on the Senate floor on January 23, 1958. Although Eisenhower had initially responded to Sputnik with a seemingly cavalier remark that it did not bother him "one iota," he changed his rhetoric within weeks and acknowledged increasing public concerns that the nation was unprepared to meet "certain pressing requirements."[30]

Yet, much as Johnson may have been tempted to use the investigation as an opportunity to set the stage for the 1960 election, he chose the bipartisan path. He described the subcommittee's basic motivations just as his subcommittee released the report:

> The Senate Preparedness Subcommittee today concluded its current series of hearings into the satellite and missile programs with

the adoption of a unanimous report. That statement expressed the sense of unity that the committee has as to the urgent need for strengthening our country's defenses. It expressed the kind of unity which I believe Americans desire. We tried to state the facts which give cause for foreboding and the facts which give cause of hope. We stated those facts not as members of political parties but as servants of the Senate reporting to the Senate and to the people of the Nation.[31]

Such was the explanation for a heavyweight investigation that escalated the space race. Yet, even as the report argued for more powerful rockets and warheads, strategic planning, and engineers, it also hinted at the need to separate peaceful space exploration from nuclear war. Eisenhower followed the recommendation when he created the National Aeronautics and Space Administration in April 1958.

Readers should note that this investigation could have been packaged with the 1956 Air Force preparedness inquiry but for the role of Sputnik and the clear focus on defense organization in the review. Whereas the Air Force review produced a highly partisan presentation about the alleged missile gap and the need for a much larger defense budget, the Sputnik review turned to a bipartisan assessment of the Defense Department's basic organization and the creation of an entirely new agency to head the U.S. space program. Although the proposal was barely noticed at the time, the investigation provided the early momentum toward the creation of the National Aeronautics and Space Administration. At least for the Sputnik investigation, organizational rivalries at the Defense Department, not its meager budget, were the problem of greatest concern.

GOVERNMENT REORGANIZATION (1947)

Herbert Hoover's first National Commission on Organization of the Executive Branch provides a forgotten example of blue-ribbon investigation done well—long, broad, serious, thorough, visible, high leverage, and durable. Although the commission was created in late 1947 by House Republicans to uncover New Deal scandals, President Truman surprised his adversaries by appointing a widely disparaged Republican president as chairman, who in turn surprised his party allies by building a more rational, effective government.[32] Authorized after a short set of hearings by the Senate Committee on Expenditures in Executive Departments, the investigation is easily defined as a Senate inquiry that used a commission as its venue. The 1947 commission finished its work in 1949 and was followed by a second commission in 1953.

Notwithstanding eleven other members, including nationally known figures such as Sen. George Aiken (R-Vt.), former ambassador Joseph Kennedy, and Sen. John L. McClellan (D-Ark.), Hoover was singularly in charge of what became a one-man commission. He directed all of the commission's twenty-four task forces, vetted all of its 273 recommendations, and supported every reorganization plan that Truman sent to Congress along the path to a great deal of impact.[33]

Having been a talented administrator during his earlier days of World War I relief efforts and then as secretary of commerce under presidents Warren Harding and Calvin Coolidge, Hoover may have viewed the commission as a way to redeem his reputation for failing to stem the economic catastrophe that emerged during his presidency. Whether motivated by self-interest, patriotic duty, or the chance to exercise his considerable administrative skills, Hoover's work earned ten weights out of eleven, the only deduction being the absence of any discernible public interest in the issue.

Although the commission had maximum impact on its own through the many Truman and Eisenhower reorganization plans, it continues to exercise historical influence to this day.[34] It was the obvious model for the successful investigations of Defense Department fraud, government mismanagement, and obsolete military bases and has been referenced in at least three major efforts to create a second Hoover Commission over the past twenty years, one of which became law only to be voided under a special provision that allowed George W. Bush to exercise a de facto veto within ninety days of his inauguration. Obama referenced the need for reorganization in his 2011 State of the Union address:

> We live and do business in the Information Age, but the last major reorganization of the government happened in the age of black-and-white TV. There are 12 different agencies that deal with exports. There are at least five different agencies that deal with housing policy. Then there's my favorite example: The Interior Department is in charge of salmon while they're in fresh water, but the Commerce Department handles them when they're in saltwater. I hear it gets even more complicated once they're smoked.[35]

Middleweights

The middle tier of my list also contains many well-known investigations of government breakdowns such as the alleged communist infiltration of government (1948), airport safety (1952), the need for a new Office of Management and Budget and a new Environmental Protection Agency (1969), the deadly siege at Ruby Ridge, Idaho (1995), and campaign finance abuses in the Clinton reelection campaign (1997). Once again, all of these investigations have their stories to tell, as do the two other middleweights discussed below.

PEARL HARBOR (1945)

Pearl Harbor was hardly a new topic when the Senate opened its investigation in 1945. To the contrary, Pearl Harbor had been hashed and rehashed in the press during the war and had already produced extensive investigations by the Army, Navy, and a blue-ribbon commission led by Supreme Court Justice Owen Roberts. The reports were of mixed value in resolving the doubts about the surprise attack, however: the Navy blamed the Army, the Army blamed the Navy, and the Roberts Commission found the commanders of the Army and Navy bases in Pearl Harbor guilty of "dereliction of duty."[36] If there was any agreement across the classified reports, it resided in a sharp critique of the secretary of state, Cordell Hull, for his November 26, 1941, ultimatum to the Japanese, which the Army described as "the document that touched the button that started the war."[37]

The 1945 investigation was touched off by Truman's late-August decision to release all classified reports and eventually earned a five-point footprint score for its leadership, visibility, seriousness, thoroughness, and leverage.

With Republicans moving quickly to criticize the Roosevelt-Truman prewar strategy, Senate Democrats mustered enough votes to create the Joint Committee to Investigate the Pearl Harbor Attack, thereby taking the lead role in the eleven-month review. Truman's future vice president, Alben Barkley (D-Ky.), chaired the Joint Committee on the Investigation of the Pearl Harbor Attack. Given the political consequences of a negative review, Barkley kept a very tight rein on the investigation, which was short, relatively narrow, not especially complex, and soon forgotten as investigations of communism in government and the motion picture industry took precedence.

The committee absolved every senior official possibly involved in the attack. Specifically, the committee found no evidence to support charges that the president or the secretaries of state, war, or Navy "tricked, provoked, incited, cajoled, or coerced Japan into attacking this Nation in order that a declaration of war might be more easily obtained from the Congress." Having concluded that "virtually everyone was surprised that Japan struck the Fleet at Pearl Harbor," the committee moved on to assess the underlying dynamics of collecting and sharing intelligence. Building on the testimony of the Pacific Fleet's commander-in-chief, Admiral Husband E. Kimmel, and his war plans officer, Admiral Charles H. McMorris, the committee argued that officers in both Washington and Hawaii knew an attack was at least a possibility and fully understood that war was imminent, but failed to act:

> Beyond serious question Army and Navy officials both in Hawaii and in Washington were beset by a lassitude born of 20 years of peace. Admiral Kimmel admitted he was affected by the "peace psychology" just like "everybody else." As expressed by Admiral McMorris, "We were a bit too complacent there." The manner in which capable officers were affected is to a degree understandable, but the Army and Navy are the watchdogs of the Nation's security and they must be alert at all times, no matter how many the years of peace.
>
> As indicated in the body of this report, there was a failure in the War and Navy Departments during the night of December 6–7 to be properly on the qui vive consistent with the knowledge that the Japanese reply to our Government's note of November 26 was being received. The failure of subordinate officials to contact the Chief of Staff and Chief of Naval Operations on the evening of December 6 concerning the first 13 parts of the 14-part memorandum is indicative of the "business as usual" attitude. Some prominent military and navy officials were entertaining and, along with other officers, apparently failed to read into the 13 parts the importance of and necessity for greater alertness.[38]

What followed was a long inventory of mistakes made almost entirely in Hawaii.[39]

The committee also criticized the intelligence and war plans divisions of the then-separate Department of War and Department of the Navy for their failure to give "careful and thoughtful attention to the intercepted messages from Tokyo to Honolulu of September 24, November 15, and November 20 (the harbor berthing plan and related dispatches) and to raise a question as to their significance . . . If properly appreciated, this intelligence should have suggested a dispatch to all Pacific outpost commanders supplying this information, as [Army chief of staff] General George C. Marshall attempted to do immediately upon seeing it."[40]

With little impact on the intelligence agencies beyond a stiff call for coordination, the investigation is best remembered as an admirable effort to clear the air by building on Truman's willingness to release all of the secret investigations that were conducted after World War II began.[41] Moreover, the committee's twenty-five principles for preventing future surprise attacks were framed as little more than platitudes about effective supervision and intelligence management and were offered in "the earnest hope that something constructive may be accomplished that will aid our national defense and preclude a repetition of the disaster of December 7, 1941."

Accordingly, principle no. 2 reminded the intelligence community that "supervisory officials cannot take anything for granted in the alerting of subordinates," principle no. 7 reminded officers that "complacency and procrastination are out of place where sudden and decisive action are of the essence," principle no. 10 argued, "there is no substitute for imagination and resourcefulness on the part of supervisory and intelligence officials," principle no. 11 argued, "communications must be characterized by clarity, forthrightness, and appropriateness," principle no. 15 stated, "there is great danger of being blinded by the self-evident," and principle no. 20 concluded, "personal or official jealously will wreck any organization." Perhaps most notable, given the failure of imagination that preceded the 9/11 terrorist attacks,[42] the list was entirely hortatory.

Even as it highlighted the same failure of imagination that would haunt the nation in the days that followed the 9/11 attacks, the committee majority refused to blame President Roosevelt and his vice president for any lassitude of their own. As a result, three of the committee's four Republicans dissented from the final report, which reflected the investigation's intense partisanship and the durability of its recommendations.[43]

HURRICANE KATRINA (2005)

The Hurricane Katrina investigation is a second highly visible example of a middleweight inquiry. For starters, the investigation was certainly urgent and therefore highly visible. The category-three hurricane roared ashore on Monday, August 29, 2005, and almost immediately overwhelmed the poorly designed levees erected to protect much of New Orleans, creating what some called the worst civil engineering disaster in U.S. history. According to the Pew Research Center, 73 percent of Americans paid very close attention to the news as the hurricane washed away vast stretches of the Gulf coast, killed more than 1,800 people, and left $80 billion in damage.[44]

Americans watched as the catastrophe unfolded on every network and cable news channel, thereby building the base for a highly visible investigation. Americans watched when the president surveyed the catastrophe on Wednesday during an Air Force One flyover; when CNN's Anderson Cooper showed the desperation in the flooded Ninth Ward, described the agony of the 3,000 citizens trapped without food, water, and working toilets in the New Orleans Superdome, and replayed the pleas for 40,000 troops. And they watched when

Bush finally toured the disaster zone on Friday and congratulated beleaguered Federal Emergency Management Agency (FEMA) director and immediate past president of the International Arabian Horse Association, Michael Brown, for doing a "heck of a job." Brown was gone by September 9.

The images were played again and again as Congress began its investigation of what went wrong both before and after the hurricane hit. With the Senate Homeland Security and Governmental Affairs Committee as the primary investigator, the hearings were quick and thorough. Led by Sen. Susan Collins (R-Maine), the committee conducted twenty-two hearings over the eight-month review, took testimony from more than 400 witnesses, and reviewed almost 900,000 pages of documents along the way to its polished final report.[45] As the committee concluded, the suffering did not occur in a vacuum: "Instead, it continued longer than it should have because of—and was in some cases exacerbated by—the failure of government at all levels to plan, prepare for, and respond aggressively to the storm. These failures were not just conspicuous; they were pervasive."[46]

The Senate was not the only player in the overall investigation. The House began its own investigation just one day after the Senate by creating its Select Bipartisan Subcommittee to Investigate the Preparation for and Response to Hurricane Katrina. Driven to beat the Senate to the finish line, the subcommittee only held nine hearings before releasing its short, but even shinier, report titled "A Failure of Initiative."[47]

The only problem with the House Select Bipartisan Committee was that it was not bipartisan at all: Democrats refused to participate in the effort, largely under instructions from House minority leader Nancy Pelosi (D-Calif.). According to my respondents, the select committee and its chairman, Tom Davis (R-Va.), made every effort to bring the Democrats on board, but Pelosi remained adamant that the effort was merely a shield for protecting the "culture of corruption, cronyism, and incompetence that has marked the Republican leadership in Washington, D.C."[48]

The Senate's investigation eventually earned a five-point footprint for its breadth, complexity, visibility, seriousness, and thoroughness, but lost six points for (1) its length (the investigation lasted barely seven months), (2) a little-known leader (Collins had just become committee chairman and was at the helm of her first major investigation), (3) lack of freedom to investigate (the investigation was under constant assault from Senate Republicans and the White House), (4) lack of high leverage (two other investigations were in the horse race for the primary investigatory lead), (5) lack of durability (the committee's report was quickly shelved after a relatively light reorganization of FEMA), and (6) lack of bipartisanship (six Democrats wrote a final dissent excoriating the White House for withholding information that they believed would have expanded the investigation to meatier political issues).[49]

Lightweights

Even the lightweights in box 3-1 include highly visible inquiries surrounding controversies such as communist infiltration of Hollywood (1947), conduct of the Korean War (1951), the Federal Bureau of Investigation's "Abscam" bribery sting that snared one senator and five House members (1982),[50] the federal government's siege of the Branch Davidian compound outside Waco, Texas (1995), and the alleged Reagan 1980 campaign effort to prevent an "October Surprise" in the Iran hostage crisis (1992). And they, too, have their own stories to tell, as do two other lightweights discussed below.

SHERMAN ADAMS MISCONDUCT (1957)

The investigation of White House chief of staff Sherman Adams was the first of two sensational investigations launched and led by the same subcommittee under the same mandate and at almost the same time. Both investigations began with fire alarms from both inside government (Adams) and outside (quiz show rigging), pursued blame setting at every turn, and produced little more than visibility.

The Adams investigation is particularly important, however, because it was designed to create partisan advantage. Although contemporary critics of Congress often decry the "parliamentarization" of the investigatory process that produces blame setting during divided government and quietude during unified government, the Adams investigation strongly suggests that this parliamentization has long existed. The parliamentarization may be increasing of late, but it is not new.

More important, however, the Adams investigation derailed what could have been a much broader, complex investigation of all federal regulatory agencies that House speaker Sam Rayburn (D-Tex.) had hoped would create a vast catalog of malfeasance for future ethics legislation. Although the House Government Operations Committee requested control of the investigation, Rayburn gave the mandate to the Committee on Interstate and Foreign Commerce and its Special Subcommittee on Legislative Oversight instead.[51] Rayburn explained his decision just before the House reauthorized the subcommittee on April 11, 1957:

I might say this with reference to the question of overlapping: The Committee on Government Operations has done some wonderful work on some of these matters. But it does not follow that it is the proper function of that committee to go into it like the Committee on Interstate and Foreign Commerce Committee would . . . I might say, as I have said it on this floor before—and I know Members have heard me say this—I served on the Committee on Interstate and Foreign Commerce when it worked on and developed practically all the laws that are proposed to be investigated ... If there is a committee in the Congress, a committee capable as a result of the work they have been doing, capable of making a thorough investigation of these laws and the execution of the laws administratively, certainly it is the Committee on Interstate and Foreign Commerce.[52]

Rayburn's hopes for a thorough investigation were soon thwarted by controversy. The subcommittee's first chairman, Rep. Morgan M. Moulder (D-Mo.), resigned for "personal reasons" after firing the subcommittee's well-connected chief counsel for leaking a secret memo alleging bribery and corruption at the Federal Communications Commission.[53]

Only months later, the subcommittee's second chairman, Rep. Oren Harris (D-Ark.), was pilloried in a "Washington Merry-Go-Round" column by future Pulitzer Prize winner Jack Anderson. According to Anderson, Harris had buried a nascent investigation of "the second most powerful man in the government—President Eisenhower's crisp, curt overseer, Sherman Adams."[54] Calling Adams "Sherm the Firm" at one point, Anderson's chronology of corruption revealed a thinly veiled quid pro quo between Adams and a shadowy textile lobbyist named Bernard Goldfine. Thus what started out as a broad investigation of regulatory agencies narrowed to a blame-setting investigation designed primarily to embarrass the president.[55] With Eisenhower backing away from his embattled assistant, Adams resigned on September 22, saying:

A campaign of vilification by those who seek personal advantage by my removal from public life has continued up to this very moment. These efforts, it is now clear, have been intended to destroy me and in so doing to embarrass the Administration and the President of the United States. An easy and obvious way to bring such an attack to an end is to remove the target.[56]

Beyond Adams, the subcommittee could claim few other victories from its eighty-nine days of hearings and 11,306 pages of testimony. Its final report was quickly shelved, and its muddled proposal for bureaucratic tightening across the federal government's far-flung regulatory empire never reached the House floor.

CLINTON CONDUCT (1995)

Given all the publicity surrounding Bill Clinton's indiscretions and misbehavior, it may be surprising that the multipronged investigation shows up near the very bottom of my list. Indeed, it received only two points—one for its length (six years) and one for its drip-drip-drip visibility. Although Clinton's impeachment is much higher on the list, the ongoing inquiries of White House misconduct had no discernible impact on government performance.

Under the helm of Bill Clinger (R-Pa.), chairman of the newly renamed House Government Reform and Oversight Committee, the investigation appears in retrospect to be more serious and potentially very influential. Although Clinger was unquestionably under pressure to contribute his share of ideas to the new majority's "assault book" of charges against the president, his brief investigatory engagement was motivated primarily by a sense that the drumbeat of allegations revealed a much larger disregard for ethical conduct. "He never really wanted to do it," one of my respondents said. "He just didn't have a choice given the charges. They were occupying too much space out there. They either had to be disposed of or the committee would never get on with its agenda."

Clinger was only one of many chairmen subjected to these limits on the freedom to investigate, however.[57] According to an April 29, 1996, *Roll Call* article, the Republican leadership had instructed all committee chairs to catalog potential investigatory topics in three categories: "waste, fraud, and abuse in the Clinton administration," "influence of Washington labor union bosses/corruption," and "examples of dishonest or ethical lapses in the Clinton administration." The memo containing the call to action was supposedly marked "urgent" and asked committee staff to "review pertinent GAO [Government Accounting Office] reports, Inspector General reports, or committee investigative materials or newspaper articles for departments and agencies within your jurisdiction that expose anecdotes that amplify these areas."

His 1997 successor to the chairmanship, Dan Burton (R-Ind.), showed no such reluctance to pursue Clinton. "It was all about the party and breaking Bill Clinton," the same respondent argued. "He just hated the president. It was as personal as it was political." Using his unilateral authority to issue committee subpoenas, Burton went after every hint of scandal—did the president trade burial plots in Arlington cemetery for campaign contributions, erase e-mails to cover up his misbehavior, give favors and nights in the White House Lincoln bedroom to contributors, and even use White House holiday cards as thinly veiled fundraising requests?

According to the committee's ranking Democrat, Henry Waxman, Burton's agenda was clear: "These allegations typically had three features in common: they made for dramatic headlines; they consumed considerable resources to investigate; and they ended up being completely unsubstantiated."[58] Lacking any weight beyond length and visibility, the conduct investigations produced a meager two-point footprint.

Despite its historical significance, Clinton's 1998 perjury investigation was only marginally heavier than Burton's conduct reviews. The product of a four-year investigation by independent counsel Kenneth Starr (a former federal judge and solicitor general), the investigation drifted from one allegation to another before finally seizing on allegations that Clinton had perjured himself in denying a sexual affair with White House intern Monica Lewinsky.[59] According to the final 400-page report, which was filled with lurid details about Clinton's sexual habits, Starr came to a widely publicized point:

> In this case, the President made and caused to be made false statements to the American people about his relationship with Ms. Lewinsky. He also made false statements about whether he had lied under oath or otherwise obstructed justice in his civil case. By publicly and emphatically stating in January 1998 that "I did not have sexual relations with that woman" and these "allegations are false," the President also effectively delayed a possible congressional inquiry, and then he further delayed it by asserting Executive Privilege and refusing to testify for six months during the Independent Counsel investigation. This represents substantial and credible information that may constitute grounds for an impeachment.[60]

With Starr's report in hand, the House Judiciary Committee's impeachment investigation began on October 8 and ended barely two months later when the committee approved four articles of impeachment. With Clinton and Starr both on the cover of *Time* as the magazine's men of the year, the House approved two of the four articles on December 19. Clinton's Senate trial on charges of perjury and obstruction of justice began on January 7, paused for the president's awkward State of the Union address, and concluded on February 9. Clinton was acquitted on both charges along party-line votes on February 12.

Despite reams of evidence and testimony, the House impeachment investigation was brief, narrow, simple, led by a virtual unknown investigator (Illinois Republican Rep. Henry Hyde), tightly controlled by the Republican leadership, not remotely interested in exploring the quality of Starr's evidence or intent, and, in my judgment, not at all serious. At the same time, the investigation was undeniably visible, thorough (down to every detail of Lewinsky's infamous blue dress), high leverage, and historically influential. Described as such, the Clinton impeachment inquiry earned a four-point footprint score. It will clearly remain a signal moment far into the future, but would be on few lists of good investigations.

Works in Progress

A handful of my investigations are so recent that they may yet fall off any future list. The next mining accident will rekindle the long-running effort to investigate and regulate the industry, for example, while the Gulf oil spill inquiry will likely continue for a bit longer, as Congress receives updates on costs and consequences.

Consider two examples of works in progress that were still alive in early 2013.

FAST AND FURIOUS (2011)

The Fast and Furious "gun-walking" investigation was the first inquiry launched and led by the new chairman of the House Committee on Oversight and Government Reform, Darrell Issa (R-Calif.). Begun in February 2011 after several whistle-blowers approached Sen. Charles Grassley (R-Iowa) with allegations of a cover-up, Issa soon took the lead as the investigation descended into a partisan battle eerily similar to the Clinton conduct inquiries.[61]

Partisan or not, the review was long, visible, and durable and generated high leverage for action. By October 2012, the committee had issued two subpoenas, held four hearings, deposed twenty-six whistle-blowers, generated three dozen press releases, examined 7,600 pages of documents, built its own website, and persuaded the full House to cite attorney general Eric Holder for contempt of Congress. It was the first contempt citation of a sitting cabinet officer in U.S. history.

Fast and Furious was not a new idea, however. It was vaguely similar to "Operation Wide Receiver," a 2006 Bush administration program designed and executed by the Justice Department's Bureau of Alcohol, Tobacco, and Firearms (ATF). The biggest difference perhaps is that Wide Receiver came late in a second term and involved fewer guns and no visibility, while Fast and Furious came late in a first term and was linked to the death of a U.S. agent.

Regardless of its origins, Fast and Furious was in direct conflict with the ATF's interdiction policy. Instead of making an immediate arrest when a "straw purchaser," or go-between, illegally bought a weapon, ATF agents were ordered to follow the guns as they "walked" into the gun-smuggling stream and up to the top of Mexico's notorious Sinaloa drug cartel.

The idea was that the higher-ups would be caught with the weapons and charged with conspiracy, drug trafficking, money laundering, and other felonies, thereby cutting "off the head of the snake," as the ATF's special agent in charge described the ultimate goal.[62] Arrests would be delayed, the ATF promised, but the perpetrators would be caught and the 2,000 sniper rifles, "AK47-type" automatic weapons, and handguns would be retrieved.

In reality, most of the weapons soon disappeared into the increasingly vicious Mexican drug wars, while others were only retrieved at the scene of a violent crime. Tragically, two of the weapons were found on December 14, 2010, near the body of slain U.S. Border Patrol agent Brian Terry. With front-line agents besieging Congress for action, the program was abandoned, the House investigation began, the U.S. attorney for Arizona was fired, and the ATF's director resigned six months later.

The investigation might have ended then but for the Justice Department's February 4 letter stating that the ATF "makes every effort to interdict weapons that have been purchased illegally and prevent their transportation to Mexico," not to mention a terse "hell, no" denial from the bureau's Phoenix Field Division.[63] The more the Justice Department tried to backtrack from these initial denials, the more Issa wanted to know about the attorney general's role in reshaping the story about the operation, which he later called the product of "felony stupid bad judgment."[64] Issa's concern was only heightened ten months later when the Justice Department withdrew its letter because it contained "inaccuracies."[65]

Frustrated by what he saw as election-year stonewalling, Issa accused Holder of a cover-up only hours before the committee issued its October 11, 2011, subpoena demanding all Justice Department documents and e-mails related to the operation:

> Mr. Attorney General, you have made numerous statements about Fast and Furious that have eventually been proven to be untrue. Your lack of trustworthiness while speaking about Fast and Furious has called into question your overall credibility as Attorney General. The time for deflecting blame and obstructing our investigation is over. The time has come for you to come clean to the American public about what you knew about Fast and Furious, when you knew it, and who is going to be held accountable for failing to shut down a

program that has already had deadly consequences, and will likely cause more casualties for years to come.

Operation Fast and Furious was the Department's most significant gun-trafficking case. It related to two of your major initiatives—destroying the Mexican cartels and reducing gun violence on both sides of the border. On your watch, it went spectacularly wrong. Whether you realize yet or not, you own Fast and Furious. It is your responsibility.[66]

The investigation was predictably divisive, with Democrats working to defend the administration as the election year progressed, even producing their own staff report in early 2012 clearing Holder and his high-level lieutenants of any wrongdoing.[67] Issa was undeterred, however, and began building the case for the contempt citation. He released his draft citation and background memorandum on May 3, 2012.

Measured by the eleven weights, the investigation was long, free to investigate, and visible and created high leverage for action during its first eighteen months, but it still had not established its breadth, complexity, seriousness, thoroughness, and durability by the end of 2012 and was never going to be bipartisan.[68] Issa would argue that the investigation could only be serious and thorough with full access to Justice Department's documents and e-mails, but the record suggests that the inquiry was less interested in the systemic problems that led to the failed operation in the first place than in the attorney general's involvement in both approving the operation and denying its failure.

The attack produced more than rhetoric, however. It also involved a constitutional showdown when the administration invoked executive privilege on June 20 to shield the Justice Department from the October 11 subpoena.

More controversy was sure to follow. Within hours, the committee voted 23-17 along party lines to forward its contempt citation to the full House. The *New York Times* summarized the quarrel in an editorial the next day, arguing that the investigation had blossomed into a full-fledged fiasco: "Executive privilege cannot and should not be allowed to shield the executive branch from regular, valuable Congressional oversight. There was no reason the House committee and the Justice Department could not work out a deal to produce the documents requested or some form of them. Instead, they show again that every issue, large or small, can be turned into ammunition for political combat."[69]

Nevertheless, the House soon approved the contempt citation in a lopsided 255-67 vote as Democrats left the chamber in droves. The U.S. attorney for the

District of Columbia soon announced that he would not and could not pros-
ecute the case given the president's claim of executive privilege, thereby assuring that the investigation would continue at least until the November election,
if not beyond.[70] Indeed, Mitt Romney even described the operation as "the
biggest failure we've had in regards to gun violence" in an October town hall
presidential debate.[71] His comments were soon followed by the October 29
release of a joint staff report titled *Fast and Furious: The Anatomy of a Failed
Operation*, prepared for Issa and Grassley.[72]

SOLYNDRA CORPORATION (2011)

The Solyndra investigation began just after the Fast and Furious investigation and started out in the House Energy and Commerce Committee's
Subcommittee on Oversight and Investigations. Led by a little-known, about-
to-retire chairman, Rep. Cliff Stearns (R-Fla.), and with the full support and frequent participation of the full committee's chairman, Fred Upton (R-Mich.), the
investigation produced six hearings, two subpoenas, and thirty-five press
releases over its two-year review. The investigation also featured a thirty-minute
hearing on September 23, 2011, that began with fiery opening statements from
Upton and Stearns and ended minutes later after Solyndra's president and chief
executive officer Brian Harrison and his chief financial officer both invoked
their Fifth Amendment rights against self-incrimination.[73]

The investigation was built on allegations that the Obama administration
had pressured the Department of Energy to make the $535 million loan guar-
antee despite early signals that the company was in financial trouble and then
interfered to delay Solyndra's collapse prior to a vice presidential visit just
before the 2010 midterm elections. Although the investigation never found
firm evidence of White House interference prior to the loan closing on
November 3, 2010, the majority staff did reach a broad finding in what the
committee and subcommittee called a final report on August 12, 2012:

> After an extensive investigation which included reviewing over
> 300,000 pages of documents, interviewing numerous individuals
> who played a role in the Solyndra loan guarantee, and holding five
> hearings before the Subcommittee on Oversight and Investigations,
> it is clear DOE [Department of Energy] should never have issued the
> loan guarantee to Solyndra and that DOE violated the plain lan-
> guage of the law when it restructured the terms of the loan guaran-
> tee and subordinated the taxpayers' interest to the interests of two
> private equity investors . . . Solyndra should stand as a cautionary

tale of what happens when an Administration ties itself to a project so closely that it becomes the poster child of its signature economic policy: when that project fails, interests other than the taxpayers' come into play. In fact, throughout the Committee's investigation, Administration officials and representatives of Solyndra made public statements trumpeting the company right up until the time it filed for bankruptcy in September 2011.[74]

Like Fast and Furious, the Solyndra investigation had all the hallmarks of a long-running, bitterly partisan investigation. Yet it also received significant support from liberal and conservative editorial boards alike, most notably at the *New York Times*, which titled its November 25, 2011, commentary "The Solyndra Mess." Although the *Times* chastised the committee's failure to produce evidence of political favoritism, it also argued that allegations about the Obama administration's effort to prevent a political disaster "were not unfounded."[75]

Also like Fast and Furious, the Solyndra investigation depended in part on the sluggish White House response to its subpoenas and was clearly designed to expose White House interference in the loan decision just before Vice President Biden's visit to the plant. Although the George W. Bush administration engaged in similar tampering in 2006, the alleged effort to delay Solyndra's bankruptcy, employee firings, and default until after the midterms was ill considered, if not strictly illegal.

Finally, also like Fast and Furious, the Solyndra investigation was narrow, not particularly complex, led by a little-known chairman, operated with little freedom to investigate, was not particularly thorough, and produced little durability beyond its use as a cudgel in the 2012 presidential campaign.

Obviously, the investigation was not bipartisan, and even Energy and Commerce Republicans noted the underlying political motivations. "Our staff will continue to dig into it and see," Rep. Jim Jordan (R-Ohio) remarked in late March 2012. "But what I hope happens is we stop doing these kind of things. Ultimately, we'll stop it on Election Day, hopefully. And bringing attention to these things helps the voters and citizens of the country make the decision that I hope helps them as they evaluate who they are going to vote for in November."[76]

As if to prove that a scandal is a terrible thing to waste, the House Oversight and Government Reform Committee soon took control of the flagging investigation. According to a March 20, 2012, staff report titled "The Department of Energy's Disastrous Management of Loan Guarantee Programs," Solyndra was just the beginning of the committee's hunt for further scandal. "This report will demonstrate how DOE loan commitments exposed taxpayer funds to excessive risk as a result of DOE's bias toward approving loans without regard to warning signs," the majority staff argued in the first paragraph of its executive summary:

> After conducting a substantial review of the Department of Energy's (DOE) loan guarantee program, it is clear that the significant losses absorbed by taxpayers as a result of Solyndra's collapse [are] just the beginning. The investigation conducted by the House Committee on Oversight and Government Reform has uncovered numerous examples of dysfunction, negligence, and mismanagement by DOE officials, raising troubling questions about the leadership at DOE and how it has administered its loan guarantee programs.[77]

Solyndra may yet live on past the end of the Obama administration if the House Oversight and Government Reform Committee and Issa continue the investigation. At least through the end of 2012, Issa put his energy into Fast and Furious, leaving Solyndra on hold for possible resurrection if and when the Holder subpoena worked its will.

A NEW LOOK AT BLUE-RIBBON COMMISSIONS

The twenty-eight blue-ribbon commissions reviewed in this analysis provide an opportunity to resolve, or at least advance, the debates about the role of presidential and congressional blue-ribbon commissions as an investigatory instrument. Although the literature on commissions has been characterized by some as "scarce" and "under-tilled," enough theory and data are in play to have established several major findings.

This small field of study has made significant progress, for example, in defining terms, and no one has made a more important contribution in doing so than Amy B. Zegart. Working off a daunting list of commissions that were created between 1981 and 2001, Zegart set three criteria for calling a commission a commission: (1) it had to be ad hoc, not permanent, meaning that it could not last more than four years, (2) it had to have been officially established, be it through executive order, directive, legislation, or formal appointment, but could have been created by a range of actors from the president, senior agency officers, one chamber of Congress, and even one or two members of Congress, and (3) it had to operate at least partially outside of government with at least three members, one of whom had to be a private citizen.[78]

After setting the limits, Zegart then joined a short list of scholars who have attempted to categorize blue-ribbon commissions by purpose or type. Thomas Wolanin began the process with three categories (policy analysis, educational, and "window dressing"), followed by Terrence R. Tutchings with three (corporate-governmental, public interest, and balanced), David Filtner with two (educational and legitimizing), Kenneth Kitts with three (procedure-oriented, situation-oriented, or crisis-oriented), Zegart with three (agenda, information, and political constellation), James P. Pfiffner with three (investigative and information gathering, policy agenda, and organizational reform), and Jordan Tama with two (crisis and agenda).[79] Three may be the preferred number, but the difference is obviously in the details.

Comparing Commissions

Much as one can admire these past efforts, especially those with relatively large numbers of cases, I did not start my project to study blue-ribbon commission. At least for this book, a commission was and still is just one of several venues for investigation that often have several different characteristics, leave very different footprints, and have different levels of impact.

Nevertheless, measured by the investigatory characteristics described in all three demographic overviews in this book, the twenty blue-ribbon commissions created by presidents and the eight created by Congress have very distinct characteristics compared to the other competing venues for investigations. As such, they offer a chance to explore at least some of the conventional wisdom about how blue-ribbon commissions achieve weight and impact.

Recall from chapter 2, for example, that commissions became a more popular destination after Watergate, rising from eight before Nixon's resignation to twenty after. There were just two commissions during the entire post–World War II period, another six during the Great Society era, and ten each during the congressional resurgence and divided government periods. Commissions were also more likely to be found in first terms (seventeen to eleven) and to be launched in presidential or midterm election years (seventeen to eleven again). Also recall that twenty of my twenty-eight blue-ribbon commissions were created by the presidency, compared with just seven by the Senate and one by the House. Commissions are the exclusive tool for ad hoc presidential investigations, an occasional tool for the Senate (one-seventh of its total), and a very rare event for the House (one out of the thirty-one investigations on the list).

Moreover, contrary to theories that commissions are somehow an escape from the partisanship associated with today's divided government, there is no discernible pattern in the use of commissions under different conditions of party control—for example, 61 percent of investigations in commissions occurred during divided government compared with 64 percent of investigations in other venues, while 25 percent of investigations in commissions occurred during divided congresses compared with 14 percent of investigations in other venues.

Investigatory characteristics provide more context for understanding why commissions might be so attractive to presidents and Congress during recent decades.

—Ten of the commissions were sparked by a fire alarm and eighteen by a police patrol. Although eight of the presidential commissions were launched by a crisis such as urban riots, the Kent State killings, and the 9/11 attacks, the other twelve developed over a longer period as presidents considered the need for some way either to accelerate a national conversation or to dispose of a lingering issue.

—Nineteen of the commissions focused on domestic issues, while nine involved foreign issues. There was no difference in the use of commissions as a proportion of investigations of domestic or foreign issues in any venue.

—Fifteen of the commissions focused on process breakdowns such as defense fraud, waste, and abuse, while thirteen involved policy breakdowns such as Social Security financing. There were no commissions on personal misconduct.

—Fifteen of the commissions focused on repairing a past breakdown such as Internal Revenue Service taxpayer abuse, while thirteen turned to preventing a future breakdown such as terrorist attacks. Presidential commissions were more likely than congressional commissions to focus on prevention, however. All eight of the congressional blue-ribbon commissions centered on repair, while thirteen of the twenty presidential blue-ribbon commissions focused on prevention. This pattern suggests that presidents may have been using their commissions to explore and legitimize future action or simply to "kick the can down the road," as members of the 2010 Simpson-Bowles deficit reduction commission often put it.

—Twenty-one of the commissions focused on fact finding, while just seven focused on blame setting. By contrast, forty-eight of the investigations conducted in venues other than commissions, such as committees and subcommittees, focused on blame setting, compared with just twenty-four focused on fact finding. However, six of the seven blame-setting commissions came from the presidency, not Congress. Presidents seemed quite willing to launch commissions designed to find the "wrongdoers," whether in the Kennedy assassination, urban riots, or the *Challenger* and *Columbia* accidents.

Given the earlier demographic analysis, it is no surprise that commissions would have heavier footprints than other venues. On average, for example, the commissions had a 6.9-point footprint, compared with a 4.4 for their peers. If commissions were the perfect instruments for finding answers to government breakdowns, of course, they would have scored much higher on average. But they are not always the heavier option.

On the positive side of the good investigation, commissions tend to be broader than competing venues (61 percent versus 31 percent), to take on more complex issues (75 percent versus 25 percent), to have well-known leadership (57 percent versus 28 percent), and to be much more serious (89 percent versus 46 percent), thorough (75 percent versus 50 percent), and durable (57 percent versus 29 percent) and much more bipartisan (89 percent versus 42 percent). On the negative side, compared with other venues, commissions are more likely to last less than a year (57 percent versus 38 percent), barely more likely to have the freedom to investigate (57 percent versus 51 percent), and barely less likely to produce high visibility (61 percent versus 63 percent). They show no advantage on leverage (68 percent for each). In short, they may be heavier, but they would not be the choice for all breakdowns, and some show the clear markers of a "window dressing" investigation, such as lack of visibility, seriousness, thoroughness, leverage, and durability.

Another Inventory of Examples

The value of commissions is easier to detect in the three weight classes discussed above. Just 11 percent of investigations by commissions were lightweights, compared with 40 percent of investigations in other venues. Although the two groups were about equal in their proportion of middleweights (39 percent for commissions versus 36 percent for other venues), commissions had a substantial edge in producing heavyweights (50 percent versus 25 percent).

As with the earlier vignettes on weight classes, which included Hoover's government reorganization effort, the following histories show how commissions create their footprints based in large part on their purpose and methodology.

HEAVYWEIGHTS

Many blue-ribbon heavyweights are described elsewhere in this book, but two deserve a deeper review here to show how highly charged issues sometimes take commissions toward unexpected results.

Start with the National Advisory Commission on Civil Disorders, which was created by Lyndon Johnson and chaired by Governor Otto Kerner (D-Ill.). The investigation was triggered by a long list of riots that started in Los Angeles in 1965, spread to Chicago in 1966, and jumped to Newark and Detroit in

1967. Launched by executive order on July 27 as Detroit burned, Johnson demanded answers to three basic questions: "What happened? Why did it happen? What can be done to prevent it from happening again?"[80]

The commission responded with an onslaught of social science data showing the impact of poverty on urban anger.[81] The commission responded with one of the most memorable opening arguments in blue-ribbon history:

> This is our basic conclusion: Our nation is moving toward two societies, one black, one white—separate and unequal.
>
> Reaction to last summer's disorders has quickened the movement and deepened the division. Discrimination and segregation have long permeated much of American life; they now threaten the future of every American.
>
> This deepening racial division is not inevitable. The movement can be reversed. Choice is still possible.[82]

The commission's final report moved quickly to its impassioned call for reform and a long list of recommendations for bringing the nation together. If book sales are any measure of potential durability, the investigation held up well in the first few years, at 2 million copies and climbing. But it was generally dismissed by Johnson, who was said to be angry about the lack of support for his Great Society programs and civil rights legislation. Johnson never said a thing about the commission, however, and is said to have sent a senior White House aide to greet Kerner in the White House lobby to receive the report.[83]

Nevertheless, the report did have some leverage on Capitol Hill, where the Senate began building new low-income housing legislation based on the report. And it had lasting, if not high-impact, support for decades. This momentum was soon interrupted by another round of more than 100 riots following Martin Luther King's assassination. The investigation earned a nine-point footprint, nonetheless, including one point for its durability.

Next, think of the three commissions established in the years before the 9/11 attacks. Unlike the 1996 White House Commission on Aviation and Security chaired by Vice President Al Gore in the wake of the TWA Flight 800 disaster, the three terrorism commissions established two years later not only focused on the future, but also argued that nonstate terrorism was a clear threat inside the United States.

None of the three was more important to the call for action than the 1998 U.S. Commission on National Security in the Twenty-First Century co-chaired by former senators Gary Hart (D-Colo.) and Warren Rudman (R-N.H.). Authorized by the secretary of defense, the Hart/Rudman Commission was the last of the three majors to join the call for action, but it became the primary one through sheer force of leadership. Without denigrating the heavy lifting done by the Advisory Panel to Assess Domestic Response Capabilities for Terrorism Involving Weapons of Mass Destruction chaired by former Virginia Republican governor James S. Gilmore III or the National Commission on Terrorism chaired by former U.S. ambassador L. Paul Bremer III, the Hart-Rudman Commission claimed the lion's share of visibility and created an aura of seriousness and thoroughness commensurate with the threats at hand. It also produced a prescient statement of coming consequence in its very first report titled "New World Coming":

> In the years ahead, borders of every sort—geographical, communal, and psychological—will be stressed, strained, and compelled to reconfiguration. As the elements and vulnerabilities of national power shift, they will often leave current institutional arrangements at loggerheads with reality. Already the traditional functions of law, police work, and military power have begun to blur before our eyes as new threats arise.
>
> Notable among these new threats is the prospect of an attack on U.S. cities by independent or state-supported terrorists using weapons of mass destruction. Traditional distinctions between national defense and domestic security will be challenged further as the new century unfolds, and both conventional policies and bureaucratic arrangements will be stretched to and beyond the breaking point unless those policies and arrangements are reformed.[84]

MIDDLEWEIGHTS

Other middleweight commissions are also discussed in the book, but two more show the role of blue-ribbon commissions in addressing technical issues.

Start with the 1979 Three Mile Island Commission that was created by executive order two weeks after the March 28 partial nuclear meltdown at the Dauphin, Pennsylvania, power plant. The accident provoked intense public concern and heavy media coverage of the subsequent investigations (for example, 753 *New York Times* articles in the year following the accident, starting with eighty-three in the first week alone). It also generated $51 million in ticket sales and four Academy Award nominations for *The China Syndrome*, which hit movie theaters just twelve days after the meltdown.[85]

With Dartmouth College president John Kemeny at the helm, the commission took what one nuclear industry representative called a "proceed, but proceed with caution," approach.[86] As if to punctuate its aversion to media coverage, the commission released its final report on Christmas Day with a handful of small-scale recommendations that led with a modest reorganization of the Nuclear Regulatory Commission.[87]

The commission also restricted its review solely to Three Mile Island, not to the nuclear power industry more complexly embraced. As if to illustrate this point, the commission's preface to its final report spent almost as much space describing what it did not do as what it did:

> We did not examine the entire nuclear industry . . . We have not looked at the military applications of nuclear energy. We did not consider nuclear weapons proliferation . . . We have not dealt with the question of the disposal of radioactive waste or the dangers of the accumulation of waste fuel within nuclear power plants adjacent to the containment buildings . . . We made no attempt to examine the entire fuel cycle, starting with the mining of uranium. And, of course, we made no examination of the many other sources of radiation, both natural and man-made, that affect all of us . . . We have not attempted to evaluate the relative risks involved in alternate sources of energy . . . We did not attempt to reach a conclusion as to whether, as a matter of public policy, the development of commercial nuclear power should be continued or should not be continued. That would require a much broader investigation, involving economic, environmental, and political considerations.[88]

Although the Three Mile Island investigation was visible, serious, thorough, and bipartisan, it did not tackle the underlying political complexity of the breakdown, focusing mostly on technical issues surrounding the failed cooling system. The investigation also had a little-known, but technically savvy, leader, lacked the freedom to investigate (it was constrained by the White House and the nuclear power industry), exerted little pressure for its muted recommendations, and produced little durability. The investigation generated a four-point footprint score as a result.[89] However, its recommendations were even less aggressive than the Nuclear Regulatory Commission's, which had already imposed a voluntary moratorium on further plant construction by the time the commission finished its work. Not surprising given its footprint and lack of leverage, it easily earned a one-point impact score for negligible effect.

Turn next to the Presidential Commission on the Human Immunodeficiency Virus (HIV) Epidemic, which was created by Reagan's executive order on June 24, 1987. As directed by the order, the commission presented its report exactly one year later. Led by a former chief of naval operations, James D.

Watkins, the commission's final report started with an entire page devoted to John Donne's meditation "No Man Is an Island" and continued with 600 recommendations, some substantive and others hortatory.[90]

However, even its chairman recognized the lack of hard facts on which to base policy: "Semen, blood, and ignorance surround this epidemic," he said at one point, "and we were in the last category."[91] Washington generally received the report with a warm embrace, but little direct commitment. And though the report did support increased research spending, it sought to balance the needs of HIV victims and society as a whole. "To slow or stop the spread of the virus, to provide proper medical care for those who have contracted the virus, and to protect the rights of both infected and non-infected persons requires a careful balancing of interests in a highly complex society." Not too much action, the report seemed to say, but not too little.

As for the twenty recommendations that the commission singled out in its preface for special attention, many were no doubt well supported by the evidence, but too broad for action. After telling Americans that the term "AIDS" should be replaced by "HIV infection," the commission's top twenty became ever more specific, including calls for federal protection against discrimination, privacy protections, more nursing scholarships, increased research funding, better training for health care professionals, and greater attention to ethical issues such as the "responsibility of all citizens to treat HIV-infected persons with respect and compassion."[92] Ultimately, the commission's greatest impact may have been an acknowledgment that the federal government had been late to the issue, and negligent in its support.

To this day, it is not clear how many of the recommendations were implemented and which ones had any lasting effect. Although the effort was broad, free to investigate, serious, and thorough and accepted the complexity of the issue, it lacked the other markers of a heavyweight investigation, perhaps most notably a lack of sure bipartisanship due to the appointment of alleged Reagan allies who fought to protect the administration's record. The ultimate hero of the effort turned out to be Watkins. Like many commission chairmen and women, Watkins was not an expert on HIV when he gaveled the commission to order, but he proved an eager student and eventually led the investigation through a serious, thorough, and bipartisan review, and to a unanimous conclusion.

LIGHTWEIGHTS

There are just three lightweight commissions among the twenty-eight on the list. But like the Three Mile Island commission, two quick vignettes suggest that they suffered largely because they had little freedom to investigate the breakdowns at hand.

Start with the 1970 investigation of the Kent State University tragedy. Created by executive order on June 13, 1970, the commission was chaired by former Pennsylvania Republican governor William Scranton. Widely viewed as window dressing, the review was triggered by the killings of four Kent State students after young, poorly trained national guardsmen fired a deadly volley into a group of students protesting the U.S. incursion into Cambodia. The Nixon administration might have sidestepped the issue but for the killing of two Jackson State students by local police only weeks later.

At first read, the commission's final report seems more like a college lecture on civil society than an investigatory summary. Indeed, the very first page of the report critiques the confusion associated with the term "campus unrest." According to the commission, the term meant all things to all people, vacillating between the "the desirable and the abhorrent, between activities which the university and society should encourage or must tolerate, and those which they must seek to prevent and must deal with firmly."[93]

Moreover, the commission made few substantive recommendations, brushed off allegations that the national guardsmen acted without cause, and mostly avoided the minute-by-minute timetables so frequently associated with many of the fire alarm investigations profiled in this book. In a sense, the commission was neither a fact-finding nor a blame-setting exercise. It had too little time for the former and very little desire for the latter.

Yet on a second reading, the report feels much more courageous, even to the point of taking a direct shot at the president. Indeed, the commission directed its toughest recommendation to the president. Urging the president to "exercise his reconciling moral leadership" to end the violence and explain the underlying causes of campus unrest. "To this end, nothing is more important than an end to war in Indochina," the commission argued. "Disaffected students see the war as a symbol of moral crisis in the nation which, in their eyes, deprives even law of its legitimacy."[94]

Obviously, the White House was not pleased. Republicans joined en masse to mount their own attacks on the report, and Vice President Spiro T. Agnew called the commission's report "imprecise, contradictory, and equivocal."[95] Having taken a much tougher stand than most observers expected, the commission was anything but window dressing. To the contrary, the commission's report put the onus on the president and managed to bring a visible and bipartisan conclusion to bear on the national debate. Nevertheless, it was short, narrow, and defined the breakdown in narrow terms and only created weight through its visibility in the wake of the tragedy and its bipartisanship. The report may have been aggressive, but the investigation was a disappointment in resolving the lingering doubt about why the shots were fired during the protests.

Turn next to the 2003 shuttle *Columbia* investigation, which was designed to repair a program that was already scheduled for termination. The investigation was launched on February 2, barely a day after the shuttle was torn apart upon reentry, and was initially led by an eight-member board appointed by the National Aeronautics and Space Administration (NASA) administrator, Sean O'Keefe. Facing allegations that O'Keefe had packed the board with NASA supporters and staffed it with senior managers involved in the flight and at the urging of the board's chair, the White House took quick ownership of the effort by adding former astronaut and *Challenger* commission member Sally Ride and four other members to what was now a de facto presidential blue-ribbon commission.

Rearmed and repurposed somewhat, the Columbia Accident Investigation Board proceeded with NASA "can-do" bravado, deploying 120 staffers, borrowing another 400 engineers, reviewing 30,000 documents, conducting 200 interviews, and managing a website that received 40 million (yes, 40 million) hits during the short review. The investigation was no doubt serious, bipartisan, and visible. And it was studiously consumed with fact finding, albeit mostly regarding the technical failure and safety system and, arguably, without the freedom, expertise, or interest to pursue questions of accountability, White House budget cutting, and the administrator's own involvement in flight management decisions. As the board argued in its final report, complex systems fail in complex ways, leading many investigations astray: "Too often, accident investigations blame a failure only on the last step in a complex process, when a more comprehensive understanding of that process could reveal that earlier steps might be equally or even more culpable."[96]

Moreover, like the 1986 *Challenger* accident discussed in chapter 4, the blame was easy to assign—a piece of foam insulation the size of a briefcase had broken off the tip of the shuttle's liquid fuel tank and struck the shuttle's left wing with such force that it tore off a large patch of heat-deflecting tiles. As one investigator later put it, the shuttle's wing "rang like a bell" when the foam broke off 82 seconds after lift-off. Although the foam only weighed two pounds, more or less, it struck the wing at roughly 500 miles an hour, exerting a ton of force.[97]

Yet, even with the culprit identified and an explicit acknowledgment that this was an accident rooted in the same history that destroyed *Challenger*, the board devoted just 16 pages of its 248-page report to organizational causes, including an introduction to organization theory, a quick review of past NASA management reforms, a discussion of the Navy's submarine reactor safety system, and a one-page primer on the dangers of PowerPoint presentations.[98]

The board was hardly naïve about politics and lobbying and signaled its concerns about the "original compromises that were required to gain approvals for the Shuttle, subsequent years of resource constraints, budgeting priorities, schedule pressures, mischaracterization of the Shuttle as operational rather than development, and lack of an agreed upon national vision for human space flight." But what was the board to do about unraveling that record? Although the board did suggest more disciplined risk analysis and tighter reporting chains, it rarely strayed from solving the "before the flight" and "before the return to flight" technical problems that would allow the shuttle to fly again. Space flight is a dangerous and complex undertaking, the board said over and over, and *Columbia* proved the point.[99]

However, the real question was not whether space flight is risky, but whether NASA took risks that were beyond acceptable. After all, this was not the first time that foam had struck a shuttle. As another former *Challenger* commissioner, Richard P. Feynman, argued in unsolicited testimony, the answer was all in the hierarchy:

> It appears that there are enormous differences of opinion as to the probability of a failure with loss of vehicle and of human life. The estimates range from roughly 1 in 100 to 1 in 100,000. The higher figures come from the working engineers, and the very low figures from management. What are the causes and consequences of this lack of agreement? Since 1 part in 100,000 would imply that one could put a Shuttle up each day for 300 years expecting to lose only one, we could properly ask "What is the cause of management's fantastic faith in the machinery?"[100]

It was the core question never answered as the shuttle program moved toward its inevitable end, leaving the board with little to show for its effort despite its acknowledgment of a tragedy revisited and its own bit of the same "groupthink" that some experts believe was the root cause of both shuttle catastrophes.[101]

Explaining Commission Footprints

Advanced statistical analysis of the twenty-eight commissions is risky at best given the small number. Moreover, advanced analysis turns out to be entirely futile. None of the investigatory characteristics produced any significant if/then significance in my regressions. Nor did the measure of history and party control.

Nevertheless, commission designers are always free to use the four statistically significant yes-no relationships between the investigatory characteristics and footprints for cautious advice:

—Put Congress in the lead. The eight congressionally sponsored commissions simply had a better track record as exemplars of the "good commission" than presidential commissions, in part perhaps because Congress only creates commissions as a last resort and therefore designs them carefully to be effective, not window dressing.

—Put the Senate in the lead. Among the congressional commissions, Senate-sponsored commissions also have a better track record than House-sponsored peers, in part because the Senate tends to emphasize the bipartisanship and overall commitment of commissions to results.

—Focus on repair. Because repairs often involve an urgent crisis such as Social Security reform or the 9/11 attacks, they appear to model the good commission.

The overall results presented here should remind investigators that commissions are just one of several venues available for their work. The question is not why commissions create weight, but whether they are the best venue for the good investigation under given circumstances. Moreover, although Watergate did create a dividing line in the number of commissions, it did not reveal any significant difference before and after, in part because there were so few commissions before Watergate.

EXPLAINING FOOTPRINTS

Returning to all 100 investigations on my list, this section of the chapter addresses a single, but hardly simple, question: How do history, investigatory characteristics, and party control affect the weight of an investigation, and, therefore, what can investigators do to increase the odds of a good investigation?

There are two ways to answer this question: (1) correlations between potential predictors and each of the eleven weights and (2) statistical competitions using regressions, which pit a group of measures such as investigatory characteristics against each of the eleven weights and the overall footprint score to see which ones matter most in predicting overall weight. The adjusted

R^2 provided at the top of each regression shows the overall strength of each competition in explaining footprints. Most of the competitions earned very high marks on this measure, but, as with many regressions, substantial variation is always left unexplained.

A First Answer

Once again, correlations provide a useful tool for exploring the relationships between history, investigatory characteristics, and party control as potential predictors and footprints as the potential consequence. However, most of the significant relationships involve investigatory characteristics.

HISTORY

There were seven significant correlations between my historical measures and the eleven weights. Freedom to investigate declined after Watergate, while leverage rose (periods show the same pattern, which is not surprising). In turn, breadth and complexity both rose in a president's second term.

Despite the earlier, but generally modest, percentage-by-percentage effects on several footprints, presidential term produced just one significant correlation (freedom to investigate), while election year produced none. Since history cannot be changed, investigators cannot find any advice in these relationships, but they can be aware of the potential weights created by starting their work in a second term.

INVESTIGATORY CHARACTERISTICS

Investigatory characteristics produced a long list of significant relationships with each of the eleven weights. Six of the correlations involved commissions, which produced positive associations with breadth, complexity, well-known leadership, seriousness, durability, and bipartisanship. Another six involved fact finding, which produced positive associations with complexity, well-known leadership, seriousness, thoroughness, leverage, durability, and bipartisanship, while blame setting showed the same associations in the opposite direction as fact finding's pure opposite.

In turn, another four involved fire alarms, which produced negative associations with seriousness, thoroughness, and bipartisanship, but a positive association with visibility, while police patrols showed the same associations in the opposite direction as fire alarm's opposite. Finally, four involved personal misconduct, which produced negative associations with the freedom to investigate, seriousness, thoroughness, and bipartisanship.

Again assuming more broadly that investigatory characteristics might predict each of the eleven weights, investigators might take note of the following speculative advice based on the strongest correlations in the analysis:

—If investigators want a long investigation, they should look to Congress, not the presidency, and avoid fact finding.

—If investigators want a broad investigation, they should avoid the House and use a commission.

—If investigators want a complex investigation, they should avoid Congress, avoid full committees and subcommittees, use a commission, and focus on fact finding.

—If investigators want well-known leadership at the helm, they should avoid the House, use a commission, ignore fire alarms, and focus on fact finding.

—If investigators want the freedom to investigate, they should avoid the use of full committees and steer away from investigations of personal misconduct.[102]

—If investigators want a visible investigation, they should pay attention to fire alarms.

—If investigators want a serious investigation, they should look to the presidency, not Congress, avoid full committees, use a commission, avoid fire alarms, avoid investigations of personal misconduct, and focus on fact finding.

—If investigators want a thorough investigation, they should avoid full committees, use a commission, ignore fire alarms, avoid investigations of personal misconduct, and focus on fact finding.

—If investigators want to create a high-leverage investigation, they should target a process breakdown.

—If investigators want a durable investigation they should use a commission and focus on fact finding.

—If investigators want a bipartisan investigation, they should look to the presidency for the lead, avoid the House, avoid full committees, use a commission, ignore fire alarms, avoid investigations of personal misconduct, and focus on fact finding.

PARTY CONTROL

Finally, there were just five strong relationships between party control and the eleven weights. One involved the freedom to investigate, which had a strong relationship with investigations launched and led in a Democratic Congress, while the other four involved thoroughness, which had strong positive relationships with investigations that occurred during (1) unified party control of government, (2) unified Democratic control of both branches of government, (3) unified party control of both chambers of Congress, and (4) Democratic control of Congress.

Four of these relationships disappeared, however, when Watergate was used as a dividing line in the analysis. There were no strong relationships between party control and the eleven weights in the forty-two investigations that occurred before Watergate and just one relationship between thoroughness and a Democratic Congress after Watergate. Although this relationship did meet the test of statistical significance, it was far from the highest level, leaving the relationship between party control and the eleven weights almost null.

A Second Answer

The second method for predicting footprints uses a statistical tool called regression, which is more precisely labeled ordinary least squares regression (OLS). Simply described, regression pits a group of independent measures such as investigatory characteristics against a dependent measure such as the eleven-point footprint score to see which ones have the greatest statistical power. In theory, the results of these statistical competitions or tournaments should help investigators to make choices as they begin their search for answers about what happened and how to produce high impact. Readers will find technical details on interpreting regressions in the endnote attached to this sentence.[103]

The following pages summarize three regressions using investigatory characteristics to predict footprints. The first section attempts to predict each of the eleven characteristics using all of the investigations on my list (tables D-1 through D-11 in appendix D); the second section attempts to predict the final eleven-point footprint score, again using all of the investigations (table D-12); while the third and final section attempts to predict the final eleven-point score among the forty-four investigations that occurred after Watergate and during divided government, meaning the prevailing conditions that are likely to hold in the immediate future (table D-13).

INVESTIGATORY CHARACTERISTICS → ELEVEN FOOTPRINT WEIGHTS

The first set of competitions presented here uses institutional home, venue, trigger, issue, breakdown, purpose, and method to predict each of the eleven footprint weights. Footprints are assumed to be the first product of investigatory characteristics, not vice versa, but it can be argued that some desired footprints such as visibility drive the choice of characteristics such as venue and method.

All but one of the regressions produced lessons for investigators, although it not always clear that investigators have the power to take action on every recommendation. All of the results listed here are presented in order of their statistical significance, accompanied by a piece of advice to investigators.

—There were two significant predictors of longer investigations: giving Congress the lead and avoiding fact finding. Congress usually has the time and institutional memory to mount long-running investigations and tends to stretch out blame-setting investigations as long as possible, perhaps in the search for partisan advantage.

—There were four significant predictors of broader investigations: using a blue-ribbon commission, giving Congress the lead, avoiding process break-downs, and picking a domestic issue. Commissions and Congress have the resources and mandates to examine broad causes and consequences, process breakdowns are often narrow by nature, and domestic issues may provide more opportunity to explore the systemic issues underlying failure.

—There were two significant predictors of complex investigations: using a commission and avoiding a process breakdown. Commissions generally have the authority to range widely, but many process breakdowns involve relatively simple missteps.

—There was just one significant predictor of having well-known leadership at the investigatory helm: focusing on fact finding. Finding the facts is one way investigators become well known, especially if the facts lead to a noticeable fix.

—There was only one significant predictor of having the freedom to investigate: avoiding investigations of personal misconduct. The ethical lapses associated with misconduct are so threatening to the party in power during unified government that investigators rarely operate with the freedom to investigate.

—There was just one significant predictor of visibility: avoiding police patrols, which means paying attention to fire alarms. Doing so makes perfect sense given the media attention associated with the events that excite the investigatory fire brigades.

—There was just one significant predictor of seriousness: picking a domestic issue. This is not to suggest that foreign issues generate more frivolous inquiries, but domestic issues often require confrontations with existing interests and heavy lobbying surrounding complex topics.

—There was just one significant predictor of thoroughness: using fact finding.

—There was just one significant predictor of leverage: giving Congress the lead. Again, the result makes perfect sense, if only because Congress has so much firepower to convert investigatory findings into action.

—There were two significant predictors of durability: using a commission and avoiding process breakdowns. Commissions tend to produce reports with very long shelf lives, not to mention having very long-living members who continue to lobby for their findings well past the last meeting. In contrast, process breakdowns rarely have the appeal to stay in play—they either fix the problem and disappear or fail to fix the problem and disappear.

—There were no significant predictors of bipartisanship among the investigatory characteristics tested in my analysis.

These predictions create a series of investigatory dilemmas. If investigators want visibility and durability, for example, they are well advised to pay attention to fire alarms, but if they want length, they are well advised to focus on police patrols. If they want to attract well-known leaders, create leverage, and ensure durability, they should give Congress the lead; if they want the freedom to investigate, they are well advised to avoid investigations of personal breakdowns, which are often tightly controlled by their institutional and party leadership; and if they want to tackle a complex issue and create durability, they should use a commission.

INVESTIGATORY CHARACTERISTICS → ELEVEN-POINT FOOTPRINT SCORE

All of these choices depend on what Congress and the president want, but one pattern seems clear from the correlations: fact finding, not blame setting, is the best strategy for creating the kind of long, serious, thorough, and bipartisan investigations codified in the standard definition of the good investigation.

This hypothesis is well tested in a competition pitting these investigatory characteristics against each other in predicting overall footprints. Here, the analysis is not between the investigatory characteristics and each of the eleven weights, but between the investigatory characteristics and the final eleven-point score (table D-12).[104]

There are four significant predictors of the theoretical good investigation, the fourth of which is close enough to the statistically significant borderline to be counted as a predictor:

—Give Congress the lead. Congress appears to have the institutional memory, resources, and commitment to produce the good investigation, but may be losing it as partisanship increases.

—Use a commission. Commissions offer the opportunity to stitch together more of the basic ingredients of good investigations and appear to have the durability to create eventual impact. Very few congressional investigations produce best-selling books, after all.

—Avoid investigations of personal misconduct. These investigations are often driven by partisan goals with little concern for the quality of the process.

—Use fact finding to seek the answers.

Paying attention to police patrols or fire alarms simply does not matter to footprints. Nor does focusing on repair or avoiding full committees and subcommittees.

Separate regressions of history and party control showed only one predictive relationship with footprint. Although party control did not generate a single notable relationship with footprint, first-term investigations produced a strong relationship.

INVESTIGATORY CHARACTERISTICS → ELEVEN-POINT FOOTPRINT SCORE DURING PREVAILING CONDITIONS

No one knows for sure how the investigatory climate will change in the future, but for now it is likely to be shaped by the polarizing winds that have buffeted Congress and the presidency over the past two to three decades. According to the *National Journal*, congressional polarization reached a thirty-year high in 2010 and stayed there in 2011.

The polarization was most pronounced in the Senate, where no Democrat had a voting record to the right of any Republican and no Republican had a voting record to the left of any Democrat. The House had a handful of "betweeners," as *National Journal* labels them, but its three-sentence headline for both chambers was the same: "Polarization remains endemic. Lawmakers march in lockstep with their party. Heretics are purged."[105]

Divided government is not a predictor of polarization—to the contrary, it is best viewed as one of many possible consequences as the electorate moves back and forth in search of comity. Nevertheless, it is the best available measure at my command for imagining one possible investigatory future, especially when combined with Watergate to create a bit of historical recency as investigators muse about designing heavyweight inquiries.

Looking just at the forty-four divided government investigations that occurred after Watergate, investigators should consider two predictors of a higher footprint score (table D-13):[106]

—Use fact finding. Facts may be in the eye of the beholder today, but they still weigh heavily in creating the good investigation.

—Focus on repair. Repairing bureaucracies and policies appears to offer more opportunity for creating heavyweight investigations, in part because prevention has less of the grand appearance of an urgent breakdown.

As this advice suggests, if investigators have any choice at all in these highly polarized times, they should seek to insulate their work against the vicissitudes of divided government by sticking to the facts. Given all the things they cannot control, fact finding is very much within reach, and it is a learnable skill.

Before concluding this chapter, it is useful to note the differences between the earlier regression of all 100 investigations and this analysis of the post-Watergate, divided-government pool. At least during divided government in the post-Watergate era, neither a congressional home nor a commission venue mattered to an investigation's footprint. Both were simply knocked out.

This statistical dismissal may seem particularly surprising given some of the earlier findings in this chapter, not to mention the enduring celebration of the Social Security, *Challenger*, and 9/11 commissions. Although the use of commissions did very well in suggesting an if-then relationship in the percentages and correlations, the final competition strongly suggests that the footprints of the future will not be strongly related to where an investigation occurs, why it is triggered, or even what kind of breakdown occurs. Rather, footprints under continued conditions of divided government will likely be determined by how an investigation operates. Perhaps investigators can find some hopeful reassurance in knowing that their early choices about how to proceed might actually matter.

CONCLUSION

This chapter provides encouragement for those still searching for the good investigation, at least as measured by footprint. Simply put, the good investigation does exist, albeit often without the nonpartisanship that so many advocates believe is essential to the art of doing it right. However, if investigators are in search of the heaviest footprint possible, the competitions presented in this chapter suggest that institutional home, venue, breakdown, and method matter most to an exemplary review.

As the next chapter argues, the ultimate question is not whether an investigation measures up against the template of the good investigation, but whether it creates impact toward repairing the breakdown at hand or preventing a breakdown in the future. And here, the good investigation matters greatly. Simply stated, the higher the footprint, the greater the impact.

One answer can be found in a more rigorous definition of impact and a defensible measure of how an investigation might affect government performance. Much as some experts assume that the good investigation always produces impact, very good investigations can produce negligible impact, while very bad investigations can generate significant change.

Moreover, impact can have either positive or negative consequences for government performance, which is arguably the ultimate subjective judgment. For example, some would argue that the investigation of communists in government had a great deal of positive impact, while others would most certainly argue that the investigation left a scar that undermines government performance to this day. In turn, some would argue that the celebrated *Challenger*, Watergate, and 9/11 investigations either dodged significant issues that would have improved performance or produced bureaucratic solutions that have muddied accountability.

FOUR

Making Investigations Count

Even though advocates occasionally use terms such as "constructive" to describe the good investigation, their focus has long been on how investigations should work, not on whether investigations actually improve government performance.

Investigations done right have inherent value, however. They thicken the legislative record for judicial interpretation, identify vulnerabilities and breaking points, help solve the delegation dilemma, strengthen constitutional checks and balances, create credible deterrence against misconduct, make the case for a watchful eye on process, policy, and conduct, and may even increase public trust in government. Done poorly, however, they undermine the faithful execution of the laws, demean the constitutional system, and increase the probability of future failures, all of which reduce the consent of the governed.

Yet, doing an investigation right does not always produce impact. Even exemplary investigations can fail to produce needed bureaucratic reforms, policy repairs, reversals in course, enhanced accountability, new agendas, and the resolution of lingering doubts. Some investigations have significant impact in pursuing one or more of these goals, while others have little or no impact at all.

Consider the early years of the Iraq War inquiry as an example of how not to do an investigation well, or at the very least not with consistency and impact. Although the Iraq War investigation as a whole ranks near the very top of both boxes 3-1 and 4-1, the early years of the inquiry were anything but long, broad, complex, serious, thorough, or durable.

This weightlessness was not caused by the lack of investigatory targets, which included prewar intelligence failures, the use of "enhanced interrogation techniques," and the Abu Ghraib prisoner abuse.

Nor was it due to the complete collapse of congressional activity. Matched with a president of their own party, House and Senate Republican majorities held seventy-one hearings on the Iraq War during the 108th Congress (2003–04), and another eighty-five in the 109th (2005–06).[1]

Even though a brief set of hearings can produce a great deal of impact, few of these early inquiries produced more than cursory discomfort. To the contrary, the hearings were generally spotty and poorly linked, and affirmed the president's Iraq War strategy. One scholar even argued that the lack of deep oversight marked an "abdication" of congressional responsibility.[2] Congress and the president's blue-ribbon commissions simply looked away.[3]

As if to prove the role of divided party control in restoring separated-powers government, the investigatory agenda expanded rapidly after Democrat majorities recaptured Congress in the 2006 midterm elections. Matched against a president of the other party, House and Senate Democratic majorities held 183 hearings on the Iraq War in the 110th Congress (2007–08), more than doubling the number of hearings during the parliamentary period from 2003–06.

Democrats soon proved quite capable of parliamentary deference, however. Matched with a president of their own party after the 2010 presidential election, House and Senate Democratic majorities held just ninety-one hearings on the war in the 111th Congress (2009–10), in part because they did not want to undermine their de facto prime minister.

The question, therefore, is why the overall Iraq War investigation eventually ended up so high on the list of heavyweight investigations with a fair amount or a great deal of impact. The answer is the Iraq Study Group. Funded in part through a $1 million appropriation driven forward by Rep. Frank Wolf (R-Va.), the de facto blue-ribbon commission was co-chaired by Lee Hamilton (D-Ind.) and former secretary of state James A. Baker III (R). Hosted by the United States Institute of Peace (a government agency), it began its work on March 15, 2006, and released its report just nine months later on December 6.

Defined as the primary investigation within the large package summarized in appendix B, the Iraq Study Group was notably effective in influencing the war strategy. It also codified the accepted wisdom regarding the eventual withdrawal of U.S. forces. Coming at a moment of reassessment in the midst of despair, the Iraq Study Group drew harsh conclusions about the "grave and

deteriorating" conditions in Iraq, appropriately couched in respectful acknowledgment of the bravery and sacrifice of U.S. and Iraqi soldiers.[4]

Despite its remarkably short timeline, the effort had a long shelf life and
the reputation to sustain it. Its report was still in play as the Obama administration worked to enforce a timetable for withdrawal, and it influenced military strategy in the Afghanistan War. It also affected the transfer of senior
military commanders such as General David Petraeus to the increasingly hot
Afghan battlefield.[5]

Similarly, the President's Commission on Care for America's Returning
Wounded Warriors also had a brief life but significant impact. Created by executive order on March 6, 2007, as wounded warriors streamed home from Iraq
and Afghanistan with grievous injuries, the commission was led by retired Sen.
Bob Dole (R-Kans.) and former Clinton secretary of health and human services
Donna Shalala, both of whom refused to participate unless the president agreed
in advance to implement their recommendations. One of my respondents close
to the commission leadership said that the co-chairs did not want a "dead-end"
commission: "Either the president was committed or he wasn't. If he wouldn't
guarantee implementation, we all had better things to do."

The effort was clearly designed to repair a broken bureaucracy and is particularly notable for its muscular twenty-seven-page report titled "Serve, Support, Simplify." The commission was launched barely two weeks after the
scandal at the Walter Reed Army Hospital hit the front-page of the *Washington
Post* on February 18, 2007. The *Post* began with a story about a single soldier:

> Behind the door of Army Spec. Jeremy Duncan's room, part of the
> wall is torn and hangs in the air, weighted down with black mold.
> When the wounded combat engineer stands in his shower and looks
> up, he can see the bathtub on the floor above through a rotted hole.
> The entire building, constructed between the world wars, often
> smells like greasy carry-out. Signs of neglect are everywhere: mouse
> droppings, belly-up cockroaches, stained carpets, cheap mattresses.[6]

The brief but serious and thorough investigation produced six broad recommendations and a precise path to implementation built around specific
action steps, as well as a short report that contained sixty-six "shoulds" and
twenty-two "musts."[7] Although many of the recommendations were implemented immediately, the commission was matched against a highly insulated
"iron-triangle" bureaucracy, which limited its ultimate impact score to a fair
amount, but not yet a great deal.[8]

The commission's durable recommendations continue to build impact,
however, as the Department of Veterans Affairs (VA) continues to add more

mental health services. However, even as the VA announced a long-overdue and commission-endorsed expansion of its staff in April 2012, its inspector general reported that only half of combat veterans receive an initial mental health evaluation within the department's two-week required window, making the average wait fifty days.[9] Whether the additional personnel will reduce the wait is still in doubt, leaving the commission's ultimate impact also in limbo.

Although the commission's work clearly continues to create investigatory effects and is almost certain to remain an exemplar of the good investigation, speed was of the essence as the Iraq and Afghanistan wars continued to produce an onslaught of vexing injuries such as brain trauma and post–traumatic stress disorder, while treatment was rarely available without long waits.[10] "The pace of change is frustratingly slow," Rep. Henry Waxman (D-Calif.) said at the end of the summer. "Still, the horror stories about problems with the military's health care system continue."[11]

Despite these examples, impact is rarely so obvious. Instead, it requires difficult judgments based on a blend of objective and subjective readings about what happened both during and after each investigation. Difficult though such judgments are, they are essential for answering whether and how investigations matter to government performance. Acknowledging that investigations can produce pure public goods in maintaining constitutional checks and balances, solving delegation dilemmas, and keeping a watchful eye, the ultimate test of a good investigation is its impact in finding the answers about a breakdown and either repairing it or preventing a similar breakdown in the future.

This chapter answers the question by introducing a simple measure of impact to rate each of my 100 investigations. The chapter moves forward with a demographic overview of how impact varies by time, investigatory characteristics, and party control, and discusses the specific destinations of impact. After another demographic overview of these destinations, the chapter ends with a statistical analysis of what determines impact by focusing primarily on destinations, footprints, and investigatory characteristics. As this final analysis clearly suggests, the path to a high amount of impact during the recent period of divided government starts with a commitment to fact finding and a focus on repair.

MEASURING IMPACT

Scholars may be reluctant to define impact, but not former members of Congress such as Lee Hamilton. Speaking at a 1999 Congressional Research Service oversight workshop, he provided a short list of specific investigatory impacts such as ferreting out waste, fraud, and abuse, culling the agenda of obsolete programs, and making sure government is working.[12]

Hamilton was not interested in simply describing the basic activities of oversight. Rather, he set the tactic of "thorough, continuing oversight" in a broader constitutional context:

> Oversight is designed to throw light on the activities of government. It can protect the country from an imperial presidency and an arrogant bureaucracy, it can expose and prevent misconduct, and maintain a degree of constituency influence in an administration . . . It is designed to look at everything the government does, expose it, put the light of publicity on it, supervise the execution of the laws, monitor, supervise the execution and implementation of public laws to assure that the laws are faithfully executed.[13]

Assuring that the laws are faithfully executed involves more than bringing transparency to government, however, which Hamilton clearly understood when he took each of his investigatory assignments over the years. Much as he worked to explore the underlying problems that laid the foundations for the Iran-Contra scandal, the 9/11 attacks, and Iraq debacle, he was always concerned about impact. "He never began an investigation for any other purpose than changing the status quo," one of my respondents said. "He wanted to make a difference. That's why he was always in demand. You knew what you were getting with him—an answer and a recommendation. If you didn't want that, you wouldn't ask him."

Ranking Impact

Generously assuming that each of my 100 investigations was also launched to achieve some kind of impact, did they achieve their purpose?

My answers are based on a careful reading of the historical record during and after each investigation. The adoption of individual recommendations was clearly important to this reading and mirrored Jordan Tama's effort to track the overall impact of his selected national security commissions within two years of completion—an effort I describe in the endnote attached to this sentence.[14]

However, some of my investigations, such as the Kennedy assassination review, did not produce recommendations per se, which usually but not always led to a low impact score, while others, such as the Pearl Harbor inquiry, produced so many recommendations that they are virtually impossible to track. Moreover, Tama's two-year deadline seemed much too short for the investigations covered by this book. Although some investigations, such as the traffic safety inquiry, resulted in almost instant change, others, such as Hoover's government reorganization review, took years, even decades, to reach fruition.

Therefore, I looked for both short-term and long-term "tracks" of impact embedded in legislation, executive orders, reorganizations, process or policy proposals, budget initiatives, major addresses, endorsements, public statements, further oversight, and other initiatives designed to repair or prevent a process breakdown, personal misconduct, or policy breakdown.

As such, I followed Thomas Wolanin's analysis on scoring the ultimate impact of presidential commissions. Wolanin is far from satisfied with the standard measure of impact—whether a problem was solved at some point after a commission reported—if only because commissions cannot be easily credited with grand problem solving.

Instead, Wolanin asks whether the president issued a statement of support, lobbied members of Congress, delivered a major message, drafted major legislation, listed recommendations in the budget or State of the Union address, issued an executive order, signed a final bill, or implemented a policy. In short, did the president do anything but applaud? As Wolanin writes, "If there is a correspondence between a commission's recommendations and changes in government policy (particularly if these developments are accompanied by evidence linking the commission to the changes or the President's views), then the commission will be judged to have some impact."[15]

My reading of each investigation's legislative and executive history produced a simple four-point impact score not unlike Wolanin's: (1) little or none, (2) some, (3) a fair amount, or (4) a great deal. Using this measure, sixteen investigations produced a great deal of impact, twenty-four produced a fair amount, thirty-one produced some, and twenty-nine produced little or none. Using a two-point, low-high measure, sixty investigations produced low impact (little or none plus some), while forty produced high impact (a fair amount plus a great deal).

Although most of the judgments found in box 4-1 were relatively easy to make, two were extremely difficult: communists in government and the Clinton impeachment/perjury inquiry. In the first case, some would argue that the investigation had great effects through its lasting fear and intimidation, while others would argue that the investigatory fervor was shallow and self-aggrandizing. I accepted the former argument and gave the investigation a three-point impact score.

Similarly, some would argue that the Clinton impeachment investigation stained the presidency for decades to come and set future precedents for investigations of presidential misconduct, while others would argue that the investigation was merely the capstone for the trivial conduct reviews and a

BOX 4-1. Federal Investigatory Impacts of 100 Investigations,
from the Most to the Least Influential, 1945–2012

Great deal of impact
(impact score 4)

Government reorganization (1947)
Bureau of Internal Revenue corruption
   (1951)
Air Force preparedness for the cold war
   (1956)
Government information management
   (1963)
Crime in America (1965)
Traffic safety (1965)
Conduct of the Vietnam War (1966)
Watergate (1973)
Intelligence agency abuses (1975)
Social Security financing crisis (1981)
Defense Department fraud, waste, and
   abuse (1985)
Savings and loan crisis (1987)
Base closing and realignment (1988)
Preventing terrorist attacks (1998)
Enron collapse (2001)
9/11 terrorist attacks (2002)

Fair amount of impact
(impact score 3)

Communists in government (1948)
Airport safety (1952)
Sputnik launch (1957)
Munitions lobby (1959)
Drug industry practices (1959)
Kennedy assassination (1963)
Executive branch reorganization (1969)
Energy shortages (1973)
Welfare fraud (1975)

General Services Administration
   corruption (1978)
Educational quality (1981)
Strategic missile forces (1983)
Space shuttle *Challenger* accident (1986)
Government mismanagement (1989)
Tobacco industry practices (1993)
Technology transfers to China (1997)
Clinton impeachment (1998)
Year 2000 technology problem (1998)
Conduct of Iraq War (2003)
Government response to Hurricane
   Katrina (2005)
Steroid abuse in baseball (2005)
Quality of care for wounded warriors
   (2007)
2008 financial collapse (2008)
Stimulus oversight (2009)

Some impact
(impact score 2)

World War II procurement fraud (1945)
Communists in Hollywood (1947)
Reconstruction Finance Corporation
   mismanagement (1950)
Organized crime in America (1950)
Conduct of Korean War (1951)
Justice Department operations (1952)
Federal Housing Administration
   mismanagement (1954)
Campaign finance corruption (1956)
Sherman Adams misconduct (1957)
Labor racketeering (1957)
Quiz show rigging (1959)
Lobbying by foreign governments (1962)

BOX 4-1. Federal Investigatory Impacts of 100 Investigations, from the Most to the Least Influential, 1945–2012 (continued)

Some impact (cont.)

State Department security procedures (1963)

Urban riots (1967)

Superfund implementation (1981)

Abscam congressional sting (1982)

Central America policy (1983)

Wedtech defense procurement decision (1986)

White House Iran-Contra program (1987)

Indian Affairs corruption (1988)

Housing and Urban Development scandal (1989)

Vietnam prisoners of war (POWs) and missing in action (MIAs) (1991)

U.S. intelligence agencies in the post–cold war era (1994)

Ruby Ridge siege (1995)

Aviation security and safety (1996)

Internal Revenue Service taxpayer abuse (1996)

1996 campaign finance abuses (1997)

Department of Homeland Security implementation and operations (2003)

Abramoff lobbying tactics (2004)

Gulf oil spill (2010)

Deficit reduction (2010)

Little or no impact
(impact score 1)

Pearl Harbor (1945)

Agriculture commodity speculation (1947)

Atomic Energy Commission operations (1949)

Dixon-Yates power contract (1954)

Agriculture commodity leasing (1962)

Defense Department stockpiling (1962)

Military "muzzling" (1962)

TFX fighter aircraft contract (1963)

Ku Klux Klan activities (1965)

Central Intelligence Agency financing of private organizations (1967)

Kent State campus unrest (1970)

Justice Department antitrust settlement (1972)

Nixon pardon (1974)

South Korean lobbying (1977)

Three Mile Island nuclear accident (1979)

Bombing of Beirut Marine barracks (1983)

Government response to the human immunodeficiency virus (HIV) epidemic (1987)

1980 "October surprise" (1992)

Whitewater allegations (1995)

Waco Branch Davidian siege (1995)

Gulf War syndrome (1995)

Clinton conduct (1995)

Secret arms shipments to Bosnia (1996)

White House energy task force (2001)

Space shuttle *Columbia* accident (2003)

U.S. attorney firings (2007)

Mine safety (2007)

Solyndra Corporation (2011)

Fast and Furious gun-walking operation (2011)

soon-forgotten event that barely affected public opinion. Once again, I accepted the former argument and gave the investigation another three-point impact score.

It is also important to note that some impacts did not last—the 1951 Bureau of Internal Revenue investigation produced immediate impact, but did not hold over the following decades. It was part of the Watergate investigation, for example, and eventually returned to the headlines and investigatory docket in 1996. Similar criticisms can be made of the Social Security and *Challenger* investigations, both of which held for a decade or two before further breakdowns. So, too, for the ongoing drumbeat of procurement failures, lobbying scandals, and campaign finance breaches.

Second Guessing

The lingering challenge is how to convert the historical record into my four-point measure of impact. After all, it is one thing to measure the implementation of a recommendation and quite another to determine whether that implementation made a difference in curing the breakdown at hand. Doing so involves a series of very difficult questions, many likely to generate significant ideological debate.

Can impact be judged as either helpful or harmful, for example? "I think you could use more discussion of the possible negative impact of investigations on government performance," Mayhew wrote me of his reading of alternative histories of supposedly high-impact investigations. "In the case of the Communist hearings, for example, one stylized story is that they ruined U.S. policy toward China for quite a while by banishing from the government anybody who knew anything about China and by putting a political pox on recognition of 'Red China.'"[16]

Can this judgment change over time? As Mayhew also argued, the Church Committee investigation of intelligence agency abuses that I celebrate in the next chapter of this book could also be interpreted as quite damaging: "Another stylized story out there is that the Church/Pike investigations constrained and, generally speaking, devastated the intelligence agencies with the result that they were demoralized, incompetent, and asleep once the terrorism problems surfaced in the 1990s."

Finally, even if the impact is helpful and remains so over time, does the benefit outweigh the cost? Instead of giving the 1956 Air Force preparedness investigation a high impact score because the defense budget went up, Mayhew asks whether the recommendation for more spending was helpful: "In retrospect, we seem to know that the US was staying pretty well ahead of the USSR in military terms in the 1950s, that Eisenhower knew that and acted accordingly, and that, in particular, the 'missile gap' seized on by Kennedy was fantasy."

Respectfully asked, did Hoover's reorganization produce the promised efficiency embedded in the "science of administration" of the times, or merely extend the sclerosis associated with the "proverbs of administration" that Herbert A. Simon so successfully debunked in 1946?[17] Was the 1998 terrorism investigation a success because its recommendations were adopted after the 9/11 attacks, or a failure because its work was not widely read until 3,000 Americans were killed in the attacks? And was the subsequent 9/11 commission a success because it convinced Congress to create a director of national intelligence, or a failure because it could not demolish the bureaucratic silos that led to the 2009 Christmas Day bombing plot?

To cap the soul-searching, even when investigatory recommendations are executed faithfully and quite apparent in the historical record, it is not always clear that the breakdown was actually fixed, deterrence was created, or future problems were prevented. Did the 1983 Social Security reform hold long enough to be scored as having a high amount of impact? I believe the answer is yes. Did the 1985 *Challenger* recommendations hold? I believe the answer is mostly yes, but the can-do culture of the National Aeronautics and Space Administration (NASA) was never diffused. Did the 1951 Bureau of Internal Revenue investigation have a substantial effect on performance? I believe the answer is yes, too.

So answered, other investigations produced either works in progress or murky impacts—the 2008 investigation of the financial collapse most certainly produced a massive reversal in course on banking policy, but whether its legislative remedy will be fully implemented and ultimately successful is beyond the question of investigatory impact. Based on this and other cases, readers are forewarned that more recent investigations are difficult, though not impossible, to score. The question is whether an investigation produced sensible advice that either repaired the breakdown at hand or prevented a breakdown in the future.

These judgments are no doubt in the eye of the beholder and should be viewed as more speculative than final. These judgments should also be viewed as conservative. As noted above, only sixteen investigations received a four-point impact score, compared to twenty-nine that received a one-point score. When in doubt, I always erred on the side of a lower impact score, especially when assessing recent investigations where the outcome is still uncertain.

A DEMOGRAPHIC OVERVIEW OF IMPACT

Investigatory impacts have many potential drivers, including history, investigatory characteristics, and party control. Footprints also play a role here in a simple cause-and-effect chain that leads directly to impact. According to the conventional definition of the good investigation, the attributes of goodness flow in, and impact flows out.

There is considerable room for debate about what comes first in creating investigatory impacts. Again given the investigatory conditions that exist at the start of an investigation, should Congress and the president look for well-known leadership first? Define the object of the investigation broadly or narrowly? Provide significant freedom to investigate? Pursue a serious and thorough investigation? Aim for a long shelf life? Encourage maximum bipartisanship? The list of potential advice is seemingly endless. Perhaps leaders are the key to the freedom to investigate and bipartisanship, for example, or perhaps the nature of the breakdown determines who becomes the leader.

This is not to dismiss investigatory impact on future party control, however. Many investigations are designed to shape upcoming elections and campaign debates through highly visible allegations such as the bomber gap at the heart of the 1956 Air Force preparedness inquiry. But I have not included electoral results as a destination for impact, although readers could easily use bipartisanship as a strong hint of political intentions.

As with so many of the measures used in this book, my judgments of investigatory impact involved interpretations, not indisputable evidence. Moreover, my question was not whether an investigation's impact was in the national interest, but whether it reached its intended destination. Although I cannot forecast the ultimate impact of any given investigation, especially the works in progress discussed in chapter 3, I made a determined effort to follow the historical leads as far as possible.

Footprints

Footprints offer a first measure for exploring the demographics of impact. Simply asked, do any of the supposed components of the good investigation matter at all to impact? It is a question too rarely asked. Even though the Project on Government Oversight (POGO) reminds congressional investigators that there is a difference between "the quality and the quantity of investigations," its oversight manual generally explores quality in operational terms. So do the Congressional Research Service, Congressional Quarterly, and most scholars.[18]

Nevertheless, there is ample evidence in the following pages that foot-prints do matter to impact. Once again, the evidence comes from the search for yes-no relationships between the eleven footprint weights and impact. At least according to the correlations, this suggests that the investigation done right is also the investigation done well: ten of the eleven correlations between the footprint weights and impact were both positive and significant, while just one was negative and significant.

Length was the only one of the eleven relationships that did not produce a relationship with impact—short investigations such as the mistreatment of wounded warriors can have very large impacts, while long investigations such as communist infiltration of the motion picture industry can have very little. In addition, the only weight that barely made the cut of statistical significance was visibility—less visible investigations of allegations such as government information management can generate very large impacts, while highly visible allegations such as Clinton misconduct and perquisites can have very little.

Once past the correlations, simple percentage comparisons offer a more accessible way to outline potential if-then relationships between the eleven weights and the four levels of impact.

—Longer investigations were more than twice as likely as shorter inves-tigations to produce a great deal of impact (21 percent versus 9 percent), while shorter investigations were significantly more likely to produce little or no impact (35 percent versus 25 percent).

—Broad investigations were much more likely than narrow investiga-tions to produce a great deal of impact (36 percent versus 3 percent), while narrow investigations were significantly more likely to produce little or no impact (44 percent versus 5 percent).

—Complex investigations were seven times more likely than simple investigations to produce a great deal of impact (33 percent versus 5 percent), while simple investigations were significantly more likely to produce little or no impact (44 percent versus 5 percent).

—Well-known leadership at the investigatory helm was much more likely to produce a great deal of impact than having less-known leadership (31 per-cent versus 8 percent), while less well-known leadership was far more likely to produce little or no impact (43 percent versus 3 percent).

—Having the freedom to investigate was much more likely to produce a great deal of impact than having little or no freedom (28 percent versus just 2 percent), while restricted freedom was five times more likely to produce lit-tle or no impact (50 percent versus 11 percent).

—Visible investigations were only slightly more likely than their less visible peers to produce a great deal of impact (19 percent versus 11 percent) and slightly more likely to produce little or no impact (35 percent versus 25 percent).

—Serious investigations were much more likely than less serious investigations to produce a great deal of impact (27 percent versus 0 percent), while less serious investigations were much more likely to produce little or no impact (46 percent versus 17 percent).

—Thorough investigations were much more likely than less thorough investigations to produce a great deal of impact (27 percent versus 0 percent), while less thorough investigations were much more likely to produce little or no impact (46 percent versus 16 percent).

—High-leverage investigations were much more likely than low-leverage investigations to produce a great deal of impact (22 percent versus 3 percent), while low-leverage investigations were more likely to produce little or no impact (53 percent versus 18 percent).

—Durable investigations were much more likely to produce a great deal of impact than less influential investigations (43 percent versus 0 percent), while less influential investigations were fifteen times more likely to produce little or no impact (46 percent versus 0 percent).

—Bipartisan investigations were only slightly more likely than partisan investigations to produce a great deal of impact (19 percent versus 13 percent), but less bipartisan investigations were twice as likely to produce little or no impact (41 percent versus 19 percent).

Measured using Watergate as a dividing line, history showed mixed effects on these relationships. Whereas the pre- and post-Watergate comparisons revealed little variation between impact and five of the weights (length, well-known leadership, visibility, durability, and bipartisanship), the comparisons produced substantial variation between impact and the other six weights (breadth, complexity, freedom to investigate, seriousness, thoroughness, and leverage). The freedom to investigate was more likely to produce a great deal of impact after Watergate (23 percent before versus 38 percent after), while breadth (47 percent versus 29 percent), complexity (42 percent versus 31 percent), seriousness (38 percent versus 22 percent), thoroughness (35 percent versus 24 percent), and leverage (30 percent versus 18 percent) were less likely to produce a great deal of impact after Watergate. These six post-Watergate changes suggest that the environment surrounding investigatory impact may have become so hostile that investigations simply cannot achieve significant results regardless of their "goodness."

History

Just as history played a minimal role in the demographic profile of investigatory footprints, it also played a minimal role in shaping the four-point and low-high impact scores used below. Although history may have indirect effects on many of the relationships discussed later in this chapter, it does not have strong direct effects one to one.

Start with the four historical periods. Although impact increases and decreases across the four periods, the variation is not strong enough to declare any grand finding. The percentage of investigations with a great deal of impact rose from just 13 percent during the post–World War II period to 26 percent during the Great Society period, but then dropped to 19 percent during the congressional resurgence and to 10 percent during the divided government. Even these small differences smooth out in the low-high combinations, when the percentage of high-impact investigations rose from 35 percent to 42 percent, 44 percent, and 41 percent through the four historical periods, respectively.

Turn next to Watergate. Despite its reputation as the starting point of the congressional resurgence, Watergate did not produce any difference in impact (19 percent of investigations before Watergate produced a great deal of impact compared with 14 percent after). Moreover, even this slight difference reverses in the low-high combinations, with 38 percent of the investigations before Watergate accorded a high level of impact compared with 43 percent after.

Turn next to presidential terms. Given the presidential election cycle, first-term investigations may trade the good investigation for visibility even at the cost of higher impact. Although this notion is barely supported in the percentage of first- and second-term investigations with a great deal of impact (13 percent versus 21 percent), it receives much stronger support in the percentage of first- and second-term investigations with a high amount of impact (31 percent versus 56 percent). Unfortunately, there are simply not enough cases to test the notion of electoral incentives blended with party control to prove or disprove the case.

Finally, turn to election years. Once again, one might expect election-year investigations to be laden with electoral incentives, but this analysis of impact does not show it. Just 15 percent of election-year investigations achieved a great deal of impact, compared with 17 percent of nonelection-year investigations. This pattern of insignificant differences is repeated in the low-high combinations (investigations with "some" impact or "little or none" in the low category versus investigations with "a fair amount" or "a great deal" in the high), at 38 percent with a high amount of impact for investigations begun in election years and 43 percent for those begun in nonelection years.

Investigatory Characteristics

Investigatory characteristics show stronger relationships with impact, but are often mediated by history. Simply explained, some investigatory characteristics show stronger relationships with impact earlier in the periods covered by this book, while others show stronger relationships later.

However, Watergate revealed only four changes in the relationships between impact and investigatory characteristics, all of which showed greater strength before Watergate than after: investigations conducted by full committees produced more impact before than after (22 percent before versus 7 percent after), as did investigations of personal misconduct (36 percent versus 0 percent), investigations that focused on prevention (21 percent versus 0 percent), and investigations that used a blame-setting methodology (17 percent versus 6 percent).

INSTITUTIONAL HOME

Institutional home produced little effect on impact. The two branches produced almost equal percentages of investigations with a great deal of impact (18 percent for Congress versus 15 percent for the presidency), but the presidency held a slight edge in impact using the low-high comparisons (50 percent versus 39 percent). Similarly, although Senate investigations were no more likely than House investigations to produce a great deal of impact (18 percent versus 16 percent), the Senate showed somewhat larger impacts than the House in the low-high comparisons (43 percent versus 32 percent).

VENUE

Investigatory venue produced significant effects on impact. Commissions produced the largest percentage of investigations with a great deal of impact (25 percent), followed by full committees (13 percent), special congressional bodies (13 percent as well), and subcommittees (12 percent). These patterns were amplified in the low-high combinations, where commissions produced the largest amount of high impact (61 percent), followed by full committees and subcommittees (39 percent each) and special congressional bodies (19 percent).

TRIGGER

Investigatory trigger produced few effects on impact. Fire alarm and police patrol investigations produced almost equal levels of a great deal of impact (15 percent and 18 percent, respectively), while policy patrol investigations were more likely than fire alarms to produce a high amount of impact in the low-high comparisons (49 percent versus 35 percent).

ISSUE

Investigatory issue did not produce any significant effects on impact.

BREAKDOWN

There were no differences in impact between investigations of process and policy breakdowns on either the four-point score or low-high comparisons, but there was a significant difference between investigations of process and policy breakdowns versus investigations of personal misconduct. Investigations of process and policy breakdowns were more likely than investigations of misconduct to produce a great deal of impact (15 percent, 20 percent, and just 8 percent, respectively) or a high amount of impact (44 percent, 48 percent, and 16 percent). Much as personal conduct investigations produced high visibility, they rarely produced significant impacts on government performance.

PURPOSE

Investigatory purpose produced mixed effects as well. Investigations that focused on repair were only slightly more likely to produce a great deal of impact than investigations that focused on prevention (20 percent versus 10 percent). This was a pattern repeated in the low-high comparisons, where repair barely led prevention. However, as noted later in this chapter, there was more significant variation by purpose when more specific forms of repair and prevention are compared.

METHOD

Finally, investigatory method produced significant effects on impact. As already hinted in the analysis of footprint scores and impact, fact finding was more likely to produce a great deal of impact than blame setting (22 percent versus 11 percent), and the differences were even greater in the low-high combinations (56 percent with a high amount of impact for fact finding versus 29 percent for blame setting).

Party Control

Viewed across a variety of measures, party control had mixed effects on impact under both the four-point and low-high measures. As the following list shows, divided government is not a barrier to impact:

—Divided government produced a slightly larger percentage of investigations with a great deal of impact (18 percent for divided versus 14 percent for unified), and added to the margin in the low-high comparisons (46 percent high impact versus 36 percent).

—Democratic control of government produced a somewhat larger percentage of investigations with a great deal of impact (17 percent during Democratic control versus 0 percent during Republican control), but Republican control reversed the edge in the low-high comparisons (50 percent during Republican control versus 32 percent during Democratic).

—Republican control of the presidency produced a slightly higher percentage of investigations with a great deal of impact (18 percent during Republican presidencies versus 14 percent during Democratic), and an even larger margin in the low-high comparisons (48 percent versus 32 percent).

—Divided party control of Congress produced a somewhat larger percentage of investigations with a great deal of impact (24 percent during divided control versus 15 percent during unified control), but unified control made up all but one point of the difference in the low-high comparisons (41 percent for divided versus 40 percent for unified).

—Democratic control of both chambers produced a slightly higher percentage of investigations with a great deal of impact (17 percent during Democratic control versus 9 percent during Republican control), but this small effect disappeared when investigations with a fair amount of impact were added into the low-high comparisons (40 percent during Democratic control versus 39 percent during Republican control).

—Democratic control of the House produced nothing significant in the percentage of investigations with a great deal of impact (17 percent during Democratic control versus 14 percent during Republican). And even this slightest of differences tightened to just one percentage point in the low-high comparisons (40 percent during Democratic control versus 39 percent during Republican control).

—Finally, Democratic control of the Senate produced a somewhat larger percentage of investigations with a great deal of impact (19 percent during Democratic control versus 11 percent during Republican control), but even this slight difference disappeared completely in the low-high comparisons (40 percent versus 40 percent).

A QUESTION FINALLY ANSWERED, MOSTLY

Several of these relationships shifted slightly when compared before and after Watergate, moving toward parity. Although divided government was linked to higher-impact investigations both before and after Watergate, the difference with unified government narrowed from 12 to 7 percentage points. Divided control of Congress was also associated with greater impact than unified control before and after Watergate, but the difference also narrowed from 38 to 7 percentage points. At the same time, Republican presidents remained ahead of Democratic presidents in producing higher-impact investigations both before and after Watergate. Given the lack of before-and-after-Watergate effects, Mayhew's *Divided We Govern* analysis is confirmed again. Divided government does not appear to make a strong difference in shaping impact.[19]

With one major exception, the party control matchups produced little variation in impact:

—The fourteen matchups between House Democratic majorities and Republican presidents produced just two investigations with a great deal of impact (14 percent), and four with little or none (29 percent).

—The seven matchups between House Republican majorities and Democratic presidents produced just one investigation with a great deal of impact (14 percent), but four with little or none (57 percent). If improving government performance was their goal, the House Republicans were by far the least successful.

—The fourteen matchups between Senate Democratic majorities and Republican presidents produced four investigations with a great deal of impact (29 percent), and just two with little or none (14 percent).

—The ten matchups between Senate Republican majorities and Democratic presidents produced one investigation with a great deal of impact (10 percent), and three with little or none (30 percent).

House Republican majorities created the major exception. Their investigations not only had the lowest percentage of freedom, visibility, durability, and bipartisanship, they also trailed House Democratic majorities by 21 percentage points in the number of investigations with either some, a fair amount, or a great deal of impact. The number of investigations in this analysis may be small, but the result supports part of Parker and Dull's argument. Matched against Democratic presidents, House Republican majorities create the most quarrelsome investigations and the least rewarding outcomes, if rewarding means better government, of course.

THE INDIRECT EFFECTS OF PARTY CONTROL ON IMPACT

Despite its mixed direct effects on investigatory impact described above, party control can and does work its will on impact as a "hidden hand," too. If it can shape footprints such as the freedom to investigate and durability, it might also shape investigatory characteristics through a chain of indirect effects from party control → investigatory characteristics → impact.

—Divided government produced larger percentages of high impact than unified government among investigations conducted by Congress (42 percent versus 32 percent), the presidency (55 percent versus 44 percent), and the House or the Senate (35 percent versus 25 percent).

—Divided government produced larger percentages of high impact investigations conducted by special congressional bodies (25 percent versus 0 percent), subcommittees (45 percent versus 31 percent), or commissions (65 percent versus 46 percent), but not full committees (29 percent versus 44 percent).

—Divided government produced larger percentages of high impact when the investigations were sparked by fire alarms (40 percent versus 27 percent) or police patrols (52 percent versus 41 percent).

—Divided government produced larger percentages of high impact when investigations focused on foreign issues (50 percent versus 18 percent).

—Divided government produced larger percentages of high impact when investigations targeted process breakdowns (48 percent versus 29 percent) or personal misconduct (22 percent versus 0 percent), but not policy breakdowns (47 percent each).

—Divided government produced larger percentages of high impact when investigations set course for repair (53 percent versus 29 percent) but not prevention (32 percent versus 44 percent).

—Divided government produced larger percentages of high impact when investigations used fact finding as their methodology (69 percent versus 31 percent), but unified government produced larger percentages when investigations used blame setting (38 percent versus 24 percent).

Once past these differences, divided and unified government produced roughly equal percentages of high impact in all other categories of investigatory characteristics.

This analysis clearly suggests that divided government is a powerful force for higher impact when it works through certain investigatory characteristics. Assuming now that the chain moves from divided government → investigatory characteristics → impact, Mayhew would be absolutely right that Congress is quite capable of producing high-impact investigations during divided government.

However, it remains to be seen whether these patterns from 100 hand-selected investigations would hold for the 1,000 that Parker and Dull studied. The two databases are so different in both their content (significant investigations versus sets of hearings) and the costs of deep analysis (very high for any given investigation or set of hearings) that we may never know the full answer. What is clear is that party control exerts indirect influence on the ultimate consequence of investigatory choices, sometimes slightly, sometimes dramatically. And that alone suggests the need for further analysis well beyond simple counts of hearings and pages of testimony, both of which are easy to collect, but only reveal a tiny sliver of the story.

THE SIX DESTINATIONS OF IMPACT

Investigators rarely launch their work with grand references to the separation of powers and the need to force the president to execute the laws faithfully. Rather, investigators mostly talk about hoped-for impacts in one or more of the following destinations: (1) reforming broken bureaucracies, (2) repairing failed policies, (3) reversing course on national strategies, (4) enhancing accountability, (5) setting the agenda for future action, and (6) resolving doubts about a particular event.

As noted later in this chapter, these six destinations are extensions of my standard measure of investigatory purpose—the first three destinations are forms of repair, while the second three are forms of prevention. Although some readers might view resolving doubts as a form of repair, I believe the effort is better viewed as a way to help the nation move past an event or controversy and onto other priorities, thereby preventing delay. But this is a judgment call that can be contested without disturbing the findings presented below.

Done well, the good investigation not only finds the answers about bureaucratic breakdowns. It also fixes them, be it through complete restructuring such as the top-to-bottom realignment of the Bureau of Internal Revenue discussed below, creation of entirely new units such as the Environmental Protection Agency, or restructuring of the government's far-flung hierarchy through reorganizations driven by investigations such as the Hoover Commission.

The good investigation not only finds the answers about policy breakdowns. It fixes them, too, be it by creating new legislation such as lobbying registration, campaign finance disclosure, and banking reregulation or by revitalizing laws that have lost their effect with the passage of time or failed to keep pace with realities such as the frustrations associated with fighting unwinnable wars.

Finally, the good investigation not only examines future breakdowns by government or outside actors such as corporations and other nations. It also prevents them, be it through firing warning shots across the bow of private industries, such as the motion picture industry and professional baseball, establishing new systems for deterring misconduct and maladministration, such as the Offices of Inspectors General (OIGs) and new performance measurement tools, preparing Congress and the presidency for future action on issues such as traffic safety, tobacco regulation, and terrorism, and resolving "who-done-it" controversies over events and conditions such as assassinations, urban riots, the human immunodeficiency virus (HIV), prisoners of war, mine disasters, and oil spills, all of which can eventually lead to bureaucratic and policy repairs.

Simply described, the good investigation launches itself after a breakdown of some kind, creates a set of investigatory characteristics, produces a footprint of its throw weight, and ultimately finds the answers needed to repair the breakdown or prevent future breakdowns.

The good investigation can and sometimes does change destinations while it continues, but its primary purpose is generally revealed at the start and thus can be considered as a driver of footprints, investigatory characteristics, and impact. Thirty-three of my investigations sought bureaucratic reforms, another twenty pursued policy repairs, six attempted to reverse course, fourteen attempted to enhance accountability, fifteen engaged in agenda setting, and twelve worked to resolve doubts.

As the following examples suggest, each of these destinations has a somewhat different modus operandi and impact. Although some investigations blended more than one destination, each had a primary destination as it began its journey toward hoped-for impact. Acknowledging that at least some of my 100 investigations such as the Ku Klux Klan inquiry were more for show than for impact, I assigned a destination to each nonetheless.

Reforming Bureaucracies

Thirty-three of my 100 investigations focused on fixing government bureaucracies at individual agencies such as the Defense Department, larger groups of agencies such as federal regulatory commissions, or government as a whole.

Bureaucratic reform may be the easiest impact to achieve. After all, it involves a reasonably well-defined breakdown, target, and potential remedy. Nevertheless, some political scientists would argue that bureaucratic breakdowns are inevitable. According to Terry M. Moe's theory of public bureaucracy, for example, it is no surprise that legislative losers might burden a new program or agency with needless bureaucracy. The surprise is that legislative winners also favor what Moe calls "complex, restrictive, often bizarre administrative arrangements that insulate their creations from control by opponents."[20] Just as losers operate in the present to undermine implementation, winners operate in the future to protect their victory for as long as possible. It is a perfect recipe for future breakdowns.

Consider two examples of bureaucratic reforms.

BUREAU OF INTERNAL REVENUE CORRUPTION (1951)

Like the Hoover Commission, discussed in chapter 3, the 1951 investigation of what was then known as the Bureau of Internal Revenue was designed to fix a broken agency.[21] Also like the Hoover Commission, it was an exemplar of the good investigation and would have earned an eleven-point footprint but for the relative obscurity of its leader, Rep. Cecil R. King (D-Calif.).

The investigation was launched and led by King's House Ways and Means Subcommittee on Administration of the Internal Revenue Laws and was sparked by allegations of bribery, "shakedowns," the exploitation of "soft touches," and the rise of criminal cliques at the top of the bureau. The bureau was still staffed under a spoils system and was clearly rife with corruption.

Having begun with an isolated, or "one-off," hearing on fraud in the bureau's St. Louis office, the investigation was eventually authorized by a House resolution and given sweeping authority and a handsome budget to conduct a wide-ranging review. Despite the bureau's complaint that the investigation would compromise tax collection by injecting politics into the process, the investigation covered a short but broad range of bureaucratic malfeasance that led to more than 166 resignations in 1951 alone.[22]

The investigation also generated headlines the old-fashioned way, through one allegation after another about lies, bribes, free vacations, and even fur coats (a frequent topic in corruption cases during the decade). Driven forward in 101 hearings over the next two years, the investigation had a great deal of impact and clearly attempted to change the organization's ethical culture with its call to change the agency's name to the Internal Revenue Service. However, it continued to spark investigations over the decades and was reprised in the 1996 investigation of taxpayer abuse.

THE CHALLENGER ACCIDENT (1986)

The 1986 investigation of the shuttle *Challenger* disaster earned its three-point impact score through a bureaucratic reform, albeit one supplemented by new deterrence systems. Led by former Republican secretary of state William Rogers, the Presidential Commission on the Space Shuttle *Challenger* Accident was created by executive order on February 3, 1986, six days after the shuttle exploded barely a minute into its flight.[23] The seven astronauts of shuttle mission 51-L had no advance warning of disaster, but at least some were still alive when their capsule hit the ocean three minutes later. As the reality sank in, a NASA spokesman acknowledged the disaster with a haunting phrase: "Obviously a major malfunction."[24]

As the commission discovered, the technical culprit was plain to see in the small puffs of black smoke that came from the aft joint of the shuttle's right-side booster rocket milliseconds after ignition.[25] The puffs signified the complete erosion of the rubber O-ring that was designed to seal the joint against "blow-by" as the rocket's frame bulged ever so slightly under initial pressure. The puffs soon grew into a giant torch that cut through the rocket's aft attachment to the liquid hydrogen fuel tank. Still attached to the tank by its forward station, the rocket began to rotate at 72.2 seconds, hit the tank at 73.124 seconds, and ignited the deadly explosion at 73.137 seconds.[26]

The technical cause of the failure was also obvious in the record low temperatures that bathed *Challenger* on the morning of the launch. Although the evidence was destined to emerge as the televised hearings wound on, commission member Richard P. Feynman made the case with a simple on-the-dais experiment on February 11.[27] Pulling two short strands of O-ring from his pocket, the Nobel Prize–winning physicist began the experiment by simply asking for a glass of ice water.

> I get my ice water, I don't drink it! I squeeze the rubber in the C-clamp and put them in the glass of ice water. After a few minutes, I'm ready to show the results of my little experiment. I reach for the little button that activates my microphone . . . I press the button for my microphone, and I say, "I took this rubber from the model and put it in a clamp in ice water for a while." I take the clamp out, hold it up in the air, and loosen it as I talk: "I discovered that when you undo the clamp, the rubber doesn't spring back. In other words, for more than a few seconds, there is no resilience in this particular material when it is at a temperature of 32 degrees. I believe that has some significance for our problem."[28]

Having shown that the O-ring could not have "seated" during the first few moments of the flight, the commission moved on with further testimony about the technical design and eventually recommended a complete overhaul of the solid-rocket motor, redesigned joints, as well as a new escape mechanism for future flight crews.

The commission was hardly finished with its work, however. After drilling through the technical facts, the commission soon turned to NASA's organizational culture and what it would later describe as "an accident rooted in history." Building on thirteen hearings, 160 interviews, and 122,000 pages of documents, the commission concluded that NASA and its contractor, Morton Thiokol, accepted the risk of a catastrophic accident because they "came to accept erosion and blow-by as unavoidable and an acceptable flight risk."[29] As Feynman said at the commission's April 3 hearing, NASA was playing "a kind of Russian roulette . . . It flies and nothing happens. Then it is suggested, therefore, that the risk is no longer so high for the next flights. We can lower our standards a little bit because we got away with it last time . . . You got away with it but it shouldn't be done over and over again like that."[30]

Alongside its brutal criticism of NASA's cavalier dismissal of repeated warnings about the O-rings and other "criticality-one" risks that could result in the loss of life, the commission hammered the agency for the same kinds of communication failures that contributed to the Pearl Harbor and 9/11 breakdowns discussed elsewhere in this book. According to the commission's final report, the flawed decision-making process was the "contributing cause of the accident." According to the commission's fact finding, the process produced a decision to launch "based on incomplete and sometimes misleading information, a conflict between engineering data and management judgments, and a NASA management structure that permitted internal flight safety problems to bypass key Shuttle managers."[31]

The commission also provided moment-by-moment details on NASA's effort to suppress dissent on the night before the launch and Thiokol's own demand that its director of engineering take off his engineer's hat and put on his manager's hat to "accommodate a major customer."[32] Much as the commission sought to address the failures through recommendations for a new inspection system and maintenance schedule, a less ambitious flight schedule, and a greater role for astronauts in management decisions, its major recommendation focused on a distant future when the shuttle would no longer be the primary vehicle for manned space flight. This final recommendation was not fully implemented until the shuttle *Atlantis* landed twenty-five years later on July 11, 2011.

The commission's recommendations were not self-executing, however. They were so diffuse in nature that NASA had to appoint an internal commission, headed by a former Apollo program director, retired Air Force general Samuel Phillips, to lead a National Academy of Public Administration implementation team.[33]

The key question is whether the investigation produced lasting change in NASA's can-do, fly-at-all-costs culture.[34] The answer is yes in the short term, but no in the long term. NASA eventually returned to its old habits.

On the one hand, there is little doubt that the investigation produced immediate changes in both shuttle design and basic operations. NASA returned to space with a safer shuttle, a new process for reviewing launch decisions, a lighter flight schedule, and greater astronaut participation in the safety process. As such, the investigation had very high immediate impact, if only by forcing NASA to trim its launch schedule.

On the other hand, the 2003 shuttle *Columbia* tragedy showed that lax oversight had returned to the fore. "It's the same damn thing," Rogers Commission member Air Force General (Ret.) Donald Kutyna argued in 2003. "They didn't learn a thing. We had nine O-rings fail, and they flew. These guys had seven pieces of foam hit, and it still flew."[35] The *Challenger* investigation made the shuttle program safer for fifteen years or so, but the launch process was still flawed, and NASA's organizational culture soon emerged unscathed.[36]

Repairing Policies

Twenty of my investigations focused on policy repairs. Just as bureaucracies fail, so do public policies. Some fail because they simply cannot be implemented (as opposed to suffering from incompetent implementation), while others fail because they create the delegation dilemma. But regardless of the cause, investigations often lead to adjustments in existing policy. These repairs are not to be confused with the basic changes in course discussed below, which involve fundamental reversals of agreed-upon strategies.

Consider two examples of policy repairs.

AIR FORCE PREPAREDNESS FOR THE COLD WAR (1956)

The 1956 investigation of Air Force preparedness for the cold war was led by one of the investigatory giants of the era: Senate Armed Services Committee Air Force Subcommittee chairman Stuart Symington (D-Mo.). It was launched in February 1956 when another investigatory giant, Richard Russell (D-Ga.), and his Democratic majority used their authority to create Symington's subcommittee. The investigation lasted 360 days, but nonetheless produced forty-one public and private hearings and generated significant leverage during a period marked by heightened anxiety about the Soviet Union's military buildup.[37]

With three other Democratic presidential hopefuls on the full committee in addition to Symington—Lyndon B. Johnson (D-Tex.), Estes Kefauver (D-Tenn.), and Henry M. "Scoop" Jackson (D-Wash.)—Symington was given a free hand to develop the harshest critique possible of the Eisenhower administration's stewardship. As the *New York Times* noted in a front-page article titled "Airpower Is a Political Issue Too," Symington was already being mentioned as a dark-horse Democratic presidential candidate and used the hearings to cement his foreign policy credentials.[38] Politically inspired hearings are not necessarily narrow or obscure, of course, but Symington's effort was clearly designed to raise his own visibility.

The investigation produced two major findings regarding air power. First, the United States did not have enough bombers to go head-to-head in a nuclear war with the Soviets, and second, the Eisenhower administration had created the "bomber gap" by vacillating between preparing for limited versus unlimited war.[39]

The investigation also produced an item-by-item description of what it called a misguided focus on quality, not quantity. According to the subcommittee's inventory, the United States trailed the Soviet Union on virtually every measure of superiority, including aircraft production, aircraft in operational units, fighter planes, light and heavy bombers, tankers, jet engines, scientific personnel, high-energy physics research facilities, housing, "new scientific type weapons," air bases, active Air Force personnel, and ballistic missiles.[40] The subcommittee's finding was short and simple: "The vulnerability of the United States to sudden attack increased greatly during the past decade, and this vulnerability will continue to increase in the foreseeable future."[41]

Despite its eight-point footprint score, the investigation's partisan edge hardly squares with the notional characteristics of the good investigation. To the contrary, the final report is best described as a harsh indictment of the Eisenhower administration and an aggressive justification for both quantity and quality. It was an expensive blend even before Sputnik spiked the defense budget six months later.

Thus if the investigation's destination was a spending repair, it clearly achieved its goal and earned a four-point impact score solely for this result. At the same time, the investigation also produced significant political impact by giving Kennedy's 1960 presidential campaign ample opportunity to claim that the United States was facing a missile gap "on which we are gambling with our future."[42]

SOCIAL SECURITY REFORM (1981)

The 1981 Social Security investigation is a second exemplar of policy repair. Forged in controversy, the National Commission on Social Security Reform labored under an extraordinarily tight deadline to rescue the cash-strapped program from what many believed was impending bankruptcy, although technical bankruptcy was never possible. It was the specter of collapse that allowed negotiators to reach consensus around a final "package of pain" that gave every constituency group a reason to claim victory even as it suffered defeat.

The commission was created by executive order in December 1981 in a desperate effort to move public attention off the president's early proposal to cut Social Security benefits. Reagan's proposals were hardly radical—several turned up in the final rescue package. Nor was Reagan the only actor on the rescue stage. Congress had already tried and failed to fix the financing crisis in 1977, and Rep. Jake Pickle (D-Tex.) and his House Ways and Means Subcommittee on Social Security had started work on another rescue even before Reagan was inaugurated. So noted, Reagan's proposals had a fatal political flaw. Driven to create the image, if not the substance, of a balanced budget, Reagan's proposals were to take effect immediately, giving older Americans no time to plan for the future and Democrats a potent opportunity to blunt the administration's momentum.

Pushed hard by Sen. Daniel Patrick Moynihan (D-N.Y.), Democrats and Republicans joined to condemn the president's proposals in a unanimous "sense of the Senate" resolution on May 20 and began preparing for a summer of bitter hearings. "It was like a bunch of duck hunters waiting in the bushes with the ducks too high to hit," a Reagan administration official told me in 1984 as I was researching my book *Artful Work: The Politics of Social Security Reform*. "Along came this old turkey, and that was it."[43] Reagan abandoned his package the next day.

As fast as Reagan tried to back away from the proposals, Democrats continued their assault through the summer as eight congressional committees began hearings on Social Security's future.[44] Although every hearing featured fiery rhetoric about the president's alleged attempt to balance the budget on the backs of the elderly, none was more heated than the Senate Finance Committee's July hearing on the president's retreat from his original proposals. As ranking member on the Finance Committee's Social Security Subcommittee, Moynihan opened his questioning of the secretary of health and human services, Richard Schweiker, with a scathing and uncharacteristically personal attack:

> I am sorry to have to say, Mr. Secretary, that the administration in the last forty-eight hours has been conducting a campaign of political terrorism on this subject. You have described a basically sound social insurance program as on the verge of going broke, and it is not. You have discussed difficulties that will have to be resolved in the middle

of the twenty-first century as if they were upon us this afternoon. You have disavowed positions the administration took with the utmost political enthusiasm just months ago.[45]

Once finished with his opening statement, Moynihan moved on to his blistering direct examination: Did the president still support a 10 percent benefit cut for current retirees, a 40 percent cut for future retirees, a reduction in disability benefits, a freeze in the annual cost-of-living adjustment, and an increase in the retirement age?

Moynihan continued down his list of questions until his heaviest shot. Was it not true, he asked the beleaguered Schweiker, that the Social Security cuts were designed to plug a gaping hole in the federal budget? "You found yourself facing a long series of deficits," he told Schweiker. "Are you not, sir, in all truth, being told, 'Take away from the retired people of America. Take it out of their household budgets and put it into the President's budget to make that budget look better'?"[46]

Even as congressional Democrats continued the attack, Moynihan and other senior Democrats began thinking about how to balance the enormous political advantage created by Reagan's misstep with the need to reassure older Americans that their retirement checks were safe. Many Democrats wanted to use Social Security as a wedge issue in both the 1982 and 1984 elections, but Moynihan and House Speaker Thomas P. "Tip" O'Neill (D-Mass.) chose the national interest.

After weeks of give-and-take, the Democratic majority reached a seemingly simple agreement with the Republicans: Democrats would support a fifteen-member National Commission on Social Security Reform as a way to calm worried beneficiaries, while Republicans agreed to enact a one-year "patch" to keep Social Security solvent, thereby allowing Democrats to run on the issue in 1982, but not in 1984. The commission was created under Executive Order 12335, December 16, 1981.

Ordinarily, Reagan's order would have signaled the presidency's lead role as an investigatory home. However, Senate majority leader Howard Baker (R-Tenn.) forced Reagan's hand. Although many Democrats favored a longer-term patch that would keep the issue alive long enough to defeat Reagan in 1984, Moynihan and O'Neill agreed to the blue-ribbon option provided that the commission would not make any recommendations until after the 1982 midterm elections. Thus the commission is best viewed as a congressionally sponsored investigation with clear restrictions on the appointments—five from the Senate majority leader, five from the speaker of the House, and five, including the chairman, from the president.

What followed was a long year of controversy and constant negotiation as the commission struggled to reach agreement. With time running out and no compromise in sight, a small group of House, Senate, and White House negotiators formed the "Gang of Nine" to find enough tax increases and benefit cuts to keep Social Security running through the early 2000s. Operating under the commission's flag, the gang produced its $170 billion package only days before the commission's charter expired in January 1983.[47]

House Ways and Means Committee ranking member and pivotal Gang of Nine negotiator Barber Conable (R-N.Y.) described the package with perfect understatement just before final passage on March 24, 1983: "I think we all relinquished some long cherished objectives in this process. It was painful, but the sacrifice was well worth the effort and the result. This conference report may not be a work of art, but it is artful work."[48]

The final compromise managed to offend every interest group at the table. Business groups opposed acceleration of scheduled payroll tax increases, the American Association of Retired People opposed benefit cuts, and labor unions opposed increases in the retirement age. Because no one solution produced enough money by itself to solve the crisis, the gang had produced a nearly perfect "house of cards." As Conable told me at the time, "Some things just aren't pretty to watch or easy to do. I've never seen a glamorous opossum or a graceful giraffe. Divorces are never comfortable. The seriously overweight should stay away from short shorts. Deep mud doesn't make for light movements. A politician has a hard time looking relaxed when found with his hand in the cookie jar."[49]

The artful work clearly succeeded in averting the impending crisis and earned the investigation a four-point impact score. However, everyone involved knew that the reforms could not hold once the baby boom generation started to retire. Thirty years of relative security was the best the investigation could guarantee, which was no small achievement given the tenor of the times.

Reversing Course

Six of my investigations involved investigations designed to reverse the strategies that had produced the Vietnam and Iraq wars, the savings and loan crisis, the Enron collapse, the 2008 financial catastrophe, and the national debt impasse. Such investigations are clearly an affront to the incrementalism that so often marks the policy process and are perhaps the most arduous investigatory path to follow. Driven in part by sunk costs often tallied through casualties and spending, Congress and presidents generally favor staying the course through fine-tuning and occasional adjustment. Although the six investigations can be defined as an especially intense form of policy repair, I have singled them out here because of their ambitious goals.

Consider two examples of this highly contentious task.

VIETNAM (1966)

The Vietnam War produced the most prominent investigation in this category, in part because it involved such large sunk costs in lives and treasure. Led by Sen. J. William Fulbright (D-Ark.) and his Committee on Foreign Relations, the eight-year investigation laid a foundation for the eventual withdrawal of U.S. troops. Although Fulbright voted for the 1964 Gulf of Tonkin Resolution authorizing U.S. military action, he came to doubt the Johnson administration's strategy and articulated a new destination in his 1966 book, *The Arrogance of Power*:

> I do not question the power of our weapons and the efficiency of our logistics; I cannot say these things delight me as they seem to delight some of our officials, but they are certainly impressive. What I do question is the ability of the United States, or France or any other Western nation, to go into a small, alien, undeveloped Asian nation and create stability where there is chaos, the will to fight where there is defeatism, democracy where there is no tradition of it, and honest government where corruption is almost a way of life. Our handicap is well expressed in the pungent Chinese proverb: "In shallow waters dragons become the sport of shrimps."[50]

Fulbright was not the only one involved in Vietnam War investigations, however. Sen. John Stennis (D-Miss.) also had his doubts about the war, but he was much more an advocate of policy repair than a reversal in course. It is a point well made by Joseph A. Fry in his book *Debating Vietnam: Fulbright, Stennis, and Their Senate Hearings*. Referring to the competing positions of the two Senate giants, Fry concludes that neither the parallel investigations nor other House and Senate efforts forced Lyndon Johnson to veer fundamentally from his middle-of-the-road, guns-and-butter policy.[51]

This history raises significant questions about the impact of the Vietnam War investigation. Did it make any difference in the course of the war? Did it alter public opinion? Did it shape Johnson's decision not to seek reelection? Did it contribute to Hubert Humphrey's slim defeat? To Nixon's "peace-with-honor" exit?

The answers are not altogether clear. However, there is significant historical evidence that the investigation preceded the growing public demand for resolution. Fulbright was hard at work on his book well before the 1968 Tet

Offensive, which rocked public opinion and added fuel to the antiwar movement, while Stennis was preparing hearings for mid-1966.

Despite Fry's careful analysis, it seems reasonable to argue that Fulbright's investigation changed the course of history through its aggressive fact finding and occasional blame setting. His investigation was not only long, broad, complex, linked, and composed of multiple, nearly simultaneous hearing sets, it was also thorough, operated with significant freedom to investigate, was mostly nonpartisan, produced intense media coverage that included dozens of televised hearings, and generated enormous visibility.

More to the point of impact, the investigation shaped the growing consensus on the need to end what Fulbright believed was an unwinnable and immoral war. The investigation continues to generate modest impacts, in part regarding the development and execution of Iraq and Afghanistan policy. As such, the investigation and its many hearing sets can be safely coded as a high-impact inquiry, in part because of the legitimacy accorded to questioning the war.

THE 2008 FINANCIAL COLLAPSE (2008)

The 2008 financial collapse is one of the most significant events in recent history. It was sudden, global, and economically disastrous. It also created the greatest recession in the nation's history. Technically defined by traditional measures of economic growth, the recession began in 2007 and ended in mid-2009, but it continued to exert its force on financial markets, unemployment, and international debt markets through 2012 and beyond. Punctuated by the fall of Lehman Brothers in September 2008, the crisis spread quickly across the financial sector as the housing market collapsed and mortgage securities plummeted. Four years later, the detritus was still visible, as central banks across the world fought the sovereign debt crisis.

The crisis produced immediate action at both ends of Pennsylvania Avenue. For its part, the Treasury Department cobbled together the $700 billion Troubled Asset Relief Program (TARP) to prop up the banks as credit markets froze; Congress authorized the spending under the Emergency Economic Stabilization Act of 2008 and outsourced oversight to the Congressional Oversight Panel, Congressional Budget Office, Government Accountability Office, and a new special inspector general for TARP. At the same time, the Federal Reserve Board pulled every monetary lever and opened every lending window within reach to stave off a full-blown panic. Throughout, the five-member Congressional Oversight Panel was the lead TARP investigator. Chaired by future Massachusetts Democratic senator Elizabeth Warren, the panel released thirty separate oversight reports between November 2008 and March 2011 and clearly contributed to the broader investigation discussed below.[52]

For its part, Congress soon acted, too. With the markets still in free fall, Sen. Christopher J. Dodd (D-Conn.) and Rep. Barney Frank (D-Mass.) entered an investigatory mode in November. Their parallel investigations ran for just over a year, but led directly to the Dodd-Frank Restoring American Financial Stability Act of 2010. Although the overall investigation produced bureaucratic reforms, policy repairs, enhanced accountability, and agenda setting, I believe the primary investigatory destination was reversing the course of banking deregulation. Although both chambers were front-and-center during the banking investigation, my reading of the record suggests that the Senate Committee on Banking, Housing, and Urban Affairs was the lead investigator, a decision supported by the start dates of the two inquiries and the Banking Committee's role in designing the final bill. Dodd's Senate Banking Committee edged out Frank's House Committee on Banking and Financial Services by starting its investigation only days before. Dodd held the first of his seventy-nine hearings, with former Federal Reserve Board chairman Paul A. Volcker as his lead witness on February 4, 2009, while Frank opened the first of at least fifty hearings six days later, with Federal Reserve Board chairman Ben Bernanke as his lead witness.[53]

The investigation did not begin in either committee, however. Henry Waxman and his House Committee on Oversight and Government Reform held the first investigatory hearing on the crisis barely a month after Lehman collapsed. Despite his aggressive and well-publicized effort to force former Federal Reserve Board chairman Alan Greenspan to apologize for his earlier participation in deregulation—illustrated by the lengthy excerpt from testimony in the endnote attached to this sentence—the catastrophe was beyond Waxman's jurisdiction and soon passed to the Dodd and Frank committees.[54]

Dodd and Frank also conducted their own blame-setting hearings early on. However, their main focus was on a large-scale reversal in course built on fact finding. After more than 120 hearings, hundreds of depositions, interviews, and months of digging, they finally produced a sixteen-title, 2,319-page bill that was enacted in a divisive split-party vote on July 15, 2010. According to the Senate Banking Committee's legislative history, fifty of its eighty hearings focused on assessing the types of reform needed to prevent a future crisis. Although its legislative report is laden with references to the failure of government oversight and policy and was obviously designed to prepare Congress for legislative action, the underlying tone throughout the House and Senate debate was reversing the banking deregulation effort. Dodd made the point when he introduced his draft legislation on November 10, 2009:

It is the job of this Congress to restore responsibility and accountability in our financial system to give Americans confidence that there is a system in place that works for and protects them . . . The financial crisis exposed a financial regulatory structure that was the product of historical accident, created piece by piece over the decades with little thought given to how it would function as a whole and unable to prevent a threat to our economic security . . . I will not stand for attempts to protect a broken status quo, particularly when those attempts are made by some of the same special interests who caused this mess in the first place.[55]

In 2012, however, the jury was still out on the investigation—although it clearly succeeded in creating a very heavy footprint, its impact remains in question. The so-called Volcker rule that would prohibit banks from purchasing investments with their own capital, borrowed or earned, remains under fire as being either too tough or too weak. The rule was the product of an extensive and aggressive investigation by Sen. Carl Levin (D-Mich.) and his Permanent Subcommittee on Oversight (the direct descendant of the Truman World War II procurement inquiries). Levin's investigation was nothing short of brilliant. Deploying every tool available, including aggressive use of the subcommittee's subpoena power, Levin and the subcommittee's ranking Republican, Sen. Tom Coburn (R-Okla.) produced a 640-page final report that continues to exert leverage on the regulatory process and stands as yet another of the subcommittee's exemplary investigations.[56] Given its late entry into the debate, the subcommittee's main role has been to force deeper consideration of possible remedies, but it may be weakened in doing so when Levin retires in 2014.

However, even if the Volcker rule is eventually promulgated (as of spring 2013 it is already two years late), it will face further obstacles as weakened regulatory agencies such as the Securities and Exchange Commission, among others, begin to enforce the provision. Moreover, the rule will face continued opposition even if implemented, including court challenges and evasion. This is one investigation where a bureaucratic reform should have accompanied the policy fix, but did not. Thus future bureaucratic breakdowns are almost inevitable, but do not diminish the investigation's immediate success in creating a three-point impact score.[57]

Before closing this brief history, it is useful to juxtapose the Dodd-Frank investigation against the simultaneous and the president's mostly forgotten Financial Crisis Inquiry Commission headed by former California state treasurer Phil Angelides. Widely heralded by the media as the second coming of the 1932 "Pecora Commission," which investigated the causes of the 1928 stock market crash, the Angelides Commission was late in its launch and was late with its report. Divided along partisan lines, haphazard in approach, and poorly staffed, the commission held its first meeting almost nine months after the Dodd-Frank investigations began and issued its final report six months after the Dodd-Frank bill passed. A *New York Times* summary made particular note of the commission's organizational problems: "Along with partisan disagreements, the commissioners themselves acknowledged that the panel was hampered by a haphazard approach and a lack of time and resources. In early 2010 the panel's executive director stepped aside and a top investigator resigned, frustrated by delays in assembling a staff."[58]

Enhancing Accountability

Fourteen of my investigations involved efforts to enhance accountability. This form of impact involves two options: sending warning shots and creating deterrence. The former is usually directed toward outside entities such as the motion picture industry or baseball in part because government eschewed action even in the face of obvious abuse, while the latter is generally directed toward government fraud, waste, and abuse or personal misconduct.

Warning shots almost always carry the threat of future legislation, but such threats are rarely taken seriously in the short term. In contrast, deterrence almost always produces either new mechanisms for preventing future breakdowns or evidence of misbehavior that might lead to resignations or impeachment. Eleven of my investigations focused on these two paths for enhancing accountability.

WARNING SHOTS

Consider two examples of investigations designed to force action through warning shots.

Quiz Show Rigging (1959)

Having disposed of the Sherman Adams case in 1957, Oren Harris (D-Ark.) and his House Subcommittee on Legislative Oversight moved quickly to another front-page scandal. The investigation began in early 1959 with allegations that quiz shows such as Twenty-One, Dotto, The $64,000 Question, and Tic Tac Dough had been rigged to favor charismatic contestants such as Charles Van Doren, who won $115,000 when his opponent, Herbert Stempel, agreed to name *On the Waterfront* rather than *Marty* as the Academy Award's best picture of 1955.[59]

Whatever his hopes for restarting his large-scale investigation of federal regulatory agencies, Harris took the narrow, simple path again. "The scandal over phony quiz shows is now entering its second year with no sign of a let-up in the publicity free-for-all that has accompanied exposure of the rigged television games," *New York Times* columnist Jack Gould wrote on August 9, 1959. "Obviously the legislative committees have stumbled on an intriguing gambit that should be productive of headlines for several more years . . . For some time, roughly since the eager Greeks first ventured on stage, there has been an urgent need for the elimination of entertainment that isn't what it promises to be. Congress should have a ball."[60]

The Senate Interstate and Foreign Commerce Committee tried several times to open its own inquiry, but Harris was faster and arguably sharper. He quickly discovered, for example, that New York County (basically, Manhattan) had impaneled a grand jury in September 1958 to investigate quiz show rigging and petitioned the district attorney for what turned out to be exclusive access to the sealed records. The records provided a treasure trove of evidence and allowed Harris to focus on the most sensational charges and most compelling witnesses. "Instead of having to call 20 witnesses," he said at the start of the subcommittee's October 9 televised hearing, "we can do it by calling only one or two."[61]

Having taken the lead by cornering the grand jury minutes, the House investigation continued for another year. All told, the quiz show investigation held twenty-four hearings, questioned 140 witnesses, and forced the Federal Communications Commission's chairman to resign. Its most celebrated hearing came on November 2, when Van Doren appeared before the subcommittee and a national television audience to confess his role in the quiz show scandal. The first five minutes of his opening statement is the stuff of which Academy Awards are often made.[62]

I would give almost anything I have to reverse the course of my life in the last 3 years. I cannot take back one word or action; the past does not change for anyone. But at least I can learn from the past.

I have learned a lot in those 3 years, especially in the last 3 weeks. I've learned a lot about life. I've learned a lot about myself, and about the responsibilities any man has to his fellow men. I've learned a lot about good and evil. They are not always what they appear to be. I was involved, deeply involved, in a deception. The fact that I, too, was very much deceived cannot keep me from being the principal victim of that deception, because I was its principal symbol.

There may be a kind of justice in that. I don't know. I do know, and I can say it proudly to this committee, that since Friday, October

16, when I finally came to a full understanding of what I had done and of what I must do, I have taken a number of steps toward trying to make up for it.

I have a long way to go. I have deceived my friends, and I had millions of them. Whatever their feeling for me now, my affection for them is stronger today than ever before. I am making this statement because of them. I hope my being here will serve them well and lastingly.[63]

The confession never quite dispelled what Harris called the "national shock" created by the scandal, the investigation did produce amendments to the Federal Communications Act that prohibited quiz show rigging and pay-to-play bribes, or payola, for shows such as American Bandstand.[64] Otherwise, it was narrow, not particularly complex, and more of a distraction from Sputnik and the cold war than a serious, thorough, and durable investigation by a well-known chairman.[65] Although the scandal still resonates today, the investigation itself is best described as a platform for what Gould called "tantalizing testimony" and earned a two-point impact score.[66]

Steroid Abuse in Professional Baseball (2005)

The 2005 investigation of steroid abuse in baseball was almost inevitable given the swirl of allegations surrounding some of the game's most celebrated players. It was also certain to be explosive, especially given George W. Bush's denunciation of steroid abuse in his 2004 State of the Union address, the Justice Department's investigation of baseball's all-time home-run champion Barry Bonds, and publication of heavily promoted books such as José Canseco's *Juiced: Wild Times, Rampant 'Roids, Smash Hits,* and *How Baseball Got Big.*[67]

Whether a lagging indicator of public interest or the final platform for resolution, the House investigation was clearly designed to force baseball either to act on its own or to face tough federal action under pending legislation, although neither of the competing proposals—the Clean Sports Act and the Professional Sports Integrity and Accountability Act—received more than passing attention. Launched in March 2005 with a hearing titled "Restoring Faith in America's Pastime," the House Oversight and Government Reform Committee's investigation met all expectations for controversy, as baseball icons such as Barry Bonds, Roger Clemens, Mark McGuire, Rafael Palmeiro, and Sammy Sosa faced intense questioning about their use of steroids and other human growth hormones.[68] Although committee chair Tom Davis (R-Va.) later acknowledged that the committee could not be an "arbiter of credibility" and would not be lured into attaching "a coefficient of credibility to different witnesses," he also concluded that several witnesses had lied in "spectacular fashion" in what he viewed as an "unfortunate battle of wills, memories, and reputations."[69]

The investigation was clearly framed from the beginning as a warning shot. Appearing together on *Meet the Press* just days before their first hearing, Davis and Waxman described steroid abuse as a national crisis. "Kids are dying from steroids," Waxman said. "They're looking up to these major league leaders in terms of the enhancements that they're using. And we have to stop it." Davis followed with a warning to baseball: "There's a cloud over baseball, and perhaps a public discussion of the issues, with witnesses testifying under oath, can provide a glimpse of sunlight."[70]

The first question here is whether the warning shot produced the intended effect on baseball, thereby preventing further government regulation.

There is no doubt that the investigation itself was durable. It was also still widely respected for its seriousness, thoroughness, freedom to investigate, and bipartisanship. And it was still exerting leverage in the wake of its early role in forcing professional baseball to launch an internal investigation chaired by former Sen. George J. Mitchell (D-Maine) and implement a voluntary testing system.[71] As such, the first four years of the investigation created a noticeable response by baseball and earned a three-point impact score.

The next question is whether its warning shot began to fade once the new chairman, Rep. Darrell Issa (R-Calif.), moved onto a long list of other scandals and "perp walks" after. The warning shot clearly faded in spring 2012 when a federal jury acquitted pitching great Roger Clemens of lying to Congress about his alleged drug use,[72] and faded even further in early winter when the National League's most valuable player, Ryan Braun, escaped suspension despite a positive drug test.[73]

Nevertheless, the system also showed surprising resiliency. More than two dozen players were suspended for using performance-enhancing drugs in 2013, for example, including Yankee all-star Alex Rodriquez and Braun, while Hall of Fame voters denied entrance to a short list of tainted players in 2013, including Barry Bonds, the single-season and career home-run record leader who broke Hank Aaron's seemingly insurmountable record in 2007 even as the congressional investigation began to dig in. "That's the ultimate goal for every major leaguer," said one of my respondents. "If that's in jeopardy because you used drugs, that's going to make a difference."

DETERRENCE

Consider two examples of investigations designed to create new systems for enhancing deterrence: welfare fraud and government mismanagement.[74]

Welfare Fraud (1975)

The 1975 welfare fraud investigation earned its impact score through the creation of an entirely new regime for detecting and deterring government fraud, waste, and abuse. Launched with a handful of occasional congressional hearings about fraud, waste, and abuse across the federal landscape, the investigation produced legislation creating quasi-independent Offices of Inspector General (OIGs) in most federal departments and agencies and earned a three-point impact score.[75]

The Senate sparked the more visible fraud investigation with a brief set of hearings on "Medicaid mills." Led by the Senate Special Aging Subcommittee on Long-Term Care, this first piece of the welfare fraud investigation featured the results of a sting operation centered largely in New York City, which was in line for a major federal bailout and operated the largest Medicaid program in the nation. According to the subcommittee's review, the city contained dozens of Medicaid mills that billed the government for false complaints and phantom patients.[76] To emphasize its concerns as Congress worked to create a bailout for New York City, the subcommittee used italics in drawing attention to its dramatic summation:

Despite alternate alarms sounded by generations of officeholders and despite an equal number of press releases indicating progress toward establishing accountability, the fraud and the abuse continue in blatant fashion. This situation can no longer be tolerated in view of New York City's fiscal crisis and the commitment of taxpayers' dollars in the form of loans insuring the city's solvency.[77]

Notwithstanding its outrage, the final report had little to say about possible reform, and the investigation would have received a one-point impact score if it had ended there. However, the House Committee on Government Operations soon launched a more substantive, but far less visible, investigation led by little-known Rep. L. H. Fountain (D-N.C.) and his Subcommittee on Intergovernmental Relations and Human Resources.

Fountain was nothing if not persistent and was an experienced investigator. He had led the 1962 investigation of agriculture commodity fraud that put Texas businessman Billie Sol Estes in prison for selling nonexistent commodity leases to clueless investors and produced a constant stream of police patrol hearings over the next fourteen years before turning to welfare fraud.[78]

A tireless advocate of independent government auditing, Fountain seized the welfare issue as another opportunity to expand government deterrence.

Based on back-to-back hearings from April to June 1975, the investigation produced a damning report and a call for a new quasi-independent OIG that would operate from the very top of the Department of Health, Education, and Welfare. Motivated by what it called wasteful expenditure of "huge amounts of tax dollars" and "further concern that fraud and abuse may be seriously impairing the effectiveness of the programs," the subcommittee focused its attention on the administrative infrastructure for detecting fraud, waste, and abuse inside the department.[79]

Fountain soon moved forward on a vast expansion of what would become dozens of OIGs across government. Although the inspectors general were presidential appointees subject to Senate confirmation, they reported to Congress and the president alike (a requirement that the Justice Department argued was unconstitutional[80]) and were authorized to set their agenda, hire their own staff, and collect any information they needed to compile their audits, investigations, and evaluations. Congress created twelve OIGs under Fountain's 1978 Inspector General Act and added another fifteen in 1988; the number stood at seventy-three in 2012.[81] As if to prove the investigation's durability, Congress began thinking about an OIG for the judicial branch in 2006. The resulting expansion of special OIGS to cover everything from tax administration (TIGTA) to Afghanistan reconstruction (SIGAR) also supports the three-point impact score.

The score would have been one point higher if the OIGs could prove that they actually deter fraud, waste, and abuse. However, the OIGs have long relied on simple measures such as dollars saved or funds put to better use for documenting their success, measures that prompted Congress to amend the 1978 act to require a more disciplined accounting. As part of Reagan's "war on waste," for example, the OIGs often measured their success through what I have described elsewhere as a "statistical body count" of new audits and investigations.[82] Although the onslaught of activity no doubt produced at least some of the visible odium of deterrence referenced earlier in this book, it was directed to ex post accountability, not ex ante prevention.

Moreover, the quality of the individual inspectors general and the performance of their offices have been uneven at best. Despite notable successes in both ex ante and ex post accountability at the Agriculture, Health and Human Services, Interior, and Justice departments, for example, other offices have behaved more like poodles than junkyard dogs, as the analogy goes, after years of politicization by Democratic and Republican presidents alike.[83] As if to demonstrate the continued executive branch opposition to the inspector general concept, many OIGs were decimated by staffing caps and cuts during the Clinton administration's "reinventing government" campaign, while the

George W. Bush administration deliberately left many inspector general posts unfilled, a practice the Obama administration has continued.[84]

Nevertheless, the 1975 welfare fraud investigation continues to produce impact through incremental adjustments, including a 2008 amendment giving inspectors general a seven-year term, protection from political interference, and a job description that requires "integrity and demonstrated ability in accounting, auditing, financial analysis, law, management analysis, public administration, or investigations."

The statute also required presidents to notify Congress no later than fifteen days in advance of an inspector general's removal, prohibited inspectors general from receiving cash awards or bonuses, which severed a potential source of executive influence, and gave each OIG a separate budget line.[85] As Sen. Claire McCaskill (D-Mo.) explained the legislation just before final passage, the inspectors general "are a first line of defense on behalf of taxpayers and against Government waste and inefficiency. They are the first line of defense because they are inside Federal agencies." As she continued, "Inspectors general inside Federal agencies are facing mountains of waste and inefficiency. If they are to do their jobs the way Congress intended, they must be independent, and their work must be immediately accessible to the public."[86]

Government Mismanagement (1989)

The four-year investigation into government mismanagement produced its impact by strengthening the federal government's performance monitoring systems. Launched and led by the Senate Governmental Affairs Committee, the investigation paralleled several other management investigations that were conducted before, during, and after the inquiry and led by committee chair John Glenn (D-Ohio), including Defense Department fraud, waste, and abuse (1985), obsolete military bases (1988), and the Housing and Urban Development scandal (1989). According to a LexisNexis search of congressional publications from 1983 to 1993, Congress held more than 1,500 hearings and passed thirty-five public laws under the broad subject of "government efficiency" over the decade.

Management reform was clearly in the air, as were critiques of virtually every federal operating system. A dozen committees and subcommittees held hearings on their piece of the problem, including procurement, information technology, financial systems, and even the sluggish presidential appointments process. With the Reagan administration's hortatory "war on waste" over, Congress turned to the more serious task of building legislative remedies.

With Glenn in the lead, the 1989 Senate investigation achieved its impact through a long list of new statutes, most notably the 1990 Chief

Financial Officers Act, the 1994 Government Performance and Results Act, and the 1994 authorization of Vice President Al Gore's reinventing government campaign.

The first of these statutes established chief financial officer posts in all federal executive agencies and required every department and agency to produce a consolidated financial statement each year; the second created an entirely new performance measurement system; and the third laid the basis for an eight-year, again mostly hortatory, effort to cut the number of federal employees, spur innovation, eliminate agency red tape, and streamline management systems. Along with a long list of complementary statutes, the investigation created a broad deterrence system built on new reporting and measurement requirements, earning a three-point impact score.

Alongside the many hearings, disjointed though they sometimes seemed, the investigation also involved at least two presidential commissions: (1) the 1982 Private Sector Survey on Cost Control, chaired by J. Peter Grace, chairman and chief executive officer of W. R. Grace and Company, and (2) the 1993 National Performance Review chaired by Al Gore. The Grace Commission was appointed by Reagan and exhorted to "be bold," while Clinton established the National Performance Review as a presidential advisory body.

Both produced their share of recommendations for action, some of which produced modest impact, others of which were soon forgotten. Although the Grace Commission claimed that its recommendations would produce $2 trillion in savings, there is no firm evidence that it produced any savings at all.

In turn, the Gore reinventing government effort was immediately dismantled when the Bush administration entered office and is now buried in a cyber cemetery at the University of North Texas. The two commissions had very different approaches to investigating government performance, the first heavily focused on reducing waste and the second on liberating federal organizations from needless rules and oversight. However, both embraced the general notion that government should be more accountable for its performance.[87]

Setting the Agenda

Fifteen of my investigations involved efforts to set the agenda for future action. This kind of impact is not necessarily measured in the short term by new legislation or regulations, but by the rise of a given issue as "an idea in good currency" for longer-term action.[88]

Consider two examples of investigations that set the future agenda.

GOVERNMENT INFORMATION MANAGEMENT (1963)

At first glance, the 1963 investigation of government information plans and policies appears to be a relatively insignificant investigation. But as chapter 2 notes, the investigation laid the foundation for passage of the Freedom of Information Act and continues to propel demands for heightened government transparency. Given the enduring success, the 1963 investigation earned a four-point impact score.

The investigation was triggered by allegations that the Kennedy administration had managed the news during the Cuban missile crisis, but actually reflected long-held concerns about information policy dating back to the formation of the Special Government Information Subcommittee of the House Government Operations Committee in 1955. As its chairman, John E. Moss (D-Calif.), said at the start of the brief investigation, his subcommittee had been following the issue for eleven years before the latest Kennedy administration allegations emerged. Although there was clearly a fire alarm on the surface, the investigation was one in a long inventory of police patrol inquiries regarding information management across government. Moss's opening statement at the first of his 1963 hearings made the case quite clearly:

> Management of the facts of Government becomes the center of public interest and a target of criticism particularly in a time of crisis. I am referring to the short-of-war type of crisis or emergency.
>
> Subcommittee investigations long ago led me to the conclusion that in this concept Government information policies often are extemporized rather than based on carefully preconceived plans that should be made available and understandable to the public and news media in advance.
>
> The recent Cuban crisis is a classic example. This period, with its attendant confusion of news handling, brought into focus the need for careful advance planning for the purpose of keeping the public accurately informed without, at the same time, playing into the hands of our opponents.[89]

Moss's hearings tackled the relatively narrow "who-did-what" facts of the case, which was the most visible part of his subcommittee's many hearings. When viewed as a discrete investigation, however, the hearings produced a clear finding: the federal government needed a systematic policy for releasing information. There would always be information that was too sensitive to release, but selective manipulation of the facts was not only self-serving, but also misleading.

The hearings covered much more than the Cuban missile crisis. Moss pivoted off his opening hearing on the case to similar allegations regarding the Office of Emergency Planning, the Defense Department, and NASA. And as if he anticipated the future cascade of good news from Vietnam, Moss conducted a 419-page hearing on May 24 entirely on early allegations that the Kennedy administration was overselling success.

The point here is not to revisit my earlier description of this forgotten investigation, but to highlight its role in shaping the 1966 Freedom of Information Act. Moss authored and sponsored the House version of the act, led five subcommittee hearings justifying passage, drafted the full committee's legislative report, and was the lead negotiator in the final compromise with the Senate. More important for scoring his investigation's impact, his 1963 hearings generated many of the cases used to push the final proposal forward and were cited repeatedly in the House and Senate legislative reports that accompanied the bill to the floor.[90]

TRAFFIC SAFETY (1965)

The traffic safety investigation created its impact by forging a new consensus on the need to regulate a long-protected industry. Launched by Sen. Abraham Ribicoff (D-Conn.) and his Senate Government Operations Subcommittee on Executive Reorganization, the investigation was sparked by Ralph Nader's best-selling book *Unsafe at Any Speed*.[91] Although Nader succeeded in making the General Motors (GM) Corvair a household synonym for danger, the Senate investigation prepared Congress for action.

The eleven-hearing, fifty-witness investigation ended just days before the one-year mark and created an eight-point investigatory footprint for its breadth, freedom to investigate, visibility, seriousness, thoroughness, leverage, durability, and bipartisanship. Its footprint would have been even heavier but for its length, relatively narrow focus, and Ribicoff's junior status. He was no doubt a well-known political figure and would earn a 1966 *New York Times* profile calling him "a cautious crusader," but Ribicoff was still an unknown investigator when he called the subcommittee to order on March 22, 1965."[92]

Nevertheless, the investigation shows the link between footprints and impact. It clearly carried more than enough weight to set the agenda for eventual action, which was carried forward by the House and Senate Commerce committees in hearings that began in March 1966. Even before the investigation ended, it had already prompted the Johnson administration to outline its own proposal for new traffic safety rules on March 2, 1966. The president not only embraced many of the proposals floating through Ribicoff's hearings, but also proposed creation of a Department of Transportation to consolidate the federal government's far-flung inventory of safety programs that were then buried in five departments and three agencies.[93] Although there was plenty of amending ahead, the subcommittee had clearly crystallized the demand for action.

Despite its eventual four-point impact score, the investigation itself lumbered on with little drama. Except for a final hearing on GM's secret investigation of Nader's personal life, the hearings involved the standard list of witnesses who gave standard testimony, answered standard questions, and appeared in standard order, with federal agencies first, industry executives second, and Nader third.

Placed on the investigatory hot seat, the government and industry executives used the same lines over and over. As the secretary of commerce said at the very top of the first of the subcommittee's eleven hearings, traffic fatalities were everyone's and no one's fault:

> Most traffic accidents happen to normal people driving in a normal way on normal roads in all kinds and makes of cars. There isn't a special type of person or road or car that accounts for most accidents. It isn't the drunk or the young; it isn't the convertible or the ill-maintained car; and it isn't the road with curves or grades that account[s] for significant numbers of accidents. Mainly, it is the fact that drivers are being asked to make judgments they can't make well; to make decisions faster than is humanly possible; and to make changes in steering and speed more accurately than they possibly can.[94]

In other words, cars don't kill drivers, drivers kill drivers.

The subcommittee's growing base of information proved otherwise. According to industry records, almost 9 million cars, or one in five cars that had been manufactured and sold, were recalled for quality checks between 1960 and 1966. The data put the lie to the bad-driver argument: "It shatters once and for all the myth that accidents are invariably caused by bad driving," Ribicoff said. "From now on, we must be concerned—not just with the 'nut behind the wheel,' but with the nut in the wheel itself."[95]

If Ribicoff and his colleagues expected Nader to create broad media coverage, they were mistaken. Nader is said to have helped to design the investigation, and his formal statement was a model of thoughtful argument,[96] but his live testimony frequently strayed from traffic safety issues to his views of environmental destruction, automobile sales strategies, cosmetic advertising, and human motivation. At one point, for example, he argued that automobile advertising was not "aimed at the reason of men, but at their ids and hypogastria." The comment prompted a short discussion of automobile advertising and the definition of just what the terms mean. Sen. Carl T. Curtis (R-Neb.) got the digression rolling by teasing Nader: "If I ever bought a car for those reasons, nobody explained it to me."[97]

Even the quick hearing on GM's investigation of Nader was a disappointment to news-hungry reporters. GM admitted that it had hired private investigators to comb Nader's professional associations, but denied any role in keeping Nader awake at night with endless phone calls or interviewing girlfriends about his sexual behavior. Some argue that Ribicoff's comments on this aspect of the hearing made the overall investigation slightly longer than a year.[98]

This last hearing was no doubt controversial, but was far from the capstone Ribicoff wanted. Nevertheless, he was able to start that hearing with a clear statement of his hoped-for impact: "I think our inquiry has been helpful. It has shed light on important matters that have long been only dimly understood . . . And at the same time, the hearings have quickened the determination of the experts in many quarters to make highway travel as safe as possible, as soon as possible."[99] And that is precisely what the investigation produced.

Resolving Doubts

Twelve of my investigations were primarily centered on resolving doubts about a controversy or event. Again, many of these investigations were also concerned about repair and other forms of deterrence and prevention. But their primary impact resided in a hoped-for end to ongoing debates about who did what. Roughly three-fifths of these investigations used fact finding to reach their final judgments, while the rest used blame setting.

THE KENNEDY ASSASSINATION (1963)

The investigation of the Kennedy assassination was designed in part to end the debate about who killed the young president on November 22, 1963. The question was not just about who pulled the trigger, however. It also involved allegations that there were other shooters, accomplices, moneymen, and high-level conspirators.

President Johnson was the driving force behind the blue-ribbon President's Commission on the Kennedy Assassination. With a long list of investigations either under way or about to be launched in the House, Senate, and Justice Department, Federal Bureau of Investigation (FBI), and even the state of Texas, Johnson preempted the chaos through his executive order creating the commission. According to Robert A. Caro's detailed account of the commission, Johnson acted both to reassure the country and to protect himself from charges that he was somehow involved in the assassination—after all, was he not in Texas when Kennedy was killed?[100]

Johnson's intention to put the doubts to rest was clear in his courtesy phone calls to congressional leaders on November 29, only hours before he created the commission. As his two phone calls to Sen. Richard Russell (D-Ga.) that day amply suggest, Johnson was not to be denied in recruiting his close allies to the seven-member body. When he first called Russell at 4:05 p.m., his old friend was compliant as Johnson explained the need for a commission:

> We're trying to avoid all the House committees . . . and Bobby Kennedy has got his ideas . . . so I've about concluded that I can get people pretty well together and I talked to the leadership on trying to have the three branches . . . on about a seven-man board . . . I think it would be better than the Judiciary running one investigation, the House running another investigation . . . and having four or five going opposite directions.[101]

Johnson called Russell again four hours later to tell him that he wanted him to be his "man on that Commission." Russell again resisted the president's request:

> Well now, Mr. President, I know I don't have to tell you of my devotion to you, but I just can't serve on that Commission ... with Chief Justice Warren . . . I don't like that man. I don't have any confidence in him at all . . .

But Johnson gave the leader of the southern Democrats no choice:

> Dick . . . it has been announced and you can serve with anybody for the good of America and this is a question that has a good many more ramifications than on the surface and we've got to take this out of the arena where they're testifying that Khrushchev and Castro did this and did that . . . you're going to lend your name to this thing . . . I gave the announcement . . . it is already in the papers and you're on it and you're going to be my man on it.[102]

Russell clearly did not know that Johnson had already made the announcement sometime between the two calls, nor did he know that Warren had accepted the chairmanship. By the time he called Russell a second time, at 8:55 p.m., his old friend was furious: "You ought to have told me you were going to name me." After a short "did" and "did not" exchange between the two legislative giants, Johnson said he was "begging" Russell to serve. Russell's response was a classic summation of the Johnson style: "You've never begged me," he told the president. "You've always told me."[103]

Russell was not the only reluctant member of the commission, however. Chief Justice Earl Warren demurred as well, but agreed to chair the effort after meeting with Johnson only hours before the president's announcement.[104] According to one of my Johnson-era respondents, Warren finally relented under withering pressure and began building the commission's investigatory infrastructure the next day.[105] With a full-time staff of eighty-seven supported by more than 210 FBI and Secret Service agents, the commission produced its 888-page report less than a year later. It also produced twenty-five volumes of evidence that were not fully released until the 1990s. Although Warren protected his freedom to investigate, albeit within a fairly narrow definition of the key questions at hand, the commission reached Johnson's hoped-for conclusion nonetheless: Lee Harvey Oswald, and Lee Harvey Oswald alone, fired the shots that killed Kennedy.[106]

The commission's logic was simple: Oswald owned the rifle that fired the three shots, carried it into the book depository, was at the window when the shots were fired, had the skill needed to fire three shots in quick order as Kennedy passed below, left his fingerprints on the rifle, later killed Dallas policeman J. D. Tippit in an apparent attempt to escape, resisted arrest, and repeatedly lied to the police. The commission also rejected the swirl of conspiracy theories involving Cuba, organized crime, a second shooter positioned on a grassy knoll ahead of the motorcade, the military-industrial complex, and the Central Intelligence Agency (CIA) with three simple words: "Oswald acted alone."[107]

Despite its unequivocal conclusion, the commission never fully convinced the public that Oswald had acted alone. Nor did the commission end the investigatory activity, which fueled at least four other investigations over the next twenty years:

—The first was launched in 1968 by Attorney General Ramsey Clark and endorsed the commission's finding that Oswald fired the shots that killed Kennedy, a point never questioned by any of the investigations.

—The second was launched in 1975 by Gerald Ford's executive order. Headed by Vice President Nelson Rockefeller, it endorsed all of the commission's findings.

—The third was also launched in 1975 as part of Sen. Frank Church's (D-Idaho) broad investigation of CIA abuses, which is discussed in chapter 5. Unlike the Warren Commission and its progeny, the Church Select Committee to Study Government Operations with Respect to Intelligence concluded that the FBI and CIA may have withheld crucial evidence from the commission and that the FBI was clearly pressured to refute the conspiracy theories. However, the committee also concluded that it had seen no evidence of any conspiracy involving Cuba or regarding the commission's broad conclusions. The fact that intelligence agencies may have failed to inform the commission of "certain information" did not lead the Church investigation to conclude that there had been a conspiracy.[108]

—The fourth was launched in 1975 by the House Select Committee on Assassinations, which affirmed the Warren Commission's finding that Oswald fired the shots that killed the president but concluded that there was a high probability that two shooters fired shots at the president, one from behind the motorcade and the other from the front.

The House Select Committee investigation was the most aggressive of the four in concluding that there was a "high probability" that two gunmen fired at the president."[109] Its challenge to the Warren Commission was based almost entirely on a police radio recording from a heavily worn "dictabelt." However, even the committee's own experts disputed the evidence, which one said provided a fifty-fifty probability at best.[110]

Nevertheless, the 1975 investigations put the assassination back in the news, while questioning the underlying motivations of the Warren Commission even as it rejected the conspiracy theory. In doing so, this secondary investigation reduced the commission's long-term impact and fueled further speculation by a long list of doubters, perhaps most notably filmmaker Oliver Stone.[111]

Moreover, the Warren report did not settle public doubts. According to a stream of public opinion surveys forty years after the assassination, the vast majority of Americans rejected the single-shooter theory. Interviewed in November 2003, 75 percent of Americans told the Gallup poll that "others were involved in a conspiracy," 65 percent told the ABC News poll that there were "still important unanswered questions about the assassination," and 68 percent told the CBS News poll that there had been a "cover-up to keep the public from learning the truth about the Kennedy assassination."[112]

Given these polls, it is easy to argue that the Warren Commission did not resolve the public's lingering doubts. However, the polls may be rooted more in a general distrust of government than the facts at hand. The vast majority of Americans may believe that unnamed others were involved in the assassination, for example, but they do not have any culprits in mind.[113]

The Warren Commission was not perfect, however, and lost weight for its brevity, narrowness, and one-dimensional view of the shooting. Yet, it still earned a three-point impact score based on its unshakable durability. More-over, even if its findings turn sour, I could easily give the commission credit for a fair amount of impact in clearing the path for Johnson's guns-and-butter legislation. By removing the assassination from the agenda, the commission made space for legislative breakthroughs that are still in force, but no doubt under fire.

WACO AND RUBY RIDGE (1995)

The Justice Department had a very bad year in 1995, as two highly visi-ble incidents entered the investigatory arena several years after they occurred. The first of the two investigations involved the 1993 siege in Waco, Texas, while the second involved the 1992 siege near Ruby Ridge, Idaho.

Both investigations were launched only months after Republicans recap-tured Congress following almost fifty years in the minority. Both also implied that Democrats had ignored the breakdowns in parliamentary deference to the Clinton administration (Waco) or expressed a show of support for federal law enforcement (Ruby Ridge).

Waco

Led by Rep. Bill Clinger (R-Pa.) and his Committee on Government Reform and Oversight with the House Committee on the Judiciary in a sec-ondary role, the Waco investigation began on April 15, 1995, but dated back almost two years to the April 19, 1993, fiery assault on the Branch Davidi-ans compound by the Bureau of Alcohol, Tobacco, and Firearms (ATF) and the FBI.

The Waco investigation began two years after a tragic standoff between federal law enforcement and members of the Branch Davidian religious sect. Led by the House Subcommittee on National Security, International Affairs, and Criminal Justice, the investigation centered on allegations that the ATF was "grossly incompetent" and that the Department of Justice and FBI were "irresponsible" and "negligent" at the end.

The siege began on February 28, 1995, after ATF agents attempted to search the Davidian residential compound. Unaware that the sect's leader, David Koresh, had been tipped off about their plans, seventy-six ATF agents stormed the compound and were met by withering gunfire. Four agents were killed and another twenty were wounded during the ninety-minute battle.

The FBI immediately took control of the siege and began negotiating with Koresh. Two months later with full knowledge and approval of Attorney General Janet Reno, the FBI launched an early morning assault on the Branch

Davidian residential compound. The siege ended after eighty men, women, and children had died from gunshots and fire.

In addition, congressional investigators eventually discovered that, contrary to its initial testimony, the FBI had used pyrotechnic tear gas grenades at the start of the assault, which may have been the source of the deadly fire. Government Reform Committee chairman Dan Burton (R-Ind.) used the new evidence to open a follow-up investigation in September 1999 that excoriated Reno for mismanaging the siege.

At virtually the same moment that Burton reopened the dormant investigation, Reno appointed former Sen. John C. Danforth (R-Mo.) to conduct an independent investigation of his own, thereby setting the stage for dueling reports. Whereas the Burton report concluded that Clinton should have demanded Reno's resignation upon release of the FBI documents, Danforth's report exonerated the FBI of the same allegations.[114]

Ruby Ridge

The Ruby Ridge investigation began on September 6, 1995, but dated back to the 1992 siege of a federal fugitive and avowed "apocalypse" ideologue named Randy Weaver. Trapped in his forest cabin on the top of Ruby Ridge on August 21, Weaver and a compatriot engaged in a running gunfight with a trio of U.S. marshals who had approached the cabin to serve an arrest warrant for having allegedly purchased two sawed-off shotguns in an ATF sting.

Although it is not clear who fired the first shots, the gunfight took a heavy toll: by the end of the second day, a deputy U.S. marshal, Weaver's wife, and his teenage son were dead. The ATF, U.S. Marshals Service, and FBI were all involved in the seven-day standoff that followed, but the FBI came under intense scrutiny for having killed Vicki Weaver.

Unlike the dueling Waco investigations, there was just one investigation of Ruby Ridge. Chaired by Sen. Arlen Specter (R-Pa. at the time), the Subcommittee on Terrorism and Government Information laid the blame for the Ruby Ridge shootings on federal law enforcement and Weaver in almost equal amounts. Weaver was to blame for provoking the confrontation, but the subcommittee minced few words in criticizing federal law enforcement as well: "Federal law enforcement professionals are held to a higher standard than ordinary American citizens. This country can tolerate mistakes made by people like Randy Weaver, but we cannot accept serious errors made by federal law enforcement agencies that needlessly result in human tragedy."[115]

Both investigations started with a singular focus on resolving doubts about federal law enforcement, in no small part because serious investigators initially led the reviews. Nevertheless, the Waco investigation was highly divisive and was the first of many House Republican investigations designed to assault the Clinton administration. "Opposition to the Waco hearings was to be expected," the final report began. "What was not expected was the extent to which the administration tried to control potential damage from the hearings." After noting that the White House had established a special "damage control team," the final report argued that the most "disturbing counter-measure" was Clinton's allegation that "the hearings were an attack on law enforcement."[116]

The partisanship is easy to identify in the hearing transcripts, which are peppered with rancor, and in the back pages of the 1979 final report, which contained multiple dissents signed by seventeen Democrats. According to the *New York Times*, the two parties had reversed their traditional positions in the hearings, with the Democrats working tirelessly to prevent the Republicans from embarrassing the administration. "The problem for the Republicans was in their conception of the hearings," then Rep. Charles E. Schumer (D-N.Y.) said. "To accomplish what they wanted, they had to make David Koresh a somewhat sympathetic figure."[117]

In contrast, the Ruby Ridge investigation produced a unanimous report. As Specter argued at the start of the investigation, this was no time for partisanship: "We have had a very close collaboration with both sides," Specter noted in gaveling the first hearing to order, "and we are pledged to conduct a nonpartisan, bipartisan inquiry on the facts without any regard to Democrats or Republicans or any political considerations or any political overtones."

As for their impact in resolving doubts, the Waco investigation produced negligible effects and received a one-point impact score. In fact, the investigation may have done more to inflame doubts than resolve them and may have contributed to Timothy McVeigh's twisted logic as he made his final preparations for the Oklahoma City bombing. Perhaps because of its bipartisanship, the Ruby Ridge investigation produced a slightly higher impact in the wake of the Justice Department's own internal reviews on the use of deadly force and received a two-point score. There will always be a restless community who sees "jack-booted government thugs" behind every tree, but the event has been long closed for most Americans.[118]

A DEMOGRAPHIC OVERVIEW OF DESTINATIONS

The six destinations share many of the characteristics already discussed in my earlier analysis of repair versus prevention as an investigatory purpose, but are part of a characteristic themselves. After all, the six destinations were carved out of my original measure of investigatory purpose as either repair or prevention. Nevertheless, the six can be compared across all of my standard demographic measures except for purpose.

Footprints

Just as investigations involve different destinations, they produce different footprints. Investigations designed to reverse the course of national policy involved the heaviest footprints at a 9.8 average, followed by setting the agenda at 6.5, reforming bureaucracies at 5.6, repairing policies at 5.3, resolving doubts at 4.6, and enhancing accountability at 4.1. Further comparisons using the low-high impact measure suggest the following patterns.

History

History produced only two effects on the six investigatory destinations.

—Investigations designed to reverse course increased steadily from none in the post–World War II period to 67 percent during divided government. The trend arguably reflects a backlash against the policy punctuations during the Great Society period and the banking and Iraq War crises.

—Investigations designed to set the agenda declined dramatically over time, dropping from 33 percent during each of the first two historical periods to 17 percent and 67 percent, respectively, in the last two.

As for presidential terms and election years, investigations designed to repair bureaucracies and public policies were slightly more likely to occur during second terms, while the other four destinations were more likely to be found in first terms. However, these historical differences were generally small and easily washed away in the if-then analysis presented below.

Investigatory Characteristics

Investigatory characteristics can be viewed as either a product or a driver of destinations. Committees and commissions that specialize in bureaucratic repair may pay more attention to one trigger or another, while process break-downs are the obvious spark for bureaucratic reform. This analysis cannot resolve the if-then path, but it does show variation across the destinations.

Start with institutional home, where Congress led the vast majority of the investigations designed to reform bureaucracies (88 percent), repair policies

(90 percent), reverse course (83 percent), enhance accountability (86 percent), and set the agenda (67 percent), while the presidency led exactly 50 percent of the investigations designed to resolve doubts, all of which involved blue-ribbon commissions.

Turn next to congressional chamber, where the House led 55 percent of the investigations designed to repair policies and 50 percent of the investigations designed to enhance accountability, while the Senate led 64 percent of the investigations designed to reform bureaucracies, 50 percent of the investigations designed to reverse course, and 60 percent of the investigations designed to set the agenda, even as the Senate had the larger percentage of investigations designed to resolve doubts (33 percent for the Senate versus 17 percent for the House).

Move next to venue, where the largest percentage of investigations designed to reform bureaucracies (39 percent) and repair policies (35 percent) occurred in subcommittees, while the largest percentage of investigations designed to enhance accountability occurred in either subcommittees or full committees (36 percent each), and the largest percentage of investigations designed to resolve doubts belonged to commissions (50 percent). Investigations designed to reverse course split equally across full committees, subcommittees, and commissions (33 percent each), and investigations designed to set the agenda split in almost equal amounts across all four venues (20 percent in full committees, 20 percent in special congressional bodies, 27 percent in subcommittees, and 33 percent in commissions).

Finally focus on triggers, issues, breakdowns, and methodology, where the six destinations varied as follows:

—Fire alarms were more likely to trigger investigations designed to repair policies (70 percent), enhance accountability (79 percent), and resolve doubts (58 percent), while police patrols were more likely to trigger investigations designed to set the agenda (80 percent), and investigations designed to reform bureaucracies or reverse course were split between the two triggers almost equally.

—Domestic issues were at the core of investigations designed to reform bureaucracies (73 percent), repair policies (65 percent), reverse course (67 percent), enhance accountability (79 percent), and resolve doubts (67 percent), while foreign issues were a somewhat larger focus in agenda setting (53 percent).

—Process breakdowns were at the core of investigations designed to reform bureaucracies (82 percent); policy breakdowns were central in investigations designed to reverse course (83 percent) and set the agenda (93 percent); the other three destinations were driven forward by a blend of process or policy breakdowns. Personal misconduct accounted for just 29 percent of investigations designed to enhance accountability, 25 percent of investigations designed to repair policies, 9 percent of investigations designed to reform bureaucracies, and none of the other destinations.

—Fact finding was more likely to be associated with investigations designed to reform bureaucracies (55 percent), set the agenda (60 percent), and resolve doubts (58 percent), while blame setting was more likely to be associated with investigations designed to repair policies (65 percent) and enhance accountability (93 percent). The two methods split equally among the investigations designed to reverse course.

Party Control

Party control produced only a handful of significant relationships among the six investigatory destinations.

For example, divided government produced a higher percentage of investigations designed to repair policies (27 percent versus 8 percent), while unified government produced a higher percentage of investigations designed to reform bureaucracies (41 percent versus 29 percent). Similarly, divided congresses produced slightly higher percentages of investigations designed to repair policies (29 percent versus 18 percent), but unified congresses produced slightly higher percentages of investigations designed to reform bureaucracies (41 percent versus 31 percent).

Although there were other differences down the list of party control measures, they were relatively small and sporadic—for example, Republican control of government produced higher percentages of investigations designed to change course (17 percent versus 5 percent) and enhance accountability (33 percent versus 13 percent), while Democratic control produced higher percentages of investigations designed to reform bureaucracies (42 percent versus 29 percent), but lower percentages of investigations designed to repair policies (7 percent versus 26 percent). The same patterns continued for the House and Senate parties, where Republican majorities produced higher percentages of investigations designed to increase accountability, while Democratic majorities produced higher percentages of investigations designed to set the agenda.

The House and Senate party matchups against presidents of the other party produced modest variations in preferences for one destination over another:

—Thirty-six percent of the matchups between House Democratic majorities and Republican presidents focused on policy repair, 29 percent on bureaucratic reform, 14 percent each on enhanced accountability and resolving doubts, and 7 percent on reversing course. Reform and repair were the dominant destinations, perhaps as Democrats tried to protect their favored programs.

—Fifty-seven percent of the matchups between House Republican majorities and Democratic presidents focused on policy repair, 29 percent on enhanced accountability, 14 percent on bureaucratic reform, and none on reversing course, setting the agenda, or resolving doubts. Repair was by far the dominant focus, perhaps as Republicans sought to constrain government.

—Thirty-six percent of the matchups between Senate Democratic majorities and Republican presidents focused on agenda setting, 29 percent on bureaucratic reform, 21 percent on policy repair, 7 percent each on reversing course and enhanced accountability, and none for resolving doubts. The preference was for agenda setting first and reform and repair second, perhaps as Democrats tried to build momentum for future action, while fixing their favored agencies and programs.

—Thirty percent each of the matchups between Senate Republican majorities and Democratic presidents focused on bureaucratic reform and enhanced accountability, 20 percent each on policy repair and resolving doubts, and none on reversing course or setting the agenda. Reform and accountability led the destinations, but Republicans were seemingly more reactive than deliberate in their choices.

Impact

The six destinations achieved very different levels of impact on my four-point impact score. Investigations designed to reverse course were the most likely to achieve a great deal of impact (50 percent), followed by investigations designed to set the agenda (27 percent), repair policies (20 percent), reform bureaucracies (20 percent), and enhance accountability and resolve doubts at 0 percent each.

This sorting is echoed in the low-high impact score where investigations designed to reverse course were the most likely to achieve a high amount of impact (83 percent), followed by investigations designed to set the agenda (60 percent), repair policies (40 percent), reform bureaucracies (39 percent), enhance accountability (36 percent), and resolve doubts (8 percent).

EXPLAINING IMPACT

This book has now reached the end of its search for answers about what causes what in the investigatory arena. Simply asked, what drives impact? How much do footprints affect impacts? What is the role of party control?

And do investigatory characteristics play a role in predicting the ultimate result of an investigation?

Noting for a last time that investigators cannot control either their time in history or which party is in control at the start of their investigation, the focus here is on what they can do in making preliminary choices about early steps—choices that often occur at the very beginning of an investigation. They can only do so much about the freedom to investigate, although well-known leaders of investigations may have the institutional muscle to resist the pressure to limit their work. They can also derive some confidence from past investigations that operated under tight control—ten of the forty-eight investigations with little or no freedom to investigate still produced a fair amount or a great deal of impact, for example. Finally, they can gain some confidence from having a well-known investigator such as Levin or Waxman—twenty-four of the thirty-five investigations with well-known leadership produced a fair amount or a great deal of impact.

A First Answer

Correlations continue to provide a first statistical tool for sorting relationships. Recall one last time, however, that correlations only reveal the presence of yes-no relationships between two measures, although these relationships may provide hints of later predictions about what matters most to impact.

The following pages do not contain any further analysis of the relationships between history, party control, and impact—none of the historical or party control measures produced any significant correlations with impact, nor did they produce any significant effects in the regressions. Party control just does not matter in these analyses, although more sophisticated techniques might reveal something profound. At least here, divided and unified we govern. And we govern in both election years and off years, first terms and second, and across the decades, divided by Watergate or not.

FOOTPRINTS

Recall that the correlations between the eleven footprint weights and the four-point impact score offer an initial glimpse of what produces an investigation done well.

As the yes-no relationships show, the durability of an investigation produced the most significant correlation with impact, followed in descending order of significance by breadth, complexity, freedom to investigate, seriousness, leadership, thoroughness, leverage, bipartisanship, and visibility, thereby stranding length as the only no-show. Given these significant relationships, it is hardly shocking that the eleven-point footprint score is strongly correlated with impact.

Investigators who wonder how their world has changed might want to compare the relationships between the eleven weights and impact before and after Watergate. As the correlations suggest, Watergate had little impact as a dividing line for sorting the relationships. However, three relationships became much stronger after Watergate:

—Well-known leadership of an investigation was modestly related to impact before Watergate, but was highly significant after. Based on these correlations, recruiting well-known leadership is even more important today than it was in the pre-Watergate years.

—Freedom to investigate followed the same pattern, rising from modest significance before Watergate to high significance after. Again based on these correlations, investigators would do well to pay maximum attention to securing this freedom, even if that means fighting their institutional leadership to gain it.

—Bipartisanship was not significantly related to impact before Watergate, but rose to modest significance after. Again based on these correlations, investigators would do well to pay at least some attention to the comity within their inquiries. It may not be the most important relationship on the list, but it is still significant.

Whether investigators can hold these relationships into the future is anyone's guess, especially given the rising tide of polarization reported by the *National Journal* in 2011. But they would be well advised to try if they wish to achieve impact. As for visibility, it does not matter to impact in either period. It may be one of the top indicators of the good investigation, especially considering the many calls for media attention in assorted investigatory manuals, but it does not hold up in the analysis thus far.

INVESTIGATORY CHARACTERISTICS

The correlations show three characteristics that had a significant yes-no relationship with impact regardless of Watergate: (1) pursuing fact finding, (2) using a commission, and (3) avoiding investigations of personal misconduct. The correlations also show at least five characteristics that became more important after Watergate, two toward a negative relationship and three toward a positive:

—Investigations launched by the House were not correlated with impact before Watergate, but were negatively correlated after Watergate.

—Investigations led by commissions were not correlated with impact before Watergate, but were positively correlated after.

—Investigations of personal misconduct were not correlated with impact before Watergate, but were negatively correlated after.

—Investigations that involved a repair of some kind (bureaucratic, policy, or a change of course) were not correlated with impact before Watergate, but were positively correlated after.

—Investigations that used fact finding as their method were not correlated with impact before Watergate, but were positively related after.

To amplify my earlier comments about history, investigatory characteristics, and party control, investigators must address the breakdown at hand. However, they often have choices about other investigatory characteristics, most notably venues, purpose, and method. They can also calibrate their investigatory agenda to monitor different kinds of breakdowns. Although some breakdowns cannot be simply ignored, others can be easily dismissed. House Republicans clearly chose to focus on Clinton's misconduct and his sordid behavior with Lewinsky, but they could have taken a different path or taken no action at all.

DESTINATIONS

One last question remains before turning to the regressions: does investigatory destination matter to impact?

The answer is mixed. Some destinations matter to ultimate impact, while others produce little more than frustration. As table D-14 shows, investigations designed to reform bureaucracies, repair policy, and enhance accountability were not associated with either higher or lower levels of impact, while investigations designed to reverse course were associated with significantly higher impact, and investigations to set the agenda and resolve doubts were associated with significantly lower impact. Congress and presidents may have plenty of experience with investigations designed to reform bureaucracies and repair policies, but their investigations did not achieve consistent success.

Viewed as a source of advice for investigators, the path to significant impact is through investigations designed to change course and set the agenda, while the path to frustration is through investigations designed to enhance accountability and resolve doubts, both of which often end in diffuse effects that are hard to uncover through the interpretations used in assigning the impact scores.

A Second Answer

These correlations lay the foundation for a final if-then analysis of the core predictors of impact. Here again, statistical regressions provide the tool for matching a group of measures against each other in an effort to predict impact, thereby helping investigators to make choices as they move toward their goal of improving government performance.

The following pages summarize four different competitions to predict the four-point impact score. The first uses each of the eleven footprint weights to predict impact among all of the investigations, the second uses investigatory characteristics to predict impact also among all of the investigations, the third uses investigatory characteristics to predict impact only among the forty-four investigations that occurred after Watergate and during divided government (prevailing conditions), and the fourth uses the six investigatory destinations described above to predict impact among all of the investigations. In reading the tables, recall that the adjusted R^2 provided at the top of each regression measures the overall power of the regression in explaining variation among the footprints. Most of the competitions earned very high marks on this measure, but, as with many regressions, substantial variation is always left unexplained.

THE 11 FOOTPRINT WEIGHTS → IMPACT

Investigatory footprints are a central force in shaping impact and can be viewed as a mediating force in a simple path from investigatory characteristics → footprints → impact. But whether as mediators or independent predictors, the eleven weights play an important role in explaining ultimate investigatory consequences.

As table D-15 shows, three of the weights show significant effects on impact, the third of which is just over the statistical borderline:[119]

—Focus on durability. Produce a body of work that can withstand the test of time.

—Be thorough. Get to the bottom of the breakdown.

—Stick with the investigation. Continue the inquiry for as long as it takes, even if patience is wearing thin.

The overall competition is highly significant for explaining ultimate impact, strongly suggesting that POGO is right to argue that how an investigation operates has a great deal of influence on what it produces in government performance. Although function does not follow form in perfect alignment, and bipartisanship shows no strength in predicting impact, investigators should learn an important lesson here. Doing it right, at least in creating durable, free, and longer investigations, makes a significant difference in having an impact.

Given the enormous significance of durability as a predictor here, investigators might ask what drives durability. It is one thing to suggest that they produce a lasting body of work, but quite another to offer advice on how to achieve lasting impact. Table D-16 offers five suggestions for enhancing durability, the fifth of which is just over the statistical borderline:

—Seek the freedom to investigate, which is essential to durability, which is in turn essential to impact.

—Generate visibility, which gives an investigation staying power.

—Embrace complexity, which usually involves events that can hold investigatory interest.

—Avoid bipartisanship, which appears to reduce visibility, and the persistent attention that follows it.

—Cultivate leverage, which enhances the odds of implementation, which is in turn a driver of durability through future adjustments.

As POGO emphatically argues, investigators must design an impact strategy early, execute it aggressively, and continue applying it after the investigation is over.

INVESTIGATORY CHARACTERISTICS → IMPACT

Although investigatory characteristics may play their greatest role in shaping footprints, they also have several direct effects on impact, which are presented in table D-17.

According to this competition, investigators should pay attention to three characteristics, the third of which is just slightly over the statistical borderline again:

—Use a commission. Commissions provide the political insulation to break through to impact.

—Give Congress the lead. Congress can produce high-impact investigations, but needs the motivation.

—Avoid investigations of personal misconduct. Misconduct rarely produces significant results beyond harassment and the occasional resignation.

As for the predictive power of history and party, president's term of office was the only measure that produced a significant predictive effect on impact. First terms tended to produce significantly lower impact than second terms, perhaps because presidents are quiescent as they become lame ducks. But even this relationship washes away when matched against investigatory structure and modus operandi.

INVESTIGATORY CHARACTERISTICS → IMPACT DURING PREVAILING CONDITIONS

This third competition pits each investigatory characteristic against the others among the forty-four investigations that occurred during divided government after Watergate, which is likely to persist for some time to come.

Moreover, there is new evidence that congressional polarization has been spreading into the electorate, which further raises the odds that investigators will face even greater pressure to launch partisan investigations in the future. According to the Pew Research Center, party divisions have increased dramatically over the past decade, culminating in the following summary based on a June 2012 survey:

> Americans' values and basic beliefs are more polarized along partisan lines than at any point in the past 25 years. Party has now become the single largest fissure in American society, with the values gap between Republicans and Democrats greater than gender, age, race or class divides. The parties also have become smaller and more ideologically homogeneous over this period. Republicans are dominated by conservatives, while a smaller but growing number of Democrats are liberals.
>
> The survey finds that neither party is solely responsible for the growing partisan gap. In different ways, both Democratic and Republican values have become more partisan over the past 25 years—and polarization extends to independents as well.[120]

Even if government returns to unified party control, there is little reason to expect a quick reversal of the polarization that may have made bipartisanship a distant investigatory hope. The Pew Research Center shows that partisanship, which was once viewed by Rauch as restricted to Washington elites, is now firmly established among the public writ large. Blue-ribbon commissions may be the most attractive venue for avoiding it.

As above, the competition presented in table D-18 provides modest counsel to future investigators who undertake their inquiries during divided government, assuming, of course, that divided government of tomorrow will remain highly polarized and quarrelsome. There were two significant predictors of investigatory impact among the characteristics tested here:

—Pursue repair (bureaucratic, policy, or changes in course), not prevention (accountability, preparation, or resolution of doubts). Repair offers a more precise course for impact compared with the more diffuse outcomes associated with prevention, especially the resolution of doubts.

—Focus on fact finding, not blame setting. Facts clearly make a difference in moving toward any destination.

THE SIX DESTINATIONS → IMPACT

The final competition in this book is designed to ask whether investigatory destinations help to predict impact. Broadly assuming that any investigation sparked by any trigger using any method can seek any type of impact, the question is whether one destination provides a greater chance of success than another.

Because of limitations in regression analysis of a single measure, the best way to answer the question is using a simpler technique called analysis of variance. This approach allows comparisons of all categories in a given measure such as investigatory destination. According to the results, investigators would be well advised to think hard about investigations designed to resolve doubts about controversies and seek policy repairs and to focus instead on reversing the course of national strategies or setting the agenda.

In addition, investigations tend to stall when they pursue accountability through new systems such as performance measurement that have proven frustratingly difficult to implement. Investigations also gain little when they seek to achieve bureaucratic reform, which often encounters intense resistance from inside and outside of government, or attempt to repair policies, which often generates similar resistance. However, investigators can gain a great deal of impact when they target the agenda, which lays the groundwork for new endeavors, and when they try to change course, which is clearly difficult but achievable through the kind of big-ticket investigations on my list.

A Note on Blue-Ribbon Impact

Using a commission may be the single most powerful predictor of impact among the 100 investigations, if not during the current era of divided government. However, it is not clear what makes commissions so successful.

As above, there are two ways to ask what causes commission impact, neither of which shows significant differences from the 100 investigations as a whole.

A REPEAT RESULT

The first answer involves correlations between my standard measures of an investigation's structure and modus operandi, which produced the same three significant relationship that emerged in chapter 3:

—Give Congress the lead. Congressional commissions produce the durability that begets greater impact

—Give the Senate the lead. Senate commissions have a history of greater durability than House commissions.

—Focus on repair. Commissions that pursue repairs of past or present breakdowns produce greater durability.

As with footprints, history, the other investigatory characteristics, and party control had no significant effects on commission impact.

COMMISSION FOOTPRINTS AND IMPACT

The second answer involves a regression of the relationship between footprints and impact. Although only twenty-eight commissions are on my list, thereby limiting inferences about all blue-ribbon commissions, the results show two footprints that produce significant findings, which might help investigators to design high-impact commissions.

—Focus on durability. Durable commissions exert influence on impact far into the future when their time has come.

—Go longer. Longer commissions have more impact than their shorter peers, although length here is relative. Most commissions are much shorter than noncommissions, but a little bit of extra time makes a very large difference in blue-ribbon impact.

The effect of durability was no surprise given its powerful effect in other analyses above, but the effect of length was completely unexpected. After all, most congressional and presidential commissions are shorter than non-commissions. Moreover, length did not produce any noticeable effect on impact for my entire list of 100 investigations, nor did it produce any effect on impact among the seventy-two noncommissions used for comparisons in this section.

The best explanation for the surprise is that length is a relative measure. With rare exceptions such as the Defense Base Closure and Realignment Commission and the Hoover Commission, a long commission investigation might last eighteen months. In contrast, a long noncommission investigation might last ten years as a war lingers on or suspicions of communist infiltration persist. But just because a long commission has a shorter life span than a noncommission does not mean that the length of its life span does not matter. In this case, the shorter the commission, the less the impact.

With few other answers about what drives commission impact, perhaps it is best to suggest that they be viewed as just another investigatory venue alongside full committees, joint, select, and special congressional bodies, and subcommittees. Commissions may generate very high amounts of impact, but there is a saturation point when commissions become so frequent that they must compete against each other for standing. Just read through appendix B for the evidence. As Appendix C shows, just because Congress or the president appoints a commission does not guarantee a primary role in a packaged investigation such as Hurricane Katrina, the Gulf Oil Spill, or the 2008 financial collapse.

CONCLUSION

Once again, investigators may only have so much room to maneuver when following any of this advice. They may want the freedom to investigate and can certainly fight for it, but they may be tightly constrained by their congressional or presidential mandates and simple electoral politics. They may also want to mount a thorough review, but might not have access to the key actors who have the evidence needed for impact. And even if they hope to explore the complexity of their issue, the triggering event may be so narrow and the leverage for action so intense that they might not be able to embrace the issue fully.

Nevertheless, even minority party members have options for breaking free from majority control. They might not have the committee gavel, but they can often generate enough visibility to drive the leadership back. They might not have immediate access to testimony, but they can write minority staff reports. And they might not have institutional resources for a full investigation, but they can ask congressional support agencies for relief. In 2001, for example, House Democrats pressured the Government Accountability Office to sue the George W. Bush administration for documents related to Vice President Richard "Dick" Cheney's secret 2001 Energy Task Force. Although GAO withdrew from the fight when the federal courts upheld the administration's claim of executive confidentiality, the Democratic minority had found a new path around a compliant, yet controlling Republican majority.[121]

Ultimately, investigators must grapple with doing the best with what they have. They may be constrained by prevailing conditions and a host of limitations, but they can build investigations with a fighting chance of having a greater impact. As the final chapter of this book strongly suggests, they must find a way to embrace the broad principles of the investigation done well and the impact achieved. Although each investigation follows a somewhat different path, sign-posts along the way can be used as benchmarks for criticism and applause. Add in a strong measure of reflection, and the possibilities for finding answers and improving performance are well within reach.

FIVE

Creating High-Impact Investigations

A central lesson of this book is that investigations can be very well done, but not have a significant impact on government performance. Moreover, even when doing it right matters, not all aspects of the good investigation carry equal weight in repairing or preventing a breakdown. Visibility is no doubt a valued investigatory goal, for example, but has little bearing on impact. Neither does complexity, seriousness, thoroughness, or even bipartisanship. An investigation can meet almost every test of "doing it right," yet still fall short. Absent durability, failure is almost guaranteed.

Moreover, even high-impact investigations can be works in progress. It is still not clear, for example, whether the massive Department of Homeland Security or beleaguered Office of the Director of National Intelligence that emerged from the 9/11 investigation will provide durable protection against terrorism. To the contrary, the two agencies have proven to be unwieldy bureaucracies with little of the hoped-for excellence needed for impact.

Nor is it clear that the repairs from past investigations will always hold for long. Impact can be fleeting when the topic involves government fraud, waste, and abuse, for example, and may not hold much beyond a decade or two even on celebrated investigations involving Social Security rescues, intelligence agency abuses, presidential aggrandizement, taxpayer abuse, space programs, or automobile safety. Congress and presidents seem to have a special gift for repeating the same errors in execution over and over, even as history challenges settled programs with ease.

Finally, even when an investigation fails, it can have impact by creating a turning point in history, albeit sometimes barely noticeable and often more a consequence of changes already set in motion than a clear break toward setting the agenda or resolving doubts.

In 1965, for example, the House Un-American Activities Committee (HUAC) changed course from its long-running search for communists in government to a detailed examination of the Ku Klux Klan. The change was driven almost entirely by the appointment of Rep. Charles Longstreet Weltner (D-Ga.) as HUAC's new chair. Although Weltner received little support for his efforts to expose the Klan's racist activities and never received even a hint of support for his Organizational Conspiracies Act of 1967, he nonetheless used his chairmanship to raise issues that HUAC had long avoided. The committee was disbanded in 1975.[1]

The history of modern congressional and presidential investigations reveals similar patterns in investigatory conduct. If not unique, each investigation has its own twists and turns as it moves forward. This variation is often set by the basic choices made as investigators frame the problem at hand, assess the political environment, and begin their work in determining ownership and venues, responding to triggers, defining the issue at hand, establishing purpose, and adopting an appropriate method for fixing the initial government breakdown.

Yet even as they work to increase the odds of impact, all investigations are shaped to some extent by prevailing norms and mandates. It is not at all clear that congressional investigators have much choice over their initial venue, for example, although plenty of cases in this book demonstrate the significant competition that arises as different venues seek to control a given breakdown, not the least of which involves the growing use of presidential commissions.

Moreover, many investigatory choices are beyond immediate control, most notably the freedom to investigate, bipartisanship, and the availability of a well-known, often insistent leader. Even well-known leaders can be intimidated by threats of removal from strong-willed party majorities and leaders such as House Speaker Newt Gingrich (R-Ga.), who bullied his committee chairs into fruitless investigations of White House misconduct.

Nevertheless, investigators still work within strict boundaries and with little-known leaders and can use their external political capital to force the fact finding that is so important to ultimate impact. Although they may have limited choices in the search for answers, their choices appear to make a significant difference in both shaping investigatory footprints and producing ultimate impact.

The rest of this chapter examines the general findings of this book in more detail before turning to the core underpinnings of the high-impact investigation. These investigatory norms speak to general commitments that investigators bring to their efforts at the very beginning of their work. They need not always commit to creating a heavyweight investigation, although there is plenty of evidence that footprints are a strong predictor of impact, but they do need to recognize their historical and institutional role in creating the public good inherent in their endeavors. And they need not always produce a great deal of impact, although this must always be their goal if government is to improve. In any event, their efforts affect the long-term reputation of investigations as a tool for the faithful execution of laws, even ones not yet enacted.

A PERSONAL OPINION

Having read so much investigatory history over the life of this project, I inevitably formed my own opinions about each investigation on my list. Not surprising, I came to admire some investigations much more than others.

Intelligence Agency Abuses (1975)

It is impossible to single out one investigation in this book as the best of the best, but I often return to the Church Committee's 1975 investigation of intelligence agency abuses as a model of the high-impact investigation.

By my reading, the investigation not only met all of the attributes of the good investigation, but also generated durable results. It did both good and well. Much as some may argue that it weakened intelligence agencies for a half century and was part of the "Vietnam syndrome" that chilled the use of "hard power" to advance U.S. interests, it most certainly pushed the Central Intelligence Agency (CIA) back from its long-standing engagement in patently illegal activities.

Tasked by the Senate in early 1975 to investigate domestic spying by the CIA, the Select Committee to Study Governmental Operations with Respect to Intelligence Activities eventually put a host of other agencies under its investigatory microscope, including the National Security Council, Federal Bureau of Investigation (FBI), Internal Revenue Service (IRS), and Defense Department. No issue was off-limits as Sen. Frank Church (D-Idaho) led the investigation through at least 126 public hearings, untold secret hearings, and at least forty meetings en route to a fourteen-volume final report.[2] The investigation was unquestionably long, broad, complex, visible, serious, thorough, high leverage, influential, and bipartisan. It also produced lasting impact through creation of the House and Senate intelligence committees, which continue to monitor the nation's intelligence agencies to this day, eventual passage of the Foreign Intelligence Surveillance Act, and creation of the Foreign Intelligence Surveillance Court (and the United States Foreign Intelligence Surveillance Court of Review).[3]

The investigation was launched at a nearly perfect point in history for an aggressive review.[4] The FBI's director, J. Edgar Hoover, had just died, and a new CIA director had just arrived, which created a rare opportunity to unveil each agency's recent history. Lyndon Johnson had just died, too, and Nixon had resigned in disgrace, which created a rare opportunity to explore presidential motives dating back to Franklin D. Roosevelt. Finally, even though Democrats held three- to four-seat majorities on all but two of the Senate's full committees, majority leader Mike Mansfield (D-Mont.) gave his party just one extra seat on the Church Committee, which created at least some incentive for bipartisanship.[5]

Even before it started, the issue gained a measure of visibility when the *New York Times* ran Seymour Hersh's sensational allegations about domestic spying:

> The Central Intelligence Agency, directly violating its charter, conducted a massive, illegal domestic intelligence operation during the Nixon Administration against the antiwar movement and other dissident groups in the United States, according to well-placed Government sources.
>
> An extensive investigation by the *New York Times* has established that intelligence files on at least 10,000 American citizens were maintained by a special unit of the C.I.A. that was reporting directly to Richard Helms, then the Director of Central Intelligence and now the Ambassador to Iran.[6]

Hersh's article merely set the stage for the Church Committee's work, but it created intense public interest, which gave the investigation at least some political insulation, a sense of urgency, and the specter of further coverage if Church did not move quickly.

With this wind at its back and a "hall of fame" committee that included Howard H. Baker Jr. (R-Tenn.), Barry M. Goldwater (R-Ariz.), Philip A. Hart (D-Mich.), Charles McC. "Mac" Mathias Jr. (R-Md.), Walter Mondale (D-Minn.), and John G. Tower (R-Tex.), the investigation ranged freely across a long list of topics, building a bipartisan case against the intelligence community's "unsavory and vicious tactics."[7] "This inquiry could have been distracted by partisan argument over allocating the blame for intelligence excesses," Church wrote in the introduction to the committee's final report. "Instead, we have unanimously concluded that intelligence problems are far more fundamental. They are not the product of any single administration, party, or man."[8] This bipartisanship was especially important to the unanimous approval of Mondale's brutal assessment of the intelligence community's disregard for the "niceties of law," which merited a special note of thanks from Church.

Not only did the Church Committee have absolute freedom to examine any allegation of illegal, improper, or unethical activity, it was also empowered to investigate specific allegations as its fact finding continued. Although the committee acknowledged that "a year was not enough time to investigate everything,"[9] it nonetheless examined a staggering inventory of scandals:

—The Nixon administration's "Houston Plan" to infiltrate antiwar organizations

—The CIA's CHAOS domestic spying operation against alleged dissident groups and the unauthorized possession of toxic agents

—The FBI's COINTELPRO program to penetrate domestic political organizations and five-year "no holds barred" campaign to "neutralize" Dr. Martin Luther King Jr.

—The Internal Revenue Service's second readings of selected tax returns filed by suspected dissidents

—CIA assassination plots against the Congo's Patrice Lumumba, the Dominican Republic's Rafael Trujillo, Vietnam's Ngo Dinh Diem, and Chile's René Schneider

—At least eight plots to kill Fidel Castro with poison pills, pens, bacterial powders, and "other devices which strain the imagination."[10]

John le Carré could not have written anything more riveting.

With undisputed freedom to investigate, the committee's list of core investigatory questions was formidable, even intimidating: Which governmental agencies have engaged in domestic spying? How many citizens have been targets of governmental intelligence activity? Where do the targets fit on the spectrum between those who commit violent criminal acts and those who seek only to dissent peacefully from national policy? Have intelligence agencies been used to serve the political aims of presidents, other high officials, or the agencies themselves? Have intelligence agencies acted outside the law? Have intelligence agencies followed due process and the rule of law?[11]

The committee answered these and other questions in a single sentence backed up by 50,000 pages of testimony: "Too many people have been spied upon by too many Government agencies and too much information has been collected."[12]

The investigation achieved its heavy footprint and high impact through a mix of fact finding, bipartisanship, and strong leadership, all points emphasized by Frederick A. O. Schwarz Jr., who joined the pending investigation as chief counsel. According to Schwarz, who had not known Church, facts were at the heart of eventual success: "Without facts, oversight will be empty," he argues in drawing the distinction between blame setting and fact finding. "Congressional committees or citizen commissions that fail to recognize this distinction make splashes, but not waves." Instead of asking who did it, the great investigation should ask how did it happen and what can be done to keep it from happening again?[13]

Communists in Hollywood (1947)

Just as it is impossible to single out the best of the best, it is equally difficult to identify the worst of the worst. Yet I often return to the 1947 investigation of communists in Hollywood as an exemplar of an investigation done poorly without any effect beyond ending dozens of careers without reason.

The Hollywood Ten investigation, as it came to be known, has been chronicled in a long list of books, films, and documentaries and is best remembered for its venal tone, abusive tactics, and the one question that HUAC asked over and over: "Are you or have you ever been a member of the Communist Party?" Many witnesses dodged the question, but some invoked their First or Fifth Amendment rights in refusing to answer.

It is still unclear what motivated the investigation, although the chance to mingle with Hollywood stars was no small perquisite. Led by Rep. J. Parnell Thomas (R-N.J.), a virtually unknown member who became HUAC chairman at the start of the year, the motion picture investigation was merely one of many inquiries involving outside groups such as World War II veterans, farmworkers, and trade unions. Thomas only lasted two years on HUAC, however, and soon came under fire from Jack Anderson and Drew Pearson for taking kickbacks from a phantom office employee. He was convicted of fraud and resigned in 1950.[14]

(Ironically, Thomas took the Fifth during his grand jury testimony. Ironically again, Thomas refused to testify at his trial and pled no contest as the evidence piled up. Ironically, a final time, Thomas served his eighteen-month prison term. Ironically a final time, he served his sentence in the same Danbury, Connecticut, prison as two of the Hollywood Ten who were convicted of contempt of Congress.)

These future ironies notwithstanding, Thomas launched the investigation on July 24 with a string of forty-eight subpoenas to future witnesses, including nineteen "unfriendlies." Thomas justified the subpoenas with characteristic anticommunist rhetoric:

> The committee is well aware of the magnitude of the subject it is investigating. However, it is the very magnitude of the scope of the motion-picture industry that makes this investigation so necessary. We all recognize, certainly, the tremendous effect that moving pictures have on their mass audiences far removed from the Hollywood sets. We all recognize that what the citizen sees and hears in his neighborhood movie house carries a powerful impact on his thoughts and behavior. With such vast influence over the lives of American citizens as the motion-picture industry exerts, it is not unnatural—in fact, it is very logical—that subversives and undemocratic forces should attempt to use this medium for un-American purposes.[15]

Others saw less patriotic forces at work. Some argued that the investigation was an expression of persistent anti-Semitism toward Jewish studio executives, others viewed it as an attack on the Screen Actors Guild and organized labor more generally, and still others saw as it an astute effort by the industry chieftains to gain greater control of their actors and deflect potential government censorship.[16]

Whatever the hidden intent, the investigation was long, visible, and influential. At the same time, it was shallow, tightly controlled, not particularly serious, anything but thorough, and filled with partisanship.[17]

More to the point of the good investigation, the hearing record is filled with innuendo, hearsay, and what some legal scholars describe as fundamental violations of constitutional rights. Writing in 1951 at the height of HUAC's broad investigation of communists in government, legal scholar Robert K. Carr argued that HUAC—acting "out of its desire to put the accusing finger on specific individuals whom it deems guilty of subversive activity"—was usurping the functions of administrative and judicial agencies already tasked with monitoring misconduct. Carr also noted that the committee's staff regarded themselves as a little FBI, in part because ex-FBI agents were so strongly integrated into HUAC's investigatory operation as a "detective agency."[18]

Carr's argument was similar to Walter Gellhorn's 1947 "report on a report" that emerged from HUAC's investigation of the Southern Conference for Human Welfare, which was created in 1938 to promote Franklin D. Roosevelt's economic agenda. Publishing in the *Harvard Law Review*, Gellhorn defined the good investigation as the simple product of "fair-minded men, striving dispassionately to arrive at the truth." But given his reading of the record, the inquiry was anything but fair and dispassionate:

> The Committee on Un-American Activities has seemingly been unwilling to tolerate those whose estimates of current problems do not match its own. Instead, it has, as in the present report, sought to intimidate or destroy by attacks upon individual reputations. Persons so attacked can rarely defend themselves against accusers who enjoy a legislative immunity and are therefore not answerable for even malicious or grossly careless misstatements.[19]

The investigation of communists in Hollywood gave HUAC yet another opportunity to act as a grand jury. Some of its star witnesses, such as Robert Montgomery, agreed that there was a "lunatic fringe" in Hollywood, but would not name names. Others, such as Ronald Reagan and George Murphy, also talked about colleagues who had been used by the communists, but would not name names either. Finally, still other star witnesses, such as Gary Cooper, evaded questions about scripts and screenwriters. Although an avowed anti-communist who peppered his remarks with references to "pinkos," Cooper refused to implicate his colleagues, as seen in the following exchange:

> Staff investigator. Have you ever observed any communistic information in any scripts?
> Mr. Cooper. Well, I have turned down quite a few scripts because I thought they were tinged with communistic ideas.
> Staff investigator. Can you name any of those scripts?
> Mr. Cooper. No; I can't recall any of those scripts to mind.
> Staff investigator. Can you tell us—
> Mr. Cooper. The titles.
> The chairman. Just a minute. Mr. Cooper, you haven't got that bad a memory.
> Mr. Cooper. I beg your pardon, sir?
> The chairman. I say, you haven't got that bad a memory, have you? You must be able to remember some of those scripts you turned down because you thought they were Communist scripts.
> Mr. Cooper. Well, I can't actually give you a title to any of them; no.
> The chairman. Will you think it over, then, and supply the committee with a list of those scripts?
> Mr. Cooper. I don't think I could, because most of the scripts I read at night, and if they don't look good to me I don't finish them

or if I do finish them I send them back as soon as possible to their author.[20]

Although several famous witnesses such as Walt Disney were convinced that the communists had provoked labor unrest at their studios, the hearings were on course for a null result until the Hollywood Ten (a group of directors, producers, and screenwriters) were called to testify on their communist sympathies. Citing their First Amendment rights to free speech through prior agreement not to invoke the Fifth Amendment, the ten refused to testify and were cited for contempt of Congress, convicted, and sent to prison.

More important, they were blacklisted from the industry as studio after studio pledged not to hire anyone suspected of communist ties, a commitment enshrined in the December 1947 "Waldorf Agreement," drafted in secret by forty-eight studio executives at New York City's Waldorf Astoria Hotel, promising that they would not "knowingly employ a Communist or a member of any party or group which advocates the overthrow of the government of the United States by force or by any illegal or unconstitutional methods."[21] The blacklist grew with each new round of hearings as once-unfriendly witnesses, such as future lifetime achievement Academy Award winner Elia Kazan, recanted their earlier testimony and named names. By 1951, the list numbered 200–300, perhaps most notably eighty-four writers, costumers, producers, and animators who signed an amicus brief supporting the Hollywood Ten's unsuccessful Supreme Court appeal of their contempt convictions.[22]

This is not the book to chronicle the impact of the investigation in destroying reputations and striking fear into the motion picture industry. Suffice it to say, however, that the investigation itself had passing impact as the anticommunist scare waned. Visible though it was, the investigation is perhaps best remembered for its negligible quality and enormous personal cost. There is little dispute that communists worked in Hollywood, but Reagan was on point in his 1947 testimony: "I believe that, as Thomas Jefferson put it, if all the American people know all of the facts they will never make a mistake."[23] HUAC never tested Reagan's hypothesis.

A SHORT INVENTORY OF FINDINGS

Acknowledging once again that the competitions described in this book leave a large amount of statistical variation yet to be explained, at least five results are supported both by the statistical analysis and by the historical record discussed above.

First, heavy footprints and higher impact occur under both divided and unified government. At least for congressional and presidential investigations of the executive, divided party control has little influence on investigatory impact. Although unified government might produce less intensive congressional and presidential investigations, party control simply does not matter greatly in driving footprints and impact. As the previous analyses strongly suggest, it is time to move away from counting the number of investigations or pages of hearing testimony and toward considering deeper measures of what, when, where, how, and why party control might make any difference at all to investigatory activity.

Second, Watergate marks a point of departure for certain kinds of investigations. Freedom to investigate declined after Watergate, while partisanship increased. These barriers to the good investigation have not prevented high-impact results, however, particularly when investigators create a fact finding norm or choose a favorable venue such as a blue-ribbon commission as a source of what G. Calvin Mackenzie has called the political "by-pass surgery" that might encourage greater bipartisanship and consensus building.[24]

Mackenzie's description is well supported by the results of the party control comparisons. Of the twenty-eight commissions on my list, impact increased dramatically during divided government, rising from 20 percent with a great deal of impact during unified government to 65 percent during divided government and from 25 percent during unified congresses to 41 percent during divided congresses. This effect was particularly pronounced among the twenty investigations conducted by commissions after Watergate with a great deal of impact during both divided government and divided congresses across the two periods: 33 percent and 41 percent, respectively, in the pre-Watergate era versus 25 and 63, respectively, in the post-Watergate period.

Third, durability is one of the most important investigatory outputs for eventual impact. Given the vicissitudes of the freedom to investigate and partisanship, generating long-lasting findings deepens the pool of ideas in good currency that can be taken up by future investigators and policymakers alike. Simple, narrow topics may have the highest yield for immediate implementation, but broad, complex topics appear to generate the most durability, if only because they produce longer inventories of possible action as future investigators move to the arduous task of developing recommendations.

Fourth, fact finding has significant effects on impact, perhaps refreshingly so. The modus operandi of the good investigation described in chapter 3 does matter to impact and is confirmed by the analysis contained in chapter 4. Investigators should take note that fact finding resides not in visibility, but in leadership and the freedom to investigate. Wherever it comes from, however, fact finding is the primary path to impact. Without the facts, it is difficult to make the case for impact.

Fifth, as just noted, having well-known leadership at the helm of an investigation is a significant contributor to the successful monitoring of government. But what does "well-known leadership" mean? Does it merely record the throw weight of a given individual? Or does it imply experience, legislative acumen, investigatory skill, skilled staffers, effective strategies, and ability to build consensus? Although leadership is difficult to measure, these attributes appear time and again in the 100 investigatory histories.

THE GOOD INVESTIGATION REVISITED

Buried in the microanalysis presented in this book are at least six broad characteristics that capture a sense of the good investigation. Even if a good investigation produces hoped-for effects by its simple launch, the effective monitoring of government involves a mix of commitment, readiness, insulation, perseverance, persuasiveness, and standing.

Commitment

High-impact investigations begin with a clear commitment to finding the answers to the breakdown at hand regardless of who might get hurt. Much as the good-government community sees great impact in the simple exercise of checks and balances, the 100 investigations presented in box 3-1 were also designed to produce better government, whether through bureaucratic reforms, policy repairs, changes in course, enhanced deterrence, agenda setting, or the resolution of doubt.

As Congressional Research Service expert Morton Rosenberg argues, this commitment drives all aspects of the good investigation:

> Every letter, every phone call, every meeting, every hearing, should having some well-defined purpose. "How am I furthering understanding or resolutions of the matter," should be the question of every step of an ongoing investigation. And oversight inquiry should be viewed as a staged process. That is, understand that you're going from one level of persuasion or pressure to the next, to find the who, what, when, where and why of a particular situation under inquiry.[25]

Commitment involves many options and resulting footprints, of course. But, as noted earlier, seriousness may be the most important indicator. Although seriousness was knocked out as a predictor of impact, it nonetheless produced a very high yes-no relationship and can be used to support Rosenberg's view that investigations should further understanding and resolution.

Lyndon Johnson's President's Commission on Law Enforcement and Administration of Justice is an appropriate example of a highly committed investigation. Created on July 23, 1965, the commission was one of Johnson's four commissions on my list and perhaps the most visible.[26] Johnson had originally hoped that former Republican presidential candidate Thomas E. Dewey would chair the effort, but he was apparently unwilling to accept. Reportedly faced with no Republican options, Johnson eventually selected his attorney general, Nicholas Katzenbach, who was later implicated in an effort to constrain the Warren Commission's work. Katzenbach was clearly conflicted—he was a political mover and shaker and very much a Johnson loyalist. Yet the commission was anything but shy about its work and included a long list of independent thinkers, including Yale's Kingman Brewster, future Watergate prosecutor Leon Jaworski, future Supreme Court justice Lewis F. Powell, and future secretary of state William Rogers.[27]

Based on his reading of the commission's short life, historian Hugh Davis Graham gave the effort extremely high marks in his comparison of Johnson's blue-ribbon commissions:

> Katzenbach's commission was so superbly led and staffed, and the total effort was so brilliantly orchestrated by the masterful chief legislator in the White House, that the Katzenbach Commission remains a prime example of the presidential commission's strategic potential. It carefully and professionally nurtured consensus between hard-line demands for crackdown and constitutional solicitude for civil liberties and due process. The result was a bumper harvest: the Omnibus Crime Control and Safe Streets Act of 1968, the Gun Control Act of 1968, and the Juvenile Delinquency Prevention and Control Act of 1968.[28]

At the same time, the commission's staff director and future Watergate deputy prosecutor and Harvard Law School dean, James Vorenberg, was far less enthusiastic. Writing in the Atlantic Monthly five years after the commission finished its work, Vorenberg argued that crime had steadily increased in the wake of the "inevitable hostility to change in any large bureaucracy" and the use of crime as a tool for electioneering.[29] To the extent that impact is measured by agenda setting for future legislative action, the commission deserves its four-point score, but if impact is measured by how well the repair actually worked over the long term, the investigation might be given a lower rating, as crime rates have ebbed and flowed with economic and social conditions and correctional institutions eventually came under fire by Katzenbach himself.[30]

The question here is whether the effort had the commitment needed for ultimate success. The answer clearly seems to be yes. Katzenbach was a reluctant chairman, but he was at the helm of a very large endeavor that called on three national conferences, conducted five opinion surveys, and interviewed what it labeled "tens of thousands of persons" en route to a ten-volume report divided into sections on trends, victims, juvenile delinquency, police behavior, the courts, the prison system, organized crime, narcotics, drunkenness, and firearms.[31]

More to the point of the value of commitment, the commission earned an eight-point footprint score, lacking only a well-known leader (Katzenbach was not a brand name by any measure), the freedom to investigate (Johnson watched the commission's every move), and visibility (crime was clearly a highly visible national issue, but the commission was rarely covered and often denigrated as a show horse designed to support Johnson's agenda).

Readiness

Readiness is one of the most frequent themes in calls for the good investigation. It was mentioned in all of my not-for-attribution interviews with former members of Congress, members of blue-ribbon commissions, and investigatory staffers. There is no substitute for getting the facts straight before the first hearing.

Many of the 100 top investigations followed this principle. "There should never be a hearing before its time," a Senate staffer told me. "There may be other investigations already under way, but the way to achieve credibility is to collect every document possible. Read them. Digest them. Prepare the committee's agenda based on what you know. Don't let witnesses set the agenda. Facts are the way to pin them down—documents, e-mails, etc."

In addition, many of my respondents said that readiness involves a broad, comprehensive approach. As Lee Hamilton argues, oversight has to probe well beyond the four corners of the page. "There are a vast number of activities of the federal government that never get into the newspaper, but it is still the task of Congress to look into them. Oversight that is driven by whether we can get cameras into the hearing room is not going to get the job done."[32]

Again, Rosenberg is the expert. "The first rule of successful oversight is that there must be in most instances intensive preparation. Nothing should be left to chance. Rarely should an inquiry, for instance, begin with a subpoena for documents or for testimony at a hearing. Formal compulsory process should be the product of urgent need after a sufficient period of fact gathering and source checking. Pay attention to details."[33]

The 1959 investigation of the munitions lobby was built on just such details. Upon first reading, the investigation of the employment of retired military officers is one of the least exciting investigations on my list. Surprisingly, however, the House Armed Services Special Investigations Subcommittee, and its little-known chairman, Rep. Edward Hebert (D-La.), produced one of the most sophisticated and influential investigations of the period. Although relatively few retired commissioned officers were employed by Washington lobbying firms and defense manufacturers at the time, their potential role in lobbying their former employers seemed unpatriotic at best, and corrupt at worst.

Moreover, the investigation set a precedent by using social science research to make its case. How many general or flag officers had retired between 1953 and 1959? How many were working for the defense industry? How many were involved in some kind of lobbying? How much were they paid? What had they done in the armed services? What contracts did they work on? And most significant, as the subcommittee framed the question, did any have discussions "concerning the sale, use, adaptation, improvement, suitability, development, or research of any article, plan, process, or program with any office or employee of the Department of Defense?"[34]

The subcommittee's data collection involved surveys of four groups: the 100 largest defense prime contractors, the entire list of retired military officers, all Defense Department acquisition personnel, and a sample of trade association executives and lobbyists. Forwarded to each group with a brief invitation from the subcommittee's chairman and a franked return-address envelope, the questionnaires produced all the data needed to fuel the investigation's twenty-four hearings and its case for post–public service ethics reform.

Given a methodology that was unheard of on Capitol Hill at the time, the subcommittee's facts were unassailable. According to the subcommittee's data cards, 261 former general and flag officers and another 485 colonels and Navy captains were employed by the defense industry as of June 30, 1959, many of whom worked under "incentive-type" engagements.

The subcommittee did not stop its search with surveys, however. It also invited witnesses who would give the subcommittee the opportunity to obtain a cross section of industries and spot check the questions based on size, location, and nature of the contract and business in addition to other variables. Acknowledging that there was no coercion to complete the surveys, the subcommittee verified the sworn testimony of a sample of the respondents.[35] The subcommittee also used cross-tabular analysis to search for gaps in the responses.

Armed with the data, the subcommittee pursued allegations of bribery, graft, and conflicts of interest within the munitions lobby. The subcommittee's final analysis from the survey and its subsequent hearings suggested significant problems in the federal government's ethics statutes:

> We were impressed with the obvious inconsistencies in testimony. Some might have a more felicitous term.
>
> For example, when discussing influence, some retired officers contended that the retired officer is a "has-been"; that he has no influence; and that his personal contact is resented by active duty personnel. These witnesses contended that the fact of being retired was, in itself, a handicap, if not a deterrent.
>
> But these confident conclusions were watered down by most of these witnesses, who, while testifying that they knew of no instances of attempted influence on themselves while on active duty, nevertheless agreed that a "cooling-off" period was desirable.
>
> It is just a little difficult to reconcile these assurances about "has-beens," when it is agreed that they could stand to be "cooled off" for, say, 2 years . . . Surely industry is not hiring historians at lush salaries. Industry buys what the employee knows. It buys knowledge which can be converted into sales for a profit.[36]

The subcommittee's extensive preparation and unassailable facts dovetailed with an equally thorough investigation by the House Judiciary Committee, both of which led to a recodification of the existing ethics statutes. However, the recodification did not include the subcommittee's proposals, which were passed by the House but died in the Senate. Despite the setback, the proposals eventually found their way into the 1978 Ethics in Government Act twenty years later and govern employment by former military and civilian employees to this day. Hence, the investigation received a six-point footprint score and achieved a fair amount of impact, in no small part because of its careful preparation. This long delay in repair and prevention is quite familiar among the other three dozen durable investigations discussed in this book—the Hoover Commission recommended creating a highly mobile senior executive service in the early 1950s, but the idea remained untouched until passage of the 1978 Civil Service Reform Act, while the Katzenbach report continues to generate legislative debate to this day.

Insulation

Investigations often involve confrontations with sensitive political and bureaucratic behemoths. Even the most astutely bipartisan investigation can produce intense opposition among the individuals and agencies being investigated. Hence investigations must be insulated against the potential backlash from investigated parties and their congressional and presidential guardians.

The opposition to thorough investigations has actually fueled the growth of an "investigation-protection" industry of lawyers and lobbyists who seek to disrupt, delay, and divide bipartisan efforts such as the 1996 investigation of campaign finance. As one of my respondents told me, "I've heard wonderful stories about lobbyists going to Capitol Hill to urge an investigation to generate business. That's always been the case. However, there are now lobbyists who also go to Capitol Hill to stop investigations by amplifying partisanship. The mere threat of investigation allows lobbyists to troll for business, and it's not always to support an investigation."

Facing yet another major scandal, the Clinton administration made every effort to dilute the charges by alleging parallel Republican misconduct. Thus, despite initial pleas for bipartisanship from Senate Governmental Affairs Committee chairman Fred Thompson (R-Tenn.), the investigation soon descended into a partisan shouting match between the White House and Republican party. Yet, even though the investigation ended in stalemate, its failure actually created modest momentum toward the 2003 Bipartisan Campaign Reform Act, and thereby earned a two-point impact score.

The 1997 campaign finance hearings raise the question of whether partisanship is the key ingredient for investigatory failure. Long before the hearings began, the Senate Governmental Affairs Committee had a tradition of bipartisan investigation. According to Elise Bean, the Democratic staff director and chief counsel of the committee's Permanent Subcommittee on Investigations, bipartisanship involves full participation and disclosure across party lines:

> [The majority and minority on our committee] work together. One side or the other takes the lead. If we're taking the lead, there's at least one person on the other staff who's assigned to our investigation. They attend all the meetings. They're welcome to do as much document review as they can manage; a lot of times they leave that to us, because it's our investigation. After we get key documents and summarize them, we tell them all about it. Our counterparts are

always fully informed and we find that circumvents a lot of problems. Some people we investigate try to go to the other party and cause trouble, but if we're working together, that doesn't happen.[37]

The campaign finance investigation clearly broke with tradition. Hamstrung by a one-year deadline, the Republican majority complained frequently about partisan "stonewalling" by the Democratic National Committee (DNC) and the Clinton White House. In turn, Democrats complained about interference from the Republican National Committee (RNC) and a phalanx of Republican campaign consultants. As the final majority report concluded on March 5, the tight deadline "virtually invited witnesses to engage in obstructive tactics, perhaps none more so than the DNC and the White House. This obstruction, combined with the sheer complexity of the investigation, made this deadline the single greatest obstacle faced by the Committee's inquiry."[38]

According to the majority report, the stonewalling was exacerbated by the mysterious "disappearance" of more than forty-five witnesses who "either fled the country or refused to cooperate by citing their Fifth Amendment privilege against self-incrimination." As Thompson complained, the president took no action "whatsoever" to convince these witnesses to cooperate. "It is clear that we are going to have two reports," he later told the *Washington Post*. "We could revisit all those old heartaches and throw some more stones if we choose to. I thought I could pull everybody together. But I couldn't do it."[39]

In the end, all eight of the committee's Republican members endorsed the final report, while all seven Democrats dissented. As *Washington Post* reporter Guy Gugliotta concluded, Democrats took "pains to find a Republican transgression to match every Clinton misstep, complain again of Republican insensitivity to minority demands, subpoenas, witnesses, and hearing time, and accuse the RNC of orchestrating 'the most elaborate scheme' to funnel foreign money illegally into the U.S. elections."[40]

Insulation comes in many forms, of course. Many of the senior staffers I interviewed mentioned the need for a strong, highly purposed chairman as a backstop. Some even did so in their Project on Government Oversight (POGO) interviews by referring to weaknesses in their own leadership. "My boss was not fast on his feet," a Republican staffer told POGO on the condition of anonymity. "I had to learn how to do several things simultaneously to compensate for that because he would ask a question at a hearing [and] could not figure how to counterpoint the answer—because he was not fast on his feet. So what I had to learn to do was think for him and speak for him, without me actually doing the speaking."[41]

Perseverance

Perseverance is often casually revealed in counts of hearings, witnesses, and pages of testimony. Although some investigations produce heavy footprints with a handful of hearings over a short period of time, thereby refuting the majority's frustrations in the 1997 campaign finance investigation, many involve a long-haul philosophy. "For God's sake, do not think that hearings are the be-all and end-all of your oversight," Senate Committee on Finance counsel Dean Zerbe told POGO. "We think our letters, getting material, getting that out to the public, having a public discussion about what they're doing, and getting detailed answers is often a much more successful way to get things accomplished."[42]

The number of hearings, witnesses, and questions is best viewed as a blunt, often temporary, indicator of perseverance, however. Perseverance is also revealed in the number of linked investigations conducted by the same and different committees led by the same and different chairs over longer periods of time. It is a point well made in Tama's research on national security commissions and advisory groups, which includes highly visible efforts such as the 9/11 Commission and alongside soon-forgotten inquiries such as the National Advisory Commission on Children and Terrorism.[43]

Some of Tama's investigations were included on my list, while others were too small to join it. Nevertheless, the persistent focus on terrorism is obvious and well worth noting as an example of the power of perseverance in shaping ultimate impact. Tama supports the argument in his own analysis of ultimate impact:

> The conventional wisdom is that commissions rarely induce changes in government policies. I have found that this conventional wisdom is correct concerning one class of panels, but wrong with respect to another. Commissions formed to advance an agenda in the absence of a crisis tend not to trigger policy changes because the status quo in Washington is very difficult to overturn. In the wake of a crisis, however, commissions often do catalyze change by using their distinctive political credibility to prod Congress and the president to agree on important reforms. Crisis commissions, it turns out, are not just devices used by elected officials to deflect political pressure or avoid unwanted action; they are also underappreciated and powerful tools for making public policy.[44]

It is important to note that Tama measured the impact of each investigation in isolation, thereby understating the possible multiplier effects as each commission added to the body of "ideas in good currency" for addressing terrorism. Many of the competing hearing sets on the list ended up in the investigation résumés, but all made a dent, both small and often large, in the final reports.

Persuasiveness

The good investigation generates enough credibility, evidence, and legitimacy to create the persuasive muscle to secure high impact. In congressional and presidential investigations, this persuasion often involves the participation of key targets, advocates, and potential adopters.

At least for the key targets of an investigation, participation can be invited or compelled through a variety of techniques, including the use of subpoenas, secondary investigations by the Government Accountability Office, federal inspectors general, and the Justice Department. Several of my 100 investigations were sparked by indictments, trials, and convictions, while several others produced indictments, trials, and convictions along the way or soon after. In turn, several involved the threat of subpoenas (a "holstered weapon" that should only be used when absolutely necessary, according to one of my respondents; a "popgun," according to another; and the best threat for producing information, according to still another).

This participation and the press coverage that often follows may be the most important source of persuasion and emerges frequently in POGO's manual as an essential tool for keeping an investigation moving forward. Mayhew makes a similar case both directly and indirectly in his list of "high-publicity" investigations.[45] This coverage is best viewed as both an independent variable in generating forward movement and a dependent variable that measures potential impact. Consider Mayhew's analysis early in his chapter on high-publicity investigations:

> Precisely, how should we recognize a relevant probe? An investigation enters this chapter's data set if it generated a specified kind of content in one or more *New York Times* front-page stories, on at least twenty days (not necessarily consecutive), during any Congress between 1946 and 1990. The test for content is as follows. A front-page story becomes relevant if it featured a committee-based charge of misbehavior against the executive branch or an executive response to such a charge.[46]

Press coverage is a critical element of creating both perseverance and public appetite for action. As shown in the previous chapter, coverage creates visibility, which adds to ultimate impact. Again, Mayhew makes the point in his analysis of importance:

> But how about weighing investigations for importance? In particular, should Congress's Watergate probes, which took place during a time of divided party control, weigh more heavily than anything else? No doubt they should. But, if we take into account the overall impact of investigations on policy making, international relations, domestic political conflict, public careers, the tone of political life, and even national folklore, there is a good case for the loyalty probes of 1948–54 as at least a solid second. Those took place mostly under unified control. It was not that party control made no difference at all . . . Accused China hand Owen Lattimore became a household name. Republican Senators injected the same kind of headline-catching, anti-administration aggression into the AEC [Atomic Energy Commission] and influence peddling probes of those years. The Democratic side had its own resourceful disloyalty hunter, Pat McCarran of Nevada. That was the way things worked.[47]

The challenge is to generate press coverage without trivializing the investigation itself. At least one of POGO's respondents made the case for horror stories as the spark. "You shouldn't hold an investigative hearing unless you have a compelling horror story, a smoking gun to reveal, or an important point to make."

Yet this respondent also argued that rehearsing and forewarning witnesses were essential for maintaining momentum: "Executive witnesses should know explicitly what you want them to talk about and what materials to bring with them. Failure to be precise invites the response, 'Gee, I didn't anticipate that. We'll get back to you with the answer in writing soon.'"[48]

Horror stories can degrade an investigation, too. "You know you're losing control when witnesses start showing up in black hoods or behind screens," one respondent told me. "It creates the impression that you've got nothing else."

High visibility, and the horror stories that often fueled it, was certainly a key to investigatory momentum in the taxpayer fraud and abuse investigations that were launched and led more than thirty years apart. As noted earlier, the 1951 investigation of the Bureau of Internal Revenue was a heavyweight in investigatory history and produced a great deal of impact. But the investigation did not fix the agency for all time. Despite its new name and organizational design, the IRS was rarely out of the investigatory spotlight during the decades that followed, if only because revenue agents are among the least popular government employees. Most of the ongoing police patrol inquiries were too small to include on my list, but the 2013 attack on the IRS for flagging Tea Party applications will no doubt make a future list.

The 1996 investigation started with a blue-ribbon congressional commission co-chaired by Sen. Bob Kerrey (D-Neb.) and Rep. Rob Portman (R-Ohio), which led the primary investigation and produced a detailed inventory of reforms, including a call for a "user friendly" culture built on a new oversight board, a fixed term of office for the IRS commissioner, and new technology. The commission's final report heralded a new vision for the agency and even argued for a budget increase and tax simplification.[49]

As the primary investigatory engine, the commission produced a heavy footprint, but was one of the few near-heavyweights to produce little impact. Its work could easily have been converted into a significant bureaucratic reform, but was soon eclipsed by a much more inflammatory and highly partisan secondary investigation by the Senate Finance Committee.

Even as it drew heavily on the commission's twelve hearings and its inventory of facts, Sen. William Roth's (R-Del.) investigation was mainly about blame setting. "We are going to see a picture of a troubled agency," Roth opened the committee's first hearing exactly three months after the Kerrey-Portman Commission released its report, "one that is losing the confidence of the American people, and one that all too frequently acts as if it were above the law." Answering charges that this was just another Clinton conduct inquiry, Roth replied, "This is not IRS bashing; it is oversight. These hearings are about good government."[50] Nevertheless, at least one panel of IRS employees appeared before the committee shielded by heavy curtains and testified through voice filters to disguise their identities. As Senate Democrats argued, the "black-hooded" panel was little more than a publicity stunt designed to inflame outrage, not achieve lasting reform.

Scandals clearly ignited the 1951 and 1996 investigations, but became the backbone of major reform in the former and tepid action in the latter. Press engagement was high in both cases, but was harnessed for very different purposes in the latter. In short, coverage was a by-product of the first investigation and the goal of the second. Thus do horror stories and hidden witnesses build visibility even as they sometimes undermine credible reform.

The participation of key stakeholders, and the buy-in that often goes with it, involves other tactics, including the use of star witnesses who make hearings memorable, create a "curtain raiser," and provide momentum even under tight deadlines. Moreover, as several investigatory reporters told me, the lack of access to star witnesses and information can itself create media coverage. "My interest in a witness goes up in direct proportion to how difficult it is for me to get that witness on the phone," a *Wall Street Journal* reporter told

POGO. "You guys have subpoena power, we don't. That's cool to be you—I'm jealous . . . The people who are compelling are the people I can't get to, for whatever reason, such as whistle-blowers that will only speak under the protection of a hearing situation."[51]

Standing

In an arena of constant search for credit, investigations must often seek standing as the final destination for answers. This standing gives an investigation the perceived legitimacy for eventual impact. It no doubt involves a blend of commitment, readiness, insulation, perseverance, and persuasiveness, but is more a sum of these parts.

Instead, standing is best viewed as a sense—sometimes ephemeral, sometimes in anticipation of a final resolution—that an investigation is legitimate. This legitimacy is often conveyed both by visible, respected, and well-known leadership and by a prestigious platform for review. One way to convey this seriousness is to elevate an investigation to a high-leverage venue such as a full committee or commission. Although subcommittees, task forces, and ad hoc advisory groups led some of my heaviest investigations, others were merely once-used venues for relatively quick reviews of specific events.

Here, it is useful to note both the increasing number of blue-ribbon commissions and their profile as investigatory platforms. They are not just a presidential platform, either. Congress created eight of the twenty-eight blue-ribbon commissions listed in box 3-1. Although some of these commissions were created in large measure as political cover for what political scientists call non-decisions (decisions not to act or ways to preempt congressional investigations), many turned out to have high impact nonetheless. Moreover, as polarization has increased over the past seventy years, blue-ribbon commissions have become increasingly popular, whether measured by decade, time quarters, or Watergate.[52]

Recall, for example, that two of the commissions were created during the Truman and Eisenhower administrations, six during the Kennedy, Johnson, and Nixon administrations, ten during the Ford, Carter, Reagan, and George W. Bush administrations, and ten more during the Clinton and George W. Bush administrations. Even commissions that were created almost entirely for political cover often took on a life of their own, defying congressional and presidential hopes for distraction and denial.

The 1985 blue-ribbon Commission on Defense Management is an example of a commission that eventually roared. Created in the wake of intense congressional hearings on fraud, cost overruns, and waste, the commission was widely viewed as a way to end the flood of stories about $7,500 coffee pots, $750 pliers, $650 ashtrays and toilet seats, $400 hammers, and $44 light bulbs. After all, the Reagan administration was involved in its own war on waste at the time, even as the Pentagon searched for some way to block sweeping defense reorganization.

However, the executive order creating the commission was just broad enough to invite a deep inspection of the defense establishment as a whole. Given the horror stories, the commission could have taken the well-worn path to another round of procurement reform. But the commission took seriously Reagan's order, which contained the following instructions:

> The primary objective of the Commission shall be to study defense management policies and procedures, including the budget process, the procurement system, legislative oversight, and the organizational and operational arrangements, both formal and informal, among the Office of the Secretary of Defense, the Organization of the Joint Chiefs of Staff, the Unified and Specified Command system, the Military Departments, and the Congress.[53]

The president also ordered the commission to review "the adequacy of the current authority and control of the Secretary of Defense in the oversight of the Military Departments, and the efficiency of the decision making apparatus of the Office of the Secretary of Defense"; "the responsibilities of the Organization of the Joint Chiefs of Staff in providing for joint military advice and force development within a resource-constrained environment"; "the adequacy of the Unified and Specified Command system in providing for the effective planning for and use of military forces"; and "the value and continued role of intervening layers of command on the direction and control of military forces in peace and in war."

Even without this mandate, the commission would have produced a heavy footprint if only because of its chairman's national reputation. As the former president and chief executive officer of Hewlett-Packard and a former deputy secretary of defense, David Packard brought enormous energy and focus to the effort. He used the platform to conduct thirty days of closed and public hearings, managed a staff of forty, and produced a series of interim reports that helped to propel defense reorganization into law.

The Packard Commission's final report, *A Quest for Excellence*, is well worth reading as an exemplar of breadth, clarity, and simple language. As Packard wrote in his introduction, the commission was absolutely committed to systemic, not piecemeal, reform: "Excellence in defense management cannot be achieved by the numerous management layers, large staffs, and countless regulations in place today. It depends, as the Commission has observed, on reducing all of these by adhering closely to basic, common-sense principles: giving a few capable people the authority and responsibility to do their job, maintaining short lines of communication, holding people accountable for results."[54]

As noted earlier, all blue-ribbon commissions do not produce this level of impact. The commission that followed the Three Mile Island accident was torn by dissension over the future of nuclear power, while the commissions to study the human immunodeficiency virus (HIV) and Gulf War syndrome failed to achieve particular clarity or impact. Ever was it thus, it seems. In 1971, for example, Sen. Edward Kennedy (D-Mass.) chaired a judiciary subcommittee hearing on the implementation, or lack thereof, of commission recommendations. According to Kennedy, the nation was in the midst of "a commission explosion":

> In the first decade after World War II, there were an average of one-and-a-half presidential commissions appointed each year. In the early 1960's the rate rose to two a year. Since then, Presidents have appointed commissions at a rate of over four each year, and President Nixon announced five in his first year in office. And this does not include dozens of task forces, study groups, and other executive branch advisory bodies, or the national commissions established by congressional enactment.[55]

Kennedy's concern was not just the rise in the number of commissions, but also the lack of implementation:

> It seems as though most Presidential commissions are merely so many Jiminy Crickets chirping in the ears of deaf Presidents, deaf officials, deaf Congressmen, and perhaps a deaf public. They could be the Nation's conscience, spurring us on to do what we know ought to be done, showing us the way, strengthening our determination to build a just and peaceful and productive society . . . But all too often we reject them, or ignore them, or forget them. And so, every time someone proposed a new commission, someone says, "Oh, no, not another commission," and Art Buchwald and Russell Baker and Liz Drew and Haynes Johnson have a field day toying with the modest proposal of a commission on commissions.[56]

Kennedy was unquestionably correct. However, his investigation of commissions produced little change in the "commission-itis" he criticized. Although some commissions are doomed to failure from their first breath, they have become more important over time as the freedom to investigate has declined. Although not always prominent, they often claim significant space in the policy debate, especially when they are led by well-known, courageous figures.

CONCLUSION

More than 200 years after the House appointed a special committee to dissect General Arthur St. Clair's defeat by Native Americans in Ohio, investigations remain a critical tool for addressing government breakdowns.[57] But investigations must be done well to achieve impact. None is preordained for success. Although initial targets and the choice of platform make a difference, what happens inside an investigation matters greatly to the outcome.

The question, therefore, is whether Congress and the president still have the skill and commitment to produce the good investigation. Some of my respondents were pessimistic about the answer, particularly given manipulation of committee chairmanships to create compliance or highly partisan investigations. Others warned of the "golden days" phenomenon. "The past always looks good to us because we were part of it," one former member of Congress cautioned me. "Be careful not to draw too much of what may be temporary aberrations. There's a good cadre of younger, aggressive members in Congress right now. They will get their chance."

Caveat noted, there is good reason to wonder about the future. Will investigatory journalism survive in any form as the media contraction continues? Will POGO and other independent investigatory organizations grow and prosper? Will new members of Congress last long enough to develop the courage necessary to follow every lead even if it involves a president of their own party? Will their staff gain enough expertise to drive the thorough inquiries that produce the largest impact? Will the data scrapers produce new investigatory sparks from their big data? And will blue-ribbon commissions begin to collapse as the current class of well-known leaders passes on?

The answers are still evolving. Yes, the House and Senate continue to create oversight agendas and subcommittees. Yes, presidents still enter office promising transparency and aggressive monitoring of their agencies. And yes, the current pressure to measure results may yet lead to more effective monitoring by the president's budget office and congressional appropriators.

No one knows whether today's bitter partisanship will eventually claim investigations as another victim of congressional inactivity, nor whether anyone will care. Thus, if I have one recommendation from my six years of research, it is that the investigatory process itself deserves thorough and serious monitoring. It is far better to prevent failed investigations in the future than to repair them once their damage is done.

APPENDIX A

Interview Respondents

Name	Major current or former position
Abshire, David	President of the Center for the Study of the Presidency and Congress
Allen, Tom	Congressman from Maine
Apfel, Kenneth	Commissioner of the Social Security Administration and professor in the School of Public Policy at the University of Maryland
Augustine, Norman	Undersecretary of the Army and chairman of the Review of U.S. Human Space Flight Plans Committee
Barnett, Philip	Staff director of the House Energy and Commerce Committee
Bass, Gary	Founder and executive director of OMB Watch
Berman, Mike S.	Counsel to Vice President Walter Mondale
Bowsher, Charles	Comptroller general
Brademas, John	Majority whip and congressman from Indiana
Brand, Stanley	General counsel to the Speaker of the House of Representatives
Bruel, Jonathan	Senior executive of the Office of Management and Budget
Bryan, Danielle	Executive director of the Project on Government Oversight
Burnham, David	Co-founder and co-director of the Transactional Records Access Clearinghouse
Clark, Timothy	Editor and president of *Government Executive*
Clinger, William	Congressman from Pennsylvania
Cohen, Sheldon	Commissioner of the Internal Revenue Service

Name	Major current or former position
Colvard, James	Deputy director of the Navy Office of Personnel Management
Daschle, Tom	Majority leader and senator from South Dakota
Davis, Tom	Congressman from Virginia
Devaney, Earl	Inspector general for the Department of the Interior and chairman of the Recovery Act Transparency Board
Dionne, E. J.	Columnist for the *Washington Post*
Dodaro, Gene L.	Acting comptroller general of the Government Accountability Office
Downey, Mortimer L.	Deputy secretary of transportation
Duberstein, Kenneth M.	White House chief of staff
Edsall, Thomas	Senior columnist for the *Washington Post*
Edwards, Mickey	Congressman from Oklahoma
Eizenstat, Stuart	Chief domestic policy adviser and executive director of the White House domestic policy staff
Fine, Glenn A.	Inspector general at the Department of Justice
Fisher, Louis	Senior specialist in separation of powers at the Congressional Research Service
Fong, Phyllis	Inspector general at the Department of Agriculture
Frenzel, Bill	Congressman from Minnesota
Galston, William	Senior fellow in governance studies at the Brookings Institution
Gorelick, Jamie	Deputy attorney general
Gustitus, Linda	Chief of staff to Senator Carl Levin from Michigan
Hamburger, Tom	Investigative reporter for the *Los Angeles Times*
Hamilton, Lee	Congressman from Indiana
Harper, Edwin	Deputy director of the Office of Management and Budget
Hill, Eleanor	Inspector general of the Department of Defense
Ink, Dwight A.	Assistant director for executive management at the Office of Management and Budget
Inman, Robert "Bobby"	Deputy director of the Central Intelligence Agency
Kaiser, Robert	Associate editor and senior correspondent for the *Washington Post*
Kelman, Steven	Director of the Office of Federal Procurement Policy
Kerrey, Bob	Senator from Nebraska
Kingsbury, Nancy	Managing director for applied research and methods at the Government Accountability Office
Kleeman, Rosslyn S.	Director of workforce future issues for the Government Accountability Office
Kohut, Andrew	President of the Pew Research Center

Name	Major current or former position
Kojm, Christopher	Deputy executive director of the 9/11 Commission
Koskinen, John	Deputy director for management at the Office of Management and Budget
Krumholz, Sheila	Executive director of the Center for Responsive Politics
Lebedev, Gregory	Senior adviser to the Robertson Foundation for Government
Leon, Richard	District judge in the U.S. District Court for the District of Columbia
Levinson, Lawrence	Deputy special counsel to the president
Lewis, Charles	Professor and founding executive editor of the Investigative Reporting Workshop in the School of Communication at American University
Lewis, Lorraine	Inspector general in the Department of Education
Mackenzie, G. Calvin	Distinguished professor of government at Colby College
Mann, Thomas	Senior fellow in governance studies at the Brookings Institution
McClellan, Mark	Commissioner of the Food and Drug Administration and administrator of the Centers for Medicare and Medicaid Services
McGinniss, Patricia	Chief executive officer of the Council for Excellence in Government
McPherson, Harry	Special counsel to the president
Mead, Kenneth	Inspector general of the Department of Transportation
Mihm, J. Christopher	Managing director of strategic issues for the Government Accountability Office
Miller, Ellen	Co-founder and executive director of the Sunlight Foundation
Moe, Ronald C.	Specialist in American government at the Congressional Research Service
Mondale, Walter	Vice president of the United States and senator from Minnesota
Nivola, Pietro	Senior fellow and director of governance studies at the Brookings Institution
Oleszek, Walter	Senior specialist in American national government at the Congressional Research Service
Ornstein, Norman	Resident scholar at the American Enterprise Institute
Ottinger, Lawrence	President of the Center for Lobbying in the Public Interest
Peters, Charles	Founder and editor-in-chief of the *Washington Monthly*
Pfiffner, James	Professor of public policy at George Mason University
Podesta, John	White House chief of staff
Posner, Paul	Senior analyst for budget and policy of the Government Accountability Office

Name	Major current or former position
Radin, Beryl	Special adviser to the assistant secretary for management and budget of the Department of Health and Human Services
Rausch, Jonathan	Senior writer and columnist for the *National Journal*
Reischauer, Robert	Director of the Congressional Budget Office
Rivlin, Alice M.	Director of the Congressional Budget Office and Office of Management and Budget
Robb, Charles	Governor of Virginia and senator from Virginia
Rosensteil, Tom	Founder and director of the Project for Excellence in Journalism
Schwarz, Frederick Jr.	Chief counsel to the Senate Select Committee to Study Governmental Activities with Respect to Intelligence Activities
Scowcroft, Brent	National security adviser to the president
Shalala, Donna	Secretary of health and human services
Shea, Robert J.	Associate director of the Office of Management and Budget
Shrum, Robert	Presidential campaign strategist
Sistare, Hannah	Staff director and counsel of the Senate Governmental Affairs Committee
Stockton, Peter	Chief investigator for the chairman of the House Energy and Commerce Committee
Talbott, Strobe	Deputy secretary of state
Thompson, Fred	Senator from Tennessee
Thurber, James	University distinguished professor of government and director of the Center for Congressional and Presidential Studies at American University
Tofel, Richard	General manager of ProPublica
Tolchin, Martin	Founder of *The Hill* and Politico.com
Tolchin, Susan J.	Professor of public policy at the Institute of Public Policy at George Mason University
Truluck, Phillip	Executive vice president of the Heritage Foundation
Volcker, Paul A.	Chairman of the Federal Reserve
Walker, David	Comptroller general and president and chief executive officer of the Peter G. Peterson Foundation
Wegman, Richard	Chief counsel and staff director of the Senate Committee on Governmental Affairs
Wellford, W. Harrison	Executive associate director of the Office of Management and Budget

APPENDIX B

Sources

The sources used in this book are summarized in the following pages.

Source	Content	Coverage
CONGRESS	*A History of Notable Senate Investigations*, U.S. Senate, Virtual Reference Desk, 2004.	1859–2004
	Organization of the Congress. Final Report of the House Members of the Joint Committee on the Organization of Congress. Committee on the Organization of Congress. Joint, H. Rpt. 103-413, December 1993.	Lists of major investigations developed by Congress
CONGRESSIONAL QUARTERLY	*Congress and the Nation*, vols. 1–12.	1789–2012
	Congressional Quarterly Almanacs, annual volumes.	Lists of major investigations indicated by designation as such or depth of coverage
	Congressional Quarterly Weekly, selected dates.	
	Congressional Quarterly's Guide to Congress, 6th ed., CQ Press, 2007.	
CONGRESSIONAL RESEARCH SERVICE	*Congressional Oversight Manual*, CRS Report for Congress, Frederick M. Kaiser, Walter J. Oleszek, and Todd B. Tatelman, Updated June 10, 2011, RL30240.	1973–2011
	Staff Depositions in Congressional Investigations, CRS Report for Congress, Jay Shampansky, Updated December 3, 1999, 95-949, at notes 16 and 18.	Lists and examples of major investigations
	Authority and Rules of Senate Special Investigatory Committees and Other Senate Entities, 1973–97, Senate Committee on Rules and Administration, S.Doc. 105-16, 105th Cong. 1st sess., 1998.	
	Providing Special Investigative Authorities for the Committee on Government Reform and Oversight, Committee on Rules, H.Rept. 105-139, at App. A., 1997.	

SCHOLARS

Source	Description	Years
Daniel Bell, "Government by Commission," *The Public Interest*, 1996.	Examples of major presidential commissions	1946–66
Frederick M. Kaiser, "Congressional Oversight of the Presidency," *Annals of the American Academy*, 1988.	Examples of major congressional investigations	1946–88
David R. Mayhew, *Divided We Govern: Party Control, Lawmaking, and Investigations, 1945–2002*, Yale University Press, 2005.	Congressional investigations (hearings) of the executive that generated twenty or more front-page *New York Times* articles	1945–2002
Norman Ornstein, "Congressional Commissions," paper prepared for the Center for the Study of the Presidency, 2009.	Examples of major blue-ribbon commissions	1945–2013
David C. W. Parker and Matthew M. Dull, Investigations, "Divided We Quarrel: The Changing Politics of Congressional Investigations," *Legislative Studies Quarterly*, 2009.	Examples of significant investigations drawn from CIS database using a detailed search string	1945–2002
James P. Pfiffner, "Presidential Commissions: Keys to Success," paper for the Center for the Study of the Presidency, 2009.	Examples of major commissions	1945–2013
Jeffrey D. Schultz, *Presidential Scandals*, Congressional Quarterly, 2000.	Examples of major investigations	1981–2006
Arthur M. Schlesinger Jr., Roger Bruns, editors, *Congress Investigates, 1792–1974*, 1975.	Comprehensive list selected to demonstrate the "expanding power and influence of this vital legislative process"	1792–1974
Jordan Tama, *Terrorism and National Security Reform: How Commissions Can Drive Change during Crises*, 2011.	Examples of major presidential commissions, including measures of impact	1981–2006
Terrence R. Tutchings, *Rhetoric and Reality: Presidential Commissions and the Making of Public Policy*, 1979.	All commissions created by presidents Truman, Eisenhower, Kennedy, Johnson, and Nixon; examples of major investigations	1946–74
Thomas R. Wolanin, *Presidential Advisory Commissions: Truman to Nixon*, University of Wisconsin Press, 1975	Examples of major presidential commissions	1945–74
Amy B. Zegart, "Blue Ribbons, Black Boxes: Toward a Better Understanding of Presidential Commissions," *Presidential Studies Quarterly*, 2004.	Examples of major presidential commissions	1981–2001
Julian E. Zelizer, *On Capitol Hill: The Struggle to Reform and its Consequences, 1948–2000*, 2004.	Examples of major investigations dealing with congressional corruption	

Investigation Résumés, 1945–2012

Investigatory committees, commissions, and so forth are presented in rough order of engagement, although it was sometimes frustratingly difficult to discern which entity moved first. General introductions to some of the more obscure investigations on this list are provided in the notes for each investigation.

Pearl Harbor (1945)

—Joint Committee on Investigation of Pearl Harbor Attack

Several investigations of Pearl Harbor occurred before the end of World War II. For example, the Roberts Commission (chaired by Justice Owen Roberts) was created by executive order on December 18, 1941, by President Franklin D. Roosevelt; the Army's Pearl Harbor Board and the Navy Court of Inquiry were "appointed pursuant to the provisions" of P.L. 78-339. Other investigations not directly authorized by the president or Congress included the Hart inquiry, the Clarke inquiry, the Clausen investigation, and the Hewitt inquiry.[1]

World War II procurement fraud (1945)

—Senate Special Committee to Investigate Contracts under the National Defense Program

Agriculture commodity speculation (1947)

—Senate Special Subcommittee on Speculation in Commodity Markets, Committee on Appropriations
—House Select Committee to Investigate Commodity Transactions

Communists in Hollywood (1947)

—House Committee on Un-American Activities

Government organization and management (1947)

—Commission on the Organization of the Executive Branch of the Government (Hoover Commission)

Communists in government (1948)

—House Un-American Activities Committee
—Senate Committee on Government Operations (McCarthy Committee)
—Senate Committee on Foreign Relations, Subcommittee on Senate Resolution 231 (Tydings Committee)
—Senate Committee on the Judiciary, Subcommittee to Investigate the Administration of the Internal Security Act and Other Internal Security Laws (McCarran Subcommittee)
—Senate Committee on Government Operations, Permanent Subcommittee on Investigations (McCarthy Committee)
—Senate Select Committee to Study Censure Charges

Atomic Energy Commission operations (1949)

—Joint Committee on Atomic Energy

Organized crime in America (1950)

—Special Committee to Investigate Organized Crime in Interstate Commerce (Kefauver Committee)

Reconstruction Finance Corporation operations (1950)

—Senate Banking and Currency Committee
—Senate Committee on Expenditures in Executive Departments, Subcommittee on Investigations

Bureau of Internal Revenue corruption (1951)

—House Ways and Means Committee, Subcommittee on Administration of the Internal Revenue Laws

Conduct of the Korean War (1951)

—Senate Committee on Armed Services and Committee on Foreign Relations (includes the General Douglas MacArthur removal from command inquiry)

Airport safety (1952)

—President's Airport Commission (General James Doolittle Commission)
—House Committee on Interstate and Foreign Commerce
—Senate Committee on Interstate and Foreign Commerce

Justice Department operations (1952)

—House Judiciary Committee, Special Subcommittee to Investigate the Justice Department
   The investigation emerged from allegations that the department was poorly managed, had "bungled" its own cleanup, and had failed to investigate several cases of vote fraud, most notably in Kansas City.

Dixon-Yates power contract (1954)

—Senate Judiciary Committee, Subcommittee on Antitrust and Monopoly
—Joint Committee on Atomic Energy

Federal Housing Administration mismanagement (1954)

—Senate Committee on Banking and Currency

Air Force preparedness for the cold war (1956)

—Senate Armed Services Committee, Subcommittee on the Air Force

Campaign finance corruption (1956)

—Senate Special Committee to Investigate Political Activities, Lobbying, and Campaign Contributions
   This reluctant investigation was sparked by a long-running stream of quiet allegations, but only intermittent hearings and interest. The Senate finally created its special committee after Sen. Francis Case (D-S.D.) reported that he had been offered a $2,500 "campaign gift" in return for undisclosed favors.[2]

Labor racketeering (1957)

—Senate Select Committee on Improper Activities in the Labor and Management Field (McClellan Committee)

Sherman Adams misconduct (1957)

—House Committee on Interstate and Foreign Commerce, Special Subcommittee on Legislative Oversight

U. S. response to the Sputnik launch (1957)

—Senate Armed Services Committee, Subcommittee on Preparedness
—House Post Office and Civil Service Committee, Subcommittee on Manpower Utilization
—House Committee on Government Operations, Special Subcommittee on Government Information (Moss Committee)
—House Committee on Appropriations, Subcommittee on Department of Defense Appropriations

Drug industry practices (1959)

—Senate Judiciary Committee, Subcommittee on Antitrust and Monopoly (Kefauver Committee)
    Part of Sen. Estes Kefauver's (D-Tenn.) broader review of monopoly and antitrust policy across government, this investigation produced major consumer reforms to regulate the prescription drug industry in the Kefauver-Harris Drug Act of 1962, which Kefauver heralded as the most important consumer legislation of the era.

Munitions lobby, the military industrial complex (1959)

—House Committee on Armed Services, Subcommittee for Special Investigations
—House Committee on the Judiciary, Subcommittee no. 5
    Dealing with the "revolving door" lobbying activities of former military and civilian department employees, this investigation contributed to 1962 legislation regulating postemployment activities.

Quiz show rigging (1959)

—House Committee on Interstate and Foreign Commerce, Special Subcommittee on Legislative Oversight
    The quiz show and payola hearings are considered a packaged investigation. As the *Congressional Quarterly* argues, the 1959 quiz show investigation "continued in 1960, dealing primarily with 'payola' and leading to enactment of legislation regulating broadcasting."[3]

Agriculture commodity leasing (1962)

—Senate Government Operations Committee, Permanent Investigations Subcommittee
—House Government Operations Committee, Subcommittee on Intergovernmental Relations

Defense Department stockpiling (1962)

—Senate Armed Services Committee, Subcommittee on National Stockpile and Naval Petroleum Reserves

Lobbying by foreign governments (1962)

—Senate Committee on Foreign Relations

Military muzzling (1962)

—Senate Armed Services Committee, Special Subcommittee on Preparedness Investigating
    This investigation dealt with allegations that the Kennedy administration was "muzzling" testimony by military officers on alleged communist infiltration of the armed services and the resulting threat to society.

Government information management (1963)

—House Committee on Government Operations, Subcommittee on Foreign Operations and Government Information (Moss Committee)
    The 1963 hearings dealt specifically with Kennedy administration policies allegedly designed to shape the news on events such as the Cuban missile crisis, but capped an eleven-year investigation.

John F. Kennedy assassination (1963)

—President's Commission on the Assassination of President John F. Kennedy (Warren Commission)
—The Clark Panel (composed of four medical experts convened by then attorney general Ramsey Clark in 1968)
—The United States President's Commission on CIA Activities within the United States (Rockefeller Commission)
—Senate Select Committee to Study Governmental Operations with Respect to Intelligence Activities (Church Committee)
—House Select Committee on Assassinations

State Department security procedures, the Otepka case (1963)

—Senate Committee on Judiciary, Subcommittee to Investigate the Administration of the Internal Security Act and Other Internal Security Laws

TFX fighter aircraft contract (1963)

—Senate Government Operations Committee, Permanent Investigations Subcommittee

Traffic safety (1965)

—Senate Committee on Government Operations, Subcommittee on Executive Reorganization
—House Committee on Interstate and Foreign Commerce
—Senate Committee on Commerce

Crime in America (1965)

—President's Commission on Law Enforcement and Administration of Justice (Katzenbach Commission)
—Senate Committee on Government Operations, Permanent Subcommittee on Investigations
—National Commission on the Causes and Prevention of Violence (Eisenhower Commission)
—House Select Committee on Crime

The Eisenhower Commission covered areas that overlapped significantly with other major presidential investigations, including the Warren, Kerner, and Scranton commissions. The investigation is not formally linked to these commissions since its impetus was unique and its focus broader, including (a) assassinations, (b) "the causes of disrespect for law and order—disrespect for proper authority in the home and disrespect for public officials—and of violent disruptions of public order by individuals and groups," and (c) "sensible and practical actions to control or prevent these outbreaks of violence." These topics are related to violence and crime in the United States.

Ku Klux Klan activities (1965)

—House Committee on Un-American Activities

Conduct of the Vietnam War (1966)

—Senate Committee on Foreign Relations (Fulbright Committee)
—Senate Armed Services Committee (Stennis Committee)
—House Foreign Affairs Committee

—House Committee on Armed Services
—House Committee on Armed Services, Subcommittee on Armed Services Investigating
—House and Senate Appropriations committees and assorted subcommittees

Additional hearings by the Joint Economic Committee (for example, economic effect of Vietnam spending, 1967), House Merchant Marine and Fisheries Committee (Coast Guard activities in Vietnam and Thailand, 1968), House Government Operations Committee (military supply systems, 1966–72), Senate Judiciary Committee (communist atrocities, 1972), and others.

Due to the intermittent nature of the Fulbright-led hearings on Vietnam and the frequent use of closed sessions, the list of hearings is likely to be incomplete. Additionally, the hearings on Laos, the Philippines, and Thailand by the Committee on Foreign Relations' Subcommittee on U.S. Security Agreements and Commitments Abroad are included despite being held at the subcommittee level. Identified hearings include the following: Supplemental Foreign Assistance FY66—Vietnam, Part 1 (1966); U.S. Policy with Respect to Mainland China (1966); Foreign Assistance, 1966 (1966); Communist World in 1967 (1967); Asia, the Pacific, and the U.S. (1967); Changing American Attitudes toward Foreign Policy (1967); Conflicts between U.S. Capabilities and Foreign Commitments (1967); U.S. Commitments to Foreign Powers (1967); Gulf of Tonkin, the 1964 Incidents (1968); Foreign Assistance Act of 1968, Part 1: Vietnam (1968); Briefing by Secretary of State William P. Rogers (1969); U.S. Security Agreements and Commitments Abroad, Part 1: the Republic of the Philippines; Part 2: Kingdom of Laos; Part 3: Kingdom of Thailand, U.S. Security Agreements and Commitments Abroad (1969); Briefing on Vietnam (1969); Vietnam Policy Proposals (1970); Vietnam: Policy and Prospects, 1970 (1970); Bombing Operations and the Prisoner-of-War Rescue Mission in North Vietnam (1970); Supplemental Foreign Assistance Authorization, 1970 (1970); Legislative Proposals Relating to the War in Southeast Asia (1971); and Causes, Origins, and Lessons of the Vietnam War (1972).[4]

Central Intelligence Agency (CIA) financing of private organizations (1967)

—President's Committee on Central Intelligence Agency Support to Private Organizations
The House and Senate elected not to hold hearings on the controversy surrounding CIA support for domestic organizations engaged in spying on its behalf.

Urban riots (1967)

—National Advisory Commission on Civil Disorders (Kerner Commission)
—Senate Government Operations, Permanent Subcommittee on Investigations
—House Committee on Un-American Activities
—House Committee on Armed Services, Special Subcommittee to Inquire into the Capability of the National Guard to Cope with Civil Disturbances

Although the McClellan hearings on riots, civil, and criminal disorders did not deal directly with the Kent State and Jackson State events, several hearings were held and a report was issued on college campus disorders. The campus-related hearings and report are linked to the Kent State student unrest investigation.

Executive branch reorganization (1969)

—President's Advisory Council on Executive Organization (Ash Council)
—Senate Committee on Government Operations

Kent State student unrest (1970)

—President's Commission on Campus Unrest (Scranton Commission)
—Senate Government Operations, Permanent Subcommittee on Investigations

Justice Department Antitrust Settlement (1972)

—Senate Committee on the Judiciary
   This investigation focused on attorney general–designee Richard Kleindienst's allegedly improper role in settling the Justice Department's antitrust case against International Telephone and Telegraph (ITT) under orders from the White House. The decision resurfaced during the later Watergate investigation, and the focus shifted to the White House itself. However, I separated this investigation from Watergate because it was quite specifically linked to pre-Watergate Justice Department activities related to the long-running ITT case.[5]

Energy shortages (1973)

—Senate Committee on Government Operations, Permanent Subcommittee on Investigations
—House Committee on Foreign Affairs, Subcommittee on Foreign Economic Policy and Subcommittee on the Near East and South Asia
—Senate Foreign Relations Committee
—Senate Interior and Insular Affairs Committee
—Joint Economic Committee Subcommittee on International Economics

Watergate (1973)

—Senate Select Committee on Presidential Campaign Activities (Ervin Committee)
—House Committee on the Judiciary
—House Committee on Armed Services, Special Subcommittee on Intelligence
—Senate Committee on the Judiciary

Nixon Pardon (1974)

—House Committee on the Judiciary, Subcommittee on Criminal Justice

Intelligence agency abuses (1975)

—Select Committee to Study Governmental Operations with Respect to Intelligence Activities (Church Committee)
—United States President's Commission on CIA Activities within the United States (Rockefeller Commission)
—House Select Committee on Intelligence (Pike Committee)

Welfare fraud (1975)

—House Committee on Government Operations, Subcommittee on Intergovernmental Relations and Human Resources
—Senate Special Committee on Aging, Subcommittee on Long-Term Care (Medicaid mills investigation)

South Korean lobbying (1977)

—House Committee on Standards of Official Conduct
—House Committee on International Relations, Subcommittee on International Organizations
—Senate Select Committee on Ethics
—Senate Select Committee on Intelligence

General Services Administration (GSA) corruption (1978)

—Senate Committee on Governmental Affairs, Subcommittee on Federal Spending Practices and Open Government
—House Committee on Government Operations, Subcommittee on Government Activities and Transportation
—Senate Committee on the Judiciary, Subcommittee on Limitations of Contracted and Delegated Authority
This investigation dealt with allegations of corruption and mismanagement in GSA's building construction, maintenance, and acquisition decisions.

Three Mile Island nuclear accident (1979)

—President's Commission on the Accident at Three Mile Island (Kemeny Commission)
—Senate Committee on the Environment and Public Works, Subcommittee on Nuclear Regulation

—House Committee on Interior and Insular Affairs, Subcommittee on Energy and the Environment

Educational quality (1981)

—National Commission on Excellence in Education (Nation at Risk)
—House Committee on the Budget, Task Force on Education and Employment
—Senate Committee on Labor and Human Resources
—House Committee on Education and Labor

The National Commission on Excellence in Education was created on August 26, 1981, and was chaired by the secretary of education, Terrel H. Bell. Neither Congress nor the president formally authorized the commission, but it was clearly adopted by the president. Indeed, the White House, not the Department of Education, released the commission's report, although the popular press, at times, attributed its creation to President Reagan.[6]

Social Security financing crisis (1981)

—National Commission on Social Security Reform (Greenspan Commission)
—Senate Finance Committee
—Senate Finance Committee, Subcommittee on Social Security and Income Maintenance Programs
—House Ways and Means Committee
—Senate Committee on Governmental Affairs, Subcommittee on Oversight of Government Management
—Senate Select Committee on Aging
—House Select Committee on Aging, Subcommittee on Human Services
—House Committee on Education and Labor, Subcommittee on Postsecondary Education
—Joint Economic Committee

Superfund implementation (1981)

—House Committee on Energy and Commerce, Subcommittee on Oversight and Investigations
—House Committee on Public Works and Transportation, Subcommittee on Investigations and Oversight
—House Government Operations Committee, Subcommittee on Environment, Energy, and Natural Resources
—House Science and Technology Committee, Subcommittee on Natural Resources, Agricultural Research, and Environment and Subcommittee on Investigations and Oversight
—House Energy and Commerce Committee, Subcommittee on Health and the Environment and Subcommittee on Commerce, Transportation, and Tourism

—Senate Committee on Environment and Public Works

—House Committee on the Judiciary

This investigation dealt with allegations that the Environmental Protection Agency (EPA) had engaged in systematic conduct designed to undermine implementation of the Superfund toxic waste cleanup program created under the 1976 Resource Conservation and Recovery Act. It led to the resignation of EPA administrator Anne Gorsuch Burford and the indictment and conviction of EPA assistant administrator Rita M. Lavelle.

Abscam congressional sting (1982)

—Senate Select Committee to Study Law Enforcement Undercover Activities of Components of the Department of Justice

—House Committee on the Judiciary, Subcommittee on Civil and Constitutional Rights

The Abscam sting involved a secret Federal Bureau of Investigations (FBI) effort to bribe members of Congress. FBI agents posed as wealthy businessmen and Arab sheiks in the operation, which targeted thirty-one members of Congress and led to the indictments of five representatives and one senator. The investigation focused on whether the sting was a violation of civil liberties and entrapment.

Bombing of Beirut Marine barracks (1983)

—House Armed Services Committee

—Department of Defense Commission on Beirut International Airport Terrorist Act, October 23, 1983 (Long Commission)

—House Committee on Foreign Affairs, Subcommittee on International Operations and Subcommittee on Europe and the Middle East

Central America policy (1983)

—National Bipartisan Commission on Central America (Kissinger Commission)

—Senate Committee on Foreign Relations

Although the Kissinger Commission is considered an executive branch investigation, the "idea of a commission was proposed in June by Sen. Henry M. Jackson (D-Wash.), Sen. Charles McC. Mathias Jr. (R-Md.), Rep. Michael D. Barnes (D-Md.), and Rep. Jack F. Kemp (R-N.Y.). They introduced legislation (Senate Resolution 158, House Resolution 240) calling on the president to appoint such a body."[7]

Strategic missile forces (1983)

—President's Commission on Strategic Forces (Scowcroft Commission)

—Senate Committee on Armed Services

Defense Department fraud, waste, and abuse (1985)

—President's Blue-Ribbon Commission on Defense Management (Packard Commission)
—Senate Committee on Governmental Affairs, Subcommittee on Oversight of Government Management
—House Committee on Energy and Commerce, Subcommittee on Oversight and Investigations
—House Committee on Armed Services, Subcommittee on Seapower and Strategic and Critical Materials and Subcommittee on Investigations
—Joint Economic Committee, Subcommittee on International Trade, Finance, and Security Economics
—Senate Committee on Governmental Affairs
—Senate Committee on Armed Services

Space shuttle Challenger accident (1986)

—Presidential Commission on the Space Shuttle *Challenger* Accident (Rogers Commission)
—House Committee on Science, Space, and Technology
—Senate Committee on Commerce, Science, and Transportation, Subcommittee on Science, Technology, and Space

Wedtech defense procurement decision (1986)

—Senate Committee on Governmental Affairs, Subcommittee on Oversight of Government Management
This investigation dealt with allegations that White House counselor and future attorney general Edwin Meese had interfered in several Defense Department contracts, including the Wedtech Corporation's $32 million Army engine contract. Meese's role in the scandal led to his resignation in 1988.

Savings and loan crisis (1987)

—House Committee on Banking, Finance, and Urban Affairs
—Senate Committee on Banking, Housing, and Urban Affairs
—House Committee on Ways and Means
—House Committee on Government Operations
—House Budget Committee
—Senate Select Committee on Ethics (Keating Five Investigation)
The savings and loan crisis includes hearings related to both the failures within the thrift industry along with the government response (the first five committees) and the investigation of alleged improprieties by senators with regard to Lincoln Savings and Loan (the last committee).

Two high-publicity hearings on this list were led by the House Committee on Banking, Finance, and Urban Affairs and focused on the Lincoln Savings and Loan Association in 1989 and the Silverado Banking, Savings, and Loan Association in 1990. The committee held more than seventy days of hearings related to the savings and loan crisis. Activity beyond 1990 continued, largely in the form of oversight conducted by the Resolution Trust Corporation, but is not included here.

U.S. government response to the HIV (human immunodeficiency virus) epidemic (1987)

—Presidential Commission on the Human Immunodeficiency Virus Epidemic (Watkins Commission)

White House Iran-Contra program (1987)

—House Committee on Foreign Affairs
—Senate Committee on Foreign Affairs
—House Select Committee to Investigate Covert Arms Transactions with Iran
—Senate Select Committees to Investigate Covert Arms Transactions with Iran
—Special Review Board (Tower Commission)
—House Permanent Select Intelligence Committee
—Senate Select Committee on Intelligence

This investigation dealt with the complicated White House operation involving secret arms sales to Iran, which were linked to the release of U.S. hostages held in Lebanon, and allegations that the Nicaraguan rebels fighting to overturn the nation's communist government had used some of the money from the arms sales. The core of the investigation dealt with efforts to determine the president's role in approving the covert operation. Although President Reagan appointed the Tower Commission days before the House and Senate created their investigatory engines, Congress was the primary investigator and clearly overshadowed the blue-ribbon review.

Although Foreign Affairs Committee chairman Rep. Dante Fascell (D-Fla.) was at the titular helm in launching the House investigation, Rep. Lee Hamilton (D-Ind.) was chairman of the House select committee that conducted the primary review, which is why the investigation earned one point for well-known leadership. However, the investigation lost footprint points because it lasted less than a year, was narrowly focused on the scandal, did not have a particularly complex issue to examine, and was definitely not bipartisan. The investigation produced twenty-seven majority recommendations that were signed by twenty-eight members and another five that were signed by eight members. Although many of the recommendations were implemented in whole or in part, it is not clear that presidents have followed either the spirit or letter of the legislative action, which is why I gave the investigation a two-point impact score.[8]

Base closing and realignment (1988)

—Defense Secretary's Commission on Base Realignment and Closure (1988, 1991, 1993, 1995, and 2005)

Indian Affairs corruption (1988)

—Senate Special Committee on Investigations of the Select Committee on Indian Affairs

Government mismanagement (1989)

—Senate Committee on Governmental Affairs
—House Committee on Government Operations
—House Budget Committee

This investigation of government performance is composed of a series of hearings and reports generated by the Senate Committee on Governmental Affairs and House Committee on Government Operations. The investigation start year is 1989 based on an observed increase in intensity and activity related to government performance by the Senate committee. A partial list of hearings for the Senate Committee on Governmental Affairs between 1986 and 1993 includes Federal Management Reorganization, Cost Control, and Loan Accounting Reform; Financial Management; OMB's Response to Government Management Failures; Measuring Program Performance: Getting the Most Bang for the Buck; Performance Measurement: Toward More Effective Government; and Federal Performance: Getting Results.

The involvement of the House Committee on Government Operations, beyond hearings on topics such as federal financial management reforms and the establishment of a chief financial officer structure, is apparent from the committee's 1992 majority staff report.[9]

Housing and Urban Development scandal (1989)

—House Committee on Government Operations, Subcommittee on Employment and Housing
—House Committee on Banking, Finance, and Urban Affairs, Subcommittee on Housing and Community Development
—Senate Committee on Banking, Housing, and Urban Affairs

Both David Mayhew and *Congressional Quarterly* identify the House subcommittee led by Rep. Tom Lantos (D-Calif.) as the primary investigation.

Vietnam prisoners of war (POWs) and missing in action (MIAs) (1991)

—Senate Select Committee on POW/MIA Affairs

—House Committee on Foreign Affairs, Subcommittee on National Security Policy and Scientific Developments
—House Select Committee on Missing Persons in Southeast Asia
—Presidential Commission on Americans Missing and Unaccounted for in Southeast Asia (Woodcock Commission, 1977)
——House Committee on International Relations, Subcommittee on Asian and Pacific Affairs
—Senate Committee on Veterans' Affairs

1980 "October surprise" (1992)

—House Task Force of Members of the Foreign Affairs Committee to Investigate Certain Allegations Concerning the Holding of American Hostages by Iran in 1980
—Senate Committee on Foreign Relations, Subcommittee on Near Eastern and South Asian Affairs
—House Committee on Post Office and Civil Service, Subcommittee on Human Resources (1984)

This investigation dealt with allegations that the 1980 Reagan presidential campaign had engaged in secret negotiations with Iran to withhold the release of the fifty-two U.S. hostages held for 444 days. The hostages were released five minutes after Reagan's inauguration in 1981. The charges were made by former National Security Council staffer Gary Sick.[10] The allegations were never substantiated.

Also known as the October Surprise Task Force, the 1980 House task force was chaired by Rep. Lee Hamilton (D-Ind.).

With regard to the 1984 subcommittee of the House Committee on Post Office and Civil Service, the "October surprise" investigation actually began in 1983 when the House Post Office and Civil Service Subcommittee on Human Resources began an investigation into "debategate," a scandal involving the alleged theft of President Jimmy Carter's debate briefing memos by a Reagan for President campaign aide who had joined the Carter campaign as a "mole." The ten-month investigation was chaired by Rep. Don Albosta (D-Mich.), eventually cost $500,000, and concluded that the allegations were true. According to the subcommittee's final report, which was approved without a single Republican vote, the papers entered the Reagan campaign through its director and future CIA head, William Casey. The subcommittee forwarded its findings to the Justice Department and called for the appointment of a special prosecutor. As expected, the Justice Department declined. Although the investigation focused almost entirely on the debate allegations, it did touch on the October surprise. However, the investigation did not draw conclusions on the issue.[11]

Tobacco industry practices (1993)

—House Committee on Energy and Commerce, Subcommittee on Health and Environment

U.S. intelligence agencies in the post–cold war era (1994)

—Commission on the Roles and Capabilities of the United States Intelligence Community (Aspin-Brown Commission)
—House Select Committee on Intelligence
—Senate Select Committee on Intelligence

This wide-ranging investigation involved analysis of the role of U.S. intelligence agencies in the post–cold war period.

Gulf War syndrome (1995)

—Presidential Advisory Committee on Gulf War Veterans' Illnesses (Lashoff Commission)
—House Committee on Veterans' Affairs
—Senate Committee on Banking, Housing, and Urban Affairs
—Senate Committee on Veterans' Affairs and Special Investigation Unit on Gulf War Illnesses
—House Committee on Government Reform and Oversight

The Senate Committee on Armed Services also held a handful of hearings on the issue from 1993 to 1997, but did not ask whether the illness was either real or caused by the war.

Ruby Ridge siege (1995)

—Senate Committee on the Judiciary, Subcommittee on Terrorism, Technology, and Government Information

Waco Branch Davidian siege (1995)

—House Judiciary Committee, Subcommittee on Crime
—House Committee on Government Reform and Oversight (Clinger Committee)
—House Committee on Government Reform and Oversight, Subcommittee on National Security, International Affairs, and Criminal Justice
—Senate Judiciary Committee
—Department of Justice, Special Counsel Inquiry (Danforth Committee)
—House Committee on Government Reform (Burton Committee)

White House conduct (1995)

—House Committee on Government Reform and Oversight
—Senate Committee on the Judiciary

Whitewater allegations (1995)

—Senate Special Committee to Investigate Whitewater Development Corporation and Related Matters
—House Committee on Banking, Finance, and Urban Affairs
—Senate Committee on Banking, Housing, and Urban Affairs
—House Committee on Banking and Financial Services
   This complicated investigation involved allegations that then-governor of Arkansas Bill Clinton and his wife, Hillary Clinton, had engaged in illegal and improper activities in structuring an Arkansas land deal called Whitewater.

Secret arms shipments to Bosnia (1996)

—House Committee on International Relations, Select Subcommittee to Investigate the U.S. Role in Iranian Arms Transfers to Croatia and Bosnia (Iranian Green Light Subcommittee)
—Senate Select Committee on Intelligence
   This investigation involved allegations that Clinton had given the "green light" to secret arms shipments from Iran to Bosnian Muslims then fighting for survival.

Aviation safety and security (1996)

—White House Commission on Aviation Safety and Security (Gore Commission)

Internal Revenue Service taxpayer abuse (1996)

—National Commission on Restructuring the Internal Revenue Service (Kerrey-Portman Commission)
—Senate Committee on Governmental Affairs
—Senate Committee on Finance

Technology transfers to China (1997)

—Commission to Assess the Organization of the Federal Government to Combat the Proliferation of Weapons of Mass Destruction (Deutch Commission)
—Senate Committee on Governmental Affairs, Permanent Subcommittee on Investigations
—Joint Economic Committee
—Senate Committee on Governmental Affairs
—Senate Select Committee on Intelligence
—House Committee on National Security and Committee on International Relations (joint investigation)
—Senate Committee on Commerce, Science, and Transportation

—House Select Committee on U.S. National Security and Military-Commercial Concerns with the People's Republic of China
—House Committee on Science
—Special Investigative Panel of the President's Foreign Intelligence Advisory Board (PFIAB, the Rudman Report)
—House Committee on Commerce, Subcommittee on Oversight and Investigations
—Senate Committee on Governmental Affairs
—Senate Committee on Armed Services
—Senate Committee on Energy and Natural Resources
—House Committee on Armed Services, Subcommittee on Military Procurement and Full Committee
—House Permanent Select Committee on Intelligence
—Senate Committee on the Judiciary, Subcommittee on Administrative Oversight and the Courts

The investigation concentrated on technology transfers to China, but included a tangle of unrelated allegations raised in diffuse hearings regarding satellites, computers, spying, and nuclear proliferation.[12]

1996 campaign finance abuses (1997)

—Senate Committee on Governmental Affairs
—House Committee on Oversight and Government Reform

Clinton impeachment (1998)

—House Committee on the Judiciary
The majority of hearings were jointly held before the two House subcommittees.

Preventing terrorist attacks (1998)

—Advisory Panel to Assess Domestic Response Capabilities for Terrorism Involving Weapons of Mass Destruction (Gilmore Commission)
—National Commission on Terrorism (Bremer Commission)
—U.S. Commission on National Security/21st Century (Hart-Rudman Commission)

This was a highly diffuse investigation that produced dozens of recommendations in the years preceding the 9/11 attacks. The Congressional Research Service packages these commissions as "broad efforts to understand the terrorist threat," but draws no conclusions regarding the lead investigator. I put the Hart-Rudman commission in the lead given its well-known leadership, visibility, and durability in the creation of the Department of Homeland Security. Although it was not authorized by Congress or created by presidential order, Secretary of Defense William S. Cohen established the commission by departmental order in 1999. Ironically, it was the last of the three major commissions in this package, but turned out to be the most significant.[13]

Year 2000 Technology Problem (1998)

—Senate Special Committee on the Year 2000 Technology Problem
—House Committee on Government Reform and Oversight, Subcommittee on Government Management, Information, and Technology
—President's Council on Year 2000 Conversion

The President's Council on Year 2000 Conversion was not a blue-ribbon commission or a formal investigation, but it was a direct response to the Year 2000 technology problem. If excluded, the list would underestimate the attention the issue received from the executive branch because the council was an active participant in efforts to understand and respond to the potential threat to information systems.

Enron collapse (2001)

—House Committee on Financial Services, Subcommittee on Capital Markets, Insurance, and Government-Sponsored Enterprises
—Senate Committee on Finance
—Senate Committee on Commerce, Science, and Transportation, Subcommittee on Consumer Affairs, Foreign Commerce, and Tourism
—House Committee on Energy and Commerce and (1) Subcommittee on Commerce, Trade, and Consumer Protection, (2) Subcommittee on Oversight and Investigations, (3) Subcommittee on Commerce, Trade, and Consumer Protection, and (4) Subcommittee on Energy and Air Quality
—Senate Committee on Governmental Affairs
—Senate Committee on Energy and Natural Resources
—House Committee on Education and the Workforce
—House Committee on Education and the Workforce, Subcommittee on Employer-Employee Relations
—Senate Committee on Health, Education, Labor, and Pensions
—Senate Committee on Banking, Housing, and Urban Affairs

The large number of inquiries into the collapse of Enron offers several potential primary investigators (with at least nine committees holding hearings). The House Committee on Financial Services is designated as the primary investigator because it held the first hearing on the Enron collapse and played a role in the resulting Sarbanes-Oxley Act of 2002.

White House Energy Task Force (2001)

—House Committee on Energy and Commerce

This task force investigation earned a one-point footprint score and a one-point impact score, making it just one of six investigations with this "double-double." The investigation focused on the alleged self-dealing role of campaign contributors and regulated parties as members of Vice President Dick Cheney's National Energy Policy Development Group established on January 29, 2001. The investigation was sparked on April 19, 2001, when the House Energy and Commerce Committee's ranking member, Rep. John D. Dingell (D-Mich.), and his colleague, Rep. Henry Waxman (D-Calif.), requested a formal General Accounting Office investigation.

9/11 terrorist attacks (2002)

—National Commission on Terrorist Attacks upon the United States (Kean-Hamilton Commission, also known as the 9/11 Commission)
—Senate Intelligence Committee and the House Permanent Select Intelligence Committee (joint inquiry)

Conduct of the Iraq War (2003)

—Senate Committee on Armed Services and assorted subcommittees
—House Committee on Armed Services and assorted subcommittees
—Senate Committee on Foreign Relations and assorted subcommittees
—House Committee on Foreign Affairs and assorted subcommittees
—Independent Panel to Review Department of Defense Detention Operations
—Iraq Study Group
—Independent Commission on the Security Forces of Iraq (Jones Commission)
—Senate Select Committee on Intelligence
—House Permanent Select Committee on Intelligence
—Commission on the Intelligence Capabilities of the United States Regarding Weapons of Mass Destruction (Robb-Silberman Commission)
—Senate Committee on Homeland Security and Governmental Affairs
—House Committee on Government Reform

The Iraq Study Group is included in this investigation because it was "created at the request of Congress in early 2006" and "Congress appropriated $1 million for the group."[14]

The other two commissions involved in the effort had less impact on the course of the war. The Jones Commission was largely ignored, while the Robb-Silverman Commission did not address intelligence failures in the pre–Iraq War period, for example, and it focused instead on reforms that would help intelligence agencies detect and prevent future acquisition of weapons of mass destruction by U.S. adversaries.

Department of Homeland Security implementation and operations (2003)

—Senate Committee on Governmental Affairs
—9/11 Commission (operating as the 9/11 Public Discourse Project)
—House Committee on Homeland Security
—House Committee on Government Reform
—Senate Committee on the Judiciary

—House Committee on the Judiciary
—Senate Committee on Commerce, Science, and Transportation
—House Committee on Transportation and Infrastructure

Space shuttle Columbia *accident (2003)*

—*Columbia* Accident Investigation Board (CAIB)
Congress held hearings on the space shuttle *Columbia* but largely focused on the quality and content of either the CAIB investigation or the subsequent response of the National Aeronautics and Space Agency (NASA). The Senate Committee on Commerce, Science, and Transportation held a joint hearing on the accident with the House Committee on Science, Subcommittee on Space and Aeronautics on February 12, 2003. The Senate committee held additional hearings related to the *Columbia* accident, including NASA: Human Space Flight (2003) and Space Shuttle *Columbia* Investigation (2003). The House Committee also held hearings to review the report, including *Columbia* Accident Investigation Board Report (September 4, 2003), NASA's Response to the *Columbia* Report (September 10, 2003), and NASA's Organizational and Management Challenges in the Wake of the *Columbia* Disaster (2003).

Abramoff lobbying tactics (2004)

—Senate Committee on Indian Affairs
—Senate Committee on Finance
—House Committee on Government Reform
The Senate Finance Committee's final report was written by the minority Democratic staff, but reportedly was authorized by the committee's chairman, Sen. Charles E. Grassley (R-Iowa).[15]

Government response to Hurricane Katrina (2005)

—Senate Committee on Homeland Security and Governmental Affairs
—House Select Bipartisan Committee to Investigate Preparation for and Response to Hurricane Katrina
—White House Task Force on the Federal Response to Hurricane Katrina (Townsend Report)

Steroid abuse in baseball (2005)

—House Committee on Government Reform
—Senate Committee on Commerce, Science, and Transportation
—Independent Investigation into the Illegal Use of Steroids and Other Performance-Enhancing Substances by Players in Major League Baseball (Mitchell Report)

—House Committee on Energy and Commerce
—House Committee on the Judiciary

Other committees have taken an interest in the issue of steroid use in sports, typically legislative rather than investigative, including the House Committee on Energy and Commerce in 2005, the House Committee on the Judiciary most recently in 2004, and the Senate Committee on the Judiciary in 1973 and 1989.

The Mitchell Report was an independent investigation of steroid use in major league baseball pursued at the request of Allan H. ("Bud") Selig, the commissioner of baseball. The inclusion of an external, nongovernmental, investigation on the list reflects the visibility of the final report and the fact that the investigation was, arguably, a direct response to congressional activity on the subject.[16]

Mine safety (2007)

—House Committee on Education and Labor
—House Committee on Education and Labor, Subcommittee on Workforce Protections
—Senate Committee on Appropriations, Subcommittee on Labor, Health and Human Services, Education, and Related Agencies
—Senate Committee on Health, Education, Labor, and Pensions, Subcommittee on Employment and Workplace Safety

Quality of care for wounded warriors (2007)

—President's Commission on Care for America's Returning Wounded Warriors (Dole-Shalala Commission)
—House Committee on Oversight and Government Reform, Subcommittee on National Security and Foreign Affairs

U.S. attorney firings (2007)

—Senate Committee on the Judiciary
—House Committee on the Judiciary, Subcommittee on Commercial and Administrative Law

2008 financial collapse (2008)

—House Committee on Oversight and Government Reform
—Senate Committee on Banking, Housing, and Urban Affairs
—Senate Committee on Banking, Housing, and Urban Affairs, (1) Subcommittee on Economic Policy, (2) Subcommittee on Securities, Insurance, and Investment, and (3) Subcommittee on Financial Institutions
—House Committee on Financial Services

—House Committee on Financial Services, Subcommittee on Capital Markets, Insurance, and Government-Sponsored Enterprises
—House Agriculture Committee
—Congressional Oversight Panel (Troubled Asset Relief Program)
—Financial Crisis Inquiry Commission (Angelides Commission)[17]

Stimulus oversight (2009)

—Recovery Act Transparency and Oversight Board
—House Committee on Science and Technology, Subcommittee on Investigations and Oversight

The Recovery Act Transparency and Oversight Board was created under the American Recovery and Reinvestment Act of 2009, which included detailed assignments to other executive branch and congressional oversight bodies, including the federal Offices of Inspectors General, Congressional Budget Office, and Government Accountability Office.

Deficit reduction (2010)

—National Commission on Fiscal Responsibility and Reform (Simpson-Bowles Commission)

Gulf oil spill (2010)

—House Committee on Natural Resources
—House Transportation and Infrastructure Committee, Subcommittee on Coast Guard and Maritime Transportation
—Senate Committee on Commerce, Science, and Transportation, Subcommittee on Oceans, Atmosphere, Fisheries, and Coast Guard
—House Committee on Oversight and Government Reform
—Senate Committee on Environment and Public Works
—House Committee on Energy and Commerce, Subcommittee on Energy and the Environment
—National Commission on the British Petroleum Deepwater Horizon Oil Spill and Offshore Drilling

If President Obama hoped to prevent congressional action by appointing his National Commission on the British Petroleum Deepwater Horizon on May 21, he was more than a week late. The House Energy and Commerce Subcommittee on Oversight and Investigations had already established its investigatory lead with a hearing on May 12. Nevertheless, Obama's commission did produce a particularly important investigatory footnote two years after the accident by giving Congress a "D" and the president a "B" for failing to enact significant deep-water drilling reform: "In just the past ten months, at least three offshore oil and gas rigs around the world have experienced significant leaks, demonstrating again and again how risky this activity is and emphasizing the need for the types of controls and protections the Commission called for. The risks will only increase as drilling moves into deeper waters with harsher, less familiar environmental conditions. Delays in taking the necessary precautions threaten new disasters, and their occurrence could, in turn, seriously threaten the nation's energy security. Everyone will benefit if the needed improvements are made properly and expeditiously. For this reason, we are encouraged by the advances the industry, the Department of the Interior, and other federal agencies have made in the two years since the Deepwater Horizon catastrophe to improve the safety of offshore drilling and the nation's readiness to respond to any spills that do occur. However, much more needs to be done, particularly by Congress, which has yet to enact any legislation responding to the explosion and spill."[18]

Fast and Furious gun-walking operation (2011)

—House Committee on Oversight and Government Reform
—Senate Committee on Finance

CQ Weekly described the investigation as "the first oversight investigation of the Obama administration that has gained significant traction since Republicans took control of the House, delivering a steady drumbeat of stories on both sides of the border about alleged malfeasance and bureaucratic bungling. And it is further undermining a department whose hodgepodge of jurisdictions has made it a frequent political scapegoat and loser in turf wars with other law enforcement agencies."[19]

Solyndra Corporation (2011)

—House Energy and Commerce Committee, Subcommittee on Oversight and Investigations
—House Energy and Commerce Committee
—House Committee on Oversight and Government Reform

All of the Energy and Commerce Committee hearings were jointly held with the Subcommittee on Oversight and Investigations.

The House Committee on Oversight and Government Reform appeared to take the lead on Solyndra and other loan decisions in late winter 2012, when the House Energy and Commerce Committee put its review on hold. The Committee on Oversight and Government Reform held its first hearing on the issue on May 16, 2012, and framed the investigation as a broad review of the Energy Department's handling of the energy loan program.

APPENDIX D

Supporting Statistical Analysis

Table D-1. Investigatory Characteristics X Length

a. Summary statistics

R	R^2	Adjusted R^2	Std. error of the estimate
.450	.202	.103	.471

b. ARNOVA

	Sum of squares	Df	Mean square	F	Sig.
Regression	4.962	11	.451	2.030	.035
Residual	19.548	88	.222		
Total	24.510	99			

c. Coefficients

	Unstandardized coefficients		Standardized coefficients		
	B	Std. error	Beta	t	Sig.
(Constant)	−.087	.256		−.340	.734
Congress led	.627	.219	.506	2.860	.005
House led	.061	.116	.058	.526	.600
Full committee venue	−.001	.157	−.001	−.007	.994
Subcommittee venue	.049	.150	.047	.329	.743
Commission venue	.341	.218	.310	1.562	.122
Police patrol	.189	.112	.190	1.687	.095
Domestic issue	.069	.114	.066	.608	.545
Process breakdown	−.078	.121	−.079	−.642	.523
Personal misconduct	−.135	.178	−.089	−.761	.449
Repair	.088	.118	.087	.746	.458
Fact finding	−.241	.113	−.242	−2.128	.036

Table D-2. Investigatory Characteristics X Breadth

a. Summary statistics

R	R^2	Adjusted R^2	Std. error of the estimate
.467	.219	.121	.460

b. ARNOVA

	Sum of squares	Df	Mean square	F	Sig.
Regression	5.199	11	.473	2.237	.019
Residual	18.591	88	.211		
Total	23.790	99			

c. Coefficients

	Unstandardized coefficients		Standardized coefficients		
	B	Std. error	Beta	t	Sig.
(Constant)	−.102	.249		−.409	.684
Congress led	.466	.214	.382	2.181	.032
House led	−.202	.114	−.195	−1.777	.079
Full committee venue	−.089	.153	−.076	−.579	.564
Subcommittee venue	−.009	.147	−.009	−.063	.950
Commission venue	.497	.213	.457	2.331	.022
Police patrol	−.152	.109	−.155	−1.388	.169
Domestic issue	.220	.111	.213	1.989	.050
Process breakdown	−.248	.118	−.254	−2.097	.039
Personal misconduct	−.330	.173	−.220	−1.904	.060
Repair	.164	.115	.163	1.422	.159
Fact finding	.106	.111	.108	.960	.339

Table D-3. Investigatory characteristics X complexity

a. Summary statistics

R	R^2	Adjusted R^2	Std. error of the estimate
.558	.311	.225	.431

b. ARNOVA

	Sum of squares	Df	Mean square	F	Sig.
Regression	7.409	11	.674	3.618	.000
Residual	16.381	88	.186		
Total	23.790	99			

c. Coefficients

	Unstandardized coefficients		Standardized coefficients		
	B	Std. error	Beta	t	Sig.
(Constant)	.060	.234		.256	.798
Congress led	.358	.201	.294	1.786	.078
House led	−.066	.107	−.063	−.617	.539
Full committee venue	−.222	.144	−.191	−1.544	.126
Subcommittee venue	−.144	.138	−.139	−1.045	.299
Commission venue	.572	.200	.527	2.862	.005
Police patrol	−.032	.103	−.033	−.311	.756
Domestic issue	.065	.104	.063	.623	.535
Process breakdown	−.257	.111	−.264	−2.316	.023
Personal misconduct	−.218	.162	−.145	−1.341	.183
Repair	.150	.108	.150	1.387	.169
Fact finding	.069	.104	.070	.661	.510

Table D-4. Investigatory characteristics X leadership

a. Summary statistics

R	R^2	Adjusted R^2	Std. error of the estimate
.447	.200	.100	.455

b. ARNOVA

	Sum of squares	Df	Mean square	F	Sig.
Regression	4.552	11	.414	2.001	.038
Residual	18.198	88	.207		
Total	22.750	99			

c. Coefficients

	Unstandardized coefficients		Standardized coefficients		
	B	Std. error	Beta	t	Sig.
(Constant)	.185	.247		.751	.455
Congress led	.237	.211	.198	1.119	.266
House led	−.119	.112	−.117	−1.060	.292
Full committee venue	−.204	.151	−.180	−1.349	.181
Subcommittee venue	−.164	.145	−.161	−1.127	.263
Commission venue	.152	.211	.143	.720	.474
Police patrol	−.020	.108	−.021	−.186	.853
Domestic issue	−.019	.110	−.019	−.177	.860
Process breakdown	−.158	.117	−.166	−1.350	.180
Personal misconduct	−.103	.171	−.070	−.604	.547
Repair	.120	.114	.122	1.053	.295
Fact finding	.242	.109	.253	2.216	.029

Table D-5. Investigatory characteristics X freedom to investigate

a. Summary statistics

R	R^2	Adjusted R^2	Std. error of the estimate
.412	.170	.066	.484

b. ARNOVA

	Sum of squares	Df	Mean square	F	Sig.
Regression	4.215	11	.383	1.635	.103
Residual	20.625	88	.234		
Total	24.840	99			

c. Coefficients

	Unstandardized coefficients		Standardized coefficients		
	B	Std. error	Beta	t	Sig.
(Constant)	.154	.263		.587	.558
Congress led	.381	.225	.306	1.694	.094
House led	−.158	.120	−.149	−1.319	.190
Full committee venue	−.160	.161	−.135	−.990	.325
Subcommittee venue	.130	.155	.123	.840	.403
Commission venue	.256	.224	.230	1.140	.257
Police patrol	−.036	.115	−.036	−.314	.754
Domestic issue	.105	.117	.099	.899	.371
Process breakdown	−.191	.125	−.191	−1.531	.129
Personal misconduct	−.377	.182	−.246	−2.070	.041
Repair	.165	.122	.160	1.353	.179
Fact finding	.080	.116	.080	.686	.495

Table D-6. Investigatory characteristics X visibility

a. Summary statistics

R	R^2	Adjusted R^2	Std. error of the estimate
.442	.196	.095	.462

b. ARNOVA

	Sum of squares	Df	Mean square	F	Sig.
Regression	4.561	11	.415	1.946	.044
Residual	18.749	88	.213		
Total	23.310	99			

c. Coefficients

	Unstandardized coefficients		Standardized coefficients		
	B	Std. error	Beta	t	Sig.
(Constant)	.664	.250		2.651	.010
Congress led	.178	.215	.148	.830	.409
House led	−.116	.114	−.113	−1.018	.311
Full committee venue	.042	.154	.037	.273	.785
Subcommittee venue	−.163	.147	−.158	−1.103	.273
Commission venue	.086	.214	.080	.402	.689
Police patrol	−.404	.110	−.416	−3.680	.000
Domestic issue	.147	.111	.143	1.320	.190
Process breakdown	−.132	.119	−.136	−1.106	.272
Personal misconduct	.060	.174	.040	.346	.730
Repair	−.084	.116	−.084	−.722	.472
Fact finding	.162	.111	.167	1.458	.148

Table D-7. Investigatory characteristics X seriousness

a. Summary statistics

R	R^2	Adjusted R^2	Std. error of the estimate
.556	.310	.223	.436

b. ARNOVA

	Sum of squares	Df	Mean square	F	Sig.
Regression	7.488	11	.681	3.586	.000
Residual	16.702	88	.190		
Total	24.190	99			

c. Coefficients

	Unstandardized coefficients		Standardized coefficients		
	B	Std. error	Beta	t	Sig.
(Constant)	.263	.236		1.114	.268
Congress led	.095	.203	.078	.472	.638
House led	.054	.108	.052	.502	.617
Full committee venue	−.218	.145	−.186	−1.499	.137
Subcommittee venue	−.196	.139	−.188	−1.412	.161
Commission venue	.272	.202	.249	1.348	.181
Police patrol	.087	.104	.088	.840	.403
Domestic issue	.226	.105	.216	2.155	.034
Process breakdown	−.079	.112	−.080	−.701	.485
Personal misconduct	−.277	.164	−.183	−1.687	.095
Repair	.112	.109	.110	1.022	.310
Fact finding	.182	.105	.184	1.737	.086

Table D-8. Investigatory characteristics X thoroughness

a. Summary statistics

R	R^2	Adjusted R^2	Std. error of the estimate
.451	.204	.104	.472

b. ARNOVA

	Sum of squares	Df	Mean square	F	Sig.
Regression	5.015	11	.456	2.044	.033
Residual	19.625	88	.223		
Total	24.640	99			

c. Coefficients

	Unstandardized coefficients		Standardized coefficients		
	B	Std. error	Beta	t	Sig.
(Constant)	.310	.256		1.209	.230
Congress led	.068	.220	.055	.308	.759
House led	−.059	.117	−.056	−.506	.614
Full committee venue	−.171	.157	−.145	−1.089	.279
Subcommittee venue	−.038	.151	−.036	−.254	.800
Commission venue	.032	.219	.029	.147	.884
Police patrol	.092	.112	.092	.819	.415
Domestic issue	.027	.114	.026	.241	.810
Process breakdown	−.022	.122	−.022	−.181	.856
Personal misconduct	−.183	.178	−.120	−1.032	.305
Repair	.194	.119	.190	1.634	.106
Fact finding	.247	.114	.248	2.176	.032

Table D-9. Investigatory characteristics X leverage

a. Summary statistics

R	R^2	Adjusted R^2	Std. error of the estimate
.371	.138	.030	.462

b. ARNOVA

	Sum of squares	Df	Mean square	F	Sig.
Regression	3.003	11	.273	1.281	.249
Residual	18.757	88	.213		
Total	21.760	99			

c. Coefficients

	Unstandardized coefficients		Standardized coefficients		
	B	Std. error	Beta	t	Sig.
(Constant)	.222	.251	.887	.378	
Congress led	.451	.215	.386	2.100	.039
House led	.087	.114	.088	.764	.447
Full committee venue	−.192	.154	−.174	−1.251	.214
Subcommittee venue	−.260	.147	−.262	−1.762	.082
Commission venue	.136	.214	.131	.636	.527
Police patrol	−.091	.110	−.097	−.827	.410
Domestic issue	.163	.111	.165	1.468	.146
Process breakdown	.078	.119	.084	.658	.513
Personal misconduct	−.142	.174	−.099	−.817	.416
Repair	.050	.116	.052	.429	.669
Fact finding	.090	.111	.096	.810	.420

Table D-10. Investigatory characteristics X durability

a. Summary statistics

R	R^2	Adjusted R^2	Std. error of the estimate
.442	.195	.095	.462

b. ARNOVA

	Sum of squares	Df	Mean square	F	Sig.
Regression	4.554	11	.414	1.942	.044
Residual	18.756	88	.213		
Total	23.310	99			

c. Coefficients

	Unstandardized coefficients		Standardized coefficients		
	B	Std. error	Beta	t	Sig.
(Constant)	−.055	.251		−.221	.826
Congress led	.511	.215	.423	2.382	.019
House led	−.044	.114	−.043	−.389	.698
Full committee venue	−.036	.154	−.031	−.234	.815
Subcommittee venue	.007	.147	.007	.049	.961
Commission venue	.579	.214	.538	2.703	.008
Police patrol	−.213	.110	−.219	−1.938	.056
Domestic issue	.056	.111	.055	.504	.616
Process breakdown	−.261	.119	−.270	−2.195	.031
Personal misconduct	−.320	.174	−.216	−1.843	.069
Repair	.039	.116	.039	.333	.740
Fact finding	.162	.111	.167	1.461	.148

Table D-11. Investigatory characteristics X bipartisanship

a. Summary statistics

R	R^2	Adjusted R^2	Std. error of the estimate
.543	.295	.207	.446

b. ARNOVA

	Sum of squares	Df	Mean square	F	Sig.
Regression	7.332	11	.667	3.350	.001
Residual	17.508	88	.199		
Total	24.840	99			

c. Coefficients

	Unstandardized coefficients		Standardized coefficients		
	B	Std. error	Beta	t	Sig.
(Constant)	.399	.242		1.647	.103
Congress led	.090	.207	.072	.434	.665
House led	−.093	.110	−.088	−.843	.401
Full committee venue	−.225	.149	−.190	−1.514	.134
Subcommittee venue	−.120	.142	−.113	−.841	.403
Commission venue	.188	.207	.170	.910	.365
Police patrol	.116	.106	.116	1.098	.275
Domestic issue	.112	.108	.106	1.041	.301
Process breakdown	.126	.115	.126	1.095	.277
Personal misconduct	−.237	.168	−.154	−1.410	.162
Repair	−.129	.112	−.126	−1.156	.251
Fact finding	.132	.107	.132	1.232	.221

Table D-12. Investigatory characteristics X overall eleven-point footprint score

a. Summary statistics

R	R^2	Adjusted R^2	Std. error of the estimate
.555	.308	.221	2.685

b. ARNOVA

	Sum of squares	Df	Mean square	F	Sig.
Regression	281.829	11	25.621	3.554	.000
Residual	634.361	88	7.209		
Total	916.190	99			

c. Coefficients

	Unstandardized coefficients		Standardized coefficients		
	B	Std. error	Beta	t	Sig.
(Constant)	1.913	1.457		1.313	.193
Congress led	3.562	1.248	.471	2.854	.005
House led	−.651	.663	−.101	−.982	.329
Full committee	−1.462	.894	−.203	−1.635	.106
Subcommittee venue	−.896	.857	−.139	−1.045	.299
Commission venue	3.114	1.245	.462	2.502	.014
Police patrol	−.497	.638	−.082	−.778	.438
Domestic issue	1.152	.647	.179	1.779	.079
Process breakdown	−1.165	.692	−.192	−1.684	.096
Personal misconduct	−2.229	1.011	−.239	−2.204	.030
Repair	.825	.674	.132	1.224	.224
Fact finding	1.264	.646	.208	1.958	.053

Table D-13. Investigatory characteristics X overall eleven-point footprint score after Watergate and during divided government

a. Summary statistics

R	R^2	Adjusted R^2	Std. error of the estimate
.771	.595	.456	2.431

b. ARNOVA

	Sum of squares	Df	Mean square	F	Sig.
Regression	277.970	11	25.270	4.274	.001
Residual	189.189	32	5.912		
Total	467.159	43			

c. Coefficients

	Unstandardized coefficients		Standardized coefficients		
	B	Std. error	Beta	t	Sig.
(Constant)	−.021	1.920		−.011	.991
Congress led	1.956	1.557	.242	1.256	.218
House led	−.211	.994	−.032	−.212	.833
Full committee	−1.897	1.334	−.244	−1.422	.165
Subcommittee venue	−2.086	1.324	−.277	−1.575	.125
Commission venue	1.836	1.638	.262	1.120	.271
Police patrol	−.140	.919	−.021	−.153	.879
Domestic issue	1.614	.934	.235	1.729	.093
Process breakdown	−.008	1.000	−.001	−.008	.994
Personal misconduct	.008	1.502	.001	.006	.996
Repair	3.058	1.164	.428	2.627	.013
Fact finding	3.271	1.038	.501	3.150	.004

Table D-14. Destination X impact

Destination	Impact score all years
Reforming bureaucracies	
Correlation	.015
Sig.	.879
N	100
Repairing policy	
Correlation	−.038
Sig.	.707
N	100
Reversing course	
Correlation	.254*
Sig.	.011
N	100
Enhancing accountability	
Correlation	−.135
Sig.	.180
N	100
Setting the agenda	
Correlation	.235*
Sig.	.019
N	100
Resolving doubts	
Correlation	−.274**
Sig.	.006
N	100

** Significant at the 0.01 level.
* Significant at the 0.05 level.

Table D-15. Footprints X impact

a. Summary statistics

R	R^2	Adjusted R^2	Std. error of the estimate
.819	.670	.629	.643

b. ARNOVA

	Sum of squares	Df	Mean square	F	Sig.
Regression	73.825	11	6.711	16.254	.000
Residual	36.335	88	.413		
Total	110.160	99			

c. Coefficients

	Unstandardized coefficients		Standardized coefficients		
	B	Std. error	Beta	t	Sig.
(Constant)	1.029	.186		5.531	.000
Length	.292	.148	.138	1.967	.052
Breadth	.322	.189	.150	1.705	.092
Complexity	.003	.206	.001	.013	.990
Leader	.229	.173	.104	1.320	.190
Freedom	.193	.161	.092	1.199	.234
Visibility	.041	.163	.019	.253	.801
Seriousness	−.190	.204	−.089	−.930	.355
Thoroughness	.392	.183	.185	2.138	.035
Leverage	.212	.160	.094	1.321	.190
Durability	1.102	.196	.507	5.615	.000
Bipartisanship	.164	.149	.078	1.102	.273

Table D-16. Ten footprint weights X durability

a. Summary statistics

R	R^2	Adjusted R^2	Std. error of the estimate
.735	.540	.489	.347

b. ARNOVA

	Sum of squares	Df	Mean square	F	Sig.
Regression	12.593	10	1.259	10.459	.000
Residual	10.717	89	.120		
Total	23.310	99			

c. Coefficients

	Unstandardized coefficients		Standardized coefficients		
	B	Std. error	Beta	t	Sig.
(Constant)	−.113	.100		−1.134	.260
Length	−.091	.080	−.094	−1.149	.254
Breadth	.048	.102	.048	.469	.641
Complexity	.401	.103	.405	3.890	.000
Leadership	−.037	.093	−.037	−.400	.690
Freedom	.354	.078	.365	4.513	.000
Visibility	.179	.086	.179	2.079	.041
Seriousness	−.018	.110	−.018	−.161	.872
Thoroughness	.104	.098	.107	1.056	.294
Leverage	.165	.085	.160	1.949	.054
Bipartisanship	−.168	.078	−.173	−2.146	.035

Table D-17. Investigatory Characteristics X Impact

a. Summary statistics

R	R^2	Adjusted R^2	Std. error of the estimate
.419	.175	.072	1.016

b. ARNOVA

	Sum of squares	Df	Mean square	F	Sig.
Regression	19.301	11	1.755	1.699	.086
Residual	90.859	88	1.032		
Total	110.160	99			

c. Coefficients

	Unstandardized coefficients		Standardized coefficients		
	B	Std. error	Beta	t	Sig.
(Constant)	.924	.551		1.676	.097
Congress led	1.164	.472	.444	2.465	.016
House led	−.152	.251	−.068	−.605	.547
Full committee venue	.222	.338	.089	.657	.513
Subcommittee venue	.173	.324	.077	.532	.596
Commission venue	1.209	.471	.517	2.567	.012
Police patrol	−.216	.242	−.102	−.893	.374
Domestic issue	.215	.245	.096	.877	.383
Process breakdown	−.443	.262	−.211	−1.692	.094
Personal misconduct	−.736	.383	−.228	−1.924	.058
Repair	.188	.255	.087	.735	.464
Fact finding	.369	.244	.175	1.508	.135

Table D-18. Investigatory Characteristics X Impact After Watergate and During Divided Government

a. Summary statistics

R	R^2	Adjusted R^2	Std. error of the estimate
.634	.402	.197	.996

b. ARNOVA

	Sum of squares	Df	Mean square	F	Sig.
Regression	21.387	11	1.944	1.958	.068
Residual	31.772	32	.993		
Total	53.159	43			

c. Coefficients

	Unstandardized coefficients		Standardized coefficients		
	B	Std. error	Beta	t	Sig.
(Constant)	1.017	.780		1.303	.202
Congress led	.373	.618	.140	.604	.550
House led	−.364	.386	−.162	−.942	.353
Full committee venue	−.326	.519	−.123	−.629	.534
Subcommittee venue	−.058	.516	−.022	−.112	.912
Commission venue	.513	.658	.214	.779	.441
Police patrol	−.156	.360	−.067	−.433	.668
Domestic issue	−.035	.360	−.015	−.098	.923
Process breakdown	.039	.388	.017	.100	.921
Personal misconduct	−.073	.575	−.023	−.128	.899
Repair	.991	.440	.405	2.250	.031
Fact finding	.897	.405	.402	2.215	.034

Notes

CHAPTER ONE

1. Peter Bachrach and Morton S. Baratz, "Two Faces of Power," *American Political Science Review* 56, no. 4 (December 1962): 918.

2. This quote comes from one of the ninety-six interviews I conducted for this project. The list of respondents is presented in appendix A; see note 13 for further detail on the ground rules for these interviews.

3. See Paul C. Light, "Perp Walks and the Broken Bureaucracy," *Wall Street Journal*, April 26, 2012 (http://online.wsj.com/article/SB100014240 52702304723304577367712675249868.html?mod=googlenews_wsj).

4. These findings emerge from a statistical competition called ordinary least squares regression, which pits a set of independent measures (independent variables) against each other in predicting a single measure (dependent variable). The significance of the result for any competition is measured by the same single result in each table in the ARNOVA results and is interpreted the same way. Most of the regressions discussed in chapter 3 and 4 are highly significant, but several fall short, which suggests that there is substantial variation as yet to be explained by measures yet to be developed.

5. A fuller list of my sources is presented in chapter 2.

6. The rule involves three components. First, when a breakdown sparks *multiple, but related investigations* at the same point in time, all of the investigations are packaged into a larger whole. Second, when a breakdown generates a stream of *multiple, but related investigations* over a long period of time, all of the investigations are also packaged into a larger whole. Obviously, when a breakdown produces a *single, short-term or long-term investigation* in a single venue, it is left standing as a separate inquiry.

7. Mayhew used a similar approach in building his list of "high-publicity investigations." See David R. Mayhew, *Divided We Govern: Party Control, Lawmaking, and Investigations, 1945–2002*, 2nd ed. (Yale University Press, 2005). Mayhew's list includes thirty-one high-publicity investigations between 1946 and 1990 and another four between 1991 and 2002. All of Mayhew's investigations made my final list either as stand-alone investigations or as part of a larger package.

8. House Committee on the Judiciary, Subcommittee on Criminal Justice, "Pardon of Richard M. Nixon and Related Matters," Serial 60 (Washington: Government Printing Office, 1975), p. 92; see also Congressional Quarterly, *Congress and the Nation: 1973–1976*, vol. 4 (Washington: CQ Press, 1977) (http://library/cqpress.com/congression/catn73-000916037).

9. House Committee on the Judiciary, "Pardon of Richard M. Nixon," p. 91.

10. House Committee on the Judiciary, "Pardon of Richard M. Nixon," p. 96.

11. Government Accountability Office, "Protecting the Public's Interest: Considerations for Addressing Selected Regulatory Oversight, Auditing, Corporate Governance, and Financial Reporting Issues," GAO-02-601T (Washington, April 9, 2002).

12. Not-for-attribution interviews allowed me to identify the broad source, but not the specific name. These interviews were conducted in person or by telephone between July 2009 and January 2010 with selected follow-ups in late 2011. Many of the interviews were with individuals who had been involved in one or more of the most visible investigations, while other interviews drew on the insights of reporters and scholars who had either covered one or more investigations at the time or studied a set of investigations as a whole. As such, the interviews were designed to elicit the insights of a selected group of individuals, not a random sample of participants.

13. Paul C. Light, *The Tides of Reform: Making Government Work, 1945–1995* (Yale University Press, 1997).

CHAPTER TWO

1. The allegations were publicized in 1991 by former Carter administration National Security Council aide Gary Sick. See Gary Sick, "The Election Story of the Decade," *New York Times*, April 15, 1991 (www.nytimes.com/1991/04/15/opinion/the-election-story-of-the-decade.html). The allegations soon sparked the Senate Foreign Relations Committee investigation on my list of the 100 most significant investigations and produced an equivocal judgment. See Committee on Foreign Relations, "The 'October Surprise' Allegations and the Circumstances Surrounding the Release of the American Hostages Held in Iran," Report of the Special Counsel to Senator Terry Sanford and Senator James M. Jeffords, Senate Report 102-125 (Washington: Government Printing Office, November 19, 1992). However, as appendix C notes, the first investigation of the allegations came in 1983 as a subtext to a House investigation of allegations that the Reagan campaign had stolen a copy of Carter's debate briefing memo.

2. Proxmire gave his first award in March 1975. The award went to the National Science Foundation for an $84,000 study of why people fall in love. The complete list of

Proxmire's 140 awards is available at http://content.wisconsinhistory.org/cdm4/document.php?CISOROOT=/tp&CISOPTR=70852.

3. See, for example, Senate Committee on Governmental Affairs, "The Defense Department's Costly Failure to Properly Manage Its Inventories Continues," Senate Report 100-155 (Washington: Government Printing Office, 1989). See also House Committee on Government Operations, "Managing the Federal Government: A Decade of Decline," Majority Staff Report (Washington: Government Printing Office, December 1992). The Senate Governmental Affairs Committee reported, for example, that the Defense Department had a twenty-two-year supply of plague vaccine in storage in 1987.

4. For a concise history of the congressional Iran-Contra investigations, see Joel M. Woldman, *Congress and the Iran-Contra Affair* (Washington: Congressional Research Service, November 1988). Select committees in each chamber conducted the investigation. Although the two chambers originally wanted a joint select committee, they split on the question. My reading of the history puts the House and Hamilton in the lead. For further background on the investigation, see the note to the investigation in appendix C.

5. National Commission on Terrorist Attacks upon the United States, "The 9/11 Commission Report: Final Report of the National Commission on Terrorist Attacks upon the United States" (Washington: Government Printing Office, 2004) (http://govinfo.library.unt.edu/911/report/911Report.pdf).

6. Philip Shenon, *The Commission: The Uncensored History of the 9/11 Investigation* (New York: Twelve, 2008), p. 401.

7. Ibid., p. 406.

8. See James L. Sundquist, *The Decline and Resurgence of Congress* (Brookings, 1981).

9. The best-known history of the *Washington Post* investigation is Bob Woodward and Carl Bernstein's *All the President's Men* (New York: Simon and Schuster, 1974). The book was made into Robert Redford's 1976 film of the same title. It was nominated for seven Academy Awards, including best picture and best supporting actor and actress, but it was *Rocky*'s year.

10. See Congressional Quarterly, "Army-McCarthy Dispute and Other Congressional Investigations, 1954," in *Congress and the Nation, 1945–1964*, vol. 1 (Washington: CQ Press, 1965) (http://library.cqpress.com/catn/catn45-4-18133-976482).

11. The waffling is well documented in the final report of the Senate's special investigating subcommittee. See Senate Committee on Foreign Relations, "State Department Employee Loyalty Investigation," Senate Report 2108 (Washington: Government Printing Office, July 20, 1950), pp. 2–3.

12. Senate Committee on Foreign Relations, "State Department Employee Loyalty Investigation," p. 149.

13. The transcript is available at www.lib.berkeley.edu/MRC/murrowmccarthy.html.

14. Roger H. Davidson, "The Political Dimensions of Congressional Investigations," *Capitol Studies: A Journal of the Capitol and Congress* 5, no. 2 (Fall 1977): 41.

15. Joint Committee on the Organization of Congress, "Final Report of the Joint Committee on the Organization of Congress" (Washington, December 1993) (www.rules.house.gov/archives/jcoc2.htm).

16. Quoted in House Special Subcommittee on Government Operations, "Government News Management" (Washington, March 25, 1963), p. 23. Readers should note that some of the digitized hearings and legislative reports cited in these notes did not have visible report numbers.

17. Harold C. Relyea, "Opening Government to Public Scrutiny: A Decade of Federal Efforts," *Public Administration Review* 35, no. 1 (January-February 1945): 3.

18. White House, Office of the Press Secretary, "President Obama Establishes Bipartisan National Commission on Fiscal Responsibility and Reform" (Washington, February 18, 2010) (www.whitehouse.gov/the-press-office/president-obama-establishes-bipartisan-national-commission-fiscal-responsibility-an).

19. *Congressional Record* (Washington: Government Printing Office, May 17), p. S6771.

20. See Senate Special Committee to Investigate Whitewater Development Corporation and Related Matters, "Final Report," Senate Report 104-280 (Washington: Government Printing Office, June 17, 1996) (http://history-matters.com/archive/contents/hsca/contents_hsca_report.htm).

21. Senate Select Committee to Study Government Operations with Respect to Intelligence Activities, "Foreign and Military Intelligence," bk. 1 (Washington: Government Printing Office, April 26, 1976), pp. 10–11 (www.aarclibrary.org/publib/church/reports/book1/html/ChurchB1_0001a.htm).

22. See Terrence R. Tutchings, *Rhetoric and Reality: Presidential Commissions and the Making of Public Policy* (Boulder: Westview Press, 1979).

23. See John C. Grabow, *Congressional Investigations: Law and Practice* (New York: Prentice-Hall, 1988), for a general overview and history of congressional investigations.

24. The drip pan story can be found at Eric Lichtblau, "Earmark Put $17,000 Pans on Army Craft," *New York Times*, May 18, 2012 (www.nytimes.com/2012/05/19/us/politics/behind-armys-17000-drip-pan-harold-rogerss-earmark.html?pagewanted =all).

25. See Congressional Quarterly, "Tactical Fighter Experimental (TFX) Airplane Contract and Other Congressional Investigations, 1963," in *Congressional Quarterly Almanac, 1963* (Washington: CQ Press, 1964), p. 1763 (http://library.cqpress.com/catn/catn45-4-18133-976582).

26. House Select Committee on Assassinations, "Report," House Report 94-1781 (Washington: Government Printing Office, December 31, 1976), p. 6.

27. Ibid., p. 5.

28. Costello's testimony provided the grist for a particularly dramatic moment in Francis Ford Coppola's 1972 film, *The Godfather*. It was nominated for ten Academy Awards, and won best picture, best actor, and best actor in a supporting role.

29. Senate Special Committee to Investigate Organized Crime in Interstate Commerce, "Organized Crime in Interstate Commerce, Final Report," Senate Report 725

(Washington: Government Printing Office, August 31, 1951), p. 102 (www.nevada observer.com/Reading%20Room%20Documents/Kefauver%20Final%20Report.htm).

30. David R. Mayhew, *Divided We Govern: Party Control, Lawmaking, and Investigations, 1945–2002*, 2nd ed. (Yale University Press, 2005)

31. See Joseph A. Fry, *Debating Vietnam: Fulbright, Stennis, and Their Senate Hearings* (New York: Rowan and Littlefield, 2006), for a full history of these hearings and the underlying conflicts about how to end the war.

32. Senate, "The Truman Committee" (www.senate.gov/artandhistory/history/minute/The_Truman_Committee.htm).

33. The flying boat and the congressional hearings it ignited were featured in the 2004 Martin Scorsese film, *The Aviator*. The bio-epic about Hughes was nominated for eight Academy Awards, but it was *Million Dollar Baby*'s year.

34. Cited in Congressional Quarterly, "Un-American Activities and Other Congressional Investigations, 1947," in *Congress and the Nation, 1945–1964*, vol. 1 (Washington: CQ Press, 1965).

35. For a history of the Truman Committee and its accomplishments, including this list of activities, see Donald H. Riddle, *The Truman Committee* (Rutgers University Press, 1964).

36. See Senate Committee on Homeland Security and Governmental Affairs, Permanent Subcommittee on Investigations, "Permanent Subcommittee on Investigations Historical Background" (Washington, n.d.) (www.hsgac.senate.gov/subcommittees/investigations/about).

37. Mayhew draws this distinction as well. High-publicity investigations are not always about important issues, but they generate high publicity nonetheless. See *Divided We Govern*, p. 27.

38. The following are the twenty-five near-miss investigations that were not included in box 2-1: the "Admirals Revolt" against cancellation of a Navy super carrier (1949), the Air Force B-36 bomber budget (1949), the "Five Percenters" lobbying scandal (1949), the Truman administration's seizure of the steel industry (1951), Air Force secretary Harold E. Talbott's private business dealings (1955), the Cosa Nostra crime syndicate (1963), Defense Department fraud, waste, and abuse (1969), Office of Management and Budget director Thomas Bertram "Bert" Lance's banking history before joining the Carter administration as budget director (1977), Billy Carter's business dealings with Libya (1980), the Reagan administration's Private Sector Survey on Cost Control headed by J. Peter Grace (1982), U.S. missions in the Soviet Union (1987), the U.S. Navy's downing of an Iranian passenger jet (1988), the Bank of Credit and Commerce International scandal (1991), the relationship between Banca Nazionale del Lavoro and the U.S. Commodity Credit Corporation (1992), the Aldrich Ames spy case (1994), the Bipartisan Commission on Entitlement Reform (1993), the Commission on Protecting and Reducing Government Secrecy (1994), the Khobar Towers terrorist bombing (1996), the National Bipartisan Commission on the Future of Medicare (1997), irregularities in the 1996 Teamsters Union election (1997), pre–Iraq War intelligence (2002), White House

involvement in the Valerie Plame case (2004), 2001 anthrax attack and Project Bioshield (2007), Iraq and Afghanistan wartime contracting fraud (2008), and federal employee misconduct at the General Services Administration, Secret Service, and Transportation Security Agency (2012).

Two other investigations were simply too young to include on the list of candidates. The first involved the investigation of national security leaks that began in late spring 2012 but had not advanced to significant status by the end of the year. The investigation focused on a series of media reports detailing the president's role in approving "kill lists" of senior terrorist leaders by Central Intelligence Agency drones and the development and release of computer viruses that were used against Iran's nuclear weapons development program. See Robert Barnes, "Leak Probe Risks for Administration Depend on Two Veteran Prosecutors," *Washington Post*, June 10, 2012 (www.washingtonpost.com/politics/leak-probes-risks-for-administration-depend-on-two-veteran-prosecutors/2012/06/10/gJQANDLFTV_story.html).

39. House Committee on Government Operations, Subcommittee on Foreign Operations and Government Information, "Government Information Plans and Policies, Part 1" (Washington: Government Printing Office, March 19, 1963), p. 1.

40. See Michael R. Godon, "House Panel Delves into Libya Attack That Killed Envoy," *New York Times*, October 10, 2012 (www.nytimes.com/2012/10/11/world/africa/hearing-focuses-on-attack-that-killed-ambassador.html?hp).

41. C. P. Trussell, "Otepka Dropped as Security Aide: Held Guilty of Passing Data; Congressional Protest," *New York Times*, November 6, 1963, p. 1.

42. Senate Committee on the Judiciary, Subcommittee to Investigate the Administration of the Internal Security Act and Other Internal Security Laws, "State Department Security: 1963–65" (Washington: Government Printing Office, 1967), p. iii.

43. Otepka's story is well told in William J. Gill, *The Ordeal of Otto Otepka* (New Rochelle: Arlington House, 1969).

44. Juliana Gruenwald, "COMPUTERS: Worry Over Year 2000 Problem Has Hill Pressing for Action," *CQ Weekly*, December 20, 1997, p. 3124.

45. Rajiv Chandrasekaran, "The Budget Didn't Bite; Computers Pass Their Date with Destiny," *Washington Post*, January 1, 2000, p. A1.

46. The Senate's Special Committee on the Year 2000 Technology Problem made no secret of its desire for credit in the title of its final report, "Y2K Aftermath: Crisis Averted" (Washington: Government Printing Office, February 29, 2000).

47. The 1978 General Services Administration investigation focused in large part on kickbacks from construction firms on Public Housing Service contracts. Ironically, perhaps, Public Housing Service was the target of further derision in 2012 for its approval and sponsorship of the $823,000 Western Region's "over-the-top" Las Vegas conference.

48. Mitt Romney's mention of the Solyndra loan is referenced in Jade F. Smith, "The Early Word: New Attack," *New York Times*, May 30, 2012 (www.nytimes.com/2012/05/30/us/politics/romney-sealing-nomination-steps-up-attack-on-obama.html).

49. Thomas E. Mann and Norman J. Ornstein, *The Broken Branch: How Congress Is Failing America and How to Get It Back on Track* (Oxford University Press, 2008).

50. Norman J. Ornstein and Thomas E. Mann, "When Congress Checks Out," *Foreign Affairs* 85, no. 6 (November-December 2006): 67.

51. See Sundquist, *The Decline and Resurgence of Congress.*

52. David C. W. Parker and Matthew M. Dull, "Divided We Quarrel: The Changing Politics of Congressional Investigations," *Legislative Studies Quarterly* 34, no. 3 (August 2009): 330. Their analysis was built on a database of 1,015 major investigations from 1947 to 2004. Parker and Dull created the inventory by culling the *Congressional Information Service Index* using the following search string: (Fraud OR interest OR corrupt! OR brib! OR conflict OR illegal OR ethic! OR espionage OR self-incrimination OR alleg! OR influence OR loyalty OR sabotage OR impropriety OR favoritism OR affair OR agency OR department OR office OR president! OR public administration OR corporation OR separation of powers OR military OR executive privilege OR [NAME OF PRESIDENT] OR council OR services OR war OR abuses OR impeach OR investigat! OR congress!) AND (executive OR commission OR federal OR employees).

53. A positive relationship means that both of the measures rise and fall together, while a negative relationship means that one measure rises as the other falls. Statistical significance is defined in a relationship by the odds that it occurred by chance and is set at either the 0.05 level, which is generally interpreted as a 5 in 100 chance that the two measures are by coincidence, or the 0.01 level, which is interpreted as a 1 in 100 chance. The lack of any sign before a correlation indicates that it is positive, meaning that the two measures rise and fall together, while a negative sign indicates that they rise and fall in opposite directions. All correlations in this book were calculated using a two-tailed bivariate test.

54. Mathew D. McCubbins and Thomas Schwartz, "Congressional Oversight Overlooked: Police Patrols versus Fire Alarms," *American Journal of Political Science* 28, no. 1 (February 1984): 165.

55. John W. Kingdon, *Agendas, Alternatives, and Public Policy*, 2nd ed. (New York: Longman, 2010).

56. Frank R. Baumgartner, Christoffer Green-Pedersen, and Bryan D. Jones, "Comparative Studies of Policy Agendas," *Journal of European Public Policy* 13, no. 7: 961.

57. See Terry M. Moe, "Toward a Theory of Public Bureaucracy," in *Organization Theory: From Chester Barnard to the President and Beyond*, edited by O. E. Williamson (Oxford University Press, 1990).

58. House Committee on Government Reform, "Unsubstantiated Allegations of Wrongdoing Involving the Clinton Administration," Minority Staff Report (Washington, March 2001), p. 1.

59. Mathew D. McCubbins, "Abdication or Delegation? Congress, the Bureaucracy, and the Delegation Dilemma," *Regulation* 22, no. 2 (July 11, 1999): 31.

60. Ibid.

61. Parker and Dull, "Divided We Quarrel," pp. 335.

62. Thomas E. Mann and Norman J. Ornstein, *It's Even Worse Than It Looks: How the American Constitutional System Collided with the New Politics of Extremism* (New York: Basic Books, 2012).

63. The number of House and Senate committee staffs moved toward general parity during the post-Watergate period, falling from 1,891 House staffers in 1977 to 1,362 in 2009, while rising from 1,082 Senate staffers to 1,246 during the same period. See R. Eric Petersen, Parker H. Reynolds, and Amber Hope Wilhelm, "House of Representatives and Senate Staff Levels in Member Committee, Leadership, and Other Offices, 1977–2010," CSR Report R41366 (Washington: Congressional Research Service, August 10, 2010) (http://assets.opencrs.com/rpts/R41366_20100810.pdf).

64. See Jonathan Rauch for an early report on this program in "Demosclerosis," *National Journal*, December 5, 1992 (www.jonathanrauch.com/jrauch_articles/demo sclerosis_the_original_article/).

CHAPTER THREE

1. Henry A. Waxman, "Remarks of Henry A. Waxman," prepared for the Congressional Oversight Symposium, American University Center for Congressional and Presidential Studies, September 18, 2006, p. 2 (www.c-spanvideo.org/program/LuncheonKey).

2. Rep. Barber B. Conable used this phrase to describe the 1983 Social Security rescue as it moved toward last-minute passage; see Paul C. Light, *Artful Work: The Politics of Social Security Reform* (New York: W. W. Norton, 1985).

3. Joel D. Aberbach, *Keeping a Watchful Eye: The Politics of Congressional Oversight* (Brookings, 1990), p. 34.

4. Project on Government Oversight (POGO), *The Art of Congressional Oversight: A User's Guide to Doing It Right* (Washington, 2009), p. 5.

5. David H. Rosenbloom, "1946: Framing a Lasting Congressional Response to the Administrative State," *Administrative Law Review* 50, no. 1 (1998): 176–77.

6. Ibid., p. 187.

7. Frederick A. O. Schwarz, "Testimony on Ensuring Executive Branch Accountability" (Washington: House Committee on the Judiciary, Subcommittee on Commercial and Administrative Law, March 29, 2007), p. 3 (http://brennan.3cdn.net/e3d9efc3511768adc3_svm6bn16e.pdf); see also Frederick A. O. Schwarz Jr. and Aziz Z. Huq, *Unchecked and Unbalanced: Presidential Power in a Time of Terror* (New York: New Press, 2007).

8. See James Pfiffner, "Presidential Signing Statements and Their Implications for Public Administration," *Public Administration Review* 69, no. 2 (March-April 2009): 249–55, for a discussion of the role of signing statements in undermining congressional control.

9. These excerpts are from POGO, *Art of Congressional Oversight*, ch. 1.

10. Joel D. Aberbach, "What's Happened to the Watchful Eye?" *Congress and the Presidency* 29, no. 1 (2002): 19.

11. Ibid., p. 7.

12. Ibid., p. 13.

13. Ibid., p. 18.

14. Jordan Tama uses similar methods to measure the context and ultimate impact of fifty-one national security commissions appointed between 1981 and 2006. See Jordan Tama, *Terrorism and National Security Reform: How Commissions Can Drive Change during Crises* (Cambridge University Press, 2011).

15. Experts may disagree about the use of breadth as an indicator of footprint. As Jordan Tama argues in *Terrorism and National Security Reform,* the narrower the focus of a national security commission, the higher the impact: "Executive branch commissions have greater impact than congressional commissions because they can be appointed more quickly and tend to be less politically polarized, enabling them to reach consensus and to complete their work while a window of opportunity for reform remains open. At the same time, commissions with relatively narrow mandates spur more reform than panels of broader scope because a narrow charge makes it easier for a commission to achieve unanimity and to advocate effectively for the adoption of its recommendations." Tama's data confirm the hypothesis: eight of his ten high-impact commissions had at least two of three characteristics: establishment after a crisis, authorization by the executive branch, and narrow scope. In contrast, only two of his ten low-impact investigations showed the same pattern. Tama, *Terrorism and National Security Reform,* p. 56. Tama's concern here, however, is impact, not footprint.

16. Lantos led the 1989 investigation of the Housing and Urban Development scandal from his post as chairman of the House Committee on Government Operations, Subcommittee on Employment. Although the subcommittee was one of three congressional panels engaged in the investigation, he was clearly the principal leader of the effort. See Congressional Quarterly, "Housing and Urban Development (HUD) Scandal, 1989–1990 Legislative Chronology," in *Congress and the Nation, 1989–1992,* vol. 13 (Washington: CQ Press, 1993) (http://library.cqpress.com/congress/catn89-0000013319; doi: catn89-0000013319).

17. National Commission on Terrorist Attacks upon the United States, "The 9/11 Commission Report: Final Report of the National Commission on Terrorist Attacks upon the United States" (Washington: Government Printing Office, 2004), p. xvi (http://gov info.library.unt.edu/911/report/911Report.pdf).

18. See the National Commission on Excellence in Education, *A Nation at Risk: The Imperative for Education Reform* (Washington, April 1983) (http://datacenter.spps.org/uploads/SOTW_A_Nation_at_Risk_1983.pdf). Chaired by University of Utah president David Pierpoint Gardner, the National Commission on Excellence in Education produced a best-selling final report that is still referenced today in debates about everything from the No Child Left Behind Act, the Department of Education's ongoing Race to the Top reform competition, and the charter school movement.

19. POGO, *Art of Congressional Oversight,* p. 9.

20. Ibid., p. 7.

21. Ibid., p. 11.

22. David R. Mayhew, *Divided We Govern: Party Control, Lawmaking, and Investigations, 1945–2002,* 2nd ed. (Yale University Press, 2005); David C. W. Parker and

Matthew M. Dull, "Divided We Quarrel: The Changing Politics of Congressional Investigations," *Legislative Studies Quarterly* 34, no. 3 (2009): 493–524.

23. Thomas E. Mann and Norman J. Ornstein, *It's Even Worse Than It Looks: How the American Constitutional System Collided with the New Politics of Extremism* (New York: Basic Books, 2012), p. 44.

24. Jonathan Rauch, "Bi-Polar Disorder," *Atlantic* (January-February 2005) (www.theatlantic.com/magazine/archive/2005/01/bipolar-disorder/303665/).

25. The commission's final plan can be found in the National Commission on Fiscal Responsibility and Reform, *The Moment of Truth* (Washington, December 2010), www.fiscalcommission.gov/sites/fiscalcommission.gov/files/documents/TheMoment ofTruth12_1_2010.pdf.

26. Eric Pianen, "Super Flaw: If Only Obama Had Upheld Bowles-Simpson," *Financial Times,* November 11, 2011 (www.thefiscaltimes.com/Articles/2011/11/22/Super-Flaw-If-Only-Obama-Had-Upheld-Bowles-Simpson.aspx#page1).

27. Recall that a positive correlation means that the two measures involved rise and fall together, while a negative correlation means that the two measures rise and fall in opposite directions.

28. Anthony Downs, "The 'Issue-Attention Cycle,'" *Public Interest* 28 (Summer 1972): 38.

29. Security Resources Panel of the Science Advisory Committee, *Deterrence and Survival in the Nuclear Age,* November 7, 1957, declassified document authored by H. Rowan Gaither Jr.

30. Congressional Quarterly, "Air and Missile Review," in *CQ Almanac 1957* (Washington: CQ Press, 1958), http://library.cqpress.com/cqalmanac/cqal57-1346219.

31. *Congressional Record—Senate,* January 23, 1958, p. 878.

32. For a brief history of the commission and a call for a new Hoover Commission, see Ronald C. Moe, "A New Hoover Commission: A Timely Idea or Misdirected Nostalgia?" *Public Administration Review* 42, no. 3 (May–June 1980): 270–77. For an analysis of how the commission affected the presidency, see Peri E. Arnold, "The First Hoover Commission and the Managerial Presidency," *Journal of Politics* 38, no. 1 (February 1976): 46–70.

33. Herbert Clark Hoover, *The Hoover Commission Report on the Organization of the Executive Branch of the Government* (New York: McGraw-Hill, 1949) (http://catalog. hathitrust.org/Record/001141813). Additional commission reports can be found in the Hathi Trust digital library.

34. The three attempts came in 1988, 1998, and 2000. I was the lead Senate staffer in drafting the first attempt. Office of Management and Budget director Richard Darman persuaded President George H. W. Bush to void the provision creating the commission.

35. The speech is available at www.whitehouse.gov/the-press-office/2011/01/ 25/remarks-president-state-union-address.

36. Commission Appointed by the President of the United States to Investigate and Report the Facts Relating to the Attack Made by Japanese Armed Forces upon

Pearl Harbor in the Territory of Hawaii on December 7, 1941, "Attack upon Pearl Harbor by Japanese Armed Forces" (Washington: Government Printing Office, January 28, 1942), p. 20 (www.ibiblio.org/pha/pha/roberts/roberts.html).

37. This history can be found at Congressional Quarterly, "Pearl Harbor and Other Congressional Investigations, 1945," in *Congress and the Nation, 1945–1964*, vol. 1 (Washington: CQ Press, 1965) (http://library.cqpress.com/catn/catn45-4-18133-976423).

38. Joint Committee of the Investigation of the Pearl Harbor Attack, "Investigation of the Pearl Harbor Attack Pursuant to S. Con. Res. 27, 79th Congress" (Washington: Government Printing Office, 1946), p. 257.

39. Ibid., pp. 251–52.

40. Ibid., p. 252.

41. Ibid., p. 266.

42. Ibid., pp. 253–66. The 9/11 Commission listed the failure of imagination as the first of four failures that led to the catastrophe.

43. Despite great competition from dozens of authors, the best book on the attack remains Roberta Wohlstetter's *Pearl Harbor: Warning and Decision*, new ed. (Stanford University Press, 1962).

44. According to the Pew Research Center, Hurricane Katrina was third in news interest among 1,301 events that Pew respondents rated from 1984 to 2006. *Challenger* was still first at 80 percent, while the 9/11 terrorist attacks were second at 75 percent. The rankings were sent to me via e-mail on September 14, 2009.

45. Senate Committee on Homeland Security and Governmental Affairs, "Hurricane Katrina: A Nation Still Unprepared," Report 109-322 (Washington: Government Printing Office, April 27, 2006), www.gpoaccess.gov/serialset/creports/katrinanation. html.

46. Senate Committee, *Hurricane Katrina*, p. 2.

47. Select Bipartisan Committee to Investigate the Preparation for and Response to Hurricane Katrina, "A Failure of Initiative" (Washington: Government Printing Office, February 15, 2006) (www.gpoaccess.gov/katrinareport/mainreport.pdf).

48. Quoted by Tim Starks, "Katrina Panel Indicts Response," *CQ Weekly*, February 20, 2006, p. 488.

49. The six Democrats applauded the investigation as a model of the good investigation: "In its comprehensiveness and non-partisanship, the Homeland Security and Governmental Affairs Committee's Hurricane Katrina investigation did exactly what the American people have a right to expect from a Congressional investigation." However, the dissent contributed to a deep partisan divide that plagued both the Senate and House investigations: "We write separately here to express our additional views on three matters on which the Chairman and the Ranking Member were ultimately unable to reach a meeting of the minds . . . The Committee's efforts to understand the role the White House played in events leading up to and following the catastrophe were severely hindered by the White House's failure to comply with Committee requests for information, documents, and interviews. As a result, we learned much too little about

what the White House and the Executive Office of the President were doing during the critical days before and after Katrina struck." See Select Bipartisan Committee, *A Failure of Initiative*, pp. 667ff, for the full dissent.

50. Abscam was the FBI's code name for the operation, which involved a fake corporation called Abdul Enterprises that offered thirty-one members of Congress bribes in return for favors. Hence the contraction of "Ab" and "scam."

51. For the full text of Rayburn's remarks in giving the investigatory assignment to Moss, see House Committee on Interstate and Foreign Commerce, Subcommittee on Legislative Oversight, "Independent Regulatory Commissions," House Report 1141 (Washington, January 8, 1959), p. 4. Many of the congressional committees and subcommittees identified in this book changed their names from time to time. For example, the Committee on Government Operations began as the Committee on Government Expenditures in 1927 and changed its name to the Committee on Government Reform and Oversight in 1995, the Committee on Government Reform in 1999, and the Committee on Oversight and Government Reform in 2007.

52. House Committee on Interstate and Foreign Commerce, "Independent Regulatory Commissions," p. 4.

53. See Bernard Schwartz, "Antitrust and the FCC: The Problem of Network Dominance," *University of Pennsylvania Law Review* 107, no. 6 (April 1959): 753–95.

54. See Jack Anderson, "Congressman Harris Quashes Investigation of Sherman Adams; Assistant to President Made Calls for Textile Tycoon, Ex-Publisher Links Adams with Alleged Embezzler," *Bell Syndicate*, May 13, 1958, p. 1 (http://dspace.wrlc. org/doc/retrieve/605617).

55. House Committee on Interstate and Foreign Commerce, "Independent Regulatory Commissions," p. 76.

56. Congressional Quarterly, "Documents in Sherman Adams Controversy," in *CQ Almanac 1958* (Washington: CQ Press, 1959) (http://library.cqpress.com/cqalmanac/cqal58-1340211).

57. Damon Chappie, "GOP Leaders Ask Panels to Dig Up Damaging Info on Clinton, Unions," *Roll Call*, April 29, 1996. No page number provided.

58. Waxman, "Remarks," p. 5.

59. Hypothetically speaking, Starr's early Whitewater review might be packaged as a small contributor to the investigation conducted by the Senate's Special Committee to Investigate Whitewater Development Corporation and Related Matters, while his review of the 1993 suicide of deputy White House counsel Vince Foster would be packaged as a secondary contributor to the Clinton conduct investigation by the House Government Reform and Oversight Committee. However, neither review fits my definition of a congressional or presidential investigation.

60. Kenneth W. Starr, *The Starr Report: The Findings of Independent Counsel Kenneth W. Starr on President Clinton and the Lewinsky Affair* (New York: Public Affairs Press, 1988). The full text of the report can be found at www.washingtonpost.com/wp-srv/politics/special/clinton/icreport/srprintable.htm.

61. No doubt because Grassley was in the Senate minority, the chamber did not hold its first hearing on the issue until June 2012, leaving Issa with ample opportunity to claim the lead. The blow-by-blow history of the operation can be found in the September 2012 report of the Justice Department's Office of Inspector General. See Justice Department, Office of Inspector General, "A Review of ATF's Operation Fast and Furious and Related Matters" (Washington: Department of Justice, September 2012) (www.justice.gov/oig/reports/2012/s1209.pdf).

62. This description came from ATF's Phoenix Field Division's special agent in charge, William Newell. Sari Horwitz, "Agent Who Started 'Fast and Furious' Defends Gunrunning Operation," *Washington Post*, June 27, 2012 (www.washingtonpost.com/world/national-security/agent-who-started-fast-and-furious-defends-operation/2012/06/27/gJQAQviT7V_story_1.html).

63. The "hell, no" denial also came from Newell. See House Committee on Oversight and Government Report, "Update on Operation Fast and Furious," Staff Memorandum (Washington, May 3, 2012, p. 6) (http://oversight.house.gov/wp-content/uploads/2012/05/Update-on-Fast-and-Furious-with-attachment-FINAL.pdf).

64. Issa made the statement during the committee's June 15, 2011, hearing. See House Committee on Oversight and Government Reform, "Operation Fast and Furious: Reckless Decisions, Tragic Outcomes," Serial 112-64 (Washington: Government Printing Office, 2011), p. 165 (http://oversight.house.gov/wp-content/uploads/2012/04/6-15-11-Full-Committee-Hearing-Transcript.pdf).

65. See Justice Department, "A Review of ATF's Operation Fast and Furious," for these details.

66. Issa letter to Holder, October 10, 2011 (http://oversight.house.gov/index.php?option=com_content&task=view&id=1474&Itemid=29).

67. See Charlie Savage, "Report by House Democrats Absolves Administration in Gun Trafficking Case," *New York Times*, January 31, 2012 (www.nytimes.com/2012/01/31/us/politics/operation-fast-and-furious-report-by-democrats-clears-obama-administration.html).

68. For the flavor of the partisanship by late spring, see House Committee on Oversight and Government Reform, "Update on Operation Fast and Furious."

69. "A Pointless Partisan Fight," *New York Times*, June 20, 2012 (www.nytimes.com/2012/06/21/opinion/a-pointless-partisan-fight.html?hp).

70. Michael S. Schmidt, "No Evidence White House Covered up Guns Case," *New York Times*, June 24, 2012 (www.nytimes.com/2012/06/25/us/issa-says-no-evidence-of-white-house-cover-up-in-guns-case.html).

71. The reference can be found at www.nytimes.com/2012/10/16/us/politics/transcript-of-the-second-presidential-debate-in-hempstead-ny.html?pagewanted=all.

72. House Committee on Oversight and Government Reform and Senate Committee on the Judiciary, "Fast and Furious: The Anatomy of a Failed Operation," Joint Staff Report to Rep. Darrell E. Issa and Sen. Charles E. Grassley (Washington, October

29, 2012) (http://oversight.house.gov/wp-content/uploads/2012/10/10-29-12-Fast-and-Furious-The-Anatomy-of-a-Failed-Operation-Part-II-of-III-Report.pdf).

73. House Committee on Energy and Commerce, "Solyndra and the DOE Loan Guarantee Program," September 23, 2011, webcast available at http://democrats.energy commerce.house.gov/index.php?q=hearing/hearing-on-solyndra.

74. House Committee on Energy and Commerce, Subcommittee on Oversight and Investigations, "The Solyndra Failure," Majority Staff Report (Washington, August 2, 2012), pp. 1–2 (http://energycommerce.house.gov/sites/republicans.energycommerce. house.gov/files/analysis/20120802solyndra.pdf).

75. "The Solyndra Mess," *New York Times*, November 25, 2011, p. 34 (www.nytimes. com/2011/11/25/opinion/the-solyndra-mess.html).

76. The quote was recorded in an interview with the *Environment and Energy Daily* on March 21 2012 (www.huffingtonpost.com/2012/03/22/jim-jordan-solyndra-investigation-elections_n_1372205.html).

77. House Committee on Oversight and Government Reform, "The Department of Energy's Disastrous Management of Loan Guarantee Programs," Majority Staff Report (Washington, March 2012), http://oversight.house.gov/wp-content/uploads/2012/03/FINAL-DOE-Loan-Guarantees-Report.pdf.

78. Amy B. Zegart, "Blue Ribbons, Black Boxes: Toward a Better Understanding of Presidential Commissions," *Presidential Studies Quarterly* 34, no. 2 (June 2004): 369.

79. Thomas R. Wolanin, *Presidential Advisory Commissions: Truman to Nixon* (University of Wisconsin Press, 1975); Terrence R. Tutchings, *Rhetoric and Reality: Presidential Commissions and the Making of Public Policy* (Boulder, Colo.: Westview Press, 1979); David Filtner Jr., *The Politics of Presidential Commissions* (Dobbs Ferry, N.Y.: Transaction, 1986); Kenneth Kitts, *Presidential Commissions and National Security: The Politics of Damage Control* (Boulder, Colo.: Lynne Rienner, 1986); James P. Pfiffner, "Presidential Commissions: Keys to Success," paper prepared for the Center for the Study of the Presidency, 1979; Zegart, "Blue Ribbons"; and Tama, *Terrorism and National Security Reform*.

80. Lyndon B. Johnson, "Remarks upon Signing Order Establishing the National Advisory Commission on Civil Disorders," *Public Papers of the President: Lyndon B. Johnson, 1967–1967* (Washington: Government Printing Office, July 29, 1967).

81. See Michael Lipsky, "Social Scientists and the Riot Commission," *Annals of the American Academy of Political and Social Science* 394, no. 1 (March 1971): 72–83. Lipsky argued that much of the data were shaped to support the commission's work.

82. National Advisory Commission on Civil Disorders, *Final Report: What Happened? Why Did It Happen? What Can Be Done?* (New York: Bantam Books, 1968), p. 1.

83. "New Controversy in the Wake of the Kerner Report," *New York Times*, March 10, 1968, n.p.

84. United States Commission on National Security/21st Century, "New World Coming: American Security in the 21st Century: The Phase I Report on the Emerging Global Security Environment for the First Quarter of the 21st Century" (Wash-

ington: United States Commission on National Security/21st Century, September 15, 1999), p. 1.

85. The 1979 Robert Bridges film, *The China Syndrome*, was nominated for four Academy Awards, including best actor and best actress, but it was *Kramer v. Kramer*'s year.

86. Unnamed source quoted in "Assessment of J. Kemeny's Report from Pres. Commission on Accident at TMI," undated posting available at www.nader.org/index.php?/archives/1518-Assesment-of-J.-Kemenys-Report-from-Pres.-Commission-on-Accident-at-TMI.html.

87. President's Commission on the Accident at Three Mile Island, "Report of the President's Commission on the Accident at Three Mile Island" (Washington: Government Printing Office, October 30, 1979) (www.threemileisland.org/downloads/188.pdf).

88. Ibid., pp. 3–4.

89. See Congressional Quarterly, "Nuclear Plant Licensing," in *CQ Almanac 1979* (Washington: CQ Press, 1980) (http://library.cqpress.com/cqalmanac/cqal79-1184337).

90. Presidential Commission on the Human Immunodeficiency Virus Epidemic, *Report of the Presidential Commission on the Human Immunodeficiency Virus Epidemic* (Washington: Government Printing Office, June 1988), p. III.

91. Quoted by Dave Gilden, "Politics before Science" (www.hivplusmag.com/Story.asp?id=34&categoryid=1).

92. Presidential Commission on the Human Immunodeficiency Virus Epidemic, *Report*, pp. xvii–xix.

93. President's Commission on Campus Unrest, *Report of the President's Commission on Campus Unrest* (Washington: Government Printing Office, September 26, 1970), p. ix.

94. Ibid., p. 9.

95. See Congressional Quarterly, "Campus Unrest," in *CQ Almanac 1970* (Washington: CQ Press, 1971) (http://library.cqpress.com/cqalmanac/cqal70-1292322).

96. *Columbia* Accident Investigation Board, "Columbia Accident Investigation Board Report," vol. 1 (Washington: NASA, August 2003), p. 178 (http://caib.nasa.gov/news/report/pdf/vol1/full/caib_report_volume1.pdf, p. 6).

97. Public Broadcasting System, "Investigating a Shuttle Disaster," NOVA, September 1, 2008, interview with Scott Hubbard, member of the *Columbia* Accident Investigation Board (www.pbs.org/wgbh/nova/space/shuttle-investigator.html).

98. This reference to PowerPoint is not to belittle the impact that PowerPoint and other forms of "slideware" can have on the analytic quality of presentations. See Edward R. Tufte's analysis and overall approach to the visual presentation of information on his website, www.edwardtufte.com/tufte/powerpoint presentations.

99. For a discussion of these organizational issues and NASA's resistance to change, see Joseph Lorenzo Hall, "*Columbia* and *Challenger*: Organizational Failure at NASA, *Space Policy* 19, no. 1 (2003): 239–47.

100. Richard P. Feynman, "Personal Observations on the Reliability of the Shuttle," in *Columbia* Accident Investigation Board, *Report*, vol. 1, app. F (http://science.ksc. nasa.gov/shuttle/missions/51-l/docs/rogers-commission/Appendix-F.txt).

101. Claire Ferraris and Rodney Carveth, "NASA and the *Columbia* Disaster: Decision-Making by Groupthink?" *Proceedings of the 2003 Association for Business Communication Annual Convention* (Blacksburg, Va.: Association for Business Communication, 2003) (http://bama.ua.edu/~sprentic/672%20Ferraris%20&%20 Carveth.pdf).

102. These three correlations with freedom to investigate are just below the standard threshold of statistical significance at the 0.05 level, but are close enough (0.056 for personal misconduct investigations, 0.072 for repair investigations, and 0.078 for full committee investigations) to the threshold to be offered as advice.

103. Readers should note three technical details as they review the regressions in appendix D. First, the adjusted R^2 provided at the top of each regression indicates the overall strength of each competition in explaining footprints. Most of the competitions earned very high marks on this measure, but, as with many regressions, substantial variation is left unexplained. Second, all of the measures used in these regressions are dichotomous in nature with two values: zero (no) or one (yes). OLS regression does not allow categorical measures that make no distinction about whether they move in any specific order. Moreover, because dichotomous measures such as institutional home are mirror images and because regression automatically removes one or the other from the analysis because of the collinearity, as it is called, I have selected only one of each of the twins for the analysis. For example, I use the measure of congressionally led investigations as my predictor of how institutional home affects each of the eleven footprint weights as well as the total eleven-point final footprint score. This approach only affects the breakdown measure, which has three components (process, personal misconduct, and policy), of which I could only use two because of the collinearity among the three. However, further regressions testing personal and policy breakdowns show the same results that emerged from the use of process breakdowns, meaning no significant predictive effect for an investigation of either process or policy, but a significant effect for an investigation of personal misconduct. Third, a negative beta coefficient means that the relationship between the investigatory characteristic and footprint weight is also negative—that is, the relationship suggests that the independent measure reduces the probability that the weight will be present in a given investigation. The measure of significance attached to the ARNOVA summary for each regression is the same as for the correlations—the higher the significance, the greater the probability that the given independent measures come together to predict the dependent measure.

104. Table D-12 in appendix D presents the regression against the eleven-point footprint for all 100 investigations. A negative beta coefficient means that the relationship between the investigatory characteristic and footprint weight is also negative—that is, the relationship suggests that the independent measure reduces the probability that the weight will be present in a given investigation.

105. John Aloysius Farrell, "Divided We Stand," *National Journal*, March 1, 2012 (http://nationaljournal.com/magzine/divided-we-stand-20120223).

106. See table D-13 for the results of the final regression against the eleven-point footprint among the forty-four investigations that occurred during divided government and after Watergate.

CHAPTER FOUR

1. The number comes from a simple ProQuest search using the term "Iraq War" to cull the congressional hearing record.

2. The Iraq War seemed to confirm every fear raised by former Congressional Research Center senior scholar Louis Fisher in *Congressional Abdication on War and Spending* (Texas A&M Press, 2000).

3. The President's Commission on Care for America's Returning Warriors is a counterexample, as is the 2008 congressionally created Commission on Wartime Contracting in Iraq and Afghanistan that was established in 2008 to address the flood of fraudulent contracting during the wars. Co-chaired by former Rep. Christopher Shays (R-Conn.) and a former senior defense contract officer, Michael J. Thibault, the commission released its report in 2011. See Commission on Wartime Contracting in Iraq and Afghanistan, *Transforming Wartime Contracting: Controlling Costs, Reducing Risks* (Washington: Government Printing Office, August 2011).

4. James A. Baker III and Lee H. Hamilton, co-chairs, *The Iraq Study Group Report* (New York: Vintage Books, 2006), p. 6 (http://online.wsj.com/public/resources/documents/WSJ-iraq_study_group.pdf).

5. Jordan Tama, *Terrorism and National Security Reform: How Commissions Can Drive Change during Crises* (Cambridge University Press, 2011), pp. 188–90.

6. Dana Priest and Anne Hall, "Soldiers Face Neglect, Frustration at Army's Top Medical Facility," *Washington Post*, February 18, 2007 (www.washingtonpost.com/wp-dyn/content/article/2007/02/17/AR2007021701172.html).

7. See President's Commission on Care for America's Returning Wounded Soldiers, "Serve, Support, Simplify" (Washington, July, 2007), p. 1 (www.veteransforamerica.org/wp-content/uploads/2008/12/presidents-commission-on-care-for-americas-returning-wounded-warriors-report-july-2007.pdf).

8. Steve Vogel, "Report Says Fixes Slow to Come at Walter Reed," *Washington Post*, September 27, 2007 (www.veteransforamerica.org/wp-content/uploads/2008/12/presidents-commission-on-care-for-americas-returning-wounded-warriors-report-july-2007.pdf).

9. Veterans Administration, Office of Inspector General, "Veterans Health Administration: Review of Veterans' Access to Mental Health Care," Report 12-009-168 (Washington, April 23, 2012) (www.va.gov/oig/pubs/VAOIG-12-00900-168.pdf).

10. Vogel, "Report Says Fixes Slow to Come at Walter Reed."

11. House Committee on Oversight and Government Reform, "Third Walter Reed Oversight Hearing: Keeping the Nation's Promise to Our Wounded Soldiers, September 26, 2007" (Washington: Government Printing Office, 2008), p. 20 (http://ezproxy.

library.nyu.edu:2073/congcomp/attachment/a.pdf?_m=509f3192d995e397b8574080c
b08e1f6&wchp=dGLzVzt-zSkSA&_md5=b44543caea47be2a525af40cae0da797&ie=
a.pdf).

12. Congressional Research Service, "Congressional Oversight: A 'How-To' Series of Workshops" (Washington, June 28, July 12, and July 26, 1999), pp. 12–13.

13. Ibid., p. 11.

14. I did not attempt to count the number and implementation of recommendations from each investigation, but urge readers to examine Jordan Tama's methodology in tracking the impact of the 192 recommendations reported by the fifty-one national security commissions he studied. Tama's list covers every significant national security commission created between 1981 and 2006. His impact score is based on two criteria: (1) an objective count of each commission's success in securing full or partial adoption of its recommendations within two years of its report and (2) how 200 commission members, panel staff, and government officials rate the influence of individual panels on a scale of one to five. See Tama, *Terrorism and National Security Reform*.

Tama uses these two measures to compare the relative impact of the forty-nine advisory groups, task forces, and blue-ribbon commissions—his other two inquiries did not produce clear recommendations, if any at all.

However, Tama's analysis is difficult to replicate when other forms of investigatory outcomes are considered. Not only is his two-year window of impact relatively brief, it is not necessarily clear why unanimity would be a source of influence. On the one hand, unanimity does create greater momentum for impact. On the other hand, it does not necessarily increase investigatory impact. As discussed below, the partisanship embedded in both the creation and modus operandi of an investigation may be a critical predictor of impact.

Tama assigns a much higher impact score than I did to Reagan's 1983 Strategic Missile Commission, for example. As he notes, Reagan formed the commission for one purpose alone: to increase congressional support for a mobile missile that would be less vulnerable to a Soviet first strike. With the proposal stalled in the House, Reagan hoped that General (Ret.) Brent Scowcroft might be able to muscle enough support from his blue-ribbon commission to forge a compromise. Despite its low footprint score, the commission clearly shaped the congressional compromise on Reagan's defense strategy. As such, it has a light footprint, but produced significant impact.

15. Thomas R. Wolanin, *Presidential Advisory Commissions: Truman to Nixon* (University of Wisconsin Press, 1975), p. 131.

16. Personal communication by e-mail, December 23, 2012.

17. See Herbert A. Simon, "Proverbs of Administration," *Public Administration Review* 6, no. 1 (Winter 1946): 53–67

18. Project on Government Oversight (POGO), *The Art of Congressional Oversight: A User's Guide to Doing It Right* (Washington, 2009), p. 16.

19. David R. Mayhew, *Divided We Govern: Party Control, Lawmaking, and Investigations, 1946–1990* (Yale University Press, 1991).

20. Terry M. Moe, "Toward a Theory of Public Bureaucracy," in *Organization Theory: From Chester Barnard to the President and Beyond*, edited by O. E. Williamson (Oxford University Press, 1990), p. 147.

21. For a contemporaneous history of the investigation, see Clara Penniman, "Reorganization and the Internal Revenue Service," *Public Administration Review* 21, no. 3 (September–October 1961): 121–30.

22. This history can be found in Congressional Quarterly, "Probe of Tax Collection Scandals," in *CQ Almanac, 1951* (Washington: CQ Press, 1952), http://library.cqpress.com/cqalmanac/cqal51-889-29657-1405251.

23. Executive Order 12546: Presidential Commission on the Space Shuttle *Challenger* Accident, February 3, 1986 (http://en.wikisource.org/wiki/Executive_Order_12546).

24. William J. Broad, "The Shuttle Explodes," *New York Times*, January 28, 1984, p. A1 (www.nytimes.com/learning/general/onthisday/big/0128.html).

25. This second-by-second chronicle comes from the Presidential Commission on the Space Shuttle *Challenger* Accident, "Report of the Presidential Commission on the Space Shuttle Challenger Accident" (Washington: National Aeronautics and Space Administration, June 6, 1986) (http://history. nasa.gov/rogersrep/genindex.htm). A briefing with clear images of the flame and resulting catastrophe can be found at www.youtube.com/watch?v= UE1Xl5BtqbU.

26. Presidential Commission, *Report*, p. 19.

27. Feynman's experiment took place during the February 11, 1986, commission hearing, and can be viewed at youtube.com/watch?v=6Rwcbsn19c0.

28. Richard P. Feynman as told to Ralph Leighton, *What Do You Care What Other People Think? Further Adventures of a Curious Character* (New York: W.W. Norton, 2001), pp. 151–52.

29. Presidential Commission, *Report*, p. 148.

30. Ibid., p. 148.

31. Ibid., p. 82.

32. Ibid., p. 104.

33. I was involved in the task force as the director of studies at the academy in 1985.

34. For the flash study of the accident and the contributory nature of NASA's organizational culture, see Malcom McConnell, *Challenger: A Major Malfunction: A True Story of Politics, Greed, and the Wrong Stuff* (New York: Doubleday, 1986); for a deeper analysis, see Diane Vaughan, *The Challenger Launch Decision: Risky Technology, Culture, and Deviance at NASA* (University of Chicago Press, 1997), and Julianne G. Mahler and Maureen Hogan Casamayou, *Organizational Learning at NASA: The Columbia and Challenger Accidents* (Georgetown University Press, 2009).

35. David E. Sanger, "Loss of the Shuttle: The Context: Inertia and Indecision," *New York Times*, August 27, 2003, p. A1 (www.nytimes.com/2003/08/27/us/loss-of-the-shuttle-the-context-inertia-and-indecision.html).

36. See Charles Perrow, *Normal Accidents: Living with High-Risk Technologies* (Princeton University Press, 1999), for a thorough discussion of the high-risk problem.

37. Senate Committee on Armed Services, Subcommittee on the Air Force, "Airpower," Subcommittee Document 29 (Washington: Government Printing Office, 1957), p. 2.

38. Anthony Leviero, "Airpower Is a Political Issue Too," *New York Times*, April 22, 1956, p. A-1.

39. Ibid., pp. 5–10.

40. Ibid., pp. 5–10.

41. Ibid., p. 96.

42. See Christopher A. Preble, "Who Ever Believed in the 'Missile Gap'? John F. Kennedy and the Politics of National Security," *Presidential Studies Quarterly* 33, no. 4 (December 2003): 801–26, for a summary of how the issue evolved during the 1960 campaign.

43. Paul C. Light, *Artful Work: The Politics of Social Security Reform* (New York: Random House, 1985), p. 125.

44. The House Committees on Aging, the Senate Committee on Aging, the Joint Economic Committee, the House Aging Committee's separate subcommittees on human services and on retirement and the Subcommittee on Income and Employment, the House Ways and Means Committee's Social Security Subcommittee, and the Senate Finance Committee's separate subcommittees on Social Security and income maintenance programs and on savings, pensions, and investments.

45. Senate Committee on Finance, Subcommittee on Social Security and Income Maintenance, "Social Security Financing and Options for the Future" (Washington: Government Printing Office, 1981), pp. 18–19.

46. Ibid., p. 19.

47. I was serving at the time as an American Political Science Association congressional fellow in the office of Rep. Barber B. Conable Jr. (R-N.Y.), who was a member of both the commission and the Gang of Nine. My story of the final negotiations can be found in Light, *Artful Work*.

48. *Congressional Record—House*, March 24, 1983, p. 7395.

49. Light, *Artful Work*, p. 5.

50. J. William Fulbright, *The Arrogance of Power* (New York: Random House, 1966), p. 15.

51. Joseph F. Fry, *Debating Vietnam: Fulbright, Stennis, and Their Senate Hearings* (New York: Rowan and Littlefield, 2006), p. vii.

52. The panel's work is summarized in its final report. See Congressional Oversight Panel, "March Oversight Report: The Final Report of the Congressional Oversight Panel" (Washington: Government Printing Office, March 16, 2001) (www.gpo.gov/fdsys/pkg/CHRG-112shrg64832/pdf/CHRG-112shrg64832.pdf).

53. A comprehensive history of the investigation and subsequent legislation can be found at the Law Librarians' Society of Washington, D.C., website at www.llsdc.org/dodd-frank-act-leg-hist/. The history contains links to all documents, including legislative drafts, hearings, Congressional Research Service reports, and web commentaries.

54. The following exchange comes from House Committee on Oversight and Government Reform, "The Financial Crisis and the Role of Federal Regulators," Preliminary Transcript, Thursday, October 23, 2008, pp. 33–34 (http://oversight-archive. waxman.house.gov/documents/20081024163819.pdf).

Chairman Waxman. My question for you is simple, were you wrong?

Mr. Greenspan. Partially, but let's separate this problem into its component parts. I took a very strong position on the issue of derivatives and the efficacy of what they are doing for the economy as a whole, which, in effect, is essentially to transfer risk from those who have very difficulty—have great difficulty in absorbing it, to those who have the capital to absorb losses if and when they occur.

These derivatives are working well. Let me put it to you very specifically . . .

Chairman Waxman. So you don't think you were wrong in not wanting to regulate the derivatives?

Mr. Greenspan. Well, it depends on which derivatives we are talking about. Credit default swaps, I think, have serious problems associated with them.

But, the bulk of derivatives, and, indeed, the only derivatives that existed when the major discussion started in 1999, were those of interest rate risk and foreign exchange risk.

Chairman Waxman. Let me interrupt you, because we do have a limited amount of time, but you said in your statement that you delivered the whole intellectual edifice of modern risk management collapsed. You also said, "Those of us who have looked to the self-interest of lending institutions to protect shareholders' equity, myself especially, are in 'a state of shock, disbelief.'"

Now that sounds to me like you are saying that those who trusted the market to regulate itself, yourself included, made a serious mistake.

Mr. Greenspan. Well, I think that's true of some products, but not all. I think that's the reason why it's important to distinguish the size of this problem and its nature.

What I wanted to point out was that the—excluding credit default swaps, derivatives markets are working well.

Chairman Waxman. Well, where did you make a mistake then?

Mr. Greenspan. I made a mistake in presuming that the self-interest of organizations, specifically banks and others, were such that they were best capable of protecting their own shareholders and their equity in the firms.

And it's been my experience, having worked both as a regulator for fifteen years and similar quantities, in the private sector, especially, ten years at a major international bank, that the loan officers of those institutions knew far more about the risks involved and the people to whom they lent money, than I saw even our best regulators at the Fed capable of doing.

So the problem here is something which looked to be a very solid edifice, and, indeed, a critical pillar to market competition and free markets, did break down. And I think that, as I said, shocked me. I still do not fully understand why it happened and, obviously, to the extent that I find out where it happened and why, I will change my views. If the facts change, I will change.

Chairman Waxman. Dr. Greenspan, Paul Krugman, the Princeton Professor of Economics who just won a Nobel Prize, wrote a column in 2006 as the subprime mortgage crisis started to emerge. He said, "If anyone is to blame for the current situation, it's Mr. Greenspan, who pooh-poohed warnings about an emerging bubble and did nothing to crack down on irresponsible lending."

He obviously believes you deserve some of the blame for our current conditions.

I would like your perspective. Do you have any personal responsibility for the financial crisis?

Mr. Greenspan. Well, let me give you a little history, Mr. Chairman. There's been a considerable amount of discussion about my views on subprime markets in the year 2000, and, indeed, one of our most distinguished governors at the time, Governor Gramlich who, frankly, is, regrettably, deceased, but was unquestionably one of the best governors I ever had to deal with—came to my office and said that he was having difficulties with the problem of what really turned out to be fairly major problems in predatory lending.

Chairman Waxman. Well, he urged you to move with the power that you as Chairman of the Fed, as both Treasury Department and HUD [Housing and Urban Development] suggested, that you put in place regulations that would have curbed these emerging abuses in subprime lending. But you didn't listen to the Treasury Department or to Mr. Gramlich.

Do you think that was a mistake on your part?

Mr. Greenspan. Well, I questioned the facts of that. He and I had a conversation. I said to him, I have my doubts as to whether it would be successful.

But to understand the process by which decisions are made at the Fed, it's important to recognize what are lines of responsibilities and lines of authority are within the structure of the system. The Fed has [an] incredibly professional large division that covers consumer and community affairs. It has got probably the best banking lawyers in the business, in the legal department, and an outside counsel of expert professionals to advise on regulatory matters. And what the system actually did was to try to corral all of this ongoing information and to eventually filter into a subcommittee of the Federal Reserve Board—

Chairman Waxman. Dr. Greenspan, I am going to interrupt you. The question I had for you is you had an ideology. . . . You feel that your ideology pushed you to make decisions that you wish you had not made?

Mr. Greenspan. Well, remember, though, whether or not ideology is, is a conceptual framework with the way people deal with reality. Everyone has one. You have to. To exist, you need an ideology.

The question is whether it exists and is accurate or not. That I am saying to you is, yes, I found a flaw, I don't know how significant or permanent it is, but I have been very distressed by that fact. But if I may, may I just finish an answer to the question—

Chairman Waxman. You found a flaw?

Mr. Greenspan. I found a flaw in the model that I perceived is the critical functioning structure that defines how the world works, so to speak.

Chairman Waxman. In other words, you found that your view of the world, your ideology, was not right, it was not working.

Mr. Greenspan. Precisely. That's precisely the reason I was shocked, because it had been going for forty years or more with very considerable evidence that it was working exceptionally well.

But let me just, if I may—

Chairman Waxman. Well, the problem is that the time has expired.

55. Senate Banking, Housing, and Urban Affairs Committee, "The Restoring American Financial Stability Act of 2010," Senate Report 111-176 (Washington: Government Printing Office, April 30, 2010), p. 45. I cannot find a House report summarizing the legislative history of its effort.

56. Senate Committee on Homeland Security and Governmental Affairs, Permanent Subcommittee on Investigations, *Wall Street and the Financial Crisis: Anatomy of a Financial Collapse*, Majority and Minority Staff Report (Washington, April 13, 2011) (www.hsgac.senate.gov/download/?id=273533f4-23be-438b-a5ba-05efe2b22f71).

57. See "Financial Crisis Inquiry Commission," *New York Times*, January 25, 2011 (http://topics.nytimes.com/top/reference/timestopics/organizations/f/financial_crisis_inquiry_commission/index.html).

58. See Jesse Eisinger, "The Volcker Rule, Made Bloated and Weak," *New York Times*, February 23, 2012 (www.nytimes.com/2012/02/26/sports/baseball/ryan-braun-case-shows-problems-with-baseballs-drug-testing.html?_r=1&scp=1&sq=Longman&st=cse).

59. See Public Broadcasting Service, "The American Experience: The Quiz Show Scandal" (www.pbs.org/wgbh/amex/quizshow/peopleevents/pande01.html).

60. Jack Gould, "Long-Term Scandal: TV Quiz Investigations Enter Second Year," *New York Times*, August 9, 1959, p. 1.

61. House Committee on Interstate and Foreign Commerce, Subcommittee, "Investigation of Television Quiz Shows," pt. I, Hearings (Washington: Government Printing Office, 1960), p. 8.

62. The 1994 Robert Redford film, *Quiz Show*, was nominated for eight Academy Awards, including best picture and best director, but it was *Forest Gump*'s year.

63. House Committee on Interstate and Foreign Commerce, "Investigation of Television Quiz Shows," pt. II, p. 624.

64. House Committee on Interstate and Foreign Commerce, Subcommittee on Legislative Oversight, "Investigation of Regulatory Commissions and Agencies," *Interim Report*, Report 1258 (Washington: Government Printing Office, 1960, p. 3).

65. For Van Doren's history of the scandal, see Charles Van Doren, "All the Answers: The Quiz-Show Scandals—and the Aftermath," *New Yorker*, July 28, 2008 (www.new yorker.com/reporting/2008/07/28/080728fa_fact_vandoren).

66 . Gould, "Long-Term Scandal."

67. José Canseco, *Juiced: Wild Times, Rampant 'Roids, Smash Hits, and How Baseball Got Big* (New York: It Books, 2006).

68. For the long history of federal efforts to control steroid abuse, see George J. Mitchell, "Report to the Commissioner of Baseball of an Independent Investigation into the Illegal Use of Steroids and Other Performance Enhancing Substances by Players in Major League Baseball" (New York: Office of the Commissioner of Baseball, December 13, 2007), ch. 3 (http://files.mlb.com/mitchrpt.pdf).

69. House Committee on Oversight and Government Reform, "Weighing the Committee Record: A Balanced Review of the Evidence Regarding Performance Enhancing Drugs in Baseball," Staff Report (Washington, March 25, 2008), p. 12.

70. *Meet the Press*, transcript, March 13, 2005, p. 1.

71. Mitchell, "Report to the Commissioner of Baseball."

72. For details on the Clemens acquittal, see Juliet Macur, "Clemens Is Found Not Guilty in Perjury Trial," *New York Times*, June 18, 2012 (www.nytimes.com/2012/06/19/sports/baseball/roger-clemens-is-found-not-guilty-in-perjury-trial.html?hp); Joseph White, Pete Yost, and Frederic J. Frommer, "Clemens Acquittal Latest Blow for Sports Cases," Associated Press, April 19, 2012 (http://hosted2.ap.org/OREUG/0a6106be5ac4420893ee9bde92187155/Article_2012-06-19-Clemens%20Trial/id-4780 517f75194dd9a66b253d8009a8ff).

73. Braun was named the National League's Most Valuable Player in 2011, but ended the season having failed a routine drug test. He eventually won his appeal to overturn the test results on a technicality surrounding the transportation of his urine sample to the testing laboratory. See Jeré Longman, "A Case of Failed Drug Testing," *New York Times*, February 26, 2012 (www.nytimes.com/2012/02/26/sports/baseball/ryan-braun-case-shows-problems-with-baseballs-drug-testing.html?_r=1&scp=1& sq=Longman&st=cse).

74. For a discussion of the role of the federal inspectors general in creating what one inspector general once called "the visible odium of deterrence," see Paul C. Light, *Monitoring Government: Inspectors General and the Search for Accountability* (Brookings, 1993).

75. See Light, *Monitoring Government*.

76. Senate Special Committee on Aging, "Fraud and Abuse among Practitioners Participating in the Medicaid Program," Staff Report for the Subcommittee on Long-Term Care (Washington: Government Printing Office, 1976).

77. Ibid., pp. 3–4.

78. See House Committee on Government Operations, Subcommittee on Intergovernmental Relations, "Operations of Billie Sol Estes" (Washington: Government Printing Office, 1964).

79. See House Committee on Government Operations, Subcommittee on Intergovernmental Relations, "Department of Health, Education, and Welfare (Prevention

and Detection of Fraud and Program Abuse)" (Washington: Government Printing Office, January 26, 1976).

80. See Light, *Monitoring Government,* for a detailed description of the OIG concept.

81. For more details on how inspectors general view their jobs, see www.ignet.gov/.

82. See Light, *Monitoring Government,* again on this point.

83. See House Committee on Oversight and Government Reform, "The Politicization of Inspectors General," Minority Staff Report (Washington, January 7, 2005) (http://democrats.oversight.house.gov/index.php?option=com_content&view=article &id=2392&catid=44:legislation).

84. Paul C. Light, "Strengthening the Inspectors General," *Washington Post,* December 2, 2010 (http://views.washintonpost.com/leadership/light/2010/12/darrell-issa-inspectors-general.html); see also POGO's ongoing effort to track inspector general vacancies at www.pogo.org/resources/good-government/go-igi-20120208-where-are-all-the-watchdogs-inspector-general-vacancies1.html.

85. Public Law 110-409, Congressional Research Service summary.

86. *Congressional Record,* June 28, 2007, p. S8693.

87. For accessible histories of the Grace Commission, see W. Bartley Hildreth and Rodger P. Hildreth, "The Business of Public Management," *Public Productivity Review* 12, no. 3 (1989): 303–21, and Charles T. Goodsell, "The Grace Commission: Seeking Efficiency for the Whole People?" *Public Administration Review* 44, no. 3 (May-June 1984): 196–204; for useful assessments of Gore's National Performance Review, see James L. Sundquist, "The Concept of Governmental Management: Or, What's Missing in the Gore Report," *Public Administration Review* 55, no. 4 (1993): 398–99, and Donald F. Kettl, *Reinventing Government: A Fifth Year Report Card* (Brookings, 1999). For the original Grace Commission report, see J. Peter Grace, *War on Waste* (New York: Macmillan, 1984). For the complete inventory of reports from the National Performance Review, visit the cyber cemetery at the University of North Texas at http://govinfo.library.unt.edu/npr/.

88. See John W. Kingdon, *Agendas, Alternatives, and Public Policy,* 2nd ed. (London: Longman, 2003), for a discussion of ideas in good currency as a fundamental part of the agenda-setting process.

89. House Committee on Government Operations, Subcommittee on Foreign Operations and Government Information, "Government Information Plans and Policies," pt. 1 (Washington: Government Printing Office, March 19, 1963), p. 2.

90. According to Harold C. Relyea, the final legislation was clearly Moss's product. See Harold C. Relyea, "Opening Government to Public Scrutiny: A Decade of Federal Efforts," *Public Administration Review* 35, no. 1 (January-February 1975): 3–10.

91. Ralph Nader, *Unsafe at Any Speed: The Designed-In Dangers of the American Automobile* (New York: Grossman Publishers, 1965).

92. James F. Welsh, "When Driving He Always Uses Seat Belts, and in Politics, Ribicoff Is a Cautious Crusader," *New York Times,* June, 12, 1966 (http://select.nytimes.com/gst/abstract.html?res=F10612FA3E58107B93C0A8178DD85F428685F9&scp=1&sq=%22When%20Driving%20He%20Always%20Uses%20Seat%20Belts%22&st=cse).

93. Johnson's proposal was contained in a special message to Congress on March 2, 1966; see Gerhard Peters and John T. Woolley, "The American Presidency Project" (www.uscb.edu/ws/?pid=28114).

94. Senate Committee on Government Operations, Subcommittee on Executive Reorganization, "Federal Role in Traffic Safety, Final Report" (Washington: Government Printing Office, January 24, 1968), p. 3.

95. Ibid., p. 22.

96. Nader's role is summarized in an online book by Martin Albaum, *Safety Sells: Market Forces and Regulation in the Development of Airbags* (Insurance Institute for Highway Safety, 2005–12), pp. 9–10 (http://safetysells.org).

97. See "Federal Role in Traffic Safety," p. 1266.

98. This "special meeting" of the subcommittee, as Ribicoff himself called it, was carefully described as entirely separate from the subcommittee's overall traffic safety investigation. Here is how Ribicoff described the meeting's purpose: "I have called this special meeting today to look into the circumstances surrounding what appeared to be an attempt by General Motors Corp. to discredit Mr. Ralph Nader, a recent witness before the subcommittee. . . . There is no law which bars a corporation from hiring detectives to investigate a private citizen, however distasteful the idea may seem to some of us. There is a law, however, which makes it a crime to harass or intimidate a witness before a congressional committee. . . . Personally, I don't like to see anyone subjected to harassment, intimidation, or character assassination. But I am particularly disturbed when this sort of activity is injected into the efforts of a legislative body to deal with a vital public issue, like traffic safety." See Senate Committee on Government Operations, "Federal Role in Traffic Safety," pt. 4, p. 1380.

99. Ibid., p. 1379.

100. Robert A. Caro, *The Years of Lyndon Johnson: The Passage of Power* (New York: Alfred A. Knopf, 2012), pp. 442. Caro does not use the transcripts of Johnson's phone calls in his analysis, or at least the content of the calls is not apparent in his descriptions.

101. The phone call took place at 4:05 p.m. on November 29, 1963. A transcript of the call is available on p. 2 at www.maryferrell.org/mffweb/archive/viewer/show Doc.do?docId=889&relPageId=2. Although Johnson told Russell that he wanted someone from the Supreme Court to chair his commission and said that he didn't think he could get anyone from the Supreme Court, he had already recruited Warren at the time.

102. The phone call took place at 8:55 p.m. on November 29, 1963. Johnson also talked about Warren's refusal to serve and his successful effort to break him down. A transcript of the call is available beginning on p. 1 at www.maryferrell.org/mffweb/archive/viewer/showDoc.do?docId=912&relPageId=1.

103. A transcript of the phone call can be found again at www.maryferrell.org/mffweb/archive/viewer/showDoc.do?docId=912&relPageId=1.

104. Warren later called in his chit when he told Johnson a few years later that he wanted a favor in return—administration support for creation of the Federal Judicial

Center, an odd title in the Law Enforcement Assistance Act of 1966 that otherwise dealt with state police.

105. The order is contained in President's Commission on the Assassination of President Kennedy, "Report of the President's Commission on the Assassination of President Kennedy," app. 1 (Washington: Government Printing Office, 1964), p. 471.

106. See Donovan L. Gay, "The Assassination of President John F. Kennedy: The Warren Commission Report and Subsequent Interest" (Washington: Congressional Research Service, September 10, 1975), for an accessible background report on the history of the commission and the investigations that followed.

107. "Report of the President's Commission on the Assassination of President Kennedy," p. 22.

108. Senate Select Committee to Study Governmental Operations with Respect to Intelligence Activities, "The Investigation of the Assassination of President JFK: The Performance of Intelligence Agencies," Senate Report 94-755, bk. 5 (Washington: Government Printing Office, April 14, 1976), p. 5 (www.aarclibrary.org/publib/contents/church/contents_church_reports_book5.htm).

109. House Select Committee on Assassinations, "Report of the Select Committee on Assassinations of the U.S. House of Representatives" (Washington: Government Printing Office, 1979), p. 2.

110. The analysis was disputed by a National Academy of Sciences review panel and was deemed inaccurate by the committee's own acoustics expert. See FBI Record 124-10006-10153.

111. The 1991 Oliver Stone film *JFK* was nominated for eight Academy Awards, including best picture and best supporting actor, but it was a year for *The Silence of the Lambs*.

Whatever the Academy's judgment, the film helped convince Congress to pass the John F. Kennedy Records Collection Act of 1992. The act created an Assassination Records Review Board to declassify and release all of the Warren Commission's evidence by 1998. The 60,000 documents that followed did not provide any new support for the second-shooter theory or alleged assassination plots.

112. These polls are available at www.pollingreport.com/news3.htm#Kennedy.

113. Asked specifically about possible conspirators by the Gallup poll, 37 percent said the mafia had been involved, 34 percent said the CIA, 18 percent Lyndon Johnson, 15 percent the Cubans, and 15 percent the Soviet Union.

114. The quotes about the AFT, Department of Justice, and FBI discussed in the first paragraph of this history come from the House Committee on Government Reform and Oversight, "Investigation into the Activities of Federal Law Enforcement Agencies toward the Branch Davidians," House Report 104-749 (Washington: Government Printing Office, August 2, 1996), pp. 3–4. The dueling reports discussed in this paragraph come from House Committee on Government Reform, "The Tragedy at Waco: New Evidence Examined," House Report 106-1037 (Washington: Government Printing Office, 2000), and John C. Danforth, "Final Report to the Deputy Attorney

General Concerning the 1993 Confrontation at the Mt. Carmel Complex, Waco, Texas" (Washington: Department of Justice, November 8, 2000).

115. Senate Committee on the Judiciary, Subcommittee on Terrorism, Technology, and Government Information, "Ruby Ridge," Senate Report 522-4 (Washington: Government Printing Office, 1995), pp. 6–7.

116. House Committee on Government Reform and Oversight, "Investigation into the Activities of Federal Law Enforcement toward the Branch Davidians," Report 104-749 (Washington, August 2, 1996), p. 2.

117. Neil A. Lewis, "In Waco Hearings, Parties Undergo a Role Reversal," *New York Times*, August 3, 1995 (www.nytimes.com/1995/08/03/us/in-waco-hearings-parties-undergo-a-role-reversal.html?pagewanted=print&src=pm).

118. The description comes from a National Rifle Association fundraising letter issued on April 13, 1995; the specific quote and further history can be found at http://mediamatters.org/blog/201103100027.

119. Readers should recall that a negative beta coefficient means that the relationship between the investigatory characteristic and footprint weight is also negative—that is, the relationship suggests that the independent measure reduces the probability that the weight will be present in a given investigation.

120. Pew Research Center, "Partisan Polarization Surges during the Bush/Obama Years," Survey Report (Washington, June 4, 2012), p. 1 (www.people-press.org/values/).

121. See Bruce P. Montgomery, "Congressional Oversight: Vice President Richard B. Cheney's Executive Branch Triumph," *Political Science Quarterly* 120, no. 4 (Winter 2005–06): 581–617.

CHAPTER FIVE

1. House Un-American Activities Committee (HUAC), "The Present-Day Ku Klux Klan Movement," House Report 98-436 (Washington: Government Printing Office, December 11, 1967); see also Rowland Evans and Robert Novak, "HUAC vs. the Klan," *Washington Post*, February 9, 1965.

2. The entire inventory of reports is available at www.aarclibrary.org/publib/contents/contents_church.htm.

3. For an accessible history of the Church Committee investigation, see Frederick A. O. Schwarz Jr., "Intelligence Oversight: The Church Committee," in *Strategic Intelligence: Intelligence and Accountability*, edited by Loch K. Johnson (Westport, Conn.: Praeger, 2007), pp. 19–46.

4. Schwarz makes these points in "Intelligence Oversight," pp. 21–22.

5. See Lorraine H. Tong, "Senate Committee Party Ratios: 94th–11th Congresses," RL34742 (Washington: Congressional Research Service, November 23, 2010) (http://assets.opencrs.com/rpts/RL34752_20101123.pdf).

6. Seymour Hersh, "Huge C.I.A. Operation Reported in U.S. against Anti-War Forces, Other Dissidents in Nixon Years," *New York Times*, December 22, 1974, p. 1.

7. Senate Select Committee to Study Governmental Operations with Respect to Intelligence Activities, "Intelligence Activities and the Rights of Americans," Senate Report 94-755, bk. 2 (Washington: Government Printing Office, April 14, 1976), p. iii, www.aarclibrary.org/publib/contents/church/contents_church_reports_book2.htm.

8. Senate Select Committee, "Intelligence Activities and the Rights of Americans," p. 4.

9. Senate Select Committee to Study Governmental Operations with Respect to Intelligence Activities, "Foreign and Military Intelligence," Senate Report 94-755, bk. 1 (Washington: Government Printing Office, April 14, 1976), p. 5 (www.aarclibrary. org/publib/contents/church/contents_church_reports_book1.htm).

10. Senate Select Committee to Study Governmental Operations with Respect to Intelligence Activities, "Interim Report: Alleged Assassination Plots Involving Foreign Leaders," Senate Report 94-465 (Washington: Government Printing Office, November 20, 1975), p. 71 (http://history-matters.com/archive/contents/church/contents_church_reports_ir.htm).

11. Senate Select Committee, "Intelligence Activities and the Rights of Americans," pp. 4–5.

12. Ibid., p. 5.

13. Schwarz, "Intelligence Oversight," pp. 25, 41.

14. The allegations were made by Drew Pearson in "Washington Merry-Go-Round: Rep. Thomas Lives in a Glass House, Chairman of Un-American Activities Committee Gets Kickbacks from Employees," *Bell Syndicate*, August 4, 1948, p. 1. The lead paragraph made the case against Thomas: "One congressman who had sadly ignored the old adage that those who live in glass houses shouldn't throw stones is bouncing Rep. J. Parnell Thomas of New Jersey, chairman of the House Un-American Activities Committee. If some of his own personal operations were scrutinized on the witness stand as carefully as he cross-examines witnesses, they would make headlines of [the] kind the congressman doesn't like."

15. HUAC, "Hearings Regarding the Communist Infiltration of the Motion Picture Industry" (Washington: Government Printing Office, October 23, 1947), p. 1.

16. See, for example, Harold Brackman, "The Attack on 'Jewish Hollywood': A Chapter in the History of Modern American Anti-Semitism," *Modern Judaism* 20, no. 1 (February 2000): 1–19; Jon Lewis, "'We Do Not Ask You to Condone This': How the Blacklist Saved Hollywood," *Cinema Journal* 39, no. 2 (Winter 2000): 3–30.

17. Lewis A. Kaplan provides an insightful analysis of the patterns of House opposition to HUAC in general using congressional district data to show the effects of ideology, foreign investment, and geography. See Lewis A. Kaplan, "The House Un-American Activities Committee and Its Opponents: A Study in Congressional Dissonance," *Journal of Politics* 30, no. 3 (August 1968): 647–71.

18. Robert K. Carr, "The Un-American Activities Committee," *University of Chicago Law Review* 18, no. 3 (Spring 1951): 601–02.

19. Walter Gellhorn, "Report on a Report of the House Committee on Un-American Activities," *Harvard Law Review* 60, no. 8 (October 1947): 1194, 1233.

20. HUAC, "Hearings Regarding the Communist Infiltration," p. 220.

21. See the Research Archives of the Society of Independent Motion Picture Producers at http://cobbles.com/simpp_archive/huac_nelson1947.htm.

22. See, for example, the list of names and their sources in HUAC, *Annual Report for the Year 1952* (Washington: Government Printing Office, December 28, 1952), pp. 40–555.

23. HUAC, "Hearings Regarding the Communist Infiltration," p. 217.

24. Personal communication.

25. Congressional Research Service, "Congressional Oversight: A 'How-To' Series of Workshops" (Washington, June 28, July 12, and July 26, 1999), p. 68.

26. See Hugh Davis Graham, "The Ambiguous Legacy of American Presidential Commissions," *Public Historian* 7, no. 2 (Spring 1985): 29. Graham also counts 134 secret task forces, including the 1967 Task Force on Crime chaired by James Q. Wilson.

27. See William E. Leuchtenburg, "Records of President Johnson's Commission on Law Enforcement: Introduction," in *Research Collections in American Politics: Microfilms from Major Archival and Manuscript Collections*, edited by William E. Leuchtenburg (Bethesda, Md.: LexisNexis Academic and Library Solutions, 2004), p. vi (www.lexisnexis.com/academic/upa_cis/group.asp?g=246).

28. Graham, "Ambiguous Legacy," pp. 20–21.

29. James Vorenberg, "The War on Crime: Five Futile Years," *Atlantic Monthly* (May 1972), www.theatlantic.com/past/politics/crime/crimewar.htm.

30. Katzenbach co-chaired the Vera Institute's 2006 Commission on Safety and Abuse in America's Prisons.

31. President's Commission on Law Enforcement and Administration Justice, *The Challenge of Crime in a Free Society* (Washington: Government Printing Office, February 1967) (www.ncjrs.gov/pdffiles1/nij/42.pdf).

32. Congressional Research Service, "Congressional Oversight," p. 18.

33. Ibid., p. 67.

34. See House Committee on Armed Services, Subcommittee for Special Investigations, "Employment of Retired Commissioned Officers by Defense Department Contractors," House Document 49296 (Washington: Government Printing Office, 1960), p. 29.

35. The exact list of retired officers employed by the defense industry can be found at House Committee on Armed Services, "Employment of Retired Commissioned Officers," pp. 7–9.

36. House Committee on Armed Services, "Employment of Retired Commissioned Officers," pp. 10–11.

37. Project on Government Oversight (POGO), *The Art of Congressional Oversight: A User's Guide to Doing It Right* (Washington, 2009), p. 17.

38. The complete investigation file, including the final reports of the majority and minority, can be found at www.washingtonpost.com/wp-srv/politics/special/campfin/stories/cf030698a.htm.

39. Guy Gugliotta, "Senate Campaign Probers Release Findings," *Washington Post*, March 6, 1998, p. 6.

40. Ibid., p. 6.

41. POGO, *Art of Congressional Oversight*, p. 54.

42. Ibid., p. 9.

43. Jordan Tama, *Terrorism and National Security Reform: How Commissions Can Drive Change during Crises* (Cambridge University Press, 2011).

44. Tama, *Terrorism and National Security Reform*, p. 181.

45. David Mayhew, *Divided We Govern: Party Control, Lawmaking, and Investigations, 1945–2002* (Yale University Press, 2005), pp. 8–33.

46. Ibid., p. 9.

47. Ibid., pp. 32–33.

48. POGO, *Art of Congressional Oversight*, p. 54.

49. National Commission on Restructuring the Internal Revenue Service, *A Vision for a New IRS* (Washington, 1997). The commission was created under Public Law 104-52 on November 19, 1995, available at www.house.gov/natcommirs/report1.pdf.

50. Senate Committee on Finance, "Practices and Procedures of the Internal Revenue Service," Senate Hearing 105-190, September 23, 24, and 25, 1997 (Washington: Government Printing Office, 1997), p. 325.

51. POGO, *Art of Congressional Oversight*, p. 47.

52. See John W. Kingdon, *Agendas, Alternatives, and Public Policies*, 2nd ed. (New York: Longman Classics in Political Science, 2003), for further insights on agenda setting and legislative action.

53. Ronald Reagan, Executive Order 12526, President's Blue-Ribbon Commission on Defense Management, July 15, 1985, p. 1 (www.reagan.utexas.edu/archives/speeches/1985/71585c.htm).

54. President's Blue-Ribbon Commission on Defense Management, "A Quest for Excellence" (Washington: Government Printing Office, 1986), p. xiii.

55. Senate Committee on the Judiciary, Subcommittee on Administrative Practice and Procedure, "Presidential Commissions" (Washington: Government Printing Office, 1971), p. 1.

56. Ibid., p. 3.

57. See James Hamilton, Robert F. Muse, and Kevin R. Amer, "Congressional Investigations: Politics and Process," *American Criminal Law Review* 44, no. 3 (Summer 2007): 1115–76, for a history of past investigations and authorities.

APPENDX C

1. See Joint Committee on the Investigation of the Pearl Harbor Attack, "Investigation of the Pearl Harbor Attack," Senate Document 244, app. A (Washington: Government Printing Office, July 20, 1946), pp. 269–71.

2. See Congressional Quarterly, "Corrupt Practices Probe," in *CQ Almanac 1956* (Washington: CQ Press, 1957), http://library.cqpress.com/cqalmanac/cqal56-1347787.

3. See Congressional Quarterly, "Television Quiz Shows and Other Congressional Investigations, 1959," in *Congress and the Nation, 1945–1964*, vol. 1 (Washington: CQ

Press, 1965), http://library.cqpress.com/catn/catn45-4-18133-976543. See also W. M. Blair, "Wider TV Inquiry to Study Bribery and Paid 'Plugs,'" *New York Times*, November 7, 1959, p. A1.

4. There is no single inventory of all congressional hearings, public and private, on Vietnam and Indochina, but Edwin E. Moise has collected a forty-page list of documents, many linked to the content of specific hearings. The list compiled by Edwin E. Moise is found at http://www.clemson.edu/caah/history/facultypages/EdMoise/main.html.

5. See Congressional Quarterly, "Watergate: A Constitutional Crisis, 1972–1974 Political Overview," in *Congress and the Nation, 1973–1976*, vol. 4 (Washington: CQ Press, 1977) (http://library.cqpress.com/catn/catn73-0009170307).

6. See L. Feinberg, "Panel Urges Measures to Halt Decline of Education in America," *Washington Post*, August 26, 1983, p. A1; P. Galley, "Education Emerges as Major Issue in 1984 Presidential Campaigning," *New York Times*, June 9, 1983, p. A1.

7. See Congressional Quarterly, "Kissinger Commission," in *CQ Almanac 1983* (Washington: CQ Press, 1984) (http://library.cqpress.com/cqalmanac/cqal83-1198569).

8. For a summary of implementation almost a year after the House and Senate released its report in November 1987, see Clyde R. Mark, *Iran-Contra Affair: Status of the Recommendations Contained in the Joint Report of the House and Senate Select Committees* (Washington: Congressional Research Service, April 1988).

9. See Minority Staff, House Committee on Government Operations, "Managing the Federal Government: A Decade of Decline," CIS-NO 93-H402-1 (Washington, December 1992).

10. See Gary Sick, "The Election Story of the Decade," *New York Times*, April 15, 1991 (www.fas.org/irp/congression/1992_cr/h920205-october-clips.htm).

11. See House Committee on the Post Office and Civil Service, Subcommittee on Human Resources, "Unauthorized Transfers of Nonpublic Information during the 1980 Presidential Election" (Washington, May 17, 1984) (http://catalog.hathitrust.org/Record/011343694).

12. See S. A. Kan, "China: Suspected Acquisition of U.S. Nuclear Weapon Secrets," CRS Report to Congress RL30143 (Washington: Congressional Research Service, 2006).

13. See J. E. Lake, "Border and Transportation Security: Overview of Congressional Issues," CRS Report for Congress RL32705 (Washington: Congressional Research Service, 2004).

14. See Congressional Quarterly, "Study Group Paints Grim Picture," in *CQ Almanac 2006* (Washington: CQ Press, 2007) (http://library.cqpress.com/cqalmanac/cqal06-1421617).

15. See J. V. Grimaldi and S. Schmidt, "Report Says Nonprofits Sold Influence to Abramoff," *Washington Post*, October 13, 2006, p. A1.

16. See D. Wilson and M. Schmidt, "Baseball Braces for Tough Report from Mitchell," *New York Times*, December 13, 2007, p. D1.

17. The many hearings are listed by the Law Librarians' Society of Washington, D.C., in "Dodd-Frank Wall Street Reform and Consumer Financial Protection Act: A

Brief Legislative History with Links, Reports, and Summaries" (www.llsdc.org/dodd-frank-act-leg-hist/).

18. See Oil Spill Commission Action, "Assessing Progress: Implementing the Recommendations of the National Oil Spill Commission," written by former members of the National Commission on the British Petroleum Deepwater Horizon Oil Spill and Offshore Drilling and published by oscaction.org (http://oscaction.org/wp-content/uploads/OSCA-Assessment-report.pdf).

19. See Seth Stern, "Under the Gun, ATF's Weakness Exposed," *CQ Weekly,* July 4, 2011, p. 1425.

Index

Aaron, Hank, 162–63
Aberbach, J., 58, 61, 62–63
Abramoff, Jack, 245
Abscam operation, 97, 235, 280 n.50
Accountability, 125, 126, 187; as desti-
    nation of investigations, 145, 146,
    159–66, 178, 179, 184
Adams, Sherman, 97–99, 228
Advisory Panel to Assess Domestic
    Response Capabilities for Terrorism
    Involving Weapons of Mass
    Destruction, 111
Afghanistan, 128
Agnew, Spiro, 114
Agriculture commodity speculation,
    225, 229
Aiken, George, 92
Air Force preparedness inquiry, 91,
    134–35, 136, 150–52
Air travel. See Aviation safety and secu-
    rity
Albosta, Don, 239
American Association of Retired
    People, 154
American Bandstand, 161
American Recovery and Reinvestment
    Act, 247
Anderson, Jack, 98, 196
Angelides, Phil, 158
Antitrust law, 232
Arrogance of Power, The (Fulbright), 155
Artful Work: The Politics of Social Secu-
    rity Reform (Light), 152

Art of Congressional Oversight, The, 59
Atomic Energy Commission, 226
Attorney firings (2007), 246
Aviation safety and security, 1, 92–93,
    110, 227, 241

Bachrach, P., 2
Baker, Bobby, 25
Baker, Howard, 153, 194
Baker, James A., III, 127
Baratz, M. S., 2
Barkley, Alben, 93
Barnes, Michael D., 235
Baumgartner, F., 43
Bean, Elise, 206–07
Beirut Marine barracks bombing, 235
Bell, Terrel H., 234
Bernanke, Ben, 157
Bipartisan Campaign Reform Act, 206
Blackhawk helicopter, 21
Blame-setting investigations. See
    Method of investigation
Blue Ribbon Commission on Defense
    Management (Packard Commis-
    sion), 19, 21, 26, 213–14
Blue-ribbon commissions: classifica-
    tion, 106–07; current scholarship,
    106; defining characteristics, 106;
    effects of party control of govern-
    ment on, 87; excess capacity in, 22;
    footprints, 108–17, 118, 121,
    122–23, 188–89; future prospects,
    53; impact, 140, 188–89, 212–14;

institutional homes of, 212; investigatory characteristics, 107–08; leadership, 109, 117; number of, 107; purpose, 117; rationale, 79; trends in use of, 37, 53, 62, 107, 212
Bonds, Barry, 161, 162
Bork, Robert, 25
Bosnia, 241
Bowles, Erskine, 18, 74
Branch Davidians, 174–75
Braun, Ryan, 162, 292 n.72
Breadth of investigation: blue-ribbon commissions, 109, 118; characteristics of historically significant investigations, 66; classification of investigations by, 4, 54, 56, 58; correlation with other footprint measures, 75; historical trends, 75; impact of investigation and, 137, 182, 277 n.15; investigatory characteristics correlated with, 118, 119, 121, 251; measurement, 65–66; party control of government and, 80, 81, 84, 88, 89; president's term of office and, 118
Breakdowns in government, types of, 11–12, 17, 44; blue-ribbon commissions for investigation of, 108; breadth of investigation and, 65–66, 84; classification of investigations by, 4; complexity of investigation and, 84; destinations of investigations and, 145, 179; distribution among historically significant examples, 44; durability of investigations and, 86; footprints of investigations and, 78, 119, 121, 122, 123; freedom to conduct investigations and, 85; high-leverage investigations correlated with, 86; impact of investigation and, 4, 140, 141, 183, 186; institutional home of investigations correlated with, 39, 45; investigatory issues produced by, 43; leadership of investigation and, 85; length of investigation and, 84; method of investigation and, 44; nondecision or inaction as, 2; outcomes of good investigations, 145–46; partisanship in investigations and, 86–87; party control of government and, 51, 52, 84, 85, 87; patterns and trends, 44–45, 54; purpose of investigation correlated with, 44; seriousness of investigations and, 86; thoroughness of investigations and, 86; triggers of investigations correlated with, 42; venue of investigations correlated with, 40; visibility of investigations and, 85
Bremer, L. Paul, 111

Brewster, Kingman, 202
Broken Branch, The (Mann & Ornstein), 35
Brooks, Jack, 56
Brown, Michael, 96
Bureaucracy, government: congress's delegation of authority to, 46–47; designed to fail, 44, 147; reform of, as destination of investigations, 145, 146–50, 158, 178, 179, 183–84, 187
Bureau of Alcohol, Tobacco, and Firearms, 101, 174–75
Bureau of Internal Revenue, 34, 134, 135, 145, 147, 210, 226
Burton, Dan, 99, 175
Bush (G. H. W.) administration, 36
Bush (G. W.) administration, 35, 41, 44, 92, 101, 161, 165, 166, 189, 212, 243–44

Cabrara, Melky, 162
Campaign finance reform, 206–07, 242
Canseco, José, 161
Caro, Robert A., 171
Carr, Robert K., 197
Carter administration, 11, 36, 212, 239
Case, Francis, 227
Casey, William, 239
Castro, Fidel, 195
Central America, 235
Central Intelligence Agency, 67, 172, 173, 193, 194, 195, 231
Chambers, Whittaker, 15
CHAOS, 195
Cheney, Richard, 189, 243–44
Chief Financial Officers Act, 165–66
China: anti-communist investigations and U.S. relations with, 134; technology transfers to, 26, 38, 241–42
China Syndrome, The, 111
Church, Frank, 14, 19, 56, 173, 193–94
Church Committee. *See* Committees and subcommittees, Senate, Select Committee to Study Government Operations with Respect to Intelligence
Civil Service Reform Act, 205
Clark, Ramsey, 172
Clean Sports Act, 161
Clemens, Roger, 161
Clinger, Bill, 99, 174
Clinton, Hillary, 241
Clinton administration, 1, 36, 44, 45, 164, 166, 174, 176, 212; congressional investigations into, 12, 18–19, 39, 45–46, 67, 69, 93,

99–101, 183, 206, 241, 280 n.59; impeach-
ment proceedings, 100–01, 131–34, 242
Coburn, Tom, 158
Cohen, William S., 242
COINTELPRO, 195
Cold war, 90, 134–35, 150–52
Collins, Susan, 96
Commission on Defense Management, 212–13
Commitment to finding answers, 201–03
Committees and subcommittees, House of
Representatives: Armed Services Commit-
tee, 26, 204–05; Banking and Financial
Services Committee, 157; Committee on
Government Reform (and Oversight), 6, 8;
Energy and Commerce, 8, 26, 57, 64, 104,
247; Financial Services Committee, 8; Gov-
ernment Operations Committee, 17,
97–98, 163, 167, 238; Government Reform
and Oversight Committee, 99, 174; Government Reform Committee, 34; Interstate
and Foreign Commerce Committee, 97;
Judiciary Committee, 100, 205; Oversight
and Government Reform Committee, 32,
105, 157, 162, 248; Select Bipartisan Subcommittee to Investigate the Preparation
for and Response to Hurricane Katrina, 96;
Select Committee on Assassinations, 22,
173; Select Committee to Investigate Commodity Transactions, 225; Special Government Information Subcommittee, 167;
Subcommittee on Administration of the
Internal Revenue Laws, 147; Subcommittee
on Criminal Justice, 6–7; Subcommittee on
Foreign Operations and Information, 17,
29–32; Subcommittee on Government
Management, Information, and Technology, 34; Subcommittee on Health, 57; Subcommittee on Intergovernmental Relations
and Human Resources, 163–64; Subcommittee on Legislative Oversight, 97–98;
Subcommittee on National Security, International Affairs, and Criminal Justice, 174;
Subcommittee on Oversight and Investigations, 247; Subcommittee on Social Security, 152; Subcommittee on Terrorism and
Government Information, 175; Un-American Activities Committee, 6, 15, 25, 67,
192, 196–99, 226; Ways and Means Committee, 147, 152, 154. *See also* Venue of
investigations
Committees and subcommittees, Senate: Air
Force Subcommittee, 150–52; Appropria-

tions Committee, 225; Armed Services
Committee, 22, 26, 90–91, 150; Banking,
Housing, and Urban Affairs Committee,
157; Commerce Committee, 8; Committee
on Expenditures in Executive Departments, 91–92; Executive Expenditures
Committee, 28; Finance Committee, 152,
211; Foreign Affairs Committee, 6; Foreign
Relations Committee, 14, 25, 26, 155; Government Affairs Committee, 26, 165, 206,
238; Governmental Affairs Committee, 8,
10, 16; Government Operations Committee, 25, 28, 168; Homeland Security and
Governmental Affairs Committee, 28, 96;
Intelligence Committee, 38; Interstate and
Foreign Commerce Committee, 160; Judiciary Committee, 32–33; Permanent Sub-
committee on Investigations, 25, 28, 206;
Permanent Subcommittee on Oversight,
158; Select Committee on Intelligence
Activities, 19; Select Committee on
POW/MIA Affairs, 20–21; Select Commit-
tee to Study Censure Charges, 25–26; Select
Committee to Study Governmental Opera-
tions, 59–60; Select Committee to Study
Government Operations with Respect to
Intelligence (Church Committee), 14,
19–20, 59–60, 134, 172–73, 193–96; Social
Security Subcommittee, 152; Special Aging
Subcommittee on Long-Term Care, 163;
Special Committee on the Year 2000 Tech-
nology Problem, 34; Special Committee to
Investigate Contracts under the National
Defense Program, 225; Special Committee
to Investigate Organized Crime in Inter-
state Commerce (Kefauver Commission),
23–24, 226; Special Committee to Investigate the National Defense Program, 27;
Special Committee to Investigate Whitewater Development Corporation and Related
Matters, 18; Special Subcommittee in
Commodity Markets, 225; Special Subcommittee on Investigations, 25; Special
Subcommittee to Investigate the Administration of the Internal Security Act and
Other Internal Security Laws, 32–33; Subcommittee on Executive Reorganization,
168; Subcommittee on Oversight of Government Management, 26. *See also* Venue
of investigations
Communists in government, 1, 6, 26, 67,
92–93, 134, 192, 226; course of investiga-

tions into, 14–16, 25–26; historical significance of investigation into, 13; impact of investigation into, 131

Communists in motion picture industry, 66, 97, 196–99, 226

Complexity of investigations: blue-ribbon commissions, 109, 118, 119; characteristics of historically significant investigations, 66; classification of investigations by, 4, 54, 56, 58; correlation with other footprint measures, 75; historical trends, 75; impact of investigations and, 137, 182, 185, 191, 200; investigatory characteristics correlated with, 118, 119, 121, 252; measurement, 66; party control of government and, 80, 84, 88, 89; president's term of office and, 118

Conable, Barber B., Jr., 10, 154

Confidentiality, claims of government privilege, 60, 103

Confirmation hearings, 25

Congressional Budget Office, 156

Congressional Oversight Manual, 54

Congressional Oversight Panel, 156

Congressional Quarterly, 5, 25, 136

Congressional Quarterly Almanac, 5

Congressional Research Service, 5, 8, 17, 129, 136

Congressional resurgence, era of: blue-ribbon commissions in, 107; footprints of investigations in, 75–76; impact of investigations in, 139; institutional home of investigations in, 38; investigatory issues in, 43; methods of investigations in, 48–49; number of investigations launched during, 36, 39; packaged investigations in, 6; venues for investigations in, 41; years of, 4, 35

Contempt of Congress, 101, 103–04

Continental Congress, 21

Cooper, Anderson, 95

Cooper, Gary, 198–99

Costello, Frank, 23, 272 n.28

Cox, Archibald, 13–14

CQ Weekly, 5

Crime and violence, 1, 201–03, 230. *See also* Organized crime investigations

Cuban missile crisis, 17, 167

Curtis, Carl T., 170

D'Amato, Alfonse, 18–19

Danforth, John C., 175

Davidson, R., 16

Davis, Hugh, 202

Davis, Tom, 56, 96, 161

Debating Vietnam: Fulbright, Stennis, and Their Senate Hearing (Fry), 155

Defense spending investigations, 1, 21–22, 26–28, 204–05, 212–13, 225, 228, 229, 230, 236

Delegation of legislative authority, 46–47, 59

Democratic National Committee, 14, 207

Demographic profiles of investigations: categories, 3–4, 35; destinations of investigations and, 176–80; primary investigator as source of, 35. *See also* Historical location of investigations; Party control during investigations; Structure and process of investigations

Department of Defense, 90, 165, 168, 193, 204, 212–13, 229, 235–36

Department of Energy, 104, 105–06

Department of Health, Education, and Welfare, 164

Department of Homeland Security, 191, 244–45

Department of Housing and Urban Development, 165, 238

Department of Justice, 65, 101–02, 103, 174, 227, 232

Department of State, 14–15, 21–22, 32–34, 230

Department of Transportation, 169

Department of Veterans Affairs, 128–29

Destination of investigations: deterrence as, 162–66; distribution among historically significant cases, 146; to enhance accountability, 145, 146, 159–63, 184, 187; footprints and, 177; historical patterns, 177; identifying, for analysis, 146; impact of investigations and, 180–81, 183–84, 187–88, 263; to influence future agendas, 145, 146, 167–70, 183–84, 187–88; investigatory characteristics and, 177–79; party control and, 179–80; qualities of good investigations, 145–46; range of, 145; to reform bureaucracy, 145, 146–59, 183, 187; to repair policy, 145, 146, 150–54, 183–84; resolving doubt, 145, 146, 170–76, 184; reversal of national strategy as, 145, 146, 154–59, 183–84

Deterrence as destination of investigation, 162–66

Dewey, Thomas E., 202

Diem, Ngo Dinh, 195

Dingell, John D., 244

Disney, Walt, 199

Divided government, era of: blue-ribbon commissions in, 107; footprints of investigations in, 75–76; foreign issue investigations in, 53; impact of investigations in, 139; institutional home of investigations in, 38; methods of investigations in, 48–49; number of investigations launched during, 36, 39; packaged investigations in, 6; purposes of investigations in, 48; triggers of investigations in, 42; venues for investigations in, 41; years of, 4, 35

Divided We Govern (Mayhew), 26, 72–73, 143

Dixon-Yates power contract, 227

Dodd, Christopher J., 157, 158

Dodd, Thomas J., 33

Dole, Robert, 56, 128

Domestic issue investigations, 4; blue-ribbon commissions, 108; destination of, 178–79; distribution among historically significant investigations, 42; footprints of, 121; historical patterns, 43–44, 53–54; method of investigation in, 43; party control of government and, 52; political benefits of, 53–54; seriousness of, 85–86; subjects of, 42, 43; theory of punctuated policy equilibrium, 43

Domestic spying, 1, 12, 14, 19–20, 67, 134, 193, 194, 195, 231, 233

Downs, A., 75

Drug industry practices, 1, 34, 228

Dull, M., 5, 37, 50, 73, 143, 145, 275 n.52

Durability of investigation, 68–69, 76; blueribbon commissions, 109, 118; classification of investigations by, 4, 54, 56, 58; correlation with other footprint measures, 75; impact of investigation and, 138, 182, 185, 188, 189, 191, 200; investigatory characteristics correlated with, 118, 119, 122, 259; party control of government and, 80–81, 86, 87, 88, 89; strategies for enhancing, 185

Durbin, Dick, 74

Educational system, 234

Eisenhower administration, 16, 22, 36, 45, 90, 91, 98, 134–35, 150–51, 212, 230

Election cycle, investigations correlated with, 4, 36; blue-ribbon commissions, 107; destinations of, 177; footprint weight and, 76–77; impact of, 139–40

Emergency Economic Stabilization Act, 156

Energy crisis (1973), 232

Enron collapse and investigation, 8, 26, 154–55, 243

Environmental Protection Agency, 93, 145

Ervin, Sam, 13, 56

Estes, Billie Sol, 163

Ethics in Government Act, 22, 205

Executive Branch: assertions of secrecy privileges by, 60, 103; blue-ribbon commissions created by, 107, 117; characteristics of investigations originating in, 43–44; Congress's delegation of authority to, 59; destinations of investigations initiated by, 178; impact of investigations originating in, 140; investigations into alleged news management by, 1; investigations into organization of, 91–92, 232; investigatory capacity of, 53; number of investigations led by, 38, 39; party control of, investigation characteristics and, 49, 50, 52, 88–89, 142; presidential pardon power, 7; purposes of investigations conducted by, 47. *See also* President's term of office, investigations correlated with; *specific presidential administration*

Fact-finding investigations. *See* Method of investigation

Failure to exercise power, 2

Family Smoking Prevention and Tobacco Control Act, 57

Fascell, Dante, 237

Fast and Furious gun-walking operation, 54, 65, 101–04, 248, 281 n.61

Federal Bureau of Investigation, 22–23, 173, 174, 175, 193, 195, 235

Federal Communications Act, 161

Federal Communications Commission, 98, 160

Federal Emergency Management Agency, 96

Federal Housing Administration, 227

Federal Judicial Center, 294–95 n.104

Federal Reserve Board, 156–57

Feynman, Richard P., 116, 148, 149

Filtner, D., 107

Financial crisis (2008), 1, 26, 90, 135, 154–55, 156–58, 246–47, 289–91

Financial Crisis Inquiry Commission, 158

Fire alarm investigations. *See* Trigger of investigation

Focus of investigations, 17–18

Food and Drug Administration, 57

Footprints of investigations: assessment challenges, 54–55; blue-ribbon commissions, 108–17, 121, 122–23; correlations between measures of, 74–75, 118–20; definition, 63–64; destinations of investigations and, 177; determinants of, 4, 89–90, 124; heavyweight examples, 90–92; historical patterns, 118, 120, 262; impact of investigations and, 56–57, 61, 63, 64, 124–25, 136–38, 182–83, 184–85, 188–89; investigatory characteristics and, 77–79, 118–19, 120–24, 261–62; lightweight examples, 97–101; measures of, 4, 54, 56, 58; middleweight examples, 92–97; party control of government and, 80–89, 119–20, 126–27; political use of investigations and, 76–77; predictors of good investigations, 117–24; ranking of historically significant examples, 70–72, 77; recent and ongoing examples, 101–06; regression analysis, 120–24, 184–85, 284 n.103–04; during second term of presidency, 118; in times of political polarization, 123–24; variation in, 54. *See also specific measures of*

Ford administration, 6–8, 36, 172

Foreign Intelligence Surveillance Act, 194

Foreign Intelligence Surveillance Court, 194

Foreign policy investigations, 4, 37; blue-ribbon commissions, 108; complexity of, 84; destination of, 178–79; distribution among historically significant investigations, 42; durability of, 86; freedom to conduct, 85; high-leverage, 86; historical patterns, 43–44; leadership of, 85; length of, 84; method of, 43; party control of government and, 84, 85; seriousness of, 85–86; subjects of, 42, 43; theory of punctuated policy equilibrium, 43; trends in congressional oversight, 35, 36, 53; venues for, 40; visibility of, 85

Foster, Vince, 18, 280 n.59

Fountain, L. H., 163–64

Frank, Barney, 56, 157

Freedom of Information Act, 17, 29, 167, 168

Freedom to conduct investigations: blue-ribbon commissions, 109; classification of investigations by, 4, 54, 56, 58, 67; correlation with other footprint measures, 75; historical trends, 76, 118, 182, 200; impact of investigations and, 137, 181, 182, 185, 192; investigatory characteristics correlated with, 119, 121, 254; party control of government and, 80, 81, 85, 88, 89, 119; qualities of good investigation, 66–67

Fry, Joseph A., 155, 156

Fulbright, J. William, 26, 56, 155, 155–56

Gardner, David Pierpoint, 277 n.18

Gellhorn, Walter, 197–98

General Motors, 168, 169, 170

General Services Administration, 34, 233, 274 n.47

George, Walter, F., 227

Gilmore, James S., III, 111

Gingrich, Newt, 67, 192

Glenn, John, 10, 56, 165

Golden Fleece awards, 11–12, 270–71 n.2

Goldfine, Bernard, 98

Goldwater, Barry, 194

Good investigation: benefits of, 126; conditions for, 201–15; current capacity for, 215; example of, 57; expectations, 58–59; foundations for, 58; high-impact example, 193–96; impact and, 124–25, 126, 136; measures of, 9, 56, 126; outcomes, 145–46; predictors of, 117–24; process guidelines for, 60–61, 69, 72

Gore, Al, 110, 166

Gould, Jack, 160

Government Accountability Office, 8, 27, 156, 189

Government information management, 167–68, 229

Government mismanagement, investigations into, 1, 34, 65–66, 165–66, 226, 227, 238

Government Performance and Results Act, 166

Grace, J. Peter, 166

Grace Commission, 166

Grassley, Charles, 56, 101, 245

Great Society era: blue-ribbon commissions, 107; destinations of investigations in, 177; footprints of investigations in, 75–76; impact of investigations in, 139; institutional home of investigations in, 38; investigatory issues in, 43; number of investigations launched during, 36, 39; packaged investigations in, 6; venues for investigations in, 41; years of, 4, 35

Green-Pedersen, C., 43

Greenspan, Alan, 66, 157, 289–91

Gugliotta, Guy, 207

Gulf Oil spill, 54, 66, 247–48

Gulf War syndrome, 214, 240

Gun Control Act, 202

Hamilton, Lee, 13, 56, 127, 129–30, 203, 237, 239

Hanna Mining Company, 22

Harris, Oren, 98, 159–60

Harrison, Brian, 104

Hart, Gary, 110

Hart, Philip A., 194

Hart-Rudman Commission. *See* U.S. Commission on National Security in the Twenty-First Century

Hearst, Patty, 22–23

Hebert, Edward, 204

Helms, Richard, 194

Hersh, Seymour, 194

Hiss, Alger, 6, 15

Historical location of investigations: historical periods, 4, 35; institutional home of investigations and, 38; measures of, 4, 35; patterns in investigatory issues, 43–44; purposes of investigations and, 48; types of breakdown under investigation and, 44–45. *See also specific historical period*; Election cycle, investigations correlated with; President's term of office, investigations correlated with; Watergate, characteristics of investigations before and after

Holder, Eric, 101, 102–04

Hollywood Ten investigation, 196–99

Hoover, Herbert, 56, 91, 92

Hoover, J. Edgar, 194

Hoover Commission, 65–66. *See* National Commission on Organization of the Executive Branch

Horn, Stephen, 34

House of Representatives, investigations conducted by: blue-ribbon commissions, 107, 117; characteristics of, 38–39, 89; destinations of, 178; footprints of, 77; impact of, 140; number of, 38; party control and, 4, 49–50, 52, 83–87, 142, 143, 179–80; purposes of, 47; venues of, 40. *See also* Committees and subcommittees, House of Representatives; Institutional home of investigations

Houston Plan, 195

Hughes, Howard, 27

Hull, Cordell, 93

Human immunodeficiency virus, 112–13, 214, 237

Humphrey, George, 22

Humphrey, Hubert, 155

Hungate, William L., 7

Hurricane Katrina, 54, 95–96, 245, 279 n.44, 279–80 n.49

Hyde, Henry, 100

Identity of investigation, 19–20

Impact of investigation: commitment to results and, 201–03; definition of, 129–30; destination of investigation and, 180–81, 183–84, 187–88, 263; determinants of, 4, 136, 181–82, 191–93, 199–201; electoral cycle and, 139–40; footprint of investigation and, 56–57, 61, 63, 64, 124–25, 136–38, 181–82, 184–85, 188–89; forgotten investigations, 29; high-impact example, 193–96; historically significant investigations, 29, 131–34, 135; historical patterns, 138–39, 143, 182, 200; investigatory characteristics and, 140–41, 144–45, 183, 185–87, 266, 267; measurement and assessment of, 8, 9, 129, 130–35, 136, 286 n.14; negative consequences of, 125, 134–35, 196–99; outcomes of blue-ribbon commissions, 140, 188–89; party control and, 141–45, 181–82, 186, 200; perseverance of investigators and, 208–09; persuasiveness as factor in, 209–12; polarization in governance and, 186–87; political insulation of investigators and, 206–07; readiness to conduct investigation and, 203–05; recommendations from investigative body and, 130; standing of investigators and, 212–15; strategies for enhancing, 189–90; types of, 9. *See also* Destination of investigations

Impeachment proceedings, Clinton, 100–01, 131–34, 242

Indian affairs, 1, 238

Inspector General Act, 164

Institutional home of investigations: blue-ribbon commissions, 117; breadth of investigations and, 84; classification of investigations by, 4, 37; competition for, 37–38; complexity of investigations and, 84; destinations of investigations and, 178; durability of investigations and, 86; footprint of investigations and, 77, 119, 121, 122–23; freedom to conduct investigations and, 85; high-leverage investigations correlated with, 86; impact of investigations and, 140, 188; leadership of investigations and, 85; length of investigations and, 84; method of investigation and, 38; partisanship in investigations and, 86–87; party control of government and, 51, 84, 85; purpose of investigation and, 38, 47, 48; seriousness of investigations and, 85; thoroughness of investigation and, 86; trends, 38, 39, 53; triggers of investigations and,

38, 39, 41; type of government breakdown under investigation and, 39, 45; venue of investigation and, 38; visibility of investigations and, 85. *See also* Executive Branch; House of Representatives, investigations conducted by; Senate, investigations conducted by

Intelligence agencies and operations, U.S., 14, 19–20, 67, 93–95, 134, 172, 173, 193–96, 233, 240

Intensity of investigations, 20–21

Internal Revenue Service, 69, 193, 195, 210–11, 241

International Telephone and Telegraph, 232

Investigations, in general: abuse of authority in, 46; benefits of, 58; data sources, 217–23, 270 n.12; earliest U.S., 21, 215; forgotten examples, 1, 29–34; future prospects, 215–16; historically significant examples, 1–2, 5–6, 13, 24–26, 29, 30–31, 273–74 n.38; methodology for assessment of, 3–4, 6–8, 9, 25, 37, 117–18; opposition to, 206–07; partisan control of, 61–62; patterns and trends, 52–54, 214; versus standard oversight, 2–3, 16–17

Iran-Contra program, 12, 237, 271 n.4

Iran hostage crisis, 11, 97, 239, 270 n.1

Iraq Study Group, 127–28

Iraq War, 1, 26, 68, 126–28, 154–55, 244

Issa, Darrell, 101, 102–03, 162

Issue-attention cycle, 75

Issues. *See* Domestic issue investigations; Foreign policy investigations

It's Even Worse Than It Looks: How the American Constitutional System Collided with the New Politics of Extremism (Mann & Ornstein), 73

Jackson, Henry M., 150, 235

Jaworski, Leon, 202

Johnson, Lyndon B., 90, 194

Johnson (L. B.) administration, 36, 43, 45, 109, 150, 155, 168–69, 170–72, 202, 212, 294–95 n.101–04

Joint Committee on the Investigation of the Pearl Harbor Attack (Roberts Commission), 93, 225

Joint Committee on the Organization of Congress, 16

Joint committees or subcommittees, 4, 77

Joint Committee to Investigate the Pearl Harbor Attack, 93

Joint Economic Committee, 26

Jones, B., 43

Jordan, Jim, 105

Juiced: Wild Time, Rampant 'Roids, Smash Hits, and How Baseball Got Big (Canseco), 161

Juvenile Delinquency Prevention and Control Act, 202

Katzenbach, Nicholas, 202

Kazan, Elia, 199

Kean, Tom, 13, 56

Keeping a Watchful Eye: The Politics of Congressional Oversight (Aberbach), 58

Kefauver, Estes, 19, 23, 56, 150, 228

Kefauver-Harris Drug Act, 228

Kefauver investigations, 19, 23–24, 226, 228

Kemeny, John, 111

Kemp, Jack, 235

Kennedy, Edward, 214–15

Kennedy, John F., 151–52. *See also* Kennedy administration; Kennedy assassination investigations

Kennedy, Joseph, 92

Kennedy administration, 21–22, 212, 229; investigation into State Department security procedures during, 32–34; investigation of alleged news manipulation by, 17, 29–32, 167–68, 229; investigations launched during, 36

Kennedy assassination investigations, 19, 22, 48, 130, 170–74, 229, 294–95 n.101–04

Kent State shootings, 12, 108, 114–15, 232

Kerner, Otto, 109

Kerner Commission. *See* National Advisory Commission on Civil Disorders

Kerrey, Bob, 211

Kerry, John, 20–21

Kimmel, Husband E., 94

King, Cecil R., 147

King, Martin Luther, 110, 195

Kissinger Commission, 235

Kitts, K., 107

Kleindienst, Richard, 232

Korean War, 97, 227

Koresh, David, 174, 176

Ku Klux Klan, 12, 67, 146, 192, 230

Kutyna, Donald, 150

Labor racketeering, 228

Lantos, Tom, 66, 277 n.16

Leadership of investigations: blue-ribbon commissions, 109, 117, 118; characteristics of historically significant investigations, 66; classification of investigations by, 4, 54, 56, 58; correlation with other footprint measures, 75; historical trends, 75–76, 182; impact of investigations and, 137, 180–81, 182, 192, 201; investigatory characteristics correlated with, 118, 119, 121, 122, 253; measurement of, 66; partisanship in selection of, 74; party control of government and, 80, 81, 85, 89; political benefits, 27; political insulation of investigators and, 207; public awareness of investigations and, 19. *See also* Primary investigator

Legitimacy of investigators and investigation, 212–15

Lehman Brothers, 156

Length of investigation: blue-ribbon commissions, 109; characteristics of historically significant investigations, 66; classification of investigations by, 4, 54, 56, 58; correlation with other footprint measures, 75; historical trends, 75; impact of investigation and, 137, 188, 189; investigatory characteristics correlated with, 118, 119, 121, 122, 250; measurement of, 65; party control of government and, 80, 81, 84, 88, 89; range of, 11, 189; variation among historically significant examples, 65

Leverage for action after investigation, 4, 54, 56, 58, 68, 76; blue-ribbon commissions, 109; historical trends, 118; impact of investigation and, 138, 182; investigatory characteristics correlated with, 119, 121, 122, 258; party control of government and, 80, 81, 86, 88, 89

Levin, Carl, 56, 158

Lewinsky, Monica, 100

Libya, Benghazi attacks, 32

Lobbying, 17, 204–05, 206–07, 227, 229, 233, 245

Lumumba, Patrice, 195

Mackenzie, G. C., 200

Mann, T. E., 35, 52, 73

Mansfield, Mike, 194

Marshall, George C., 94

Mathias, Charles McC., Jr., 194, 235

Mayhew, D. R., 5, 26, 50, 72–73, 134, 143, 209, 210, 270 n.7

McCarthy, Joseph, 14–15, 16, 25

McCaskill, Claire, 165

McClellan, John L., 92, 227

McCubbins, M. D., 41, 47

McGuire, Mark, 161

McMorris, Charles H., 94

McVeigh, Timothy, 176

Media coverage: design of investigations for, 23–24; Hurricane Katrina, 95–96; impact of investigation and, 209–10; investigation of alleged manipulation of, by Kennedy administration, 17, 29–32, 167–68, 229; origins of Freedom of Information Act, 17–18; trigger of investigation and, 121

Medicaid fraud, 22–23

Method of investigation: blended, 48; blue-ribbon commissions, 108; breadth of investigation and, 84; classification of investigations by, 4, 48; complexity of investigation and, 84; destination of investigation and, 179; durability of investigation and, 86; footprint of investigation and, 79, 118, 119, 121, 122, 123, 124; freedom to conduct investigation and, 85; high-leverage investigations correlated with, 86; historical patterns, 48–49, 54; impact of investigation and, 4, 140, 141, 183, 200–01; institutional home of investigation and, 38; investigatory issue correlated with, 43; length of investigation and, 84; partisanship in investigation and, 87; party control of government and, 52, 84, 86, 87; purpose of investigation and, 47–48; seriousness of investigation and, 86; thoroughness of investigation and, 86; trigger of investigation and, 42; type of government breakdown and, 44; venue of investigation and, 40; visibility of investigation and, 85

Military base realignment and closure, 65, 165, 189, 238

Mine safety, 1, 246

Mitchell, George J., 56, 162

Mitchell Report, 245–46

Mobilization of bias, 2

Moe, Terry M., 44, 146

Mondale, Walter, 194, 195

Montgomery, Robert, 198

Morton Thiokol, 149

Moss, John E., 17, 29–32, 167–68

Moulder, Morgan M., 98

Moynihan, Daniel P., 34, 152–54

Multiple lines of investigation, 5–6, 25–26, 269 n.6

Murphy, George, 198

Murrow, Edward R., 16
My Lai, 6, 26

Nader, Ralph, 168, 169–70
National Academy of Public Administration, 10, 150
National Advisory Commission on Children and Terrorism, 208
National Advisory Commission on Civil Disorders (Kerner Commission), 19, 109–10
National Aeronautics and Space Administration, 91, 115–16, 135, 148–50, 168
National Commission on Excellence in Education, 69, 234, 277 n.18
National Commission on Fiscal Responsibility and Reform (Simpson-Bowles commission), 18, 74, 247
National Commission on Organization of the Executive Branch (Hoover Commission), 69, 91–92, 135, 145, 205, 226
National Commission on Social Security Reform, 10, 151–54, 153
National Commission on Terrorism, 111
National Commission on Terrorist Attacks upon the United States, 13
National Commission on the British Petroleum Deepwater Horizon, 247–48
National Energy Policy Development Group, 243–44
National Journal, 123
National Performance Review, 166
National Security Council, 193
Nation at Risk, 69
New York Times, 14, 19, 33, 103, 105, 151, 159, 160, 176, 194
Nicaragua, 237
Nixon, Richard, 15, 155, 194
Nixon administration, 36, 114, 156, 194, 195, 212, 214
Nixon pardon, 6–8, 65, 233
Nuclear energy industry, 111–12
Nuclear Regulatory Commission, 112

Obama administration, 18, 32, 36, 92, 102–06, 127, 128, 165, 247–48, 274 n.38
Office of Emergency Planning, 168
Office of Management and Budget, 93
Offices of Inspectors General, 2, 163, 164–65
O'Keefe, Sean, 115
Omnibus Crime Control and Safe Streets Act, 202
O'Neill, Thomas P., 153–54

Operation Wide Receiver, 101
Organizational Conspiracies Act, 192
Organized crime investigations, 23–24, 226, 272 n.28
Ornstein, N. J., 35, 52, 73
Oswald, Lee Harvey, 48, 172
Otepka, Otto, 32–34, 230
Outcomes of investigations: electoral change as goal of, 136; investigation into, 214–15; negative consequences, 125, 126, 196–99; positive consequences, 126; scope of, 1–2, 3. *See also* Footprints of investigations; Impact of investigations
Oversight and monitoring: of intelligence activities, 19–20; purpose, 130; role of Congress in, 59–60; routine, versus investigations, 2–3, 16–17; trends in Congress, 35–36, 62–63. *See also* Investigations, in general
Oxley, Mike, 8

Packaged investigations, 6, 25–26, 269 n.6
Packard, David, 213
Packard Commission. *See* Blue Ribbon Commission on Defense Management
Palmeiro, Rafael, 161
Parker, D. C. W., 5, 37, 50, 73, 143, 145, 275 n.52
Partisanship in investigations: appointment of investigators and, 74; blue-ribbon commissions, 109, 118; characteristics of historically significant investigations, 69; classification of investigations by, 4, 54, 56, 58; congressional investigations into Clinton administration, 45–46; correlation with other footprint measures, 75; effect of, on quality of investigations, 72–74, 79–80, 206–07; Enron collapse investigation, 8; evidence for, 51–52; future prospects, 123; goals of oversight and, 60; Hurricane Katrina investigations, 96; impact of investigations and, 138, 182, 185, 191; as inimical to good investigation, 69–72; investigatory characteristics correlated with, 118, 119, 122, 260; measurement, 69; party control of government and, 80, 81, 86–87, 88–89; as positive characteristic, 61–62; Ruby Ridge hearings, 176; trends, 39, 73–74, 76, 200; Waco siege hearings, 176
Party control during investigations: blue-ribbon commissions, 87, 107–08; cate-

gories of, 4, 49; characteristics of investigations and, 50–52; destinations of investigations and, 179–80; distribution of historically significant investigations, 49–50; footprints of investigations and, 80–89, 119–20, 123, 126–27; impact of investigations and, 141–43, 181–82, 186, 187, 200; indirect effects on investigation footprints, 83–87, 123; indirect effects on investigation impact, 143–45; polarization in government and, 123, 186–87; strategies for minority party members, 189–90

Payola, 161

Pearl Harbor, 1, 93–95, 130, 149, 225

Pearson, Drew, 196, 297 n.14

Pecora Commission, 158–59

Pelosi, Nancy, 96

Perseverance of investigators, 208–09

Personal misconduct investigations. *See* Breakdowns in government, types of

Petraeus, David, 128

Pfiffner, J. P., 107

Phillips, Samuel, 149

Pickle, Jake, 152

Pike, Otis, 19

Polarization in governance, 52, 73, 88–89, 123–24, 186–87

Police patrol as investigation trigger. *See* Trigger of investigation

Policy investigations. *See* Breakdowns in government, types of

Policy repair, as destination of investigation, 145, 146, 150–54, 178, 183–84

Portman, Rob, 211

Post–World War II period: blue-ribbon commissions, 107; destinations of investigations in, 177; footprints of investigations in, 75–76; foreign issue investigations in, 53; impact of investigations in, 139; institutional home of investigations in, 38; number of investigations launched during, 36, 39; packaged investigations in, 6; triggers of investigations in, 42; venues for investigations in, 41; years of, 4, 35

Powell, Lewis F., 202

Presidential Commission on the Human Immunodeficiency Virus Epidemic, 112–13

Presidential Commission on the Space Shuttle *Challenger* Accident (Rogers Commission), 1, 10, 11, 53–54, 66, 67, 90, 134, 135, 147–50, 236, 279 n.44

President's Commission on Care for America's Returning Wounded Warriors, 128–29, 285 n.3

President's Commission on Law Enforcement and Administration of Justice, 202

President's Commission on the Assassination of John F. Kennedy (Warren commission), 19, 22, 170–74, 202

President's Council on Year 2000 Conversion, 243

President's term of office, investigations correlated with, 4, 36; blue-ribbon commissions, 107; destinations of, 177; footprint weight and, 76, 118, 123; impact of, 139, 186

Prevention as goal of investigation. *See* Purpose of investigation

Primary investigator, 6, 35, 64–65

Prisoners of war, 20–21, 238–39

Private Sector Survey on Cost Control, 166

Process breakdown. *See* Breakdowns in government, types of

Professional Sports Integrity and Accountability Act, 161

Project on Government Oversight, 5, 59, 60–61, 62, 69, 72, 136, 185, 207

Proxmire, William, 11–12, 270–71 n.2

Public awareness and opinion, 279 n.44; issue-attention cycle, 75; on Kennedy assassination, 173; leadership of investigation and, 19; resolving doubt as goal of investigation, 145, 170–76. *See also* Media coverage; Visibility of investigations

Public Housing Service, 274 n.47

Punctuated policy equilibrium, 43, 44–45

Purpose of investigation: blue-ribbon commissions, 108, 117; breadth of investigation and, 84; classification of investigations by, 4, 46; complexity of investigation and, 84; delegation dilemma and, 46–47; destination of investigation and, 145; distribution of historically significant examples, 47; durability of investigation and, 86; footprint and, 78–79, 119, 123, 124; freedom to conduct investigation and, 85; high-leverage investigations correlated with, 86; historical trends, 48, 54; impact of investigation and, 141, 188; institutional home of investigations and, 38, 47, 48; leadership of investigation and, 85; length of investigation and, 84; method of investigation and, 47–48; party control of government and, 52, 84, 85, 86; prevention versus repair as, 216; range of, 12; seriousness of investigation and, 86; thoroughness of investigation and, 86; type of government breakdown and, 44; visibility of investigation and, 85. *See also* Destination of investigations

Quest for Excellence, A, 213–14
Quiz show rigging, 1, 66, 159–61, 228

Rauch, J., 73–74, 186
Rayburn, Sam, 97–98, 280 n.51
Readiness to conduct investigation, 203–05
Reagan, Ronald, 198, 199
Reagan administration, 21, 44, 69, 112–13, 164, 165, 212, 213, 286 n.14; Iran-Contra affair, 12, 237; Iran hostage crisis and, 11, 97, 239, 270 n.1; Social Security reforms, 151–54
Recommendations from investigative bodies, 130
Reconstruction Finance Corporation, 226
Recovery Act Transparency and Oversight Board, 247
Reinventing government campaign, 165, 166
Relyea, H. C., 17–18
Reno, Janet, 174–75
Repair of breakdown as goal of investigation. *See* Purpose of investigation
Republican National Committee, 207
Resolving doubt, as goal of investigation, 145, 146, 170–76, 178–79, 184
Restoring American Financial Stability Act, 157
Reversal of national strategy, as destination of investigation, 145, 146, 154–59, 183–84
Ribicoff, Abraham, 168, 169, 294 n.98
Rice, Susan, 32
Ride, Sally, 115
Rivlin, Alice, 74
Roberts, Owen, 93, 225
Roberts Commission, 225
Rockefeller, Nelson, 172
Rogers, William, 147, 202
Rogers Commission. *See* Presidential Commission on the Space Shuttle *Challenger* Accident
Romney, Mitt, 34, 104
Roosevelt (F. D.) administration, 27, 197, 225
Rosenberg, Morton, 201, 203–04
Rosenbloom, D. H., 59

Roth, William, 211
Ruby Ridge, Idaho, 1, 93, 174, 175–76, 240
Rudman, Warren, 56, 110
Russell, Richard, 150–51, 171–72, 294 n.101
Ryan, Paul, 74

Sarbanes, Paul, 8
Sarbanes-Oxley Act, 8
Savings and loan crisis, 26, 154–55, 236–37
Schneider, René, 195
Schumer, Charles E., 176
Schwartz, T., 41
Schwarz, F. A. O., 59–60, 196
Schweiker, Richard, 152–53
Scowcroft, Brent, 56, 286 n.14
Scowcroft Commission. *See* Strategic Missile Commission
Scranton, William, 114
Screen Actors Guild, 197
Secrecy privileges of government, 60, 103, 190
Securities and Exchange Commission, 158
See It Now, 16
Select committees or subcommittees, 4
Selig, Allan H., 246
Senate, investigations conducted by: blue-ribbon commissions, 107, 117; characteristics of, 38–39, 89; destinations of, 178; footprints of, 77; impact, 140, 142, 143, 144, 188; number, 38; party control and, 4, 49–50, 52, 83–87, 142, 143, 144, 179–80; purposes of, 47; venues of, 40. *See also* Committees and subcommittees, Senate; Institutional home of investigations
September 11 terrorist attacks, 12, 13, 53, 68, 90, 108, 135, 191, 244, 279 n.44
Seriousness of investigations: blue-ribbon commissions, 109, 118; characteristics of historically significant investigations, 67; classification of investigations by, 4, 54, 56, 58; correlation with other footprint measures, 75; impact of investigations and, 138, 182, 201–02; investigatory characteristics correlated with, 118, 119, 121, 256; measurement, 67; party control of government and, 80, 81, 85–86, 87, 88, 89
Shalala, Donna, 56, 128
Shays, Christopher, 285 n.3
Shenon, P., 13
Shuttle *Challenger* Accident. *See* Presidential Commission on the Space Shuttle *Challenger* Accident
Shuttle *Columbia,* 66, 115–16, 150, 245

Sick, Gary, 239, 270 n.1
Simon, Herbert A., 135
Simpson, Alan, 18, 74
Simpson-Bowles Commission. *See* National Commission on Fiscal Responsibility and Reform
Smith, Michael J., 11
Social Security, 1, 90, 134, 135, 151–54, 234
Solyndra corporation, 1, 34, 54, 64, 65, 104–06, 248
Sosa, Sammy, 161
Southern Conference for Human Welfare, 197–98
South Korea, 233
Special committees or subcommittees, 4, 18
Special congressional bodies, 4, 40, 77, 85, 140
Specter, Arlen, 175
Spruce Goose, 27, 28
Sputnik, 1, 90–91, 228
St. Clair, Arthur, 215
Starr, Kenneth, 100, 280 n.59
Stature of investigations, 18–19
Stearns, Cliff, 104
Stempel, Herbert, 160
Stennis, John C., 26, 56, 155
Steroid use in sports, 67, 161–63, 245–46, 292 n.72
Stevens, J. Christopher, 32
Stimulus spending, 247
Stone, Oliver, 173, 295 n.111
Strategic Missile Commission (Scowcroft Commission), 19, 286 n.14
Structure and process of investigations: brand identity, 19–20; characteristics of blue-ribbon commissions, 106, 107–08; destinations of investigations and characteristics of, 177–79; excess capacity, 22–23; focus, 17–18; footprints correlated with characteristics of, 77–79, 118–19, 120–24, 250–62; footprints correlated with party control conditions and characteristics of, 83–87; guidelines for, 60–61; impact of investigations and, 140–41, 144–45, 183, 185–87, 266, 267; intensity, 20–21; leadership, 64–65; linkages with prior hearings, 21–22; measures of, 4, 37; media coverage and, 23–24; stature of, 18–19; varieties of, 12. *See also specific measure of*
Subpoenas, 46, 102, 103, 104, 196–97, 204, 209
Superfund, 234–35
Symington, Stuart, 22, 150, 150–51

Tama, J., 107, 130, 208–09, 277 n.15, 286 n.14
Tax policy and collection. *See* Bureau of Internal Revenue; Internal Revenue Service
Tea Party, 211
Terrorist threat, 1, 135, 191, 208, 242
Terry, Brian, 102
TFX fighter aircraft, 230
Thomas, Clarence, 25
Thomas, J. Parnell, 196–97, 297 n.14
Thompson, Fred, 206
Thoroughness of investigations: blue-ribbon commissions, 109, 118; characteristics of historically significant investigations, 68, 76; classification of investigations by, 4, 54, 56, 58, 68; correlation with other footprint measures, 75; impact of investigation and, 191; impact of investigations and, 138, 182, 185; investigatory characteristics correlated with, 118, 119, 121, 257; party control of government and, 80, 81, 86, 87, 88, 119–20
Three Mile Island, 12, 66, 111–12, 214, 233–34
Time magazine, 15
Tippit, J. D., 172
Tobacco industry, 2, 57, 239
Tower, John G., 194
Tower Commission, 237
Traffic safety investigations, 2, 168–70, 294 n.98
Trigger of investigation: blue-ribbon commissions, 108; breadth of investigation and, 84; classification of investigations by, 4, 41; complexity of investigation and, 84; destination of investigation and, 178; durability of investigation and, 86; focus of investigation and, 17; footprint of investigations and, 77–78, 119, 121, 122, 123; freedom to conduct investigation and, 85; impact of investigation and, 140–41; institutional home of investigations and, 38, 39, 41; leadership of investigation and, 118; method of investigation and, 42; partisanship in investigation and, 86–87, 118; party control of government and, 51, 84, 86, 87; patterns before and after Watergate, 42; seriousness of investigation and, 85, 118; thoroughness of investigation and, 86, 118; trends, 53–54; type of government breakdown and, 41; types of, 41; venue of investigation and, 40; visibility of investigation and, 85, 118
Troubled Asset Relief Program, 156
Trujillo, Rafael, 195

Truman, Harry S., 27, 28, 56
Truman administration, 36, 44, 91–92, 93, 212
Tutchings, T. R., 107
Tydings, Millard E., 14

United States Institute of Peace, 127
Unsafe at Any Speed (Nader), 168
Upton, Fred, 104
Urban unrest, 108, 109–10, 231–32
U.S. Commission on National Security in the Twenty-First Century (Hart-Rudman Commission), 19, 110–11

Valley Forge, Pennsylvania, 21
Van Doren, Charles, 159–61
Venue of investigation: advantages of full committee as, 53; breadth of investigations and, 84; competition for, 192; complexity of investigation and, 84; destination of investigation and, 178; durability of investigation and, 86; footprint of investigation and, 77, 119; freedom to conduct investigation and, 85; high-leverage investigations correlated with, 86; historical location of investigation and, 41; impact of investigation and, 140, 183, 186, 192; institutional home of investigation and, 38; leadership of investigation and, 85; length of investigation and, 84; method of investigation and, 40; multi-venue investigations, 5–6; partisanship in investigation and, 86–87; party control of government and, 51, 84, 85, 86; patterns and trends, 40, 53; seriousness of investigation and, 85; thoroughness of investigation and, 86; trigger for investigation and, 40; types of, 4, 40; types of government breakdowns correlated with, 40; visibility of investigation and, 85
Vietnam War, 1, 6, 17, 20–21, 26, 90, 154–56, 230–31, 238–39, 300 n.4
Visibility of investigations: blue-ribbon commissions, 109; characteristics of historically significant investigations, 67; classification of investigations by, 4, 54, 56, 58; correlation with other footprint measures, 75, 118; historical trends, 76; identity of investigation and, 19; impact of investigations and, 137, 138, 182–83, 191; investigatory characteristics correlated with, 118, 119, 121, 122, 255; measurement, 67; party control of government and, 80, 81, 85, 87, 88

Volcker, Paul A., 157
Volcker rule, 158
Vorenberg, James, 202

W. R. Grace and Company, 166
Waco siege, 54, 97, 174–75, 176, 240
Waldorf Agreement, 199
Wallace, Henry, 27
Walter Reed Army Hospital, 128
Warning shots, 159–63
Warren, Earl, 171, 172, 294–95 n.101–04
Warren, Elizabeth, 156
Warren Commission. *See* President's Commission on the Assassination of John F. Kennedy
Washington, George, 89
Washington Post, 14, 207
Watergate, characteristics of investigations before and after, 4; blue-ribbon commissions, 37, 117; footprint, 77, 78, 79, 82–83, 118, 120, 262; impact, 138, 139, 140, 142–43, 182, 200, 267; institutional home of investigations, 39; investigatory issues, 43–44; investigatory method, 48–49; investigatory purpose, 48; number, 36, 62; partisanship, 39, 50–51; party control of government and, 81, 82–83, 120, 200; triggers of investigations and, 42; types of breakdowns, 45
Watergate scandal, 13–14, 90, 134, 232
Watkins, James D., 112–13
Waxman, Henry, 8, 46, 56, 100, 129, 157, 162, 244, 289–91
Waxman Commission, 19, 57
Weaver, Randy, 175–76
Weaver, Vicki, 175
Wedtech, 236
Welfare fraud investigations, 163–65, 233
Weltner, Charles Longstreet, 192
White House Commission on Aviation and Security, 110
Whitewater Corporation, 18–19, 241, 280 n.59
Witnesses and testimony, 23, 210, 211–12
Wolanin, T. R., 5, 131
Wolf, Frank, 127
World War II procurement fraud, 26–28, 225
Wounded Warriors, 246, 285 n.3

Y2K investigations, 1, 34, 67, 243

Zegart, A. B., 5, 106, 107
Zerbe, Dean, 208
Zwicker, Ralph W., 16